Environmental Ethics

Foundational Readings, Critical Responses

FIRST EDITION

Environmental Ethics

Foundational Readings, Critical Responses

EDITED BY Joel Jay Kassiola

cognella®

SAN DIEGO

Bassim Hamadeh, CEO and Publisher
Kristina Stolte, Senior Field Acquisitions Editor
Alisa Munoz, Project Editor
Celeste Paed, Associate Production Editor
Jess Estrella, Senior Graphic Designer
Greg Isales, Licensing Associate
Natalie Piccotti, Director of Marketing
Kassie Graves, Vice President of Editorial
Jamie Giganti, Director of Academic Publishing

3970 Sorrento Valley Blvd., Ste. 500, San Diego, CA 92121

CONTENTS

CHAPTER 9

The Proposed Concept of the "Anthropocene": Should We Accept It as Science, Reject It as Ideology, or Both?

315

Introduction

Environmental Ethics as the Exemplary Applied Ethics Field: Its Challenge to Western Domination of Nature and Proposals for a Nonhierarchical Nature-Humanity Relationship

Joel Jay Kassiola

Philosophy ought to question the basic assumptions of the age. Thinking through, critically and carefully, what most people take for granted is, I believe, the chief task of philosophy, and it is this task that makes philosophy a worthwhile activity.
—Peter Singer[1]

Vice cuts us off from reality, according to Thomas Aquinas. The arrogance of anthropocentrism cuts people off from the reality of nature ... as we ignore nature's stories and tell truncated and false studies about ourselves ... Anthropocentrism is not just a faulty value system but also a faulty way of understanding the world. In Aristotle's terms, it is an intellectual vice as well as a character vice ... If we want to live environmentally responsible lives, we will have to cultivate practices that lock in habits and ways of looking at the world that are nonanthropocentric.
—Philip Cafaro[2]

The Book's Pedagogical Inspiration

The inspiration for this collection of readings for use in a college course on environmental ethics arose from my own teaching of such a course for 15 years. Senior faculty always tell junior faculty that there should be a synergistic relationship between one's teaching and research: Excellence in teaching is achieved by conducting cutting-edge research and then applying insights learned to inform

---

1 Peter Singer, "All Animals Are Equal," *Philosophical Exchange* 5, no. 1 (1974): XXX–XXX, 111.
2 Ronald Sanders and Philip Carafo (Eds.), "Gluttony, Arrogance, Greed, and Apathy: An Explication of Environmental Vice," in *Environmental Virtue Ethics* (Lanham, MD: Roman and Littlefield, 2005), 146, 156.

one's teaching, from textbook selection to emphases in class discussion. Likewise, a faculty member's teaching should, ideally, provoke research questions to explore as well as help shape positions to be taken in one's research.

I raise this subject of the relationship between academic research and teaching because the inspiration for this book came directly from my own teaching of courses in environmental ethics that have become extremely popular with students of four-year colleges as the conditions of the environment have worsened and are being recognized by the general public, especially with regard to the urgency associated with the challenges of climate change beginning in the late 1980s. Within my teaching experience, I relied on the standard readings in the relatively young academic field of environmental ethics that began in the late 1960s with the publication of Lynn White, Jr.'s famous 1967 article "The Roots of the Environmental Crisis," and the breakthrough work by Peter Singer and Paul Taylor in the 1970s and early 1980s, and Aldo Leopold's 1949 "Land Ethic" essay. I discovered the dominant textbooks in the field and their distinguishing characteristics: extremely large anthologies, sometimes over 650 pages long that included philosophical articles such as the ones listed. They were also replete with scientific reports and analyses of the existing environmental problems: water and air pollution, depletion of natural resources, biodiversity loss, deforestation, and so on. By using these volumes in my own classes, I was able to observe their strengths and weaknesses from the students' perspective as well as my own as the instructor.

Teaching environmental ethics has led me to strive to capture the virtues of previous texts and attempt to mitigate their shortcomings in the conception of this book. I hope that *Environmental Ethics: Foundational Readings, Critical Responses* will support and enhance the learning experience for teachers and students.

Teaching environmental ethics opened my eyes to a powerful outcome. Although I teach several other courses in political and social philosophy, none of these courses has the special reaction of students reporting to me that the environmental ethics course transformed their lives and the way they see the world.

This led me to think about who enrolls in such a course and how the answer to this question should inform the structure of the course, including the choice of its textbooks. This provoked me to create an environmental ethics text for students who enroll in a course in environmental ethics, as opposed to classes in political science, geography, geosciences, or other environmental sciences. The study of ethics is distinctive to philosophy and is normally excluded from courses in these other scientific departments.

In my experience, an essential characteristic of environmental ethics students is how few of them are philosophy majors. The overwhelming majority of students in such a course are likely to never have taken a philosophy course previously, with the possible exception of a required course in critical thinking or informal logic offered by the philosophy department. Applied ethics courses in general tend to attract non-majors seeking to understand ethical issues within their chosen field of study, like business or medicine. Regarding environmental ethics, an increasingly large number of all students are concerned now about the environmental crisis, not only environmental studies, biology, political science, and geosciences majors. Typically, these students enter environmental ethics with no previous background in philosophy.

This fact has a profound impact on the nature of the student audience for the environmental ethics course, its agenda, and its readings. Most environmental ethics students are exposed to the following large subjects for the first time: the nature of philosophy, the nature of ethics and normative discourse as a whole, and, finally, scientific details of the environmental crisis.

This lack of preparation for understanding environmental ethics on the first day of class makes for a daunting set of challenges not faced by the instructor's colleagues whose advanced philosophy courses are filled by philosophy majors. Introducing new students to the world of philosophy, the nature of ethics, the current deteriorating state of our environment, and its ethical issues and dilemmas gives the environmental ethics an enormously wide and deep scope. In addition, a course on environmental ethics is likely to be not only the first, but the only philosophy course taken by many of the students. The importance of such a course and its readings is great and, therefore, demands an unusual amount of pre-course planning by the instructor with regard to the selection of topics and assignments. (See reading on the nature of ethics to begin this book and the discussion that follows.)

The Dialogical Nature of Philosophy and the Structure of This Book: Foundational Readings and Critical Responses

On the question of how the inspiration and structure of this book interrelate, I return to the significant role of the course in conveying the nature of philosophy and its problems and mode of reasoning. Since Socrates and Plato, philosophy in the West has been dialectical, or dialogical, at its core. Socrates, as depicted by Plato, is engaged in conversation with interlocutors in back-and-forth (dialectical) dialogues as a method of advancing thought toward the truth in Plato's dialogues. The continuous assertion-criticism, response-reply process provides a philosophical model of how human thinking can make progress and enlightenment can be achieved. This insight about the philosophical method of knowing is expressed in the commonplace prescription that the teaching of philosophy should occur in a conversational mode—as in Plato's dialogues—rather than in a simple declaration, as in a treatise, or in the classroom in a formal, one-way instructor lecture. Philosophical truth emerges, on this view of the subject, from the temporary results of an ongoing assertion-criticism, response-reply dialogue between different and competing positions. Within this perspective, we learn through responding to criticism: opposing advocates reacting thoughtfully to each other.

Thus, it may be asked at this point, "How does this dialogical philosophical method of knowing shape the structure of this book?" As conveyed by its subtitle, "Foundational Readings, Critical

Responses," within environmental ethics, each chapter consists of a different essential reading on a central theme within the field: from the beginning, according to Western civilization, with the Bible and Genesis, chapters 1–3; through Francis Bacon's important contribution to the hegemonic modern anthropocentrism, or, viewing nature as subordinate to and "resources" for humanity's interests because of humankind's moral superiority; through Lynn White, Jr.'s blaming Judeo-Christianity for the environmental crisis; all the way forward to the current assertion of the "Anthropocene," or, the assertion of the achievement of Bacon's vision of the domination of nature by contemporary humanity. (See foundational readings that follow.)

The readings considered "foundational" to the field are designated by the letter "A." Some academic fields have sufficiently contested natures so that establishing consensus on foundational or canonical readings would be difficult to do, as in the philosophy of art or business ethics. Not so with environmental ethics that is both young enough to be applicable and familiar to current students and yet developed enough to have a body of works from which to select as essential or of core importance to the field, or the ability to generate a large number of responses and significant impact on contemporaneous scholars when first published, and to retain that significance; in other words, they are "classics" in the field.

By examining the designated "A" readings, the composition of the foundation of the field of environmental ethics is clear and largely undisputed: Genesis 1–3, Bacon, Thoreau, White, Leopold, Singer, Taylor, and Warren are all consensus members of the environmental ethics canon that virtually all introductory discussions of the field refer to, with Lynn White, Jr.'s 1967 "Roots" article considered the origin of the field.[3] This volume uniquely expands the list of foundational readings with the emphasis on Francis Bacon's philosophy of humanity-serving science. Bacon's philosophy might be mentioned in such introductory works in environmental ethics, but these writings themselves are rarely, if ever, provided. Because I believe Bacon's anthropocentric conception of the scientific inquiry is so important to what eventually became the dominant worldview in the West (and now throughout the globalized world), this volume is distinguished, as far as I am aware, in providing selected quotations gleaned from Bacon's various methodological works. This is necessary (as opposed to an excerpt from one work) because his aphoristic philosophy of science is scattered throughout his many works and is not solely contained in one or two works.

Another unusual inclusion under the foundational readings is the "8A" reading for the subject of "Consumption and Environmental Ethics," (see chapter 8). A common criticism of the mainstream environmental social movement in the US since its inception in the 1960s has been that it ignores

---

3　See any existing environmental ethics introductory text. Most likely candidates from this group of foundational readings to be omitted from environmental ethics anthologies are the Genesis, Bacon, and Thoreau readings. What distinguishes this volume is the inclusion of these three foundational readings. In addition, this collection pointedly excludes the nonphilosophical scientific and social scientific descriptions and analyses of various environmental problems that blur the overall philosophical and ethical nature of environmental ethics and, moreover, produce an extremely large volume impossible to be used fully, or even mostly, in a one-semester course. I believe these differences from existing environmental ethics collections produce a more clearly and philosophically focused book, but more on this point later.

the connection between advocating for endless hyperconsumption in our consumer society and the detrimental consequences for the environment. Scholars seldom argue for the positive nature of the consumer way of life since the entire social order (encompassing its social institutions like the media, education, politics, etc.) proclaims the desirability of limitless consumption of luxury goods. One confronts thousands of ads every day defining material success and the competitive social status that it confers in these societies. These consumer values are hegemonic but implicit, so that no explicit argument advocating them is deemed necessary. Hence, we have no canonical statement in favor of the consumerist worldview and its ethical values.

The reading by Colin Campbell in this chapter is the most clear and profound that I know concerning the justification of our endless acts of consumption. It centers on the thesis that consuming is an important component of achieving self-identity, admittedly a universal human goal. I hope this reading by Campbell provides a good foil to the critical essay on environmental and social vices embedded within the consumer society discussed by Philip Cafaro and stimulates reflection on the ethical pros and cons of the hyperconsumer society in the developed world and aspired to by the remaining developing countries. In addition to the environmental ethical vices alleged by Cafaro, the consumer society must confront the danger of the entire human population seeking identity through luxury consumption on a finite planet.

How can the Earth provide available materials for the production of all these consumer goods and absorb the resulting byproducts such as nuclear waste, plastics, or greenhouse gases?

One final addition to the standard foundational readings is a discussion of the proposed neologism, the "Anthropocene," by scientist Paul Crutzen and his colleagues. Older introductions to environmental ethics did not even discuss this concept since it is a recent intellectual development proposed to symbolize the human domination of and responsibility for nature. Crutzen and E.G. Stoermer, in the inaugural work creating this literature, argue that we now live in a new geological age, the Anthropocene. This concept and the society it is supposed to represent may be viewed historically as the culmination of Bacon's vision of the human domination of nature through scientific knowledge. The Crutzen and Stoermer reading is the initial proposal of this increasingly popular idea among both scientists and social scientists. Supporters of this new concept consider the current era to be fundamentally different from the preceding Holocene Age, which lasted 10,000 years and is therefore deserving of a new linguistic label.

How is the dialogical nature of the volume to be achieved? I recommend the pairing of the foundational "A" readings with critical responses to the readings indicated by the designation "B," such as Carolyn Merchant's criticisms of Bacon's philosophy of science or Chaone Mallory's critique of Leopold's "Land Ethic." This structure of the book provides the framework for students to engage in discussion and write rationally persuasive essays: What is Leopold's (or any "A" foundational author's) position? What is Mallory's (or any "B" critical response author's) critique of it? Most importantly for the achievement of the epistemological (theory of knowledge) goals of the dialogically philosophical method, How do students assess the resulting debate? Or, which position, Leopold or Mallory, in the given example, seems to be superior? And, crucial to add, why? For what reasons?

This dialogical structure, modeled on the dialogical nature of philosophy, is a strong teaching method in my view. Students learn the important message that ideas and claims do not exist in a vacuum, isolated from other potentially critical views. Arguments must prevail—and possibly be enhanced—by confrontation with opposing positions for good reasons that the student should discern, reflect on, and offer.

The nineteenth-century British philosopher John Stuart Mill's "collision theory of truth" is instructive on this quintessential point. Mill's famous essay "On Liberty" is not only the paradigmatic defense of the freedom of speech, but characterizes (temporary) truth as the product of the "colliding" or confronting opposing perspectives and assessing the comparative merits of each participating argument.[4] Here, the beginning student of environmental ethics will be introduced to this dialogical or collision theory of intellectual growth and progress so vital to philosophy, especially ethics, by considering and assessing the opposing foundational readings and critical responses for each theme or issue.

Just as the volume's dialogical structure informs class discussion by debating the strengths and weaknesses of each reading and how they withstand their opponent's arguments, it can also help frame students' written work as well. The combination of foundational and critical response readings provides the instructor with an emergent format for written assignments: the debate paper. Most students in environmental ethics (as previously discussed) have never written rationally persuasive papers wherein they are expected to present, analyze, and, finally, assess, arguments by protagonists on each chapter topic, and decide for themselves which position is more convincing. They learn to be true to philosophy's essence based on "the systematic use of critical reasoning."[5] Why, or, for what reasons is this so? Most students' previous writing of papers was based on descriptive or explanatory empirical statements, so the kind of writing required for environmental studies: philosophical and ethical, will require a thorough explanation by the instructor.

One semester of environmental ethics will not be sufficient to turn novice philosophy students into skilled thinkers and writers, but it is a noble start when carried over to the students' similar courses; significant improvement can be achieved by practicing such writing, guided by the instructors' suggestions for improvement. Ideally, this book will give students opportunities to develop and refine their analytical, argumentative, and writing abilities.

---

4   See John Stuart Mill, "Of Liberty of Thought and Discussion," In *On Liberty* (Chicago: Henry Regnery, 1955). One passage that is directly relevant here is "since the general or prevailing opinion on any subject is rarely or never the whole truth, it is only by the collision of adverse opinions, that the remainder of the truth has any chance of being supplied" (76).

5   To use the words here defining "philosophy" by the author discussing the nature of ethics, Lewis Vaughn, who provides the reading that follows on this topic. The full definition of "philosophy" provided by Vaughn is: "the systematic use of critical reasoning to answer the most fundamental questions in life."

Environmental Ethics as an Exemplary Field in Applied Ethics: Human Identity and Our Relation to Nature as a Central Question

The practical importance of environmental ethics explains why it is one of the fields included within the subfield of "applied ethics." This subfield category within ethics is essential to distinguish environmental ethics from ethical theory and the typical philosophy course on ethics where various candidate theories of normative ethics and metaethics (or discourse about first-order normative ethical judgments) are examined and evaluated. (See reading on the nature of ethics.) In such a standard ethics course, familiar examples of ethical theories, utilitarianism, deontology or Kantianism, and virtue ethics, and their canonical creators, Bentham, Kant, and Aristotle, are read and discussed. In contrast, environmental ethics courses and readings apply ethical theories to the defined environmental problems in order to make value judgments, prescriptions, and obligation statements regarding the environment "to understand better our obligations to others [including nonhumans]," as Cafaro puts it in the same work as quoted in the epigraph.

This is why environmental ethics is a constituent of applied ethics like business or biomedical ethics, using ethical conceptions and principles related to their respective subject matter areas, (the capitalist business realm, the world of medicine, or other branches of professional ethics, like engineering or journalism). Applied ethics "attempts to show the implications of normative theory for specific moral issues or particular decisions in concrete circumstances," according to authors of an introductory text to ethics.[6]

Environmental ethics stands out among the other applied ethics fields in that rather than being about the behavior of members of various professions within highly limited professional roles and working environments, like businesspersons, physicians, or engineers, and so on as the provided definition emphasizes, *environmental ethics is about the central question for humanity, our identity as humans including our relation to the biophysical environment that surrounds us: animals, plants, ecosystems, and possibly the entire planet treated as one enormous ecosystem, or Gaia.*

Answers to this basic question will influence significantly the way we envision ourselves, so there is a reflexive relationship at work here: When we define one side of the relationship, it has implications for the other. Thus, how we define the nonhuman world and its relation to humanity will reflect and influence how we define ourselves. Furthermore, how we include the nonhuman world within morality, whether it has a moral relation with humans (equal or not), influences how we identify ourselves, or, how we define humanity, especially the nature of human morality, characterize our relationship, if any, with nonhuman nature. Environmentalists are heavily influenced by the recent rise and development of the science of ecology and emphasize the interdependence of all life. The

---

6   In addition to the reading on Ethics by Vaughn, see Brooke Noel Moore and Robert Michael Stewart, *Moral Philosophy: A Comprehensive Introduction* (Mountain View, CA: Mayfield, 1994), 14, for the quoted statement.

study of the relationship between humans and the more-than-human world is a practically profound one for environmental ethics. The basis of ecology, the understanding that all life is interdependent, cannot be dismissed without argument by a simple denial or the undefended assertion of separatist anthropocentrism.

The applied ethics impact of environmental ethics supports inclusion of this field as a fundamental course within the philosophy curriculum and why its textbooks should reflect the real, everyday lives of its student users. Of all of my courses in political philosophy and environmental political philosophy, no other course has generated such earnest reports of life-changing readings and discussions.

When students of environmental ethics discover this core question of the human relation to nature beyond humans and alternatives to Western anthropocentrism contained in the foundational readings, they are provoked to re-examine their own worldview, ethical judgments, and conduct regarding the environment and its components. The revolutionary thinkers Singer, Taylor, and Leopold expanded the longstanding, human-based ethics that was in place in the West since Socrates to include animals, all life, and ecosystems within morality. Furthermore, White's founding article on the blameworthiness of Judeo-Christianity for the environmental crisis and, indirectly, the importance of religion to our moral perspective on the environment, along with Warren's argument for the interdependence between environmentalism and feminism in ecofeminism both challenge the dominance of anthropocentrism, Christianity, and sexism in the West.

In all these breakthrough readings, Singer's call for philosophy to question the basic assumptions of the age (see epigraph) is certainly fulfilled. They should be required reading for the contemporary citizen to reflect on how we envision and treat nature theoretically as well as how to treat nature practically.

An environmental ethics course does not intend to turn its members into radical environmental activists, vegetarians, or vegans, but one consequence of examining the nature-humanity relationship and reasoned arguments for expansion of the ethical realm does challenge our deeply entrenched anthropocentrism. Socrates's motto for Western philosophy, "The unexamined life is not worth living," becomes relevant here, as does Singer's epigraphic comment about philosophy questioning the basic assumptions or the "taken-for-granted ideas of the age." In this case, the basic assumption of Western Civilization is the human separation from and ethical superiority to nonhuman nature leading to the rightful human domination of nature.

Two Examples of Environmental Ethics as an Applied Ethic: "Moral Agency/Patienthood" and "Equal Consideration"

Here are two examples of how environmental ethical concepts and principles can impact students by exposing them to ideas and values that are rare in mainstream modern culture.

One is the fundamental ethical concept of "responsibility" or "agency" underlying the ethical distinction between "moral agents" in contrast to "moral patients." Invariably, when discussing Singer's zoocentrism and his argument for the moral equality of all animals, a student will raise the purported counter-example of a lion (or some other predator) "naturally"—and, therefore, "rightly"—killing and devouring prey. Indeed, some philosophical opponents of zoocentrism discuss its implication of eliminating the natural predator-prey relation as a *reductio ad absurdum* of Singer's moral egalitarian expansion to all animals of moral considerability beyond humans exclusively.[7]

The moral agent/moral patient ethical distinction is decisive here. Nonhuman animals do not possess moral responsibility or moral agency because of their lack of reasoning ability, and, therefore, are not bearers of *prima facie* moral obligations of responsible agents against killing. This makes the ordinary prescription against killing not applicable to nonhuman (non-responsible) animals like lions who are merely moral patients and, therefore, not covered by ethical principles intended only for moral agents. In contrast, the normal adult human is a moral agent with ethical responsibility. Thus, this ethical distinction renders the nonhuman alleged reductio example of the lion as predator null and void as a claimed counter-example to Singer's animal egalitarian perspective.

Another telling example of an ethical principle applied to the nature-human relationship is the principle of "equal consideration," essential to all environmental ethics and its expansion of previously millennia-long, human-based ethics and superiority over nature exemplified in Singer's, Taylor's, and Leopold's ethical theories. All members of the ethical community, for example, Singer's animals, Taylor's members of the community of life, and, for Leopold, components of his category of "land," plants, animals, soils, and waters, are deserving of equal consideration. This crucially does not mean the "same" consideration, when it comes to treatment as it does in the realm of mathematics. In fact, it is the misanalogy to math that misleads actors from understanding that in the philosophical context "equality" means "fair" or "just" and not the "same" or "identical" treatment. Indeed, equal consideration could mean distinctly different ("unequal") treatment in order to be "equal" in the sense of fairness or justice, as in the case of a blind student receiving more time to take an exam than the other sighted students.

This ethical principle is vital to the environmental ethical arguments for a non-hierarchical relationship between nature and humanity that contests the Western domination of nature doctrine. "Deep" or nonhierarchical environmental ethics that deny human superiority or exceptionalism formed the foundation of the field that was built on the arguments of Singer for nonhuman animals; Taylor for all living beings including plants; Leopold for ecosystems; and Warren for her conception of ecofeminism and equal treatment for women and nature.

---

7   See, for example, Mark Sagoff, "Animal Liberation and Environmental Ethics: Bad Marriage, Quick Divorce," *Osgoode Hall Law Journal* 22(1984): 297–307.

What We Can Learn from Foundational Debates within Environmental Ethics: The Upshot of the Critical Responses

The foundational readings for this volume were largely predetermined by the historical development of the field and the ascription of "classic" or "canonical" to a particular reading. There is a remarkable consensus among environmental ethicists on who and what are considered canonical, not unlike the group of thinkers and their major works within the history of Western political philosophy (my own field of training), from Plato to Marx. There is little disagreement that Plato, Aristotle, Hobbes, Locke, Rousseau, Mill, and Marx should be considered essential to this subject and in courses addressing the historical development of the field. Differences begin to arise about whether Saints Augustine and Aquinas, or Hegel, or Kant, are to be included; and, in contemporary political philosophy the consensus collapses, so contemporary courses are greatly disparate in regard to which thinkers should be included: Jurgen Habermas? Michel Foucault? Isaiah Berlin? Max Weber? and so on.

For environmental ethics (a much younger field than political philosophy—fifty years versus 2,400 years) little contention is likely with this volume's list of "A" or foundational readings, except perhaps within the consumption topic. However, when one turns to the "B" readings or critical responses, much like the example of contemporary political philosophy, there is great choice and diversity. My criteria for inclusion for these readings of critical responses to the foundational works centered on whether the work directly addressed the foundational reading and how effective the criticism was. In addition, the candidate critical responses needed to be at the core of the foundational work. Finally, I considered whether the resulting debate focused on the central environmental ethical issue of the relation between nature and humanity. In sum, the readings considered for the critical responses portion of the volume were weighed on whether the proposed critique will spark a productive debate in readers' minds. In short, will consideration of the "A" and "B" readings generate a conceptual platform on which readers can learn important concepts, issues, and positions within environmental ethics?

Perhaps the clearest example of these criteria at work is Carolyn Merchant's critique of Francis Bacon's philosophy of science. Merchant's discussion goes to the heart of Bacon's (and later Western society's) attempt to justify the domination and exploitation of nature conceived as a female for the benefit of male-dominated seventeenth-century British society. Merchant writes,

> The "controversy over women" and the inquisition of witches—both present in Bacon's social milieu—permeated his description of nature and his metaphorical style and were instrumental in his transformation of the earth as a nurturing mother and womb of life as a source of secrets to be extracted for economic advance.[8]

---

8   Carolyn Merchant, *The Death of Nature: Women, Ecology and the Scientific Revolution* (New York: HarperOne, HarperCollins Publishers, 1983), 165.

Merchant's critique of Bacon clearly presents and opposes the central issues of Western society's sexism, scientism, and anthropocentrism. The debate between Merchant and Bacon is an ideal example of Millian "collisions," producing an opportunity to learn about environmental ethics and the world.

Or, consider Fainos Mangena's critique of Warren's ecofeminism advocacy as necessary for both an ethically acceptable feminism and environmentalism. Mangena raises the fundamental challenge that, as opposed to Warren's theory of the universal domination of both women and nature, it might be culturally limited to the West, as shown by the alternative views and roles of women, men, and nature in Africa. By raising these essential issues of cultural differences between the Eurocentric West and Africa, Mangena poses fundamental challenges to Western feminism and environmentalism and questions the conceptual integrity of the worldview of ecofeminism. Again, it is hoped that readers' consideration of this debate between Mangena's and Warren's positions will shed light on the nature of environmental ethics and ecofeminism, helping readers formulate their own positions on these issues based on evidence.

The presence of the Bible in the readings may draw criticism, so further comment seems apt. In my secular university experience, I have seen that today's mainstream undergraduate population exhibits widespread ignorance of the Bible. Most of my environmental ethics students report never having read anything in the Bible and are initially skeptical about its assignment in the course readings.

What is erroneously inferred by this large group of students is that their personal rejection of organized religion allows for a dismissal of the Bible as a relevant work to their lives and the society in which they live. Peter Harrison, in his essay on White's founding essay of environmental ethics, assesses White's alleging direct responsibility for the environmental crisis to Judeo-Christianity scripture and its anthropocentrism.

The Bible in a philosophy course on environmental ethics is not read from the perspective of a member of a religion's faithful. This approach would be wholly inappropriate in an academic discipline quintessentially dedicated to rational inquiry, thus matters of faith lie outside its purview. Instead, philosophers examine the Bible for its cultural significance: its influence on society and its values. Genesis, chapters 1–3, famously depicts the divine creation of the world and the Fall of Adam and Eve. This is why, despite the enormous Biblical exegetical (interpretative) literature—perhaps the largest single-topic literature in Western thought—such textual interpretations and debates about the *spiritual* meaning of these famous chapters of the Old Testament are not relevant for environmental ethics; however, these original texts are included here because of their enormous *cultural* significance.

As Harrison observes in his critical response, the key verse for humanity's relationship to the environment appears in Genesis 1:28. "Subdue the Earth" and "have dominion over all the animals" (or "conquer the Earth" and "be masters over all the animals," depending on the translation) functions as a divine justification for the Western anthropocentrism and domination over nature, a worldview resulting in the exploitation and consequent deterioration of the natural environment. What the agnostic or atheistic student misunderstands is that no matter what one's theological stance is, the cultural meaning and significance of the Bible remains supremely important, especially the most prominent excerpt: The Old Testament God commands Adam, representing humankind, to subdue the Earth and dominate all the animals. This verse has been used to legitimize the prevailing domination of nature worldview such that it is the *de facto* modern social paradigm, expanded worldwide with the globalization of Western capitalism and anthropocentrism. Harrison's critical response clearly raises profound issues for students to consider and reflect on.

The first critical response by Carolyn Merchant on the Biblical story of Adam and Eve and the Harrison essay commenting on White's shocking charge against Judeo-Christianity provide the reader with an excellent introduction to the social role of the Bible in the West and how it has influenced our conception of the relationship between humanity and nature. It is truly the "beginning" of Western anthropocentric thought, and as such is essential to know. If nothing else, these chapters of Genesis should demonstrate the primary cultural importance of the Bible to first-time, undergraduate readers.

Francis Bacon's ideas about scientific inquiry and knowledge are almost always omitted from environmental ethics texts. I deviate from this practice because of my belief that his renown "[k]nowledge is power" statement really translates to "scientific knowledge is power over nature." This philosophy and his envisioned quest for scientific knowledge to recover the glories of Eden after the Fall was an effort by Bacon to justify the domination of feminized nature. Thus, Bacon's philosophy of scientific inquiry, like the Bible and Genesis 1–3, is culturally profound even if the contemporary adherents to this vision of the world and science are unaware of its origin in Bacon's seventeenth-century philosophy.

Therefore, just as with the inclusion of the Bible's Genesis 1–3 reading, the selected quotations by Bacon are intended to illustrate the profound social significance of these ideas to post-seventeenth-century modernity concerning the ethically proper relationship between humanity and nature. Bacon's thoughts on the nature of scientific knowledge and humanity's self-serving reasons for seeking it were to become the hegemonic Western master narrative of the male domination of nature envisioned as female, as Merchant in her critical response to Bacon's writings points out, furthermore, as does Warren in her essay on ecofeminism.

Henry David Thoreau's reading, "Walking," represents a long and rich tradition of naturalist thought where nature is conceived as the embodiment of all that is "good, beautiful, true and right in the world."[9] This ideal vision of nature ultimately guiding human values and conduct goes back to the pre-Socratic period and continues right up to modernity where it opposes modern anthropocentrism that views nature merely a subordinate "resource" or instrument for superior human goals and interests.

Bill McKibben's path-breaking thesis in 1989—now despairing commonplace among naturalists and environmentalists who accept Thoreau's traditional dream of ideal nature—was that the naturalists' superior view of nonhuman nature was destroyed by the damaging ecological footprint of late twentieth

---

9   Paul Wapner, *Living through the End of Nature: The Future of American Environmentalism* (Cambridge, MA: MIT Press, 2010), 54. See chapter 3 of this work regarding "The Dream of Naturalism" for a detailed presentation of this dream of the naturalist tradition.

century (and, now, the twenty-first century) humanity. Advanced science and technology dominate all of the planet, including nonhuman nature, as well as causing pollution, highlighted by the urgent problems of global warming and climate change. Sadly, from McKibben's point of view, not much is left of Thoreau's inspiring nature, ending the possibility of experiencing love and joy from walking in the wilderness and observing the minute details of a massively diverse, complex, and beautiful natural environment that was independent of humanity (see reading by Thoreau).

This momentous development of the "end of nature," or, the end of the naturalist concept of nature separate from humanity made Merchant's second critical response reading from her *The Death of Nature* volume and McKibben's *End of Nature* volume converge in noting the death of the naturalist's dream and its central conception of the wild, nonhuman "nature." Both thinkers refer to the "end" or "death" of nature, but for different reasons or causes: For Merchant, it is the rise of Baconian modern science and sexism that turned living and active nature into something inert to be studied and manipulated according to human values and interests; and, for McKibben, it is modern industrial values that drive humanity's materially obsessed consumerist way of life that destroys natural ecosystems and pollutes the environment as the unprecedented increase in greenhouse gas emissions bring about global warming and climate change that impacts the entire planet.

It should be noted that both Merchant's and McKibben's grim analyses of the demise of Thoreau's wild naturalist view of nonhuman nature are grounded in modernity—modern science for Merchant, modern industrialism and materialism for McKibben. In this context, environmental ethics may be considered as a counter-hegemonic, anti-modern movement by reasserting or reclaiming nonhuman nature from the subordinate status regarding the modern conception of its relationship to humanity and to an equality with humanity in a nonhierarchical relationship as Singer (partially with respect to nonhuman animals), Taylor, Leopold, and Warren (along with women) claim in their respective environmental ethical theories.

My contribution on Chinese (Neo-)Confucian green thought adopts Lynn White's prescription for Western society to reform (Judeo-)Christianity or replace it with a substitute that supports an environmentally sustainable way of life. He opts for the former and proposes the reformative Christian ideas of Saint Francis of Assisi, which emphasize an egalitarian nature-humanity relationship. However, critics of White's brief essay have noted that White does not adequately describe what these Franciscan environmental views are, except to deny separation and superiority, thereby rejecting the Western human domination over nature inherent in the Judeo-Christian tradition going back to Genesis.

Instead, I propose White's second choice of an alternative worldview to the hegemonic anthropocentric Judeo-Christian perspective: Chinese Confucianism. I prescribe this millennia-old Confucian tradition of thought not as an alternative religion, but as a different conception of the world and combining the ancient Confucian focus on ethics (beginning with Confucius in the fifth century BCE) and Neo-Confucian perspective emphasizing cosmology and ontology (beginning in the eleventh century CE). This Confucianism provides an informative contrast between Western modernity with its central values of industrialism, materialism, individualism, and, anthropocentrism, especially significant in the context of environmental ethics and the nonhierarchical view of nature derived from the cosmological ideas of the eleventh century CE and later Neo-Confucians (see table of differences between the two worldviews in my essay). My intention here is that the alternative Confucian perspective will expose the limitations and flaws within the modern Western anthropocentric model whose foundation White contends goes back to Judeo-Christianity ecotheology and will spark thinking about an alternative conceptual framework beyond reforming Christianity, especially now that Western modernism has been globalized and the environmental crisis has worsened to the urgent point where fundamental change is necessary if an environmental catastrophe is to be avoided.

White's famous article that began the field of environmental ethics shockingly and courageously fulfilled Singer's vision of philosophy questioning the basic assumptions of the age. It embodied a challenge to dominant and taken-for-granted Christianity in the West and held its anthropocentrism responsible for the global environmental crisis. My essay may be considered as an attempt to build on White's accomplishment by proposing and examining an alternative cosmology. It is my belief that the core issue of environmental ethics is the question of the nature-humanity relationship requiring conceptions of both entities and their connection to each other. This can be creatively approached through Neo-Confucian cosmological thinking. I hope that my essay's inclusion in this volume will provoke readers to explore alternative worldviews and cosmologies to envision a sustainable and just global social order; the glorious naturalist tradition to which Thoreau was a prominent contributor is no longer a viable option.

The three pioneering philosophers, Leopold, Singer, and Taylor, and their respective critics, Chaone Mallory, Michael Fox, and William French, model the dialogical trait of philosophy. The debates between these thinkers provide excellent opportunities for the new student of environmental ethics to become familiar with the most important innovative theories in the recent expansion of long-established anthropocentric boundaries that once defined the nature-humanity relation as one-sided—to serve the needs and interests of humans. This is what Singer considers progress in ethics, the overcoming and eradicating of discrimination, or what Warren calls the "isms of domination," and unequal treatment (in the sense of unfairness). Logically, (if not chronologically), one can identify the progression from anthropocentrism to Singer's zoocentrism on to the biocentrism of Taylor, and finally the ecocentrism of Leopold—perhaps continuing to Gaiaism and even including inanimate objects in a Neo-Confucian-inspired cosmicentrism. Neo-Confucian cosmology continues the progression of expanding moral inclusiveness or considerability—or what is considered to lie within the realm of morality—to include the cosmic realm of the fundamental Neo-Confucian triad of Heaven, Earth (nature), and humanity, where Heaven is not a place but a normative ideal where inanimate objects as well as living beings are included (see my essay).

Philip Cafaro's discussion of the concept of "environmental vice" with four examples is included as a counter-point to Colin Campbell's praise for modern consumerism as a means to achieve self-discovery. Cafaro's focus on four vicious values that contribute to the environmental crisis highlights one of the most important characteristics of environmental ethics and the current environmental deterioration: It is not a circumstance that can be "solved" or "fixed" by technological innovation. "Crisis of values" highlights the current environmental crisis is in its essence a crisis of values. While the environment is widely recognized as a subject of dire conditions, the cause of these conditions is rarely recognized as lying in our values; hence, this phrase and the important consequent of requiring "fundamental value change" is crucial to the field of environmental ethics and its urgency today.

The gluttony, arrogance, greed, and apathy Cafaro selects for discussion are matters of our values, and the proper response to ethically vicious values is rejection and replacement with superior ones. Therefore, the best way to respond to the environmental challenges confronting humanity today is twofold: first, recognizing and rejecting of the misguided values that have produced our environmental problems, and second, replacing these undesirable—and unsustainable—values with desirable ones that will enhance sustainability and social justice. Environment ethicists have excelled at the negative first part of this dual process by criticizing the Judeo-Christian, modern, anthropocentric, sexist, and materialist assumptions of our age. I believe what is needed not only for a more effective field of environmental ethics, but also for a successful environmental social change movement, is the positive contribution of a prescribed alternative worldview to replace the unsustainable and unjust Western, modern industrial value system and social institutions built on them, for example, Confucian green theory.

It is fitting to close this collection of readings with the current debate over the increasingly influential concept of the "Anthropocene," given that this introductory volume to environmental ethics began with the Bible and the creation of the Earth by an all-powerful Judeo-Christian God of the Old Testament and Genesis. Thousands of years later, the secular ideology of modernism and its doctrine of anthropocentrism, or human supremacy over the natural world, seems an apt parallel. According to the originator of the concept, "Anthropocene," P.J. Crutzen and his scientific colleagues (in the reading for this text, E.F. Stoermer), contemporary humanity now controls the fate of the world and appears to have realized the dream of Bacon and the many other thinkers throughout Western history who have accepted the anthropocentric domination of a nature point of view.[10]

With humanity's population growth to unprecedented numbers and projections of even higher population levels into the twenty-second century, ongoing technological innovation fueled by continuous scientific research and development, and increasing material affluence for the billions of people left behind by the original nineteenth-century industrial creation of wealth (hundreds of millions of new middle-class consumers are predicted in China and India alone), it appears as if there truly is something new under the sun worthy of a new geological label like the "Anthropocene," indicative

---

10 Ibid., 79–105.

of humanity's new planetary dominant status. This linguistic proposal is seen by its advocates as having the virtue of expressing the new conditions present on Earth and the end of a geological era that existed for over ten thousand years. McKibben's "end of nature" needs to be recognized, the advocates of the Anthropocene idea of human domination of and responsibility for nature would argue, and, furthermore, no matter what the relation between nature and humanity may have been previously, God-dominated, human-dominated, or nature-dominated, today it does appear as if it is unquestionable that the role of humans on Earth has fundamentally changed from the pre-industrial period as all the data regarding modern consumption show.[11]

From population size to the amount of paper consumed to water use, and so on, humanity in the industrial age it seems has produced so much change as to warrant some new linguistic designation. And, moreover, since these Earthy changes—including environmental degradation—were created by humankind, it seems only right that a new conceptual label be devised to convey these historical changes. Thus, the proposed new geological age, the Anthropocene, appears appropriate and may explain its rapid rise in use since the turn of the twenty-first century when P.J. Crutzen and E.F. Stoermer first proposed it in the reading provided here.

However, the chief characteristic of philosophy questioning popular assumptions of the age or current social trends, like the idea of a new geological age reflective of humanity's domination of nature, comes to the fore in the challenges to this proposed concept, represented by the critical response by Christine Cuomo. What the Anthropocene proposal means ethically and politically are topics glaringly—and not surprisingly—omitted by the natural scientists who have embraced the term and concept. So, once again, philosophy, and ethics, in particular, and in this case, specifically, environmental ethics, are needed to examine, assess, and propose corrections to the prevailing culturally accepted beliefs and assumptions. I invite the reader to consider Cuomo's critique of the idea of the Anthropocene and weigh possible replies in rational dialogue with the opposing positions in an effort to arrive at a tentative conclusion that is closer to the truth, and one that can inform one's future actions.

Surely, the measurement of global atmospheric CO_2 is historically unprecedented and the other peak data that moved Crutzen and Stoermer to prescribe the new term to capture our historically unique circumstances cannot be denied empirically; contemporary humankind has, in fact, depleted, polluted, consumed, and transformed the natural environment to quantitative levels never experienced previously with our unprecedented numbers, material wealth, new technology, and industrial values including endless consumption and economic growth. Thus, the new material conditions do deserve to be noted and perhaps given a new designation, but, as critics like Cuomo challenge, why should the neologism created to reflect the aforementioned changes focus on humanity's domination of the Earth?

---

11   See Will Steffen, Paul J. Crutzen, and John R. McNeill, "The Anthropocene: Are Humans Now Overwhelming the Great Forces of Nature?" *Ambio,* 36, no. 8 (2007): 614–621, where empirical data showing the "global change" since the industrial revolution are provided to justify the new nomenclature, especially the graphs in figure 2 (p. 617).

As we have seen in the previous readings in this book, the anthropocentric assumption in the West since Genesis has been one of human exceptionalism and separation from nature, and, furthermore, supremacy over it. However, it is vital to note that this alleged human domination of nature has been questioned by environmental ethics' counter-assertion to this hegemonic narrative with its expansion of the human-based ethics to one of ethical equality with animals, all life, and even all ecosystems as well as between the sexes of humanity. *In this respect, environmental ethics stands as a direct challenge to the "Anthropocene" proposal despite the latter's taken-for-granted status.* Cuomo expresses this trenchant conclusion as follows:

> Perilous environmental changes and compromised systems at planetary scales are trends we should work at all costs to terminate, rather than normalize for the future. Instead of dismal science declaring "game over" for the Holocene [the geological age for the past 10,000 years], realistic science can interpret the last environmental traces of war, pollution and disruption as crucial warnings within the current epoch, encouraging ethical and empowering responses rather than fatalism and denial. … The geological signals scientists propose as the marks of a new epoch represent colonial and "neocolonial" interventions and changes that have been catastrophically harmful, and that currently threaten to produce even more extensive harm. If what is distinct about the proposed new geological phase is that it leaves physical signals like mining tailings, nuclear fallout, ocean acidification and anthropogenic species extinction, then the Anthropocene represents an atrocity rather than a promising trend.[12]

The ecotheologian Thomas Berry has proposed a different label in contradistinction to the Anthropocene, the "Ecozoic," in order to reflect a partnership between the Earth's biotic community and humanity.[13] What is important for our purposes to note about Berry's neologism is that it overcomes the human superiority and domination thesis conveyed by the "Anthropocene" and the anthropocentric viewpoint that underlies it.

A telling upshot of this debate about linguistic designations is the point to be expressed by each conceptual label. The Anthropocene continues the Western domination of nature trope since Genesis and Bacon's modern secular attempt to recreate Eden only this time without God achieved by the human enterprise of natural science. My own candidate for such a new label to reflect the (hopeful) environmental ethics-inspired rejection of Western anthropocentrism as well as the acceptance of the need to expand morality and the resulting applicability of moral equality between humans and

---

12 Christine J. Cuomo, "Against the Idea of an Anthropocene Epoch: Ethical, Political and Scientific Concerns." *Biogeosystem Technique* 4, no. 1 (2017): 4–8. 2017.

13 See Brian Swimme and Thomas Berry, *The Universe Story: From the Primordial Flaring Forth to the Ecozoic Era—A Celebration of the Unfolding of the Universe* (New York: HarperCollins Publishers, 1992), 241–261.

the other living inhabitants on Earth is "Ecosoczoic." This is a derivative of Berry's "Ecozoic" but includes the importance of human society along with the other ecological factors. The interdependence between the nonhuman environment and humanity, or inescapable "hybridity" or "entanglement"[14] between these two entities should be expressed in any label for the new age of moral development and equality. This point of the egalitarian relationship between nature and human society appears persuasive once the millennia-old anthropocentric Western worldview of human domination is shed.

It is high time to give up various "isms of domination," as Warren calls them, or false ideologies of superiority. Time to discard the long and misguided quest for human superiority and the immense harm such an aim has caused and consider fellow members of Taylor's community of life and Leopold's "plain" or equal citizens of the "land" in equal partnership with other members. In closing this introduction, I encourage readers to think of their own neologism to characterize our new era—not one that subordinates nature to humanity's will and interests, but one that has "respect for nature," as Taylor would put it.

It is the purpose of this volume to demonstrate to its readers why environmental ethics has a decisive role in this dramatic change of worldviews—or cultural revolution—beginning with Leopold's and White's challenges to the anthropocentric assumptions of our age through the path-breaking theories of Singer, Taylor, and Warren, continuing right up to the current critical responses of the assertion of our environmental vices by Cafaro and to the Anthropocene proposal by Cuomo. Hopefully, at the book's end, the reader will understand and appreciate better why I claimed environmental ethics to be the "exemplary applied ethics field."

---

14   See Damian F. White, Alan P. Rudy, and Brian J. Gareau, *Environments, Natures, and Society Theory: Towards a Critical Hybridity* (New York: Palgrave Macmillan, 2016).

CHAPTER I

An Introduction to the Nature of Ethics

1. Beginning Ethics

An Introduction to Moral Philosophy

By Lewis Vaughn

Ethics, or **moral philosophy**, is the philosophical study of morality. **Morality** refers to beliefs concerning right and wrong, good and bad—beliefs that can include judgments, values, rules, principles, and theories. These beliefs help guide our actions, define our values, and give us reasons for being the persons we are. Ethics, then, addresses the powerful question that Socrates formulated twenty-four hundred years ago: How ought we to live?

The continued relevance of this query suggests something compelling about ethics: you cannot escape it. You cannot run away from all of the choices, feelings, and actions that accompany ideas about right and wrong, good and bad—ideas that persist in your culture and in your mind. After all, for much of your life, you have been assimilating, modifying, or rejecting the ethical norms you inherited from your family, community, and society. Unless you are very unusual, from time to time you deliberate about the rightness or wrongness of actions, embrace or reject particular moral principles or codes, judge the goodness of your character or intentions (or someone else's), perhaps even question (and agonize over) the soundness of your own moral outlook when it conflicts with that of others. In other words, you are involved in ethics—you *do* ethics—throughout your life. Even if you try to remove yourself from the ethical realm by insisting that all ethical concepts are irrelevant or empty, you will have assumed a particular view—a theory in the broadest sense—about morality and its place in your life. If at some point you are intellectually brave enough to wonder whether your moral beliefs rest on coherent supporting considerations, you will see that you cannot even begin to sort out such considerations without—again—doing ethics. In any case, in your life you must deal with the rest of the world, which turns on moral conflict and resolution, moral decision and debate.

What is at stake when we do ethics? In an important sense, the answer is *everything we hold dear*. Ethics is concerned with values—specifically, *moral values*. Through the sifting and weighing of moral values we determine what the most important things are in our lives, what is worth living for and what is worth dying for. We decide what is the greatest good, what goals we should pursue in life, what virtues we should cultivate, what duties we should fulfill, what value we should put on human life, and what pain and perils we should be willing to endure for notions such as the common good, justice, and rights.

Does it matter whether the state executes criminals who have the mental capacity of a ten-year-old? Does it matter whether we can easily save a starving child but casually decide not to? Does it matter who actually writes the term paper you turn in and represent as your own? Does it matter whether young girls in Africa have their genitals painfully mutilated for reasons of custom or religion? Do these actions and a million others just as controversial matter at all? Most of us—regardless of our opinion on these issues—would say that they matter a great deal. If they matter, then ethics matters, because these are ethical concerns requiring careful reflection using concepts and reasoning peculiar to ethics.

But even though ethics is inescapable and important in life, you are still free to take the easy way out, and many people do. You are free *not* to think too deeply or too systematically about ethical concerns. You can simply embrace the moral beliefs and norms given to you by your family and your society. You can just accept them without question or serious examination. In other words, you can try *not* to do ethics. This approach can be simple and painless—at least for a while—but it has some drawbacks.

First, it undermines your personal freedom. If you accept and never question the moral beliefs handed to you by your culture, then those beliefs are not really yours—and they, not you, control your path in life. Only if you critically examine these beliefs *yourself* and decide for *yourself* whether they have merit will they be truly yours. Only then will you be in charge of your own choices and actions. The philosopher John Stuart Mill summed up the ask-no-questions approach to life pretty well: "He who lets the world, or his own portion of it, choose his plan of life for him, has no need of any other faculty than the ape-like one of imitation."[1]

Second, the morally blind attitude increases the chance that your responses to moral dilemmas or contradictions will be incomplete, confused, of mistaken. Sometimes in real life, moral codes or rules do not fit the situations at hand, or moral principles conflict with one another, or entirely new circumstances are not covered by any moral policy at all. Solving these problems requires something that a hand-me-down morality does not include: the intellectual tools to critically evaluate (and reevaluate) existing moral beliefs.

Third, if there is such a thing as intellectual moral growth, you are unlikely to find it on the safe route. To not do ethics is to stay locked in a kind of intellectual limbo in which personal moral progress is barely possible.

The philosopher Paul Taylor suggests that there is yet another risk in taking the easy road. If someone blindly embraces the morality bequeathed to him by his society, he may very well be a fine embodiment of the rules of his culture and accept them with certainty. But he also will lack the ability to defend his beliefs by rational argument against criticism. What happens when he encounters others who also have very strong beliefs that contradict his? "He will feel lost and bewildered," Taylor says, and his confusion might leave him disillusioned about morality. "Unable to give an objective, reasoned justification for his own convictions, he may turn from dogmatic certainty to total skepticism. And from total skepticism it is but a short step to an 'amoral' life. … Thus the person who begins by accepting moral beliefs blindly can end up denying all morality."[2]

There are other easy roads—roads that also bypass critical and thoughtful scrutiny of morality. We can describe most of them as various forms of subjectivism, a topic that we closely examine later on. You may decide, for example, that you can establish all your moral beliefs by simply consulting your feelings. In situations calling for moral judgments, you let your emotions be your guide. If it feels right, it is right. Alternatively, you may come to believe that moral realities are relative to each person, a view known as *subjective relativism* (also covered in a later [reading]). That is, you think that what a person believes or approves of determines the rightness or wrongness of actions. If you believe that abortion is wrong, then it *is* wrong. If you believe it is right, then it *is* right.

But these facile pathways through ethical terrain are no better than blindly accepting existing norms. Even if you want to take the subjectivist route, you still need to critically examine it to see if there are good reasons for choosing it—otherwise your choice is arbitrary and therefore not really yours. And unless you thoughtfully consider the merits of moral beliefs (including subjectivist beliefs), your chances of being wrong about them are substantial.

Ethics does not give us a royal road to moral truth. Instead, it shows us how to ask critical questions about morality and systematically seek answers supported by good reasons. This is a tall order because, as we have seen, many of the questions in ethics are among the toughest we can ever ask—and among the most important in life.

The Ethical Landscape

The domain of ethics is large, divided into several areas of investigation, and cordoned off from related subjects. So let us map the territory carefully. As the term *moral philosophy* suggests, ethics is a branch of philosophy. A very rough characterization of philosophy is the systematic use of critical reasoning to answer the most fundamental questions in life. Moral philosophy, obviously, tries to answer the fundamental questions of morality. The other major philosophical divisions address other basic questions; these are *logic* (the study of correct reasoning), *metaphysics* (the study of the fundamental nature of reality), and *epistemology* (the study of knowledge). As a division of philosophy, ethics does its work primarily through critical reasoning. Critical reasoning is the careful, systematic evaluation of statements, or claims—a process used in all fields of study, not just in ethics. Mainly this process includes both the evaluation of logical arguments and the careful analysis of concepts.

Science also studies morality, but not in the way that moral philosophy does. Its approach is known as **descriptive ethics**—the *scientific* study of moral beliefs and practices. Its aim is to describe and explain how people actually behave and think when dealing with moral issues and concepts. This kind of empirical research is usually conducted by sociologists, anthropologists, and psychologists. In contrast, the focus of moral philosophy is not what people actually believe and do, but what they *should* believe and do. The point of moral philosophy is to determine what actions are right (or wrong) and what things are good (or bad).

Philosophers distinguish three major divisions in ethics, each one representing a different way to approach the subject. The first is **normative ethics**—the study of the principles, rules, or theories that guide our actions and judgments. (The word *normative* refers to norms, or standards, of judgment—in this case, norms for judging rightness and goodness.) The ultimate purpose of doing normative ethics is to try to establish the soundness of moral norms, especially the norms embodied in a comprehensive moral system, or theory. We do normative ethics when we use critical reasoning to demonstrate that a moral principle is justified, or that a professional code of conduct is contradictory, or that one proposed moral theory is better than another, or that a person's motive is good. Should the rightness of actions be judged by their consequences? Is happiness the greatest good in life? Is utilitarianism a good moral theory? Such questions are the preoccupation of normative ethics.

Another major division is **metaethics**—the study of the meaning and logical structure of moral beliefs. It asks not whether an action is right or whether a person's character is good. It takes a step back from these concerns and asks more fundamental questions about them: What does it mean for an action to be *right*? Is *good* the same thing as *desirable*? How can a moral principle be justified? Is there such a thing as moral truth? To do normative ethics, we must assume certain things about the meaning of moral terms and the logical relations among them. But the job of metaethics is to question all of these assumptions, to see if they really make sense.

Finally, there is **applied ethics**—the application of moral norms to specific moral issues or cases, particularly those in a profession such as medicine or law. Applied ethics in these fields goes under such names as medical ethics, journalistic ethics, and business ethics. In applied ethics we study the results derived from applying a moral principle or theory to specific circumstances. The purpose of the exercise is to learn something important about either the moral characteristics of the situation or the adequacy of the moral norms. Did the doctor do right in performing that abortion? Is it morally permissible for scientists to perform experiments on people without their consent? Was it right for the journalist to distort her reporting to aid a particular side in the war? Questions like these drive the search for answers in applied ethics.

In every division of ethics, we must be careful to distinguish between *values* and *obligations*. Sometimes we may be interested in concepts or judgments of *value*—that is, about what is morally *good, bad, blameworthy,* or *praiseworthy*. We properly use these kinds of terms to refer mostly to persons, character traits, motives, and intentions. We may say "She is a good person" or "He is to blame for that tragedy." Other times, we may be interested in concepts or judgments of *obligation*—that is, about what is obligatory or a duty, or what we should or ought to do. We use these terms to refer to *actions*. We may say "She has a duty to tell the truth" or "What he did was wrong."

When we talk about value in the sense just described, we mean *moral* value. If she is a good person, she is good in the moral sense. But we can also talk about *nonmoral* value. We can say that things such as televisions, rockets, experiences, and artwork (things other than persons and intentions) are good, but we mean "good" only in a nonmoral way. It makes no sense to assert that in themselves televisions or rockets are morally good or bad. Perhaps a rocket could be used to perform an action that is morally wrong. In that case, the action would be immoral, while the rocket itself would still have nonmoral value only.

Many things in life have value for us, but they are not necessarily valuable in the same way. Some things are valuable because they are a means to something else. We might say that gasoline is good because it is a means to make a gas-powered vehicle work, or that a pen is good because it can be used to write a letter. Such things are said to be **extrinsically valuable**—they are valuable as a means to something else. Some things, however, are valuable in themselves or for their own sakes. They are valuable simply because they are what they are, without being a means to something else. Things that have been regarded as valuable in themselves include happiness, pleasure, virtue, and beauty. These are said to be **intrinsically valuable**—they are valuable in themselves.

The Elements of Ethics

We all do ethics, and we all have a general sense of what is involved. But we can still ask, What are the elements of ethics that make it the peculiar enterprise that it is? We can include at least the four factors described in this section.

The Preeminence of Reason

Doing ethics typically involves grappling with our feelings, taking into account the facts of the situation (including our own observations and relevant knowledge), and trying to understand the ideas that bear on the case. But above all, it involves, even requires, critical reasoning—the consideration of reasons for whatever statements (moral or otherwise) are in question. Whatever our view on moral issues and whatever moral outlook we subscribe to, our commonsense moral experience suggests that if a moral judgment is to be worthy of acceptance, it must be supported by good reasons, and our deliberations on the issue must include a consideration of those reasons.

The backbone of critical reasoning generally and moral reasoning in particular is logical argument. This kind of argument—not the angry-exchange type—consists of a statement to be supported (the assertion to be proved; the conclusion) and the statements that do the supporting (the reasons for believing the statement; the premises). With such arguments, we try to show that a moral judgment is or is not justified, that a moral principle is or is not sound, that an action is or is not morally permissible, or that a moral theory is or is not plausible.

Our use of critical reasoning and argument helps us keep our feelings about moral issues in perspective. Feelings are an important part of our moral experience. They make empathy possible, which gives us a deeper understanding of the human impact of moral norms. They also can serve as internal alarm bells, warning us of the possibility of injustice, suffering, and wrongdoing. But they are unreliable guides to moral truth. They may simply reflect our own emotional needs, prejudices, upbringing, culture, and self-interests. Careful reasoning, however, can inform our feelings and help us decide moral questions on their merits.

The Universal Perspective

Logic requires that moral norms and judgments follow the *principle of universalizability*—the idea that a moral statement (a principle, rule, or judgment) that applies in one situation must apply in all other situations that are relevantly similar. If you say, for example, that lying is wrong in a particular situation, then you implicitly agree that lying is wrong for anyone in relevantly similar situations. If you say that killing in self-defense is morally permissible, then you say in effect that killing in self-defense is permissible for everyone in relevantly similar situations. It cannot be the case that an action performed by A is *wrong* while the same action performed by B in relevantly similar circumstances is *right*. It cannot be the case that the moral judgments formed in these two situations must differ just because two different people are involved.

This point about universalizability also applies to reasons used to support moral judgments. If reasons apply in a specific case, then those reasons also apply in all relevantly similar cases. It cannot be true that reasons that apply in a specific case do not apply to other cases that are similar in all relevant respects.

The Principle of Impartiality

From the moral point of view, all persons are considered equal and should be treated accordingly. This sense of impartiality is implied in all moral statements. It means that the welfare and interests of each individual should be given the same weight as all others. Unless there is a morally relevant difference between people, we should treat them the same: we must treat equals equally. We would think it outrageous for a moral rule to say something like "Everyone must refrain from stealing food in grocery stores—except for Mr. X, who may steal all he wants." Imagine that there is no morally relevant reason for making this exception to food stealing; Mr. X is exempted merely because, say, he is a celebrity known for outrageous behavior. We not only would object to this rule, we might even begin to wonder if it was a genuine moral rule at all because it lacks impartiality. Similarly, we would reject a moral rule that says something like "Everyone is entitled to basic human rights—except Native Americans." Such a rule would be a prime example of unfair discrimination based on race. We can see this blatant partiality best if we ask what morally relevant difference there is between Native Americans and everyone else. Differences in income, social status, skin color, ancestry, and the like are not morally relevant. Because there are no morally relevant differences, we must conclude that the rule sanctions unfair discrimination.

We must keep in mind, however, that sometimes there are good reasons for treating someone differently. Imagine a hospital that generally gives equal care to all patients, treating equals equally. Then suppose a patient comes to the hospital in an ambulance because she has had a heart attack and will die without immediate care. The hospital staff responds quickly, giving her faster and more sophisticated care than some other patients receive. Because the situation is a matter of life and death, it is a good reason for *not* treating everyone the same and for providing the heart attack patient with special consideration. This instance of discrimination is justified.

The Dominance of Moral Norms

Not all norms are moral norms. There are legal norms (laws, statutes), aesthetic norms (for judging artistic creations), prudential norms (practical considerations of self-interest), and others. Moral norms seem to stand out from all of these in an interesting way: they dominate. Whenever moral principles or values conflict in some way with nonmoral principles or values, the moral considerations usually override the others. Moral considerations seem more important, more critical, or more weighty. A principle of prudence such as "Never help a stranger" may be well justified, but it must yield to any moral principle that contradicts it, such as "Help a stranger in an emergency if you can do so without endangering yourself." An aesthetic norm that somehow involved violating a moral principle would have to take a backseat to the moral considerations. A law that conflicted with a moral principle would be suspect, and the latter would have to prevail over the former. Ultimately the justification for civil disobedience is that specific laws conflict with moral norms and are therefore invalid. If we judge a law to be bad, we usually do so on moral grounds.

Notes

1. John Stuart Mill, *On Liberty,* 1859.

2. Paul W. Taylor, *Principles of Ethics: An Introduction* (Encino, CA: Dickenson, 1975), 9–10.

CHAPTER 2

The Foundational Biblical Beginning with All of Its Interpretative Challenges and Yet Singular Cultural Influence

2A. The Holy Bible, Genesis, chapters 1–3

1:1 In the beginning God created the heaven and the earth.

1:2 And the earth was without form, and void; and darkness was upon the face of the deep. And the Spirit of God moved upon the face of the waters.

1:3 And God said, Let there be light: and there was light.

1:4 And God saw the light, that it was good: and God divided the light from the darkness.

1:5 And God called the light Day, and the darkness he called Night. And the evening and the morning were the first day.

1:6 And God said, Let there be a firmament in the midst of the waters, and let it divide the waters from the waters.

1:7 And God made the firmament, and divided the waters which were under the firmament from the waters which were above the firmament: and it was so.

1:8 And God called the firmament Heaven. And the evening and the morning were the second day.

1:9 And God said, Let the waters under the heaven be gathered together unto one place, and let the dry land appear: and it was so.

1:10 And God called the dry land Earth; and the gathering together of the waters called he Seas: and God saw that it was good.

1:11 And God said, Let the earth bring forth grass, the herb yielding seed, and the fruit tree yielding fruit after his kind, whose seed is in itself, upon the earth: and it was so.

1:12 And the earth brought forth grass, and herb yielding seed after his kind, and the tree yielding fruit, whose seed was in itself, after his kind: and God saw that it was good.

1:13 And the evening and the morning were the third day.

1:14 And God said, Let there be lights in the firmament of the heaven to divide the day from the night; and let them be for signs, and for seasons, and for days, and years: 1:15 And let them be for lights in the firmament of the heaven to give light upon the earth: and it was so.

1:16 And God made two great lights; the greater light to rule the day, and the lesser light to rule the night: he made the stars also.

1:17 And God set them in the firmament of the heaven to give light upon the earth, 1:18 And to rule over the day and over the night, and to divide the light from the darkness: and God saw that it was good.

1:19 And the evening and the morning were the fourth day.

1:20 And God said, Let the waters bring forth abundantly the moving creature that hath life, and fowl that may fly above the earth in the open firmament of heaven.

1:21 And God created great whales, and every living creature that moveth, which the waters brought forth abundantly, after their kind, and every winged fowl after his kind: and God saw that it was good.

1:22 And God blessed them, saying, Be fruitful, and multiply, and fill the waters in the seas, and let fowl multiply in the earth.

Selections from "Genesis," The King James Bible.

1:23 And the evening and the morning were the fifth day.

1:24 And God said, Let the earth bring forth the living creature after his kind, cattle, and creeping thing, and beast of the earth after his kind: and it was so.

1:25 And God made the beast of the earth after his kind, and cattle after their kind, and every thing that creepeth upon the earth after his kind: and God saw that it was good.

1:26 And God said, Let us make man in our image, after our likeness: and let them have dominion over the fish of the sea, and over the fowl of the air, and over the cattle, and over all the earth, and over every creeping thing that creepeth upon the earth.

1:27 So God created man in his own image, in the image of God created he him; male and female created he them.

1:28 And God blessed them, and God said unto them, Be fruitful, and multiply, and replenish the earth, and subdue it: and have dominion over the fish of the sea, and over the fowl of the air, and over every living thing that moveth upon the earth.

1:29 And God said, Behold, I have given you every herb bearing seed, which is upon the face of all the earth, and every tree, in the which is the fruit of a tree yielding seed; to you it shall be for meat.

1:30 And to every beast of the earth, and to every fowl of the air, and to every thing that creepeth upon the earth, wherein there is life, I have given every green herb for meat: and it was so.

1:31 And God saw every thing that he had made, and, behold, it was very good. And the evening and the morning were the sixth day.

2:1 Thus the heavens and the earth were finished, and all the host of them.

2:2 And on the seventh day God ended his work which he had made; and he rested on the seventh day from all his work which he had made.

2:3 And God blessed the seventh day, and sanctified it: because that in it he had rested from all his work which God created and made.

2:4 These are the generations of the heavens and of the earth when they were created, in the day that the LORD God made the earth and the heavens, 2:5 And every plant of the field before it was in the earth, and every herb of the field before it grew: for the LORD God had not caused it to rain upon the earth, and there was not a man to till the ground.

2:6 But there went up a mist from the earth, and watered the whole face of the ground.

2:7 And the LORD God formed man of the dust of the ground, and breathed into his nostrils the breath of life; and man became a living soul.

2:8 And the LORD God planted a garden eastward in Eden; and there he put the man whom he had formed.

2:9 And out of the ground made the LORD God to grow every tree that is pleasant to the sight, and good for food; the tree of life also in the midst of the garden, and the tree of knowledge of good and evil.

2:10 And a river went out of Eden to water the garden; and from thence it was parted, and became into four heads.

2:11 The name of the first is Pison: that is it which compasseth the whole land of Havilah, where there is gold; 2:12 And the gold of that land is good: there is bdellium and the onyx stone.

2:13 And the name of the second river is Gihon: the same is it that compasseth the whole land of Ethiopia.

2:14 And the name of the third river is Hiddekel: that is it which goeth toward the east of Assyria. And the fourth river is Euphrates.

2:15 And the LORD God took the man, and put him into the garden of Eden to dress it and to keep it.

2:16 And the LORD God commanded the man, saying, Of every tree of the garden thou mayest freely eat: 2:17 But of the tree of the knowledge of good and evil, thou shalt not eat of it: for in the day that thou eatest thereof thou shalt surely die.

2:18 And the LORD God said, It is not good that the man should be alone; I will make him an help meet for him.

2:19 And out of the ground the LORD God formed every beast of the field, and every fowl of the air; and brought them unto Adam to see what he would call them: and whatsoever Adam called every living creature, that was the name thereof.

2:20 And Adam gave names to all cattle, and to the fowl of the air, and to every beast of the field; but for Adam there was not found an help meet for him.

2:21 And the LORD God caused a deep sleep to fall upon Adam, and he slept: and he took one of his ribs, and closed up the flesh instead thereof; 2:22 And the rib, which the LORD God had taken from man, made he a woman, and brought her unto the man.

2:23 And Adam said, This is now bone of my bones, and flesh of my flesh: she shall be called Woman, because she was taken out of Man.

2:24 Therefore shall a man leave his father and his mother, and shall cleave unto his wife: and they shall be one flesh.

2:25 And they were both naked, the man and his wife, and were not ashamed.

3:1 Now the serpent was more subtil than any beast of the field which the LORD God had made. And he said unto the woman, Yea, hath God said, Ye shall not eat of every tree of the garden? 3:2 And the woman said unto the serpent, We may eat of the fruit of the trees of the garden: 3:3 But of the fruit of the tree which is in the midst of the garden, God hath said, Ye shall not eat of it, neither shall ye touch it, lest ye die.

3:4 And the serpent said unto the woman, Ye shall not surely die: 3:5 For God doth know that in the day ye eat thereof, then your eyes shall be opened, and ye shall be as gods, knowing good and evil.

3:6 And when the woman saw that the tree was good for food, and that it was pleasant to the eyes, and a tree to be desired to make one wise, she took of the fruit thereof, and did eat, and gave also unto her husband with her; and he did eat.

3:7 And the eyes of them both were opened, and they knew that they were naked; and they sewed fig leaves together, and made themselves aprons.

3:8 And they heard the voice of the LORD God walking in the garden in the cool of the day: and Adam and his wife hid themselves from the presence of the LORD God amongst the trees of the garden.

3:9 And the LORD God called unto Adam, and said unto him, Where art thou? 3:10 And he said, I heard thy voice in the garden, and I was afraid, because I was naked; and I hid myself.

3:11 And he said, Who told thee that thou wast naked? Hast thou eaten of the tree, whereof I commanded thee that thou shouldest not eat? 3:12 And the man said, The woman whom thou gavest to be with me, she gave me of the tree, and I did eat.

3:13 And the LORD God said unto the woman, What is this that thou hast done? And the woman said, The serpent beguiled me, and I did eat.

3:14 And the LORD God said unto the serpent, Because thou hast done this, thou art cursed above all cattle, and above every beast of the field; upon thy belly shalt thou go, and dust shalt thou eat all the days of thy life: 3:15 And I will put enmity between thee and the woman, and between thy seed and her seed; it shall bruise thy head, and thou shalt bruise his heel.

3:16 Unto the woman he said, I will greatly multiply thy sorrow and thy conception; in sorrow thou shalt bring forth children; and thy desire shall be to thy husband, and he shall rule over thee.

3:17 And unto Adam he said, Because thou hast hearkened unto the voice of thy wife, and hast eaten of the tree, of which I commanded thee, saying, Thou shalt not eat of it: cursed is the ground for thy sake; in sorrow shalt thou eat of it all the days of thy life; 3:18 Thorns also and thistles shall it bring forth to thee; and thou shalt eat the herb of the field; 3:19 In the sweat of thy face shalt thou eat bread, till thou return unto the ground; for out of it wast thou taken: for dust thou art, and unto dust shalt thou return.

3:20 And Adam called his wife's name Eve; because she was the mother of all living.

3:21 Unto Adam also and to his wife did the LORD God make coats of skins, and clothed them.

3:22 And the LORD God said, Behold, the man is become as one of us, to know good and evil: and now, lest he put forth his hand, and take also of the tree of life, and eat, and live for ever: 3:23 Therefore the LORD God sent him forth from the garden of Eden, to till the ground from whence he was taken.

3:24 So he drove out the man; and he placed at the east of the garden of Eden Cherubims, and a flaming sword which turned every way, to keep the way of the tree of life.

2B. Reinventing Eden

The Fate of Nature in Western Culture

By Carolyn Merchant

> *She has taken up with a snake now. The other animals are glad, for she was always experimenting with them and bothering them; and I am glad, because the snake talks, and this enables me to get a rest. She says the snake advises her to try the fruit of that tree, and says the result will be a great and fine and noble education. ... I advised her to keep away from the tree. She said she wouldn't. I forsee trouble. Will emigrate.* —Mark Twain, "Extracts from Adam's Diary"

Two grand historical narratives explain how the human species arrived at the present moment in history. Both are Recovery Narratives, but the two stories have different plots, one upward, the other downward. The first story is the traditional biblical narrative of the fall from the Garden of Eden from which humanity can be redeemed through Christianity. But the garden itself can also be recovered. By the time of the Scientific Revolution of the seventeenth century, the Christian narrative had merged with advances in science, technology, and capitalism to form the mainstream Recovery Narrative. The story begins with the precipitous fall from Eden followed by a long, slow, upward attempt to recreate the Garden of Eden on earth. The outcome is a better world for all people. This first story—the mainstream Recovery Narrative—is a story of upward progress in which humanity gains the power to manage and control the earth.

The second story, also a Recovery Narrative, instead depicts a long, slow decline from a prehistoric past in which the world was ecologically more pristine and society was more equitable for all people and for both genders. The decline continues to the present, but the possibility and, indeed, the absolute necessity of a precipitous, rapid Recovery exists today and could be achieved through a sustainable ecology and an equitable society. This second story is one told by many environmentalists and feminists.

Both stories are enormously compelling, and both reflect the beliefs and hopes of many people for achieving a better world. They differ fundamentally, however, on who and what wins out. In the mainstream story, humanity regains its life of ease at the expense of the earth; in the environmental story, the earth is both the victim of exploitation and the beneficiary of restoration. Women play pivotal roles in the two stories, as cause and/or victims of decline and, along with men, as restorers of a reclaimed planet. But, I argue that a third story, one of a partnership between humanity and the earth and between women and men, that draws on many of the positive aspects of the two stories is also emerging. In this [reading] I develop, compare, and critically assess the roots and broad outlines of these stories.

The Christian Narrative

The Christian story of Fall and Recovery begins with the Garden of Eden as told in the Bible. The Christian story is marked by a precipitous fall from a pristine past. The initial lapsarian moment, or loss of innocence, is the decline from garden to desert as the first couple is cast from the light of an ordered paradise into a dark, disorderly wasteland to labor in the earth. Instead of giving fruit readily, the earth now extracts human labor. The blame for the Fall is placed on woman.

The biblical Garden of Eden story has three central chapters: Creation, temptation, and expulsion (later referred to as the Fall). A woman, Eve, is the central actress, and the story's plot is declensionist (a decline from Eden) and tragic. The end result is a poorer state of both nature and human nature. The valence of woman is bad; the end valence of nature is bad. Men become the agents of transformation. After the Fall, men must labor in the earth, to produce food. They become the earthly saviors who strive, through their own agricultural labor, to re-create the lost garden on earth, thereby turning the tragedy of the Fall into the comedy of Recovery. The New Testament adds the Resurrection—the time when the earth and all its creatures, especially humans, are reunited with God to recreate the original oneness in a heavenly paradise. The biblical Fall and Recovery story has become the mainstream narrative shaping and legitimating the course of Western culture.

The Bible offers two versions of the Christian origin story that preceded the Fall. In the Genesis 1 version, God created the land, sea, grass, herbs, and fruit; the stars, sun, and moon; and the birds, whales, cattle, and beasts, after which he made "man in his own image ... male and female created he them." The couple was instructed "to be fruitful and multiply, replenish the earth, and subdue it," and was given "dominion over the fish of the sea, the fowl of the air, and over every living thing that moveth on the face of the earth." This version of creation is thought to have been contributed by the Priestly school of Hebrew scholars in the fifth century B.C.E. These scholars edited and codified earlier material into the first five books (or Pentateuch) of the Old Testament, adding the first chapter of Genesis.[1]

The alternative Garden of Eden story of creation, temptation, and expulsion (Genesis 2 and 3) derives from an earlier school. Writers in Judah in the ninth century B.C.E. produced a version of the Pentateuch known as the J source, *The Book of J*, or the Yahwist version (since Yahweh is the Hebrew deity). These writers recorded the oral traditions embodied in songs and folk stories handed down through previous centuries. In addition to the Garden of Eden story, these records include the heroic narratives of Abraham, Jacob, Joseph, and Moses; the escape from Egypt; and the settlement in the promised land of Canaan.[2]

In the Genesis 2 story, God first created "man" from the dust. The name Adam derives from the Hebrew word *adama*, meaning earth or arable land. *Adama* is a feminine noun, meaning an earth that gives birth to plants. God then created the Garden of Eden, the four rivers that flowed from it, and the trees for food (including the tree of life and the tree of the knowledge of good and evil in the center). He put "the man" in the garden "to dress and keep it," formed the birds and beasts from dust, and brought them to Adam to name. Only then did he create "the woman" from Adam's rib:

"And Adam said, This is now bone of my bones, and flesh of my flesh: she shall be called Woman, because she was taken out of man."[3]

Biblical scholar Theodore Hiebert argues that the Yahwist's Eden narrative is told from the perspective of an audience outside the garden familiar with the post-Edenic landscape. The use of the word *before* in the phrases that described God making "every plant of the field before it was in the earth," and "every herb of the field before it grew" signify the pasturage and field crops of the post-Edenic cultivated land in which the listener is situated. Similarly, the phrases that note that "God had not caused it to rain upon the earth" and that "a mist from the earth" came that "watered the whole face of the ground" indicate a post-Edenic rain-based agriculture centered on cultivation of the *adama*, or arable land.[4]

The Garden of Eden described in Genesis 2, however, is a different landscape from that of the post-Edenic *adama*; it is filled with spring-fed water out of which the four rivers flow. It contains the "beasts of the field," "fowls of the air," cattle, snakes, and fruit trees, including the fig, as well as humans "to dress and keep it." The image of the garden in which animals, plants, man, and woman live together in peaceful abundance in a well-watered garden is a powerful image; it provides the starting and ending points for both plots of the overarching Recovery Narrative.

Hiebert compares the garden to a desert oasis irrigated by springs. "The term 'garden' (*gan*)," he notes, "is itself the common designation in biblical Hebrew for irrigation-supported agriculture." Irrigation agriculture was typified by the river valley civilizations of Mesopotamia and Egypt, in which rivers overflowed onto the land and water was channeled into ditches running to fields. Of the four rivers mentioned in Genesis 2, two are the Tigris (Hiddekel) and Euphrates of Mesopotamia, while the Pison and Gihon "are placed by the Yahwist south of Israel in the area of Arabia and Ethiopia (2:11–13), and have been identified by some as the headwaters of the Nile," notes Hiebert. The Edenic landscape is thus spring-fed, river-based, and irrigated, whereas the post-Edenic landscape initiated by the temptation is rain-based. Irrigation itself later becomes a technology of humanity's hoped-for return to the garden.[5]

Genesis 3 begins with "the woman's" temptation by the serpent and the consumption of the fruit from the tree of the knowledge of good and evil. (In the Renaissance this fruit became an apple, owing to a play on the Latin word bad, or *malum*, which also means apple). The story details the loss of innocence through the couple's discovery of nakedness followed by God's expulsion from the garden of Adam and his "wife," whom he now calls Eve, because she is to become "the mother of all the living." Adam is condemned to eat bread "in the sweat of thy face," and is "sent forth from the garden of Eden, to till the ground (the *adama* or arable land) from whence he was taken," the same *adama* to which he will return after death. But because Adam has listened to his wife, the *adama* was cursed. Thorns and thistles would henceforth grow in the ground where the "herb of the field" (field crops) must be grown for bread. After the couple's expulsion, God places "at the east of the garden of Eden" the cherubim and flaming sword to guard the tree of life.[6]

The landscape into which Adam and Eve are expelled is described by Evan Eisenberg in *The Ecology of Eden*. By 1100 B.C.E. the Israelites were farming the hills of Judea and Samaria in Canaan with ox-drawn scratch plows and planting wheat, barley, and legumes such as peas and lentils. They pastured sheep, goats, and cattle, and grew grapes in vineyards, olives on hillside groves, and figs, apricots, almonds, and pomegranates in orchards. "Where least disturbed," Eisenberg notes, "the landscape was [a] sort of open Mediterranean woodland ... with evergreen oak, Aleppo pine, and pistachio. ... Elsewhere this would dwindle to ... a mix of shrubs and herbs such as rosemary, sage, summer savory, rock rose, and thorny burnet. The settlers cleared a good deal of this forest for pasture and cropland." They captured water in cisterns and terraced the land to retain the rich, but shallow red soil for planting, using the drier areas for pasturage. The arid hill country in which arable and pasturage lands was mingled was therefore the landscape that would be inhabited by the descendants of Adam and Eve.[7]

Genesis 4 recounts the fate of Adam and Eve's sons, Abel ("keeper of sheep"—a pastoralist) and Cain ("tiller of the ground"—a farmer). God accepts Abel's lamb as a first fruit, but rejects Cain's offering of the "fruit of the ground," grown on the *adama*. Although the seminomadic pastoralists and farmers of the Near East often existed in mutual support, they also engaged in conflict. Cain's killing of Abel may represent both that conflict and the historical ascendancy of settled farmers over nomadic pastoralists. A second explanation stems from the fact that Israelite farms in the hill country incorporated both farming and pastoralism into a subsistence way of life. According to Hiebert, the elder son was responsible for the tilling of the land, whereas the younger son was the keeper of the sheep. Hiebert argues that God's banishment of Cain after the killing of Abel represents a prohibition against settling disputes through the killing of kin.[8]

When human beings fell into a more labor-intensive way of life, their view of nature reflected this decline. Nature acting through God meted out floods, droughts, plagues, and disasters in response to humanity's sins or bountiful harvests in response to obedience. J. L. Russell notes that the Christian interpreter Paul "regarded the whole of nature as being in some way involved in the fall and redemption of man. He spoke of nature as 'groaning and travailing' (Romans 8.22)—striving blindly towards the same goal of union with Christ to which the Church is tending, until finally it is re-established in that harmony with man and God which was disrupted by the Fall." While the term *fall* to characterize the expulsion or going forth from Eden is absent from the Bible, it becomes commonplace in the ensuing Christian tradition. Beginning with St. Augustine, the story is interpreted as a Fall that can be undone by a savior.[9]

Before the Fall, nature was an entirely positive presence. The garden, which is the beginning and end of the Recovery Narrative, is an idealized landscape. The beasts and herbs of Genesis 1 are described as "very good," as are the cattle, fowl, beasts, and trees in the Genesis 2 Garden of Eden. The dust of Genesis 2, from which "man" was formed and which was watered by "a mist from the earth," is positive in valence. The ground, from which the other creatures are made is positive as well. But after the couple disobeys God, the ground is cursed. Adam eats of it in sorrow, and it brings forth thorns and thistles.

Figure 2.1 Adam and Eve enter the enclosed, circular Garden of Eden in lockstep. The Tree of Life and the Tree of the Knowledge of Good and Evil are at the center of the Garden, watered by a fountain, while the four rivers flow from the Garden. Ludolphus de Saxonia, *Vita Christi* (Antwerp, Gerard Leeu, 1487). Courtesy of the Huntington Library, San Marino, California

Figure 2.2 In the background Eve, tempted by the serpent, holds the apple from the Tree of the Knowledge of Good and Evil as Adam looks on. In the foreground Adam and Eve, having tasted the fruit, are expelled from the Garden, no longer in lockstep, leaving the angel with the flaming sword to guard the Tree of Life. *Adam and Eve with a Serpent from Heures à l'usage de Rome*, 1488 by J. J. du Pré. Reproduced in *The Garden of Eden* by John M. Prest, 1982 and originally from *Medieval Gardens* by Sir Frank Crisp, 1924. Reference (shelfmark) 19183 d.26.

The serpent changes from being "more subtle" than the other beasts to being "cursed above all cattle and above every beast of the field." In the Christian tradition, the thorns, thistles, and serpent symbolize barren desert and infertile ground, a negative nature from which humanity must recover to regain the garden.[10]

With the Fall from Eden, humanity abandons an original, "untouched" nature and enters into history. Nature is now a fallen world and humans fallen beings. But this Fall through the lapsarian moment sets up the opposite—or Recovery—moment. The effort to recover Eden henceforth encompasses all of human history. Reattaining the lost garden, its life of ease from labor, and its innocent happiness (and, I would add, the potential for human partnership with the earth) become the primary human endeavor. The Eden narrative is, according to Henry Goldschmidt, "a story of originary presence which is subsequently usurped by difference; and then of a final presence, reinstituted, sweeping away the unfortunate misadventure."[11]

The Recovery story begins with the Fall from the garden into the desert (and the loss of an original partnership with the land), moves upward to the re-creation of Eden on earth (the earthly paradise), and culminates with the vision of attainment of a heavenly paradise, a recovered garden. Paradise is defined as heaven, a state of bliss, an enclosed garden or park—an Eden. Derived from a Sumerian word, *paradise* was once the name of a fertile place that had become dry and barren; the Persian word for park, or enclosure, evolves through Greek and Latin to take on the meaning of garden, so that by the medieval period Eden is depicted as an enclosed garden. The religious path to a heavenly paradise, practiced throughout the early Christian and medieval periods, incorporated the promise of salvation to atone for the original sin of tasting the forbidden fruit. In the Christian story, time has two poles—beginning and end, creation and salvation.[12]

The resurrection or end drama, heralded in the New Testament, envisions an earth reunited with God when the redeemed earthly garden merges into a higher heavenly paradise. The second coming of Christ was to occur either at the outset of the thousand-year period of his reign of peace on earth, as foretold in Revelation 20 (the millennium), or at the Last Judgment, when the faithful

Figure 2.3 After the expulsion from Eden, Adam is forced to till the barren ground with plow and oxen. G. B. Andreini. "Adamo," *L'Adamo, Sacra Rappresentatione* (Milan, 1617), p. 110. Courtesy of the Huntington Library, San Marino, California

Figure 2.4 After the Fall, nature becomes a disorderly wilderness in which animals, who once lived in harmony, devour each other, while Adam and Eve are forced to live in caves and clothe themselves in skins. G. B. Andreini. "Eua, Adamo," *L'Adamo, Sacra Rapresentatione* (Milan, 1617), p. 115. Courtesy of the Huntington Library, San Marino, California

were reunited with God at the resurrection. Since medieval times, millenarian sects have awaited the advent of Christ on earth.[13]

The Parousia is the idea of the end of the world, expressed as the hope set forth in the New Testament that "he shall come again to judge both the quick and the dead." It depicts a redeemed earth and redeemed humans. "The scene of the future consummation is a radically transformed earth," writes A. L. Moore. *Parousia* derives from the Latin *parere*, meaning to produce or bring forth. Hope for Parousia was a motivating force behind the Church's missionary work, both in its early development and in the New World; Christians prepared for this expected age of glory when God would enter history. Moore notes, "The coming of this Kingdom was conceptualized as a sudden catastrophic moment, or as preceded by the Messianic kingdom, during which it was anticipated that progressive work would take place."[14]

The Modern Narrative

A secular version of the Recovery story became paramount during the Scientific Revolution of the seventeenth century, one in which the earth itself became a new Eden. This is the mainstream narrative of modern Western culture, one that continues to this day—it is *our* story, one so compelling we cannot escape its grasp. In the 1600s, Europeans and New World colonists began a massive effort to reinvent the whole earth in the image of the Garden of Eden. Aided by the Christian doctrine of redemption and the inventions of science, technology, and capitalism, the longterm goal of the Recovery project has been to turn the entire earth into a vast cultivated garden. The seventeenth-century concept of Recovery came to mean more than Recovery from the Fall. It also entailed restoration of health, reclamation of land, and recovery of property. The strong interventionist version in Genesis 1 validates Recovery through domination, while the softer Genesis 2 version advocates dressing and keeping the garden through human management (stewardship). Human labor would redeem the souls of men and women, while the earthly wilderness would be redeemed through cultivation and domestication.[15]

The Garden of Eden origin story depicts a comic or happy state of human existence, while the Fall exemplifies a tragic state. Stories and descriptions about nature and human nature told by explorers, colonists, settlers, and developers present images of and movement between comic (positive) or tragic (negative) states. Northrop Frye describes the elements of these two states. In comic stories, he notes, the human world is a community and the animal world comprises domesticated flocks and birds of peace. The vegetable world is a garden or park with trees, while the mineral world is a city or temple with precious stones and starlit domes. And the unformed world is depicted as a river. In tragic stories, the human world is an anarchy of individuals and the animal world is filled with birds and beasts of prey (such as wolves, vultures, and serpents). The vegetable world is a wilderness, desert, or sinister forest, the mineral world is filled with rocks and ruins, and the unformed world is a sea or flood. All of these elements are present in the two versions of the Recovery Narrative.[16]

The plot of the tragedy moves from a better or comic state to a worse or tragic state (from the Garden of Eden to a desert wilderness). The comedy, on the other hand, moves from an initial tragic state to a comic outcome (from a desert to a recovered garden). Thus, the primary narrative of Western culture has been a precipitous, tragic Fall from the Garden of Eden, followed by a long, slow, upward Recovery to convert the fallen world of deserts and wilderness into a new earthly Eden. Tragedy is turned into comedy through human labor in the earth and the Christian faith in redemption. During the Scientific Revolution, the Christian and modern stories merged to become the mainstream Recovery Narrative of Western culture (see Table 2.1).

Table 2.1 Reinventing Eden: Narratives of Western Culture

Christian	Modern	Environmentalist	Feminist
Eden	Golden Age	Pristine Wilderness	Matriarchy or Equality
Fall	Dark Ages	Ecological Crisis	Patriarchy
Birth of Christ	Renaissance	Environmental Movement	Feminist Movement
Heaven	Enlightenment, Capitalism	Restored Earth	Emancipation, Equality

The Role of Gender

The way in which gender is encoded into the mainstream Recovery Narrative is crucial to the structure of the story. In the Christian tradition, God—the original oneness—is male, while in the garden the woman (Eve) is subordinate to the man (Adam). The fall from the garden is caused by the woman, Eve; Adam is the innocent bystander, forced to pay the consequences as his sons, Abel and Cain, are constrained to develop pastoralism and farming. While fallen Adam becomes the inventor of the tools and technologies that will restore the garden, fallen Eve becomes the nature that must be tamed into submission. In much of the imagery of Western culture, Eve is inherently connected to and associated symbolically with nature and the garden. In the European and American traditions, male science and technology mitigate the effects of fallen nature. The good state that keeps unruly nature in check is invented, engineered, and operated by men, and the good economy that organizes the labor needed to restore the garden historically has been male directed.

In Western culture, nature as Eve appears in three forms. As original Eve, nature is virgin, pure, and light—land that is pristine or barren but has the potential for development. As fallen Eve, nature is disorderly and chaotic; a wilderness, wasteland, or desert requiring improvement; dark and witchlike, the victim and mouthpiece of Satan as serpent. As mother Eve, nature is an improved garden; a nurturing earth bearing fruit; a ripened ovary; maturity. Original Adam is the image of God as creator, initial agent, activity. Fallen Adam appears as the agent of earthly transformation, the hero who redeems the fallen land. Father Adam is the image of God as patriarch, law, and rule, the model for kingdom and state.

These denotions of nature as female and agency as male are encoded as symbols and myths into land that has the potential for development but needs the male hero—Adam. But such symbols are not "essences" because they do not represent characteristics necessary or essential to being female or male. They are historically constructed meanings derived from the origin stories of European settlers and the cultural and economic practices they transported to and developed in the New World. These gender symbols are not immutable; they can be changed by exposing their presence and rethinking history.

The male/female hierarchy encoded into the Genesis texts both consciously and implicitly socializes the young into behavioral patterns. Eve, after ingesting the fruit, is told she will be ruled by her husband, and the conflation of animals with women as helpmates is also explicit. In all versions of the story, Eve became Adam's "wife" after the two became one flesh, and she is to be "ruled over" or "dominated" by her husband after she disobeys God.[17]

But there is another way to read the gendered message. In the feminist reading, Genesis 1's simultaneous creation of men and women indicates their potential equality ("male and female created He them"). Recovery, therefore, is an effort to reclaim an original gender equality or partnership. Genesis 2, on the other hand, depicts the creation sequentially, first, of a real, material male body from dust and, second, woman from the body of the male. Hence Eve is second in the order of creation, implying the subjection of woman to man.[18] But some feminists argue that Eve is not derivative of Adam; he was not awake at her creation, nor was he even consulted in advance. "Like man, woman owes her life solely to God," states Phyllis Trible, "to claim that the rib means inferiority or subordination is to assign the man qualities over the woman which are not in the narrative itself." Eve's role in initiating the Fall can also be debated. Was she the weaker, more vulnerable sex and hence susceptible to the serpent's temptation? Or, was she actually the First Scientist—the more independent and curious of the two—as in the Mark Twain epigraph earlier. In this reading, Eve was the one who questioned the established order of things and initiated change. As original biologist, Eve talks to the snake and nature rather than to God as does Adam. As prototypic scientist, Eve could hold the key to recovering Eden through a new science.[19]

While the Bible does not employ the term *partner* for the male–female relationship, today some people are rethinking the Genesis passages in terms of partnership. Theologian Ray Maria McNamara interprets the creation story in Genesis 1 in terms of a partnership between God and the earth. She notes that although God said "Let the earth bring forth grass and herb" it was actually the earth as an active partner that "brought forth grass and herb ... and the tree yielding fruit." Another contribution to a partnership interpretation is made by the Reverend William M. Boyce Jr., who offers a free translation of several of the Genesis verses. He portrays Adam and Eve as helpers, partners, and colleagues to one another and a God who views the whole of creation as very, very good.[20]

Stewardship Versus Dominion

While the role of gender is central to the story, equally critical is the question of human dominion versus stewardship of nature. If Genesis 1 is accepted as the ethical model, as it is in mainstream Western culture, then the domination of nature could be interpreted as the ideal pathway to Recovery. But if Genesis 2 represents the ethical ideal (humans as stewards over the animals), then Recovery could mean that humans are the caretakers and stewards of nature. The Bible and the Torah, in Christian and Judaic traditions, provide interesting variations on the language of the two creation stories leading to dominance or stewardship. The terms *dominion, mastery, subduing, conquering,* and *ruling* predominate in different translations of the Genesis 1 story. In order to have dominion, men and women must "be fruitful," "be fertile," "become many," "increase," "multiply," "grow in number," "have many children," and then "replenish," "fill," "fill up," and "people" the "earth" or the "land."[21] If the fall from Eden entails the loss of immortality bestowed by the tree of life, humans can henceforth attain immortality only through sexual procreation. Thus, in the mainstream story of Western culture, to recover the Garden of Eden means that people must not only convert the earthly wilderness into a garden, but must also replenish the earth by expanding the human population over space and time. The Genesis 1 ethic, claims that humans must "replenish the earth and subdue it." Or, as historian Lynn White Jr. argued in 1967, it is "God's will that man exploit nature for his proper ends."[22]

Genesis 2 presents stewardship as an ethical alternative to the domination of nature. God puts "man" into the Garden of Eden and instructs him "to dress it and to keep it." The Genesis 2:15 ethic is often interpreted as the stewardship of nature, as opposed to the Genesis 1:28 ethic of dominion or mastery. In Genesis 2, the earth is a garden—a local plot of land rather than a vast area for spatial conquest—and the man is commanded to "dress," "keep," "tend," "guard," and "watch over" it. According to ecologist René Dubos, God "placed man in the Garden of Eden not as a master but rather in a spirit of stewardship." For many religious sects wishing to embrace an ecological ethic, stewardship is the most persuasive ethic that is also consistent with biblical traditions. Stewardship is a caretaker ethic, but it is still anthropocentric inasmuch as nature is created for human use.[23] Moreover, Nature is not an actor, but is rendered docile.

Throughout most of Western history, the biblical mandates of stewardship and dominion have sometimes been explicitly separated and at other times implicitly merged. For example, medieval enclosed gardens were often protected, carefully stewarded spaces, while eighteenth-century garden estates were vast displays of dominion and power. Early American farms ranged from small patches in the forest tended mainly for family provisions to large plantations and capitalist ranches that dominated the landscape. While the former exemplify potential partnerships between humanity and the land, the latter represent the potential for human mastery over the earth. Colonists, planters, and westward pioneers often explicitly cited the Genesis 1:28 mandate in order to justify expansion. In Western culture, the Genesis 1 and 2 accounts have usually been conflated. In the mainstream Recovery project, humanity has turned the entire earth into a vast garden by mastering nature. The Genesis 1:28 ethic of dominion has provided the rationale for the Recovery of the garden lost in Genesis 2 and 3, submerging the stewardship ethic of Genesis 2:15.

When Adam and Eve tasted the fruit of the tree of the knowledge of good and evil, humans acquired their potential omniscience of nature. Wanting to become more like God, humanity has craved knowledge of everything. Since the seventeenth century, mainstream Western culture has pursued the pathway to Eden's Recovery by using Christianity, science, technology, and capitalism in concert. That human dominion over nature, however, has costs in terms of the depletion of the planet's resources.[24]

The Genesis stories provide two ethical alternatives, dominion and stewardship—both of which are anthropocentric. They do not explicitly acknowledge nonanthropocentric ethics, such as ecocentrism in which humanity is only one of a number of equal parts—an ecocentric ethic; nor is biocentrism a possibility, in which value is grounded in life itself, rather than being centered on humanity. But another form of ethics is the partnership ethic I propose that posits nature and humanity as equal, interacting, mutually responsive partners [...]. This ethic combines human actions and nature's actions in a dynamic relationship with each other. Here nature is not created specifically for human use, nor are women and animals seen as helpmates for "man." Rather, human life and biotic life exist in mutual support, reciprocity, and partnership with each other. Gardens could exemplfy places in which the practice of gardening is a caretaking of the soil and the life it generates.[25]

Environmentalist and Feminist Narratives

An alternative to the mainstream story of Fall and Recovery is told by many environmentalists and feminists. This second narrative begins in a Stone-Age Garden of Eden and depicts a gradual, rather than precipitous, loss of a pristine condition. It uses archeological, anthropological, and ecological data, along with myth and art, to re-create a story of decline. Both environmental and feminist accounts idealize an Edenic prehistory in which both sexes lived in harmony with each other and nature, but they are nevertheless compelling in their critique of environmental disruption and the subjugation of both women and nature. When viewed critically, both can contribute to a new narrative of sustainable partnership between humanity and nature.

One version of the environmental narrative is exemplified by the work of philosopher Max Oelschlaeger. Paleolithic people, he notes, did not distinguish between nature and culture, but saw themselves "as one with plants and animals, rivers and forests, as part of a larger, encompassing whole. ..." In that deep past, people in gathering/hunting bands lived sustainably and "comfortably in the wilderness," albeit within cycles of want and plenty. Contained within the sacred oneness of the *Magna Mater* (the Great Mother), hunters followed rituals that respected animals and obeyed rules for preparing food and disposing of remains. Cave paintings, for example, reveal human-animal hybrids that suggest identity with the *Magna Mater*, while the cave itself is her womb. Although myth rather than science explained life, Stone-Age peoples, argues Oelschlaeger, were just as intelligent as their "modern" counterparts.[26]

Oelschlaeger sees humankind's emergence from the original oneness with the *Magna Mater* as the beginning of a wrenching division, just as birth is a traumatic separation from the human mother. He writes, "No one knows for certain how long prehistoric people existed in an Edenlike condition of hunting-gathering, but 200,000 years or more is not an unreasonable estimate for the hegemony of the Great Hunt. Even while humankind lived the archaic life, clinging conceptually to the bosom of the *Magna Mater*, the course of cultural events contained the seeds of an agricultural revolution, since prehistoric peoples were practicing rudimentary farming and animal husbandry."[27]

Oelschlaeger's narrative is one of gradual decline from the Paleolithic era rather than a precipitous fall as depicted in the Genesis 3 story. Near the end of the last ice age, around 10,000 B.C.E., changes in climate disrupted Paleolithic ecological relations. Animals and grains were gradually domesticated for herding and cultivation, heralding a change to pastoral and horticultural ways of life, particularly in the Near East. Once humans became agriculturists, Oelschlaeger observes, "the almost paradisiacal character of prehistory was irretrievably lost." Differences between humans and animals, male and female, people and nature became more distinct.[28] Humanity lost the intimacy it once had with the *Magna Mater*: "Western culture was now alienated from the Great Mother of the Paleolithic Mind."[29]

The first environmental problems stemming from large-scale agriculture occurred in Mesopotamia. Canals stretched from the Tigris to the Euphrates, bringing fertility to thousands of square miles of cropland; but as these irrigation waters evaporated, salts accumulated in the soils and reduced productivity. Oelschlager suggests that agriculture marks a decline from an Edenic past: "If the thesis that agriculture underlies humankind's turn upon the environment, even if out of climatological exigency, is cogent, then the ancient Mediterranean theater is where the 'fall from Paradise' was staged. ..."[30]

In the Near East, the great town-based cultures emerged around 4000 B.C.E. By about 1000 B.C.E., the ancient tribes of Yahweh had become a single kingdom, ruled by David, that practiced rain-based agriculture. The God Yahweh above the earth represents a rupture with the *Magna Mater* of the Paleolithic era and a legitimization of the settled agriculture and pastoralism of the Neolithic era. The Hebrews rebelled against sacred animals as idols and placed Yahweh as the one god above and outside of nature. Time was no longer viewed as a cyclical return, but as a linear history with singular determinative events. As the "chosen people," Hebrew agriculturists and pastoralists became part of a broad-based transition from gathering/hunting to farming/herding.[31]

Ecologically, the fall from Eden, told in Genesis 2, may reflect the differences between gathering/ hunting and farming/herding initiated thousands of years earlier. In the Garden of Eden's age of gathering, Adam and Eve pick the fruits of the trees without having to labor in the earth. The transition from foraging and hunting to settled agriculture took place some 9,000 to 10,000 years ago (7000–8000 B.C.E.) with the domestication of wheat and barley in the oak forests and steppes of the Near East. Around 5,000 years ago (3200–3100 B.C.E.), fruits such as the olive, grape, date, pomegranate, and fig were domesticated. By 600 B.C.E., when the biblical stories were codified, fruit trees were cultivated throughout the Near East. The Genesis 2 story may reflect the state of farming at the time and the labor required for tilling fields as opposed to tending and harvesting fruit trees.[32]

The tilling, planting, harvesting, and storing of wheat and barley represents a form of settled agriculture in which the earth was managed for grain production. "By the time the Genesis stories were composed," writes John Passmore, "man had already embarked on the task of transforming nature. In the Genesis stories [he] justifies his actions."[33] In Genesis 1, the anthropocentric God of the Hebrews commands that the earth be subdued. This represents a rupture with the nature gods of the past that occurred during the transition from polytheism to monotheism and was codified during the years of Israelite exile in Babylon between 587 and 538 B.C.E.

During the Iron Age (1200–1000 B.C.E.), the cultures of Israel and Canaan had overlapped. Canaanite mythology included a pantheon of deities: the patriarch El; his consort and mother-goddess, Asherah; the storm-god Baal, and his sister/consort Anat. Although the worship of Yahweh predominated, Israelites also worshipped El, Baal, and Asherah. During the period of the monarchy (ca. 1000–587 B.C.E.), the figure of Yahweh assimilated characteristics of the other deities, and Israel then rejected Baal and Asherah as part of its religion. "By the end of the monarchy," states Mark S. Smith, "much of the spectrum of religious practice had largely disappeared; monolatrous Yahwism was the norm in Israel, setting the stage for the emergence of Israelite monotheism."[34]

Monotheism represented an irrevocable break with the natural world. Henri and H. A. Frankfort note that the emergence of monotheism represents the highest level of abstraction and constitutes the "emancipation of thought from myth." They write, "The dominant tenet of Hebrew thought is the absolute transcendence of God. Yahweh is not in nature. … The God of the Hebrews is pure being, unqualified, ineffable. … Hence all concrete phenomena are devaluated." Although God had human characteristics, he was not human; although God had characteristics assimilated from other deities, he was the One God, not one among many gods.[35]

From an ecological perspective, the separation of God from nature constitutes a rupture with nature. God is not nature or of nature. God is unchanging, nature is changing and inconstant. The human relationship to nature was not one of *I* to *thou*, not one of subject to subject, nor of a human being to a nature alive with gods and spirits. The intellectual construction of a transcendent God is yet another point in a narrative of decline. The separation of God from nature legitimates humanity's separation from nature and sets up the possibility of human domination and control over nature. In the agricultural communities of the Old Testament, humanity is the link between the soil and God. Humans are of the soil, but separate from and above the soil: they till the land with plows and reap the harvest with scythes; they clear the forests and pollute the rivers; their goats and sheep devour the hillsides and erode the soil. Over time, the natural landscape is irrevocably transformed. At the same time, however, nature is an unpredictible actor in the story. Noah's flood, plagues of locusts, earthquakes, droughts, and devastating diseases inject uncertainties into the outcome. Efforts to control nature come up against chaotic events that upset the linearity of the storyline and create temporary or permanent setbacks.[36]

The environmentalist narrative of decline initiated by the transition to agriculture continues to the present. Tools and technologies allow people to spread over the entire globe and to subdue the earth. The colonizers denude the earth for ores and build cities and highways across the land. Despite this destruction, however, environmentalists hope for a Recovery that reverses the decline by means of planetary restoration. The environmental Recovery begins with the conservation and preservation movements of the nineteenth century and continues with the environmental movement of the late twentieth century.

Notes

1. Roy B. Chamberlain and Herman Feldman, *The Dartmouth Bible: An Abridgment of the King James Version, with Aids to its Understanding As History and Literature, and As a Source of Religious Experience* (Boston, Mass.: Houghton Mifflin, 1961); Genesis 1:26–28; introduction, 9–10.

2. Chamberlin and Feldman, *Dartmouth Bible*, introduction, 8–9; Harold Bloom, ed., and David Rosenberg, trans., *The Book of J*, (New York: Vintage, 1990).

3. Chamberlin and Feldman, *Dartmouth Bible,* Genesis 2:7–22; introduction, 8–9. Everett Fox, ed., *The Five Books of Moses* (New York: Schocken, 1995), Genesis 2:23: "She shall be called Woman/Isha, for from Man/Ish she was taken." Adam is named in Genesis 2:19: "God formed every beast of the field, and every fowl of the air; and brought them unto Adam to see what he would call them." "Woman" is created in Genesis 2:21–22, but is not named Eve until after the couple's disobedience and punishment in Genesis 3:20: "And Adam called his wife's name Eve; because she was the mother of all living." The name Eve may have come from the Sumerian name Nin-ti, meaning "lady of the rib" or "lady of Life." See W. Gunther Plaut, ed., *The Torah, A Modern Commentary* (New York: Union of Hebrew Congregations, 1981), 30, n. 21. On the literature pertaining to the Adam and Eve story, see Michael E. Stone, *A History of the Literature of Adam and Eve* (Atlanta: Scholars Press, 1992); Gary A. Anderson and Michael E. Stone, ed., *A Synopsis of the Books of Adam and Eve,* 2d ed., revised (Atlanta: Scholars Press, 1998); Kristen E. Kvam, Linda S. Schearing, and Valarie H. Ziegler, ed., *Eve and Adam: Jewish, Christian, and Muslin Readings on Genesis and Gender* (Bloomington: Indiana University Press, 1999); Gary Anderson, Michael Stone, and Johannes Tromp, ed., *Literature on Adam and Eve: Collected Essays* (Leiden: Brill, 2000); Paul Morris and Deborah Sawyer, ed., *A Walk in the Garden: Biblical, Iconographical, and Literary Images of Eden* (Sheffield, Eng.: Sheffield Academic Press, 1992); John R. Levison, *Texts in Transition: The Greek Life of Adam and Eve* (Atlanta: Society of Biblical Literature, 2000).

4. Theodore Hiebert, *The Yahwist's Landscape: Nature and Religion in Early Israel* (New York: Oxford University Press, 1996), 32–35.

5. Hiebert, *The Yahwist's Landscape,* 53–55, quotations on 55 and 53.

6. Chamberlin and Feldman, *Dartmouth Bible,* Genesis 3:1–7, 22–24; Bill Moyers, *Genesis: A Living Conversation* (New York: Doubleday, 1996), 67; Hiebert, *The Yahwist's Landscape,* 33–35.

7. Evan Eisenberg, *The Ecology of Eden* (New York: Alfred A. Knopf, 1998), 86–89, quotation on 87.

8. J. Baird Callicott, "Genesis Revisited: Muirian Musings on the Lynn White, Jr. Debate," *Environmental Review* 14, nos. 1–2 (1990): 65–92, esp. 81. Moyers, *Genesis,* 71–76. See Genesis 1:29–30; Genesis 2:9; Genesis 3:18, 19, 23; Hiebert, *The Yahwist's Landscape,* 40–41.

9. J. L. Russell, "Time in Christian Thought," in *The Voices of Time: A Cooperative Survey of Man's Views of Time As Expressed by the Sciences and Humanities,* ed. J. T. Fraser (Amherst: University of Massachusetts Press, 1981), quoted in Max Oelschlaeger, *The Idea of Wilderness: From Prehistory to the Age of Ecology* (New Haven, Conn.: Yale University Press, 1991), 67.

10. Genesis 1:31; Genesis 2:6–7; Genesis 3:1, 14, 18.

11. Victor Rotenberg, "The Lapsarian Moment" (unpublished manuscript, University of California-Berkeley, 1993); Henry Goldschmidt, "Rupture Tales: Stories and Politics in and Around the Garden of Eden" (unpublished manuscript, University of California, Santa Cruz, 1994), quotations on 8–9; I thank Victor Rotenberg and Henry Goldschmidt for sharing their manuscripts with me. As postmodern philosopher

Jacques Derrida puts it, the story is an ontotheology "determining the ... meaning of being as presence, as parousia, as life without difference"; see Derrida, *Of Grammatology,* trans. Gayatri Chakravorty Spivak (Baltimore: Johns Hopkins University Press, 1976), 71.

12. *Oxford English Dictionary,* compact ed., 2 vols. (Oxford: Oxford University Press, 1971), vol. 1., s.v. "Eden"; vol. 2, s.v. "paradise"; Plaut, *The Torah,* 29, note 8. In the Jewish tradition, Eden is the home of the righteous after death. On time in the Christian tradition, see Oelschlaeger, *The Idea of Wilderness,* 65–66.

13. Jeffrey L. Sheler, "The Christmas Covenant," *U.S. News and World Report,* Dec. 19, 1994, 62–71, esp. 66. Religious sects differ as to forms of millennialism. Premillennialists, such as fundamentalist and evangelical Christians, believe a catastrophe or final battle of Armageddon will initiate the age of Christ on earth. Postmillennialists argue for Christ's return only after a golden age of peace on earth brought about by working within the church. Antimillennialists, who include most Protestants and Roman Catholics, do not accept the one-thousand-year reign of Christ on earth, but instead believe in a period prior to the final resurrection in which Christ works through the church and individual lives.

14. A. L. Moore, *The Parousia in the New Testament* (Leiden: E. J. Brill, 1966), 2, 3, 5, 16, 17, 20, 21, 25–26, 28. Moore notes "The divine intervention in history was the manifestation of the Kingdom of God. ... [T]his would involve a total transformation of the present situation, hence the picture of world renewal enhanced sometimes by the idea of an entirely supernatural realm" (25–26). Further, "Concerning the central figure in the awaited End-drama there is considerable variation. In some visions the figure of Messiah is entirely absent. In such cases 'the kingdom was always represented as under the immediate sovereignty of God'" (21).

15. The concept of a recovery from the biblical Fall appears in the seventeenth century. According to the *Oxford English Dictionary,* recover is "[t]he act of recovering oneself from a mishap, mistake, fall, etc."; vol. 2, s.v. "fall." See also Bishop Edward Stillingfleet, *Origines Sacrae* (London, 1662), II, i, sec 1.: "The conditions on which fallen man may expect a recovery"; William Cowper, *Retirement* (1781), 138: "To ... search the themes, important above all Ourselves, and our recovery from our fall"; and Richard Eden, *The Decades of the Newe Worlde or West India* (1555), 168: "The recoverie of the kyngedome of Granata." The term *recovery* also embraced the idea of regaining a "natural" position after falling and a return to health after sickness. It acquired a legal meaning in the sense of gaining possession of property by a verdict or judgment of the court. In common recovery, an estate was transferred from one party to another. See John Cowell, *The Interpreter* (1607), s.v. "recoverie": "A true recoverie is an actuall or reall recoverie of anything, or the value thereof by Judgement." Another meaning was the restoration of a person or thing to a healthy or normal condition, or a return to a higher or better state, including the reclamation of land. [See anonymous,] *Captives bound in Chains ... the misery of graceless Sinners, and the hope of their recovery by Christ* (1674); Bishop Joseph Butler, *The Analogy of Religion Natural and Revealed* (1736), 2: 295: "Indeed neither Reason nor Analogy would lead us to think ... that the Interposition of Christ ... would be of that Efficacy for Recovery of the World, which Scripture teaches us it was"; Joseph Gilbert, *The Christian Atonement* (1836), 1:24: "A modified system, which shall include the provision of means for recovery from a lapsed state"; James Martineau, *Essays, Reviews, and Addresses*

(1890–91), 2:310: "He is fitted to be among the prophets of recovery, who may prepare for us a more wholesome future." John Henry Newman, *Historical Sketches* (1872–73) 2:1:3:121: "The special work of his reign was the recovery of the soil."

16. On the tragic and comic visions of the human, animal, vegetable, mineral and unformed worlds, see Northrup Frye, *Fables of Identity* (New York: Harcourt Brace, 1963), 19–20.

17. Bloom and Rosenberg, *The Book of J*, 62; A. Cohen, ed., *Soncino Chumash, or, Five Books of Moses with Haphtaroth* (Hindland, Surrey, Eng.: Soncino Press, 1947), 11; Plaut, ed., *The Torah* (1981), 30; Aryeh Kaplan, trans., *The Living Torah: The First Five Books of Moses and the Haftarot* (New York: Mazanim, 1981), 9; *Tanakh* (1985), 5; Arthur S. Maxwell, *The Bible Story*, rev. ed. (Hagerston, Md.: Review and Herald Publishing Association, 1994), 47–49. Kaplan, *The Living Torah* says, "Your passion will be to your husband and he will dominate you" (Genesis 3:16). The King James version of the Bible and the 1947 *Soncino Chumash* call both the animals and the woman "help meets"; the 1981 Plaut edition of *The Torah* and the 1985 *Tanakh* refer to them as "fitting helpers"; Kaplan's 1981 *Living Torah* denotes them "compatible helpers," while Everett Fox, ed., *The Five Books of Moses* (New York: Schocken Books, 1995) uses "a helper corresponding to him." *The Book of J*, thought by Harold Bloom to have been written by a woman, calls both the animals and the woman (created to help Adam "tend" and "watch" the Garden of Eden) "partners" (Genesis 2:18, 20). The children's *Bible Story* (1994) calls them "mates," while Eve is Adam's "life companion."

18. Plaut, *The Torah*, 28, 32. Victor Roland Gold et al., eds., *The New Testament and Psalms: An Inclusive Version* (New York: Oxford University Press, 1995) translates God as Father-Mother. The Lord's Prayer (Matthew 6:9–10) thus reads "Our Father-Mother in heaven, hallowed be your name. Your dominion come."

19. Phyllis Trible, quoted in Plaut, *The Torah*, 33, n. 15. On Eve as the first scientist see Mark Twain, "Eve's Diary," in *The Diaries of Adam and Eve* (replica of the 1904–5 1st ed.), in *The Oxford Mark Twain*, ed. Shelley Fisher Fishkin (New York: Oxford University Press, 1996).

20. Ray Maria McNamara, Graduate Theological Union, Berkeley, personal communication with the author. Reverend William Moore Boyce Jr., Richmond, Virginia, a free translation of Genesis 2:18; Genesis 1:28 and 31 (1998): "Then the Lord God said: 'It is not good for humans to be alone. I will make them helpers, partners, and colleagues to each other'. ... So God created humankind in God's own image, in the image of God they were created, male and female they were created, and God saw the whole creation and indeed it was very, very good."

21. A. Cohen, *The Soncino Chumash*, 7 note. The King James version of the Bible and the *Soncino Chumash* translate the Genesis 1:28 passage in almost identical terms, using the familiar terms *subdue* and *dominion*: "And God blessed them and God said unto them: 'Be fruitful and multiply and replenish the earth and subdue it; and have dominion over the fish of the sea and over the fowl of the air, and over every living thing that creepeth upon the earth.'" Cohen notes that the Hebrew word for *subdue* could be read as applying only to the singular individual ("subdue thou it") and therefore was "addressed only to man

whose function it is to subdue, but not to woman." The New Century version of the *Bible* (1987) reads, "Have many children and grow in number. Fill the earth and be its master. Rule over the fish of the sea. ..." Here mastery and rule are the message. Plaut's edition of *The Torah* (1981) also replaces the words "subdue it" with "master it," while changing "have dominion over" to "rule." It reads, "God blessed them and God said to them, 'Be fertile and increase, fill the earth and master it; and rule the fish of the sea, the birds of the sky, and all the living things that creep on earth.'" The *Tanakh*, a new translation of the *Torah* rendered in 1985, like the 1981 Plaut version, uses "increase," "master," and "rule." Harsher, however, is the translation in Kaplan *The Living Torah*, which uses "conquer" and "dominate." The passage reads, "God blessed them. God said to them, 'Be fertile and become many. Fill the land and conquer it. Dominate the fish of the sea, the birds of the air, and every beast that walks the land.'" A new translation rendered by David Seidenberg ("Some Texts from the Torah on the Relationship between Humanity and Nature," unpublished manuscript, 1993), employs "conquer" (as does the Kaplan edition), while also translating the land as female: "And Elohim blessed them and said to them, 'bear fruit and increase and fill up the land and conquer/occupy her and prevail over the fish of the sea and over the bird of the skies and over every animal crawling on the land.'" For more information see Jeremy Cohen, *"Be Fertile and Increase, Fill the Earth and Master It." The Ancient and Medieval Career of a Biblical Text.* (Ithaca: Cornell University Press, 1989). These comparisons among Genesis 1:28 renderings in the Christian and Judaic traditions seem to confirm the mandate to populate, "subdue," "master," "rule," and "conquer" the (female) land. Encoded into Western culture, such language was used historically to justify spatial expansion, colonial territories, manifest destiny, and the westward conquest of other peoples and lands.

22. Plaut, *The Torah*, 39; Lynn White Jr., "The Historical Roots of our Ecologic Crisis," *Science* 155 (1967): 1203–7, reprinted in Ian Barbour, ed., *Western Man and Environmental Ethics: Attitudes toward Nature and Technology* (Reading, Mass.: Addison Wesley, 1973), 18–30, quotation on 25.

23. René Dubos, "Conservation, Stewardship, and the Human Heart," *Audubon*, September 1972, 21–28, quotation on 27; see also Dubos, "A Theology of the Earth," in Ian G. Barbour, ed., *Western Man and Environmental Ethics*, 43–54; Robin Attfield, *The Ethics of Environmental Concern* (New York: Scribner's, 1974); and Bruce Babbitt, "Stewards of Creation," *Christian Century*, 113, no. 16 (1996), 500–503.

24. Plaut, *The Torah*, 38.

25. Cohen, ed., *Soncino Chumash* (1947), 10; Plaut, ed., *The Torah* (1981), 30; Kaplan, ed. *The Living Torah* (1981), 9; *Tanakh* (1985), 5; Bloom and Rosenberg, *The Book of J*, 62; Seidenberg, *Some Texts from the Torah*, 1. Plaut, *The Torah*, however, changes the wording to "to till it and tend it," introducing into Eden more explicitly the possibility of agriculture. Kaplan's *Living Torah* and Fox's *Schocken Bible* use "to work it and watch it," while the 1985 *Tanakh* (again, like the Plaut 1981 version) employs "to till it and tend it." Rosenberg's 1990 translation of the *Book of J* renders the passage as follows: "Yahweh lifts the man, brings him to rest in the garden of Eden, to tend it and watch." As in his Genesis 1:28 translation, Seidenberg renders the garden as female and translates the verbs as to "work/serve and watch over" her. His translation reads, "And YHVH Elohim took the human and placed him/it in 'ayden garden to work/serve her and to watch over her." Here again the female connection to the land and garden are

made explicit, but "man" is instead rendered "human." This language interprets humanity as caretaker of the land. On biocentric ethics, see Paul Taylor, *Respect for Nature: A Theory of Environmental Ethics* (Princeton, N.J.: Princeton University Press, 1986). On ecocentric ethics, see Aldo Leopold, "The Land Ethic," in *A Sand County Almanac* (New York: Oxford University Press, 1949), 201–25; J. Baird Callicott, *In Defense of the Land Ethic: Essays in Environmental Philosophy* (Albany: State University of New York Press, 1989); and Holmes Rolston III, *Philosophy Gone Wild: Essays in Environmental Ethics* (Buffalo, N.Y.: Prometheus Books, 1986).

26. Oelschlaeger, *The Idea of Wilderness*, 11–12, 14, 16, 17–18, 20, 23, quotation on 11–12.

27. Ibid., 24.

28. Ibid., 25, 28.

29. Ibid., 60, 65, 67.

30. Ibid., 31, 39.

31. Ibid., 42, 47–48.

32. Carol Manahan, "The Genesis of Agriculture and the Agriculture of Genesis," unpublished manuscript. On the domestication of crops and the rise of settled agriculture, see David R. Harris and Gordon C. Hillman, ed. *Foraging and Farming: The Evolution of Plant Exploitation* (Boston: Unwin Hyman, 1989); Daniel Zohary and Pinhas Spiegel-Roy, "Beginnings of Fruit-Growing in the Old World," *Science* 187 (1975): 319–27.

33. John Passmore, quoted in Oelschlaeger, *The Idea of Wilderness*, p. 46.

34. Mark S. Smith, *The Early History of God: Yahweh and the Other Deities in Ancient Israel* (San Francisco: Harper Collins, 1990), xix–xxvii, quotation on xxvii.

35. Henri Frankfort, H. A. Frankfort, John A. Wilson, Thorkild Jacobsen, and William A. Irwin, *Before Philosophy: The Intellectual Adventure of Ancient Man* (Baltimore: Penguin, 1949), 241–48, 253, quotations on 241–42.

36. J. Donald Hughes, *Ecology in Ancient Civilizations* (Albuquerque: University of New Mexico Press, 1975), 20–28.

Bibliography

Anderson, Gary A. and Michael Stone, eds. *A Synopsis of the Books of Adam and Eve*. 2d ed., revised. Atlanta: Scholars Press, 1998.

Anderson, Gary A., Michael Stone, and Johannes Tromp, eds. *Literature on Adam and Eve: Collected Essays*. Leiden: Brill, 2000.

Attfield, Robin. *The Ethics of Environmental Concern*. New York: Scribner's, 1974.

Babbitt, Bruce. "Stewards of Creation." *The Christian Century*, 113, no. 16 (1996), 500–503.

Barbour, Ian G., ed. *Western Man and Environmental Ethics*: Attitudes Towards Nature and Technology. Reading, Mass.: Addison-Wesley, 1973.

Bloom, Harold, ed. and David Rosenberg, trans. *The Book of J*. Trans. Rosenberg, David. New York: Vintage, 1990.

Callicott, J. Baird. "Genesis Revisited: Muirian Musings on the Lynn White, Jr. Debate." *Environmental Review* 14, nos. 1–2 (1990): 65–92.

_____. *In Defense of the Land Ethic: Essays in Environmental Philosophy*. Albany: State University of New York Press, 1989.

Chamberlin, Roy B. and Herman Feldman. *The Dartmouth Bible, An Abridgment of the King James Version, with Aids to its Understanding as History and Literature, and as a Source of Religious Experience*. Boston: Houghton Mifflin, 1961.

Cohen, A. *The Soncino Chumash*. Hindland, Surrey, UK: The Soncino Press, 1947.

Cohen, Jeremy. *"Be Fertile and Increase, Fill the Earth and Master It:" The Ancient and Medieval Career of a Biblical Test*. Ithaca: Cornell University Press, 1989.

Derrida, Jacques. *Of Grammatology*. Trans. Gayatri Chakravorty Spivak. Baltimore: Johns Hopkins University Press, 1976.

Dubos, René. "Conservation, Stewardship, and the Human Heart." *Audubon* September 1972, 21–28.

_____. "A Theology of the Earth." In *Western Man and Environmental Ethics: Attitudes toward Nature and Technology*. Ed. Ian Barbour. Reading, Mass.: Addison-Wesley, 1973, 43–54.

Eisenberg, Evan. *The Ecology of Eden*. New York: Alfred Knopf, 1998.

Fox, Everett, ed. *The Five Books of Moses*. New York: Schocken, 1995.

Frankfort, Henri, H. A. Frankfort, John A. Wilson, Thorkild Jacobsen, and William A. Irwin. *Before Philosophy: The Intellectual Adventure of Ancient Man*. Baltimore, Md.: Penguin Books, 1949 [1946].

Frye, Northrup. *Fables of Identity*. New York: Harcourt Brace, 1963.

Gold, Victor Roland et al., eds. *The New Testament and Psalms: An Inclusive Version*. New York: Oxford University Press.

Hiebert, Theodore. *The Yahwist's Landscape: Nature and Religion in Early Israel*. New York: Oxford University Press, 1996.

Holy Bible, New Century Version. Dallas: Word Publishing, 1987.

Hughes, J. Donald. *Ecology in Ancient Civilizations*. Albuquerque: University of New Mexico Press, 1975.

Kaplan, Aryeh, trans. *The Living Torah: The First Five Books of Moses and the Haftarot*. New York: Mazanim, 1981.

Kvam, Kristen, Linda S. Schearing, and Valarie H. Ziegler, eds. *Eve and Adam: Jewish, Christian, and Muslim Readings on Genesis and Gender*. Bloomington: Indiana University Press, 1999.

Leopold, Aldo. *A Sand County Almanac*. New York: Oxford University Press, 1949.

Levison, John R. *Texts in Transition: The Greek Life of Adam and Eve*. Atlanta: Society of Biblical Literature, 2000.

Maxwell, Arthur S. *The Bible Story*. Revised ed. Hagerston, Md.: Review and Herald Publishing Association, 1994.

Moore, A. L. *The Parousia in the New Testament*. Leiden: E. J. Brill, 1966.

Morris, Paul and Deborah Sawyer, eds. *A Walk in the Garden: Biblical, Iconographical, and Literary Images of Eden*. Sheffield, Eng.: Sheffield Academic Press, 1992.

Moyers, Bill. *Genesis: A Living Conversation*. New York: Doubleday, 1996.

Oelschlaeger, Max. *The Idea of Wilderness: From Prehistory to the Age of Ecology*. New Haven, Conn.: Yale University Press, 1991.

Oxford English Dictionary. Compact edition. 2 vols. Oxford: Oxford University Press, 1971.

Plaut, W. Gunther, ed. *The Torah: A Modern Commentary*. New York: Union of Hebrew Congregations, 1981.

Rolston, Holmes III. *Philosophy Gone Wild: Essays in Environmental Ethics*. Buffalo N.Y.: Prometheus Books, 1986.

Rotenberg, Victor. "The Lapsarian Moment." Unpublished Manuscript, 1993.

Russell, J. L. "Time in Christian Thought." *The Voices of Time: A Cooperative Survey of Man's Views of Time As Expressed by the Sciences and Humanities*. Ed. J. T. Fraser. 2d ed. Amherst: University of Massachusetts Press, 1981.

Seidenberg, David. "Some Texts from the Torah on the Relationship between Humanity and Nature." Unpublished manuscript, 1993.

Sheler, Jeffrey L. "The Christmas Covenant." *U.S. News and World Report*, Dec. 19, 1994: 62–71.

Smith, Mark S. *The Early History of God: Yahweh and the Other Deities in Ancient Israel*. San Francisco: Harper Collins, 1990.

Stone, Michael E. *A History of the Literature of Adam and Eve*. Atlanta: Scholars Press, 1992.

Tanakh, A New Translation of the Holy Scriptures, According to the Traditional Hebrew Text. Philadelphia: Jewish Publication Society, 1985.

Twain, Mark. *The Diaries of Adam and Eve*. Replica of the 1904–1905 1st ed. *The Oxford Mark Twain*. Ed. Shelley Fisher Fishkin. Vol. 26. New York: Oxford University Press, 1996.

White, Lynn, Jr. "The Historical Roots of Our Ecologic Crisis," *Science* 55 (1967): 1203–7.

CHAPTER 3

The Rise of the Domination of Nature through Scientific Knowledge: The Unfortunate Importance of Francis Bacon's Philosophy

3A. Francis Bacon, Quotations from Various Works

Selections from *The Works of Francis Bacon* edited by James Spedding, Robert Leslie Ellis, and Douglas Denon Heath, Volume IV.[1]

1. Only let the human race recover that rights over nature which belongs to it by divine bequest, and let power be given it. ...[2]

2. ... I mean (according to the practice in civil causes) in this great Plea or Suit granted by the divine favour and providence (whereby the human race seeks to recover its rights over nature), to examine nature herself and the arts upon interrogatories.[3]

3. Human knowledge and human power meet in one; for where the cause is not known the effect cannot be produced.[4]

4. I may hand over to men their fortunes, now their understanding is emancipated and come as it were of age; whence there cannot but follow an improvement in man's estate, and an enlargement of his power over nature. For man by the fall fell at the same time from his state innocency and from his dominion over creation. Both of these losses however can even in this life be in some part repaired; the former by religion and faith, the latter by arts and sciences.[5]

5. ... I would address one general admonition to all; that they consider what are the true ends of knowledge, and that they seek it not either for pleasure of the mind, or for contention, or for superiority to others, or for profit, or fame, or power, or any of these inferior things; but for the benefit and use of life. ...[6]

6. The End of our Foundation is the knowledge of Causes and secret motions of things; and the enlarging of the bounds of the Human Empire, to the effecting of all things Possible.[7]

7. ... it will not be amiss to distinguish the three kinds and as it were grades of ambition in mankind. The first is of those who desire to extend their own power in their country; which kind is vulgar and degenerate. The second is of those who labour to extend the power of their country and its dominion among men. This certainly has more dignity, though not less covetousness. But if a man endeavor to establish and extend the power and dominion of the human race itself over the

---

1 New York: Cambridge University Press, first published in 1858, this edition, 2011. Pagination below is taken from this 2011 edition.

2 *Novum Organum,* First Book, Aphorism CXXIX, p. 115

3 *Preparative Towards a Natural and Experimental History,* Aphorism X, p. 263.

4 *Novum Organum,* First Book, Aphorism III, p. 47.

5 *Novum Organum,* Second Book, Aphorism LII, pp. 247–248.

6 *The Great Instauration,* Preface, pp. 20–21.

7 *New Atlantis,* edited by Rose-Mary Sargent, *Francis Bacon: Selected Philosophical Works,* Indianapolis, Indiana: Hackett Publishing Company, 1999, p. 261.

Francis Bacon, "Selections," *The Works of Francis Bacon,* vol. 4, ed. James Spedding, Robert Leslie Ellis and Douglas Denon Heath, 1858.

universe, his ambition (if ambition it can be called) is without doubt both a more wholesome thing and a more noble than the other two. Now the empire of man over things depends wholly on the arts and sciences. For we cannot command nature except by obeying her.[8]

8. ... the use of History Mechanical is, of all others, the most radical and fundamental towards natural philosophy; such natural philosophy I mean as shall not vanish in the fumes of subtle or sublime speculations, but such as shall be operative to relieve the inconveniences of man's estate. For it will not only be immediate benefit, by connecting and transferring the observations of one art to the use of others, and thereby discovering new commodities. ... nature exhibits herself more clearly under the trials and vexations of art then when left to herself.[9]

9. Among Prerogative Instances I will put in the tenth place Instances of Power ... which I also call *Instances of the Wit,* or *Hands of Man.* These are the noblest and most consummate works in each art, exhibiting the ultimate perfection of it. For since our main object is to make nature serve the business and conveniences of man, it is altogether agreeable to that object that the works which are already in man's power should (like so many provinces formerly occupied and subdued) he noted and enumerated, especially such as are the most complete and perfect, because starting from them we shall find an easier and nearer passage to new works hitherto unattempted [emphasis in original].[10]

10. I find nature in three different states, and subject to three different conditions of existence. She is either free, and follows her ordinary course of development; as in the heavens, in the animal and vegetable creation, and in the general array of the universe; or she is driven out of her ordinary course by the perverseness, insolence, and forwardness of matter, and violence of impediments; as in the case of monsters; or lastly, she is put in constraint, moulded, and made as it were new by art and the hand of man; as in things artificial.[11]

11. Now my plan is to proceed regularly and gradually from one axiom to another, so that the most general are not reached till the last; but then when you do come to them you find them to be not empty notions, but well defined, and such as nature would really recognize as her first principles, and as such as lie at the heart and marrow of things.[12]

12. There is therefore much ground for hoping that there are still laid up in the womb of nature many secrets of excellent use, having no affinity or parallelism with any thing that is now known, but lying out of the beat of the imagination, which have not yet been found out.[13]

13. Signs also are to be drawn from the increase and progress of systems and sciences. For what is founded on nature grows and increases; while what is founded on opinion varies but increases not. If therefore those doctrines had not plainly been like a plan torn up from its roots, but had

---

8   *Novum Organum,* First Book, Aphorism CXXIX, p. 114.
9   *De Augmentis, Of the Dignity and Advancement of Learning,* The Second Book, Chapter II, pp. 297–298.
10 *Novum Organum,* Second Book, Aphorism XXXI, p. 170.
11 *De Augmentis, Of the Dignity and Advancement of Learning,* Second Book, Chapter II, p. 294.
12 *The Great Instauration,* Plan of the Work, p. 25.
13 *Novum Organum,* First Book, Aphorism CIX, p. 100.

remained attached to the womb of nature and continued to draw nourishment from her, that could never have come to pass which we have seen now for twice a thousand years; namely, that the sciences stand where they did and remain almost in the same condition; receiving no noticeable increase, but on the contrary, thriving most under their first founder, and then declining. Whereas in the mechanical arts, which are founded on nature and the light of experience, we see the contrary happen, for these (as long as they are popular) are continually thriving and growing, as having in them a breath of life; at first rude, then convenient, afterwards adorned, and at all times advancing.[14]

14. But if any man there by who, not content to rest in and use the knowledge which has already been discovered, aspires to penetrate further; to overcome, not adversary in argument, but nature in action; to seek, not pretty and probably conjectures, but certain and demonstrable knowledge; I invite all such to join themselves, as true sons of knowledge, with me, that passing by the outer courts of nature, which numbers have trodden, we may find a way at length into her inner chambers.[15]

15. ... you have but to follow and as it were hound nature in her wanderings, and you will be able, when you like, to lead and drive her afterwards to the same place again ... Neither ought a man to make scruple of entering and penetrating into these holes and corners, when the inquisition of truth is his sole object. ...[16]

16. ... I think a division of this kind most useful, when propounded in familiar and scholastical terms; namely, that the doctrine of Natural Philosophy be divided into the inquisition of Causes, and the Production of Effects: Speculative and Operative. The one searching into the bowels of nature, the other shaping nature as on an anvil.[17]

17. ... I mean it [*the Great Instauration*] to be a history not only of nature free and at large (when she is left to her course and does her work her own way), such as that of the heavenly bodies, meteors, earth and sea, minerals, plants, animals, but much more of nature under constraint and vexed; that is to say, when by art and the hand of man she is forced out of her natural state, and squeezed and moulded.[18]

---

14 *Novum Organum,* First book, Aphorism LXXIV, pp. 74–75.

15 *Novum Organum,* Preface, p. 42.

16 *De Augmentis, Of the Dignity and Advancement of Learning,* The Second Book, Chapter II, p. 296.

17 *De Augmentis, Of the Dignity and Advancement of Learning,* The Third Book, Chapter III, p. 343.

18 *The Great Instauration,* Plan of the Work, p. 29.

3B. The Death of Nature

Women, Ecology, and the Scientific Revolution

By Carolyn Merchant

D isorderly, active nature was soon forced to submit to the questions and experimental techniques of the new science. Francis Bacon (1561–1626), a celebrated "father of modern science," transformed tendencies already extant in his own society into a total program advocating the control of nature for human benefit. Melding together a new philosophy based on natural magic as a technique for manipulating nature, the technologies of mining and metallurgy, the emerging concept of progress and a patriarchal structure of family and state, Bacon fashioned a new ethic sanctioning the exploitation of nature.

Bacon has been eulogized as the originator of the concept of the modern research institute, a philosopher of industrial science, the inspiration behind the Royal Society (1660), and as the founder of the inductive method by which all people can verify for themselves the truths of science by the reading of nature's book.[1] But from the perspective of nature, women, and the lower orders of society emerges a less favorable image of Bacon and a critique of his program as ultimately benefiting the middle-class male entrepreneur. Bacon, of course, was not responsible for subsequent uses of his philosophy. But, because he was in an extremely influential social position and in touch with the important developments of his time, his language, style, nuance, and metaphor become a mirror reflecting his class perspective.

Sensitive to the same social transformations that had already begun to reduce women to psychic and reproductive resources, Bacon developed the power of language as political instrument in reducing female nature to a resource for economic production. Female imagery became a tool in adapting scientific knowledge and method to a new form of human power over nature. The "controversy over women" and the inquisition of witches—both present in Bacon's social milieu—permeated his description of nature and his metaphorical style and were instrumental in his transformation of the earth as a nurturing mother and womb of life into a source of secrets to be extracted for economic advance.

Bacon's roots can be found in middle-class economic development and its progressive interests and values. His father was a middle-class employee of the queen, his mother a Calvinist whose Protestant values permeated his early home life. Bacon took steps to gain the favor of James I soon after the latter's ascent to the throne in 1603. He moved from "learned counsel" in 1603 to attorney general in 1613, privy councillor in 1616, lord keeper in 1617, and, finally, lord chancellor and Baron Verulam in 1618. His political objectives were to gain support for his program of the advancement of science and human learning and to upgrade his own status through an ambitious public career.[2]

Bacon's mentor, James I, supported antifeminist and antiwitchcraft legislation. During the "controversy over women," females had challenged traditional modes of dress considered as appropriate to their place in society. In Holland, for example, young women were criticized for wearing men's hats with high crowns. In England, the title page of a work called *Hic-Mulier or The Man-Woman* (1620) showed a woman in a barber's chair having her hair clipped short, while her companion outfitted herself in a man's plumed hat (Fig. 3.1).[3] In an attempt to keep women in their place in the world's order, King James in that same year enlisted the aid of the clergy in preventing females from looking and dressing in masculine fashions: "The Bishop of London had express commandment from the king to will [the clergy] to inveigh vehemently against the insolence of our women, and their wearing of broad-brimmed hats, pointed doublets, their hair cut short or shorn, and some of them [with] stilettos or poinards … *the truth is the world is very much out of order.*"[4] (Italics added.)

In 1616, Mrs. Turner, accomplice in the murder of Sir Thomas Overbury, had been sent to the gallows by James wearing the yellow, starched ruffs she had brought into vogue and that he detested. As the king's attorney general, Bacon participated in the controversy, since it was his role to bring charges for the poisoning of Overbury against the Countess of Somerset. Overbury had publicly (through a poem, "The Wife") opposed the romance between his close friend, subsequently Earl of Somerset, and the countess. The perfect wife, he said, was one who combined goodness, virtue, intelligence, and common sense but not too much "learning and pregnant wit," for "Books are a part of man's prerogative." Angered by his insults, and fearful of his influence, the countess contrived to poison Overbury through the help of a physician's widow, Mrs. Turner, and an apothecary named Franklin.

Bacon prepared two versions of his charge against the countess, one should she confess, the other should she plead not guilty. At the packed trial, at which some places sold for £10–50, the countess confessed, but was spared. Mrs. Turner, however, was convicted and sent to the gallows, and "as she was the person who had brought yellow starched ruffs into vogue, [it was decreed that] she should be hanged in that dress, that the same might end in shame and detestation."[5]

The Overbury case increased interest in the popular controversy over women and resulted in the publication of several editions of Overbury's poem and a number of reactions to the murder; for example, "A Select Second Husband for Sir Thomas Overburies' Wife, Now a Matchless Widow" (1616) and Thomas Tuke's "A Treatise Against Painting and Tincturing of Men and Women: Against Murder and Poysoning: Pride and Ambition" (1616).

Bacon was also well aware of the witch trials taking place all over Europe and in particular in England during the early seventeenth century. His sovereign, while still James VI of Scotland, had written a book entitled *Daemonologie* (1597). In 1603, the first year of his English reign, James I replaced the milder witch laws of Elizabeth I, which evoked the death penalty only for killing by witchcraft, with a law that condemned to death all practitioners.[6]

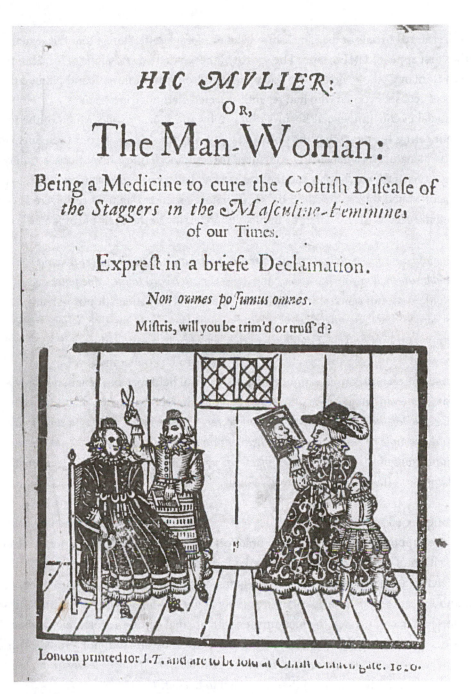

Figure 3.1 Title page from *Hic-Mulier or the Man-Woman* (London, 1620). In the clothing controversy of seventeenth-century England, women challenged society by wearing "inappropriate" dress. This 1620 polemic of anonymous authorship shows a woman modeling a man's plumed hat, while a second woman has her hair clipped short by a barber.

It was in the 1612 trials of the Lancashire witches of the Pendle Forest that the sexual aspects of witch trials first appeared in England. The source of the women's confessions of fornication with the devil was a Roman Catholic priest who had emigrated from the Continent and planted the story in the mouths of accused women who had recently rejected Catholicism.

These social events influenced Bacon's philosophy and literary style. Much of the imagery he used in delineating his new scientific objectives and methods derives from the courtroom, and, because it treats nature as a female to be tortured through mechanical inventions, strongly suggests the interrogations of the witch trials and the mechanical devices used to torture witches. In a relevant passage, Bacon stated that the method by which nature's secrets might be discovered consisted in investigating the secrets of witchcraft by inquisition, referring to the example of James I:

> *For you have but to follow and as it were hound nature in her wanderings, and you will be able when you like to lead and drive her afterward to the same place again.* Neither am I of opinion in this history of marvels that superstitious narratives of *sorceries, witchcrafts, charms,* dreams, divinations, and the like, where there is an assurance and clear evidence of the fact, should be altogether excluded. ... howsoever the use and practice of such arts is to be condemned, yet from the speculation and consideration of them ... a useful light may be gained, not only for a true judgment of the offenses of persons charged with such practices, *but likewise for the further disclosing of the secrets of nature. Neither ought a man to make scruple of entering and penetrating into these holes and corners, when the inquisition of truth is his whole object—as your majesty has shown in your own example.*[7] (Italics added.)

The strong sexual implications of the last sentence can be interpreted in the light of the investigation of the supposed sexual crimes and practices of witches. In another example, he compared the interrogation of courtroom witnesses to the inquisition of nature: "I mean (according to the practice in civil causes) in this great plea or suit granted by the divine favor and providence (whereby the human race seeks to recover its right over nature) *to examine nature herself* and the arts upon interrogatories."[8] Bacon pressed the idea further with an analogy to the torture chamber: "For like as a man's disposition is never well known or proved till he be crossed, nor Proteus ever changed shapes till he was *straitened* and *held fast,* so nature exhibits herself more clearly under the *trials* and *vexations* of art [mechanical devices] than when left to herself."[9]

The new man of science must not think that the "inquisition of nature is in any part interdicted or forbidden." Nature must be "bound into service" and made a "slave," put "in constraint" and "molded" by the mechanical arts. The "searchers and spies of nature" are to discover her plots and secrets.[10]

This method, so readily applicable when nature is denoted by the female gender, degraded and made possible the exploitation of the natural environment. As woman's womb had symbolically yielded to the forceps, so nature's womb harbored secrets that through technology could be wrested from her grasp for use in the improvement of the human condition:

> There is therefore much ground for hoping that there are still laid up in the womb of nature many secrets of excellent use having no affinity or parallelism with anything that is now known ... only by the method which we are now treating can they be speedily and suddenly and simultaneously presented and anticipated.[11]

Bacon transformed the magical tradition by calling on the need to dominate nature not for the sole benefit of the individual magician but for the good of the entire human race. Through vivid metaphor, he transformed the magus from nature's servant to its exploiter, and nature from a teacher to a slave. Bacon argued that it was the magician's error to consider art (technology) a mere "assistant to nature having the power to finish what nature has begun" and therefore to despair of ever "changing, transmuting, or fundamentally altering nature."[12]

The natural magician saw himself as operating within the organic order of nature—he was a manipulator of parts within that system, bringing down the heavenly powers to the earthly shrine. Agrippa, however, had begun to explore the possibility of ascending the hierarchy to the point of cohabiting with God. Bacon extended this idea to include the recovery of the power over nature lost when Adam and Eve were expelled from paradise.

Due to the Fall from the Garden of Eden (caused by the temptation of a woman), the human race lost its "dominion over creation." Before the Fall, there was no need for power or dominion, because Adam and Eve had been made sovereign over all other creatures. In this state of dominion, mankind was "like unto God." While some, accepting God's punishment, had obeyed the medieval strictures against searching too deeply into God's secrets, Bacon turned the constraints into sanctions. Only by "digging further and further into the mine of natural knowledge" could mankind recover that lost dominion. In this way, "the narrow limits of man's dominion over the universe" could be stretched "to their promised bounds."[13]

Although a female's inquisitiveness may have caused man's fall from his God-given dominion, the relentless interrogation of another female, nature, could be used to regain it. As he argued in *The Masculine Birth of Time,* "I am come in very truth leading to you nature with all her children to bind her to your service and make her your slave." "We have no right," he asserted, "to expect nature to come to us." Instead, "Nature must be taken by the forelock, being bald behind." Delay and subtle argument "permit one only to clutch at nature, never to lay hold of her and capture her."[14]

Nature existed in three states—at liberty, in error, or in bondage:

> She is either free and follows her ordinary course of development as in the heavens, in the animal and vegetable creation, and in the general array of the universe; or she is driven out of her ordinary course by the perverseness, insolence, and forwardness of matter and violence of impediments, as in the case of monsters; or lastly, she is put in constraint, molded, and made as it were new by art and the hand of man; as in things artificial.[15]

The first instance was the view of nature as immanent self-development, the nature naturing herself of the Aristotelians. This was the organic view of nature as a living, growing, self-actualizing being. The second state was necessary to explain the malfunctions and monstrosities that frequently appeared and that could not have been caused by God or another higher power acting on his instruction. Since monstrosities could not be explained by the action of form or spirit, they had to be the result of matter acting perversely. Matter in Plato's *Timaeus* was recalcitrant and had to be forcefully shaped by the demiurge. Bacon frequently described matter in female imagery, as a "common harlot." "Matter is not devoid of an appetite and inclination to dissolve the world and fall back into the old Chaos." It therefore must be "restrained and kept in order by the prevailing concord of things." "The vexations of art are certainly as the bonds and handcuffs of Proteus, which betray the ultimate struggles and efforts of matter."[16]

The third instance was the case of art (techné)—man operating on nature to create something new and artificial. Here "nature takes orders from man and works under his authority." Miners and smiths should become the model for the new class of natural philosophers who would interrogate and alter nature. They had developed the two most important methods of wresting nature's secrets from her, "the one searching into the bowels of nature, the other shaping nature as on an anvil." "Why should we not divide natural philosophy into two parts, the mine and the furnace?" For "the truth of nature lies hid in certain deep mines and caves," within the earth's bosom. Bacon, like some of the practically minded alchemists, would "advise the studious to sell their books and build furnaces" and, "forsaking Minerva and the Muses as barren virgins, to rely upon Vulcan."[17]

The new method of interrogation was not through abstract notions, but through the instruction of the understanding "that it may in very truth dissect nature." The instruments of the mind supply suggestions, those of the hand give motion and aid the work. "By art and the hand of man," nature can then be "forced out of her natural state and squeezed and molded." In this way, "human knowledge and human power meet as one."[18]

Here, in bold sexual imagery, is the key feature of the modern experimental method—constraint of nature in the laboratory, dissection by hand and mind, and the penetration of hidden secrets—language still used today in praising a scientist's "hard facts," "penetrating mind," or the "thrust of his argument." The constraints against penetration in Natura's lament over her torn garments of modesty have been turned into sanctions in language that legitimates the exploitation and "rape" of nature for human good. The seventeenth-century experimenters of the Accademia del Cimento of Florence (i.e., The Academy of Experiment, 1657–1667) and the Royal Society of London who placed mice and plants in the artificial vacuum of the barometer or bell jar were vexing nature and forcing her out of her natural state in true Baconian fashion.[19]

Scientific method, combined with mechanical technology, would create a "new organon," a new system of investigation, that unified knowledge with material power. The technological discoveries of printing, gunpowder, and the magnet in the fields of learning, warfare, and navigation "help us to think about the secrets still locked in nature's bosom." "They do not, like the old, merely exert a gentle guidance over nature's course; they have the power to conquer and subdue her, to shake her to her foundations." Under the mechanical arts, "nature betrays her secrets more fully … than when in enjoyment of her natural liberty."[20]

Mechanics, which gave man power over nature, consisted in motion; that is, in "the uniting or disuniting of natural bodies." Most useful were the arts that altered the materials of things—"agriculture, cookery, chemistry, dying, the manufacture of glass, enamel, sugar, gunpowder, artificial fires, paper, and the like." But in performing these operations, one was constrained to operate within the chain of causal connections; nature could "not be commanded except by being obeyed." Only by the study, interpretation, and observation of nature could these possibilities be uncovered; only by acting as the interpreter of nature could knowledge be turned into power. Of the three grades of human ambition, the most wholesome and noble was "to endeavor to establish and extend the power and dominion of the human race itself over the universe." In this way "the human race [could] recover that right over nature which belongs to it by divine bequest."[21]

The interrogation of witches as symbol for the interrogation of nature, the courtroom as model for its inquisition, and torture through mechanical devices as a tool for the subjugation of disorder were fundamental to the scientific method as power. For Bacon, as for Harvey, sexual politics helped to structure the nature of the empirical method that would produce a new form of knowledge and a new ideology of objectivity seemingly devoid of cultural and political assumptions.

Notes

1. Treatments of Francis Bacon's contributions to science include Paolo Rossi, *Francis Bacon: From Magic To Science* (London: Routledge & Kegan Paul, 1968); Lisa Jardine, *Francis Bacon: Discovery and the Art of Discourse* (Cambridge, England: Cambridge University Press, 1974); Benjamin Farrington, *Francis Bacon: Philosopher of Industrial Science* (New York: Schumann, 1949); Margery Purver, *The Royal Society: Concept and Creation* (London: Routledge & Kegan Paul, 1967).

2. Farrington, *Francis Bacon,* p. 82. James Spedding, *The Letters and the Life of Francis Bacon,* 7 vols. (London: Longmans, Green, Reader, and Dyer, 1869), vol. 3, pp. 56–66.

3. Louis Wright, "The Popular Controversy Over Women," in *Middle-Class Culture in Elizabethan England* (Chapel Hill: University of North Carolina Press, 1935), Chap. 13, pp. 493, 494; Anon., *Hic Mulier, or The Man-Woman, Being a Medicine to Cure the Coltish Disease of the Staggers in the Masculine-Feminines of Our Times* (London, 1620); Lucy Ingram Morgan, "The Renaissance Lady in England," unpublished doctoral dissertation, University of California at Berkeley, 1932.

4. "Letter of John Chamberlain," Jan. 25, 1620. Quoted in Wright, p. 493.

5. Thomas Overbury, *Miscellaneous Works,* ed. E. F. Rimbault (London: Smith, 1856), quotation on p. xxxvii; see also Spedding, *Letters and Life of Francis Bacon,* vol. 5, pp. 296–305, esp. 297, 298 n.; Violet A. Wilson, *Society Women of Shakespeare's Time* (London: Lane, Bodley Head, 1924), p. 205; Wright, p. 491.

6. James I, *Daemonologie* (New York: Barnes & Noble, 1966; first published 1597); Keith Thomas, *Religion and the Decline of Magic* (New York: Scribner's, 1971), p. 520; Wallace Notestein, *A History of Witchcraft in England from 1558 to 1718* (New York: Apollo Books, 1968), p. 101; Ronald Seth, *Stories of Great Witch Trials* (London: Baker, 1967), p. 83.

7. Bacon, "De Dignitate et Augmentis Scientiarum," (written 1623), *Works,* ed. James Spedding, Robert Leslie Ellis, Douglas Devon Heath, 14 vols. (London: Longmans Green, 1870), vol. 4, p. 296. The ensuing discussion was stimulated by William Leiss's, *The Domination of Nature* (New York: Braziller, 1972), Chap. 3, pp. 45–71.

8. Bacon, "Preparative Towards a Natural and Experimental History," *Works,* vol. 4, p. 263. Italics added.

9. Bacon, "De Dignatate," *Works,* vol. 4, p. 298. Italics added.

10. Bacon, "The Great Instauration" (written 1620), *Works,* vol. 4, p. 20; "The Masculine Birth of Time," ed. and trans. Benjamin Farrington, in *The Philosophy of Francis Bacon* (Liverpool, England: Liverpool University Press, 1964), p. 62; "De Dignitate," *Works,* vol. 4, pp. 287, 294.

11. Quoted in Moody E. Prior, "Bacon's Man of Science," in Leonard M. Marsak, ed., *The Rise Of Modern Science in Relation to Society* (London: Collier-Macmillan, 1964), p. 45.

12. Rossi, p. 21; Leiss, p. 56; Bacon, *Works,* vol. 4, p. 294; Henry Cornelius Agrippa, *De Occulta Philosophia Libri Tres* (Antwerp, 1531): "No one has such powers but he who has cohabited with the elements, vanquished nature, mounted higher than the heavens, elevating himself above the angels to the archetype itself, with whom he then becomes cooperator and can do all things," as quoted in Frances A. Yates, *Giordano Bruno and the Hermetic Tradition* (New York: Vintage Books, 1964), p. 136.

13. Bacon, "Novum Organum," Part 2, in *Works,* vol. 4, p. 247; "Valerius Terminus," *Works,* vol. 3, pp. 217, 219; "The Masculine Birth of Time," trans. Farrington, p. 62.

14. Bacon, "The Masculine Birth of Time," and "The Refutation of Philosophies," trans. Farrington, pp. 62, 129, 130.

15. Bacon, "De Augmentis," *Works,* vol. 4, p. 294; see also Bacon, Aphorisms," *Works,* vol. 4.

16. "De Augmentis," *Works,* vol. 4, pp. 320, 325; Plato, "The Timaeus," in *The Dialogues of Plato,* trans. B. Jowett (New York: Random House, 1937), vol. 2, p. 17; Bacon, "Parasceve," *Works,* vol. 4, p. 257.

17. Bacon, "De Augmentis," *Works,* vol. 4, pp. 343, 287, 343, 393.

18. Bacon, "Novum Organum," *Works,* vol. 4, p. 246; "The Great Instauration," *Works,* vol. 4, p. 29; "Novum Organum," Part 2, *Works,* vol. 4, p. 247.

19. Alain of Lille, *De Planctu Naturae,* in T. Wright, ed., *The Anglo-Latin Satirical Poets and Epigrammatists* (Wiesbaden: Kraus Reprint, 1964), vol. 2, pp. 441, 467; Thomas Kuhn, "Mathematical vs. Experimental Traditions in the Development of Physical Science," *Journal of Interdisciplinary History* 7, no. 1 (Summer 1976): 1–31, see p. 13. On the Accademia del Cimentio's experiments see Martha Ornstein [Bronfenbrenner], *The Role of Scientific Societies in the Seventeenth Century* (reprint ed., New York: Arno Press, 1975), p. 86.

20. Bacon, "Thoughts and Conclusions on the Interpretation of Nature or A Science of Productive Works," trans. Farrington, *The Philosophy of Francis Bacon,* pp. 96, 93, 99.

21. Bacon, "De Augmentis," *Works,* vol. 4, pp. 294; "Parasceve," *Works,* vol. 4, pp. 257; "Plan of the Work," vol. 4, pp. 32; "Novum Organum," *Works,* vol. 4, pp. 114, 115.

CHAPTER 4

Nonhuman Nature and Its Ending: The Naturalist Tradition and Its Current Despair

4A. Walking

By Henry David Thoreau

I wish to speak a word for Nature, for absolute Freedom and Wildness, as contrasted with a freedom and culture merely civil,—to regard man as an inhabitant, or a part and parcel of Nature, rather than a member of society. I wish to make an extreme statement, if so I may make an emphatic one, for there are enough champions of civilization: the minister and the school committee and every one of you will take care of that.

I have met with but one or two persons in the course of my life who understood the art of Walking, that is, of taking walks—who had a genius, so to speak, for *sauntering*, which word is beautifully derived "from idle people who roved about the country, in the Middle Ages, and asked charity, under pretense of going *à la Sainte Terre*," to the Holy Land, till the children exclaimed, "There goes a *Sainte-Terrer*," a Saunterer, a Holy-Lander. They who never go to the Holy Land in their walks, as they pretend, are indeed mere idlers and vagabonds; but they who do go there are saunterers in the good sense, such as I mean. Some, however, would derive the word from *sans terre* without land or a home, which, therefore, in the good sense, will mean, having no particular home, but equally at home everywhere. For this is the secret of successful sauntering. He who sits still in a house all the time may be the greatest vagrant of all; but the saunterer, in the good sense, is no more vagrant than the meandering river, which is all the while sedulously seeking the shortest course to the sea. But I prefer the first, which, indeed, is the most probable derivation. For every walk is a sort of crusade, preached by some Peter the Hermit in us, to go forth and reconquer this Holy Land from the hands of the Infidels.

It is true, we are but faint-hearted crusaders, even the walkers, nowadays, who undertake no persevering, never-ending enterprises. Our expeditions are but tours, and come round again at evening to the old hearth-side from which we set out. Half the walk is but retracing our steps. We should go forth on the shortest walk, perchance, in the spirit of undying adventure, never to return,—prepared to send back our embalmed hearts only as relics to our desolate kingdoms. If you are ready to leave father and mother, and brother and sister, and wife and child and friends, and never see them again,—if you have paid your debts, and made your will, and settled all your affairs, and are a free man; then you are ready for a walk.

To come down to my own experience, my companion and I, for I sometimes have a companion, take pleasure in fancying ourselves knights of a new, or rather an old, order—not Equestrians or Chevaliers, not Ritters or Riders, but Walkers, a still more ancient and honorable class, I trust. The chivalric and heroic spirit which once belonged to the Rider seems now to reside in, or perchance

Henry David Thoreau, Selections from "Walking," 1851.

to have subsided into, the Walker—not the Knight, but Walker Errant. He is a sort of fourth estate, outside of Church and State and People.

We have felt that we almost alone hereabouts practiced this noble art; though, to tell the truth, at least if their own assertions are to be received, most of my townsmen would fain walk sometimes, as I do, but they cannot. No wealth can buy the requisite leisure, freedom, and independence which are the capital in this profession. It comes only by the grace of God. It requires a direct dispensation from Heaven to become a walker. You must be born into the family of the Walkers. *Ambulator nascitur, non fit.* Some of my townsmen, it is true, can remember and have described to me some walks which they took ten years ago, in which they were so blessed as to lose themselves for half an hour in the woods; but I know very well that they have confined themselves to the highway ever since, whatever pretensions they may make to belong to this select class. No doubt they were elevated for a moment as by the reminiscence of a previous state of existence, when even they were foresters and outlaws.

I think that I cannot preserve my health and spirits, unless I spend four hours a day at least—and it is commonly more than that—sauntering through the woods and over the hills and fields, absolutely free from all worldly engagements. You may safely say, A penny for your thoughts, or a thousand pounds. When sometimes I am reminded that the mechanics and shopkeepers stay in their shops not only all the forenoon, but all the afternoon too, sitting with crossed legs, so many of them—as if the legs were made to sit upon, and not to stand or walk upon—I think that they deserve some credit for not having all committed suicide long ago.

I, who cannot stay in my chamber for a single day without acquiring some rust, and when sometimes I have stolen forth for a walk at the eleventh hour, or four o'clock in the afternoon, too late to redeem the day, when the shades of night were already beginning to be mingled with the daylight, have felt as if I had committed some sin to be atoned for,—I confess that I am astonished at the power of endurance, to say nothing of the moral insensibility, of my neighbors who confine themselves to shops and offices the whole day for weeks and months, aye, and years almost together. I know not what manner of stuff they are of—sitting there now at three o'clock in the afternoon, as if it were three o'clock in the morning. Bonaparte may talk of the three-o'clock-in-the-morning courage, but it is nothing to the courage which can sit down cheerfully at this hour in the afternoon over against one's self whom you have known all the morning, to starve out a garrison to whom you are bound by such strong ties of sympathy. I wonder that about this time, or say between four and five o'clock in the afternoon, too late for the morning papers and too early for the evening ones, there is not a general explosion heard up and down the street, scattering a legion of antiquated and house-bred notions and whims to the four winds for an airing—and so the evil cure itself.

How womankind, who are confined to the house still more than men, stand it I do not know; but I have ground to suspect that most of them do not *stand* it at all. When, early in a summer afternoon, we have been shaking the dust of the village from the skirts of our garments, making haste past those houses with purely Doric or Gothic fronts, which have such an air of repose about them, my companion whispers that probably about these times their occupants are all gone to bed. Then it is that I appreciate the beauty and the glory of architecture, which itself never turns in, but forever stands out and erect, keeping watch over the slumberers.

No doubt temperament, and, above all, age, have a good deal to do with it. As a man grows older, his ability to sit still and follow indoor occupations increases. He grows vespertinal in his habits as the evening of life approaches, till at last he comes forth only just before sundown, and gets all the walk that he requires in half an hour.

But the walking of which I speak has nothing in it akin to taking exercise, as it is called, as the sick take medicine at stated hours—as the swinging of dumb-bells or chairs; but is itself the enterprise and adventure of the day. If you would get exercise, go in search of the springs of life. Think of a man's swinging dumb-bells for his health, when those springs are bubbling up in far-off pastures unsought by him!

Moreover, you must walk like a camel, which is said to be the only beast which ruminates when walking. When a traveler asked Wordsworth's servant to show him her master's study, she answered, "Here is his library, but his study is out of doors."

Living much out of doors, in the sun and wind, will no doubt produce a certain roughness of character—will cause a thicker cuticle to grow over some of the finer qualities of our nature, as on the face and hands, or as severe manual labor robs the hands of some of their delicacy of touch. So staying in the house, on the other hand, may produce a softness and smoothness, not to say thinness of skin, accompanied by an increased sensibility to certain impressions. Perhaps we should be more susceptible to some influences important to our intellectual and moral growth, if the sun had shone and the wind blown on us a little less; and no doubt it is a nice matter to proportion rightly the thick and thin skin. But methinks that is a scurf that will fall off fast enough—that the natural remedy is to be found in the proportion which the night bears to the day, the winter to the summer, thought to experience. There will be so much the more air and sunshine in our thoughts. The callous palms of the laborer are conversant with finer tissues of self-respect and heroism, whose touch thrills the heart, than the languid fingers of idleness. That is mere sentimentality that lies abed by day and thinks itself white, far from the tan and callus of experience.

When we walk, we naturally go to the fields and woods: what would become of us, if we walked only in a garden or a mall? Even some sects of philosophers have felt the necessity of importing the woods to themselves, since they did not go to the woods. "They planted groves and walks of Platanes," where they took *subdiales ambulationes* in porticos open to the air. Of course it is of no use to direct our steps to the woods, if they do not carry us thither. I am alarmed when it happens that I have walked a mile into the woods bodily, without getting there in spirit. In my afternoon walk I would fain forget all my morning occupations and my obligations to society. But it sometimes happens that I cannot easily shake off the village. The thought of some work will run in my head and I am not where my body is—I am out of my senses. In my walks I would fain return to my senses. What business have I in the woods, if I am thinking of something out of the woods? I suspect myself, and cannot help a shudder when I find myself so implicated even in what are called good works—for this may sometimes happen.

My vicinity affords many good walks; and though for so many years I have walked almost every day, and sometimes for several days together, I have not yet exhausted them. An absolutely new prospect is a great happiness, and I can still get this any afternoon. Two or three hours' walking will carry me to as strange a country as I expect ever to see. A single farmhouse which I had not seen before is sometimes as good as the dominions of the king of Dahomey. There is in fact a sort of harmony discoverable between the capabilities of the landscape within a circle of ten miles' radius, or the limits of an afternoon walk, and the threescore years and ten of human life. It will never become quite familiar to you.

Nowadays almost all man's improvements, so called, as the building of houses and the cutting down of the forest and of all large trees, simply deform the landscape, and make it more and more tame and cheap. A people who would begin by burning the fences and let the forest stand! I saw the fences half consumed, their ends lost in the middle of the prairie, and some worldly miser with a surveyor looking after his bounds, while heaven had taken place around him, and he did not see the angels going to and fro, but was looking for an old post-hole in the midst of paradise. I looked again, and saw him standing in the middle of a boggy Stygian fen, surrounded by devils, and he had found his bounds without a doubt, three little stones, where a stake had been driven, and looking nearer, I saw that the Prince of Darkness was his surveyor.

I can easily walk ten, fifteen, twenty, any number of miles, commencing at my own door, without going by any house, without crossing a road except where the fox and the mink do: first along by the river, and then the brook, and then the meadow and the wood-side. There are square miles in my vicinity which have no inhabitant. From many a hill I can see civilization and the abodes of man afar. The farmers and their works are scarcely more obvious than woodchucks and their burrows. Man and his affairs, church and state and school, trade and commerce, and manufactures and agriculture even politics, the most alarming of them all,—I am pleased to see how little space they occupy in the landscape. Politics is but a narrow field, and that still narrower highway yonder leads to it. I sometimes direct the traveler thither. If you would go to the political world, follow the great road,—follow that market-man, keep his dust in your eyes, and it will lead you straight to it; for it, too, has its place merely, and does not occupy all space. I pass from it as from a bean field into the forest, and it is forgotten. In one half hour I can walk off to some portion of the earth's surface where a man does not stand from one year's end to another, and there, consequently, politics are not, for they are but as the cigar smoke of a man.

The village is the place to which the roads tend, a sort of expansion of the highway, as a lake of a river. It is the body of which roads are the arms and legs—a trivial or quadrivial place, the thoroughfare and ordinary of travelers. The word is from the Latin *villa* which together with *via*, a way, or more anciently *ved* and *vella*, Varro derives from *veho*, to carry, because the villa is the place to and from which things are carried. They who got their living by teaming were said *vellaturam facere*. Hence, too, the Latin word *vilis* and our *vile*; also *villain*. This suggests what kind of degeneracy villagers are liable to. They are wayworn by the travel that goes by and over them, without traveling themselves.

Some do not walk at all; others walk in the highways; a few walk across lots. Roads are made for horses and men of business. I do not travel in them much, comparatively, because I am not in a hurry to get to any tavern or grocery or livery-stable or depot to which they lead. I am a good horse to travel, but not from choice a roadster. The landscape-painter uses the figures of men to mark a road. He would not make that use of my figure. I walk out into a nature such as the old prophets and poets, Menu, Moses, Homer, Chaucer, walked in. You may name it America, but it is not America: neither Americus Vespucius, nor Columbus, nor the rest were the discoverers of it. There is a truer amount of it in mythology than in any history of America, so called, that I have seen.

However, there are a few old roads that may be trodden with profit, as if they led somewhere now that they are nearly discontinued. There is the Old Marlborough Road, which does not go to Marlborough now, methinks, unless that is Marlborough where it carries me. I am the bolder to speak of it here, because I presume that there are one or two such roads in every town.

At present, in this vicinity, the best part of the land is not private property; the landscape is not owned, and the walker enjoys comparative freedom. But possibly the day will come when it will be partitioned off into so-called pleasure grounds, in which a few will take a narrow and exclusive pleasure only,—when fences shall be multiplied, and man traps and other engines invented to confine men to the *public* road, and walking over the surface of God's earth shall be construed to mean trespassing on some gentleman's grounds. To enjoy a thing exclusively is commonly to exclude yourself from the true enjoyment of it. Let us improve our opportunities, then, before the evil days come.

Ben Jonson exclaims,—

> *"How near to good is what is fair!"*

So I would say,—

> *"How near to good is what is wild!"*

Life consists with wildness. The most alive is the wildest. Not yet subdued to man, its presence refreshes him. One who pressed forward incessantly and never rested from his labors, who grew fast and made infinite demands on life, would always find himself in a new country or wilderness, and surrounded by the raw material of life. He would be climbing over the prostrate stems of primitive forest trees.

Hope and the future for me are not in lawns and cultivated fields, not in towns and cities, but in the impervious and quaking swamps. When, formerly, I have analyzed my partiality for some farm which I had contemplated purchasing, I have frequently found that I was attracted solely by a few square rods of impermeable and unfathomable bog—a natural sink in one corner of it. That was the jewel which dazzled me. I derive more of my subsistence from the swamps which surround my native town than from the cultivated gardens in the village. There are no richer parterres to my eyes than the dense beds of dwarf andromeda (*Cassandra calyculata*) which cover these tender places on the earth's surface. Botany cannot go farther than tell me the names of the shrubs which grow there—the high-blueberry, panicled andromeda, lamb-kill, azalea, and rhodora—all standing in the quaking sphagnum. I often think that I should like to have my house front on this mass of dull red bushes, omitting other flower plots and borders, transplanted spruce and trim box, even graveled walks—to have this fertile spot under my windows, not a few imported barrow-fuls of soil only to cover the sand which was thrown out in digging the cellar. Why not put my house, my parlor, behind this plot, instead of behind that meager assemblage of curiosities, that poor apology for a Nature and art, which I call my front yard? It is an effort to clear up and make a decent appearance when the carpenter and mason have departed, though done as much for the passer-by as the dweller within. The most tasteful front-yard fence was never an agreeable object of study to me; the most elaborate ornaments, acorn tops, or what not, soon wearied and disgusted me. Bring your sills up to the very edge of the swamp, then (though it may not be the best place for a dry cellar,) so that there be no access on that side to citizens. Front yards are not made to walk in, but, at most, through, and you could go in the back way.

Yes, though you may think me perverse, if it were proposed to me to dwell in the neighborhood of the most beautiful garden that ever human art contrived, or else of a dismal swamp, I should certainly decide for the swamp. How vain, then, have been all your labors, citizens, for me!

My spirits infallibly rise in proportion to the outward dreariness. Give me the ocean, the desert, or the wilderness! In the desert, pure air and solitude compensate for want of moisture and fertility. The traveler Burton says of it—"Your *morale* improves; you become frank and cordial, hospitable and single-minded. … In the desert, spirituous liquors excite only disgust. There is a keen enjoyment in a mere animal existence." They who have been traveling long on the steppes of Tartary say, "On reentering cultivated lands, the agitation, perplexity, and turmoil of civilization oppressed and suffocated us; the air seemed to fail us, and we felt every moment as if about to die of asphyxia." When I would recreate myself, I seek the darkest wood, the thickest and most interminable and, to the citizen, most dismal, swamp. I enter a swamp as a sacred place,—a *sanctum sanctorum*. There is the strength, the marrow, of Nature.

4B. The End of Nature

The Future of American Environmentalism

By Bill McKibben

C hanges that can affect us can happen in our lifetime in our world—not just changes like wars but bigger and more sweeping events. I believe that without recognizing it we have already stepped over the threshold of such a change: that we are at the end of nature.

By the end of nature I do not mean the end of the world. The rain will still fall and the sun shine, though differently than before. When I say "nature," I mean a certain set of human ideas about the world and our place in it. But the death of those ideas begins with concrete changes in the reality around us—changes that scientists can measure and enumerate. More and more frequently, these changes will clash with our perceptions, until, finally, our sense of nature as eternal and separate is washed away, and we will see all too clearly what we have done. [...]

An idea, a relationship, can go extinct, just like an animal or a plant. The idea in this case is "nature," the separate and wild province, the world apart from man [sic] to which he adapted, under whose rules he was born and died. In the past, we spoiled and polluted parts of that nature, inflicted environmental "damage." But that was like stabbing a man with toothpicks: though it hurt, annoyed, degraded, it did not touch vital organs, block the path of the lymph or blood. We never thought we had wrecked nature. Deep down, we never really thought we could: it was too big and too old; its forces—the wind, the rain, the sun—were too strong, too elemental.

But, quite by accident, it turned out that the carbon dioxide and other gases we were producing in our pursuit of a better life—in pursuit of warm houses and eternal economic growth and of agriculture so productive it would free most of us from farming—*could* alter the power of the sun, could increase its heat. And that increase *could* change the patterns of moisture and dryness, breed storms in new places, breed deserts. Those things may or may not have yet begun to happen, but it is too late to altogether prevent from happening. We have produced the carbon dioxide—we are ending nature. [...]

One can, of course, argue that the current crisis, too, is "natural," because man is part of nature. This echoes the views of the earliest Greek philosophers, who saw no difference between matter and consciousness—nature included everything. The British scientists James Lovelock wrote some years ago that "our species with its technology is simply an inevitable part of the natural scene," nothing more than mechanically advanced beavers. In this view, to say that we have "ended" nature, or even damaged nature, makes no sense, since we *are* nature, and nothing we can do is "unnatural." This view can be, and is, carried to even greater lengths; Lynn Margulis, for instance, ponders the question of whether robots can be said to be living creatures, since any "invention of human beings is ultimately based on a variety of processes including that of DNA replication, no matter the separation in space or time of that replication from the invention."

But one can argue this forever and still not really feel it. It is a debater's point, a semantic argument. When I say that we have ended nature, I don't mean, obviously, that natural processes have ceased—there is sunshine and still wind, still growth, still decay. Photosynthesis continues, as does respiration. *But we have ended the thing that has, at least in modern times defined nature for us—its separation from human society.* [...]

One reason we pay so little close attention to the separate natural world around us is that it has always been there and we presumed it always would. As it disappears, its primal importance will be clearer—in the same way that some people think they have put their parents out of their lives and learn differently only when the day comes to bury them.

How will we feel the end of nature? In many ways, I suspect. If nature means ... [a] great joy at fresh and untrammeled beauty, its loss means sadness at man's [sic] footprints everywhere. But, as with death of a person, there is more than simply loss, a hole opening up. There are also new relationships that develop, and strains and twists in old relationships. And since this loss is peculiar in not having been inevitable, it provokes profound questions that don't arise when a person dies. [...]

Instead of a world where rain had an independent and mysterious existence, the rain had become a subset of human activity: a phenomenon like smog or commerce or the noise from the skidder towing logs on Cleveland Road—all things over which I had no control, either.

The rain bore a brand; it was a steer, not a deer. And that was where the loneliness came from. There's nothing there except us. There's no such thing as nature anymore—that other world that isn't business and art and breakfast is not another world, and there is nothing except us alone. [...]

All the talk about fundamental challenges to industrial civilization struck me as a trifle overblown, loopy.

But I've since learned more about the greenhouse effect. Now with the atmosphere changing thanks to our way of life, ideas like deep ecology interest me for more than philosophical reasons—they seem at least plausible. That is, they are extreme solutions, but we live in an extreme time. I cannot imagine any change more extreme than the change from four billion years of nature to year one of artifice. If industrial civilization is ending nature, it is not utter silliness to talk about ending—or, at least, transforming—industrial civilization.

We've taken, as individuals and as nations, certain moderate steps in the past few decades—created wildernesses, reintroduced eagles where they had been wiped out, cut the lead in our gasoline, and so on. But the world didn't seem to be demanding basic changes in the way we lived. Perhaps now it is. Perhaps what was for Thoreau an aesthetic choice is for us a practical one; perhaps the choice is, figuratively, if not literally, between endless rows of headless chickens and some new, very much more humble way of life [...] [A]lternatives, simply because they are more moderate, are not always more correct. It could be that this idea of a humbler world, or some idea like it, is both radical and necessary, in the way that cutting off a leg can be both radical and necessary.

CHAPTER 5

The Founding of Environmental Ethics in Judeo-Christian Ecotheology and an Alternative

5A. The Historical Roots of Our Ecological Crisis

By Lynn White, Jr.

A conversation with Aldous Huxley not infrequently put one at the receiving end of an unforgettable monologue. About a year before his lamented death he was discoursing on a favorite topic: Man's unnatural treatment of nature and its sad results. To illustrate his point he told how, during the previous summer, he had returned to a little valley in England where he had spent many happy months as a child. Once it had been composed of delightful grassy glades; now it was becoming overgrown with unsightly brush because the rabbits that formerly kept such growth under control had largely succumbed to a disease, myxomatosis, that was deliberately introduced by the local farmers to reduce the rabbits' destruction of crops. Being something of a Philistine, I could be silent no longer, even in the interests of great rhetoric. I interrupted to point out that the rabbit itself had been brought as a domestic animal to England in 1176, presumably to improve the protein diet of the peasantry.

All forms of life modify their contexts. The most spectacular and benign instance is doubtless the coral polyp. By serving its own ends, it has created a vast undersea world favorable to thousands of other kinds of animals and plants. Ever since man became a numerous species he has affected his environment notably. The hypothesis that his fire-drive method of hunting created the world's great grasslands and helped to exterminate the monster mammals of the Pleistocene from much of the globe is plausible, if not proved. For 6 millennia at least, the banks of the lower Nile have been a human artifact rather than the swampy African jungle which nature, apart from man, would have made it. The Aswan Dam, flooding 5000 square miles, is only the latest stage in a long process. In many regions terracing or irrigation, overgrazing, the cutting of forests by Romans to build ships to fight Carthaginians or by Crusaders to solve the logistics problems of their expeditions, have profoundly changed some ecologies. Observation that the French landscape falls into two basic types, the open fields of the north and the *bocage* of the south and west, inspired Marc Bloch to undertake his classic study of medieval agricultural methods. Quite unintentionally, changes in human ways often affect nonhuman nature. It has been noted, for example, that the advent of the automobile eliminated huge flocks of sparrows that once fed on the horse manure littering every street.

The history of ecologic change is still so rudimentary that we know little about what really happened, or what the results were. The extinction of the European aurochs as late as 1627 would seem to have been a simple case of overenthusiastic hunting. On more intricate matters it often is impossible to find solid information. For a thousand years or more the Frisians and Hollanders have been pushing back the North Sea, and the process is culminating in our own time in the reclamation of the Zuider Zee. What, if any, species of animals, birds, fish, shore life, or plants have died out in the process? In their epic combat with Neptune have the Netherlander overlooked ecological values in such a way that the quality of human life in the Netherlands has suffered? I cannot discover that the questions have ever been asked, much less answered.

People, then, have often been a dynamic element in their own environment, but in the present state of historical scholarship we usually do not know exactly when, where, or with what effects man-induced changes came. As we enter the last third of the 20th century, however, concern for the problem of ecologic backlash is mounting feverishly. Natural science, conceived as the effort to understand the nature of things, had flourished in several eras and among several peoples. Similarly there had been an age-old accumulation of technological skills, sometimes growing rapidly, sometimes slowly. But it was not until about four generations ago that Western Europe and North America arranged a marriage between science and technology, a union of the theoretical and the empirical approaches to our natural environment. The emergence in widespread practice of the Baconian creed that scientific knowledge means technological power over nature can scarcely be dated before about 1850, save in the chemical industries, where it is anticipated in the 18th century. Its acceptance as a normal pattern of action may mark the greatest event in human history since the invention of agriculture, and perhaps in nonhuman terrestrial history as well.

Almost at once the new situation forced the crystallization of the novel concept of ecology; indeed, the word *ecology* first appeared in the English language in 1873. Today, less than a century later, the impact of our race upon the environment has so increased in force that it has changed in essence. When the first cannons were fired, in the early 14th century, they affected ecology by sending workers scrambling to the forests and mountains for more potash, sulfur, iron ore, and charcoal, with some resulting erosion and deforestation. Hydrogen bombs are of a different order: a war fought with them might alter the genetics of all life on this planet. By 1285 London had a smog problem arising from the burning of soft coal, but our present combustion of fossil fuels threatens to change the chemistry of the globe's atmosphere as a whole, with consequences which we are only beginning to guess. With the population explosion, the carcinoma of planless urbanism, the now geological deposits of sewage and garbage, surely no creature other than man has ever managed to foul its nest in such short order.

There are many calls to action, but specific proposals, however worthy as individual items, seem too partial, palliative, negative: ban the bomb, tear down the billboards, give the Hindus contraceptives and tell them to eat their sacred cows. The simplest solution to any suspect change is, of course, to stop it, or, better yet, to revert to a romanticized past: make those ugly gasoline stations look like Anne Hathaway's cottage or (in the Far West) like ghost-town saloons. The "wilderness area" mentality invariably advocates deep-freezing an ecology, whether San Gimignano or the High Sierra, as it was before the first Kleenex was dropped. But neither atavism nor prettification will cope with the ecologic crisis of our time.

What shall we do? No one yet knows. Unless we think about fundamentals, our specific measures may produce new backlashes more serious than those they are designed to remedy.

As a beginning we should try to clarify our thinking by looking, in some historical depth, at the presuppositions that underlie modern technology and science. Science was traditionally aristocratic, speculative, intellectual in intent; technology was lower-class, empirical, action-oriented. The quite sudden fusion of these two, towards the middle of the 19th century, is surely related to the slightly prior and contemporary democratic revolutions which, by reducing social barriers, tended to assert a functional unity of brain and hand. Our ecologic crisis is the product of an emerging, entirely novel, democratic culture. The issue is whether a democratized world can survive its own implications. Presumably we cannot unless we rethink our axioms.

The Western Traditions of Technology and Science

One thing is so certain that it seems stupid to verbalize it: both modern technology and modern science are distinctively *Occidental*. Our technology has absorbed elements from all over the world, notably from China; yet everywhere today, whether in Japan or in Nigeria, successful technology is Western. Our science is the heir to all the sciences of the past, especially perhaps to the work of the great Islamic scientists of the Middle Ages, who so often outdid the ancient Greeks in skill and perspicacity: al-Rāzī in medicine, for example; or ibnal-Haytham in optics; or Omar Khayyam in mathematics. Indeed, not a few works of such geniuses seem to have vanished in the original Arabic and to survive only in medieval Latin translations that helped to lay the foundations for later Western developments. Today, around the globe, all significant science is Western in style and method, whatever the pigmentation or language of the scientists.

A second pair of facts is less well recognized because they result from quite recent historical scholarship. The leadership of the West, both in technology and in science, is far older than the so-called Scientific Revolution of the 17th century or the so-called Industrial Revolution of the 18th century. These terms are in fact outmoded and obscure the true nature of what they try to describe—significant stages in two long and separate developments. By A.D. 1000 at the latest—and perhaps, feebly, as much as 200 years earlier—the West began to apply water power to industrial processes other than milling grain. This was followed in the late 12th century by the harnessing of wind power. From simple beginnings, but with remarkable consistency of style, the West rapidly expanded its skills in the development of power machinery, labor-saving devices, and automation. Those who doubt should contemplate that most monumental achievement in the history of automation: the weight-driven mechanical clock, which appeared in two forms in the early 14th century. Not in craftsmanship but in basic technological capacity, the Latin West of the later Middle Ages far outstripped its elaborate, sophisticated, and esthetically magnificent sister cultures, Byzantium and Islam. In 1444 a great Greek ecclesiastic, Bessarion, who had gone to Italy, wrote a letter to a prince in Greece. He is amazed by the superiority of Western ships, arms, textiles, glass. But above all he is astonished by the spectacle of waterwheels sawing timbers and pumping the bellows of blast furnaces. Clearly, he had seen nothing of the sort in the Near East.

By the end of the 15th century the technological superiority of Europe was such that its small, mutually hostile nations could spill out over all the rest of the world, conquering, looting, and colonizing. The symbol of this technological superiority is the fact that Portugal, one of the weakest states of the Occident, was able to become, and to remain for a century, mistress of the East Indies. And we must remember that the technology of Vasco da Gama and Albuquerque was built by pure empiricism, drawing remarkably little support or inspiration from science.

In the present-day vernacular understanding, modern science is supposed to have begun in 1543, when both Copernicus and Vesalius published their great works. It is no derogation of their accomplishments, however, to point out that such structures as the *Fabrica* and the *De revolutionibus* do not appear overnight. The distinctive Western tradition of science, in fact, began in the late 11th century with a massive movement of translation of Arabic and Greek scientific works into Latin. A few notable books—Theophrastus, for example—escaped the West's avid new appetite for science, but within less than 200 years effectively the entire corpus of Greek and Muslim science was available in Latin, and was being eagerly read and criticized in the new European universities. Out of criticism arose new observation, speculation, and increasing distrust of ancient authorities. By the late 13th century Europe had seized global scientific leadership from the faltering hands of Islam. It would be as absurd to deny the profound originality of Newton, Galileo, or Copernicus as to deny that of the 14th century scholastic scientists like Buridan or Oresme on whose work they built. Before the 11th century, science scarcely existed in the Latin West, even in Roman times. From the 11th century onward, the scientific sector of Occidental culture has increased in a steady crescendo.

Since both our technological and our scientific movements got their start, acquired their character, and achieved world dominance in the Middle Ages, it would seem that we cannot understand their nature or their present impact upon ecology without examining fundamental medieval assumptions and developments.

Medieval View of Man and Nature

Until recently, agriculture has been the chief occupation even in, "advanced" societies; hence, any change in methods of tillage has much importance. Early plows, drawn by two oxen, did not normally turn the sod but merely scratched it. Thus, cross-plowing was needed and fields tended to be squarish. In the fairly light soils and semiarid climates of the Near East and Mediterranean, this worked well. But such a plow was inappropriate to the wet climate and often sticky soils of northern Europe. By the latter part of the 7th century after Christ, however, following obscure beginnings, certain northern peasants were using an entirely new kind of plow, equipped with a vertical knife to cut the line of the furrow, a horizontal share to slice under the sod, and a moldboard to turn it over. The friction of this plow with the soil was so great that it normally required not two but eight oxen. It attacked the land with such violence that cross-plowing was not needed, and fields tended to be shaped in long strips.

In the days of the scratch-plow, fields were distributed generally in units capable of supporting a single family. Subsistence farming was the presupposition. But no peasant owned eight oxen: to use the new and more efficient plow, peasants pooled their oxen to form large plow-teams, originally receiving (it would appear) plowed strips in proportion to their contribution. Thus, distribution of land was based no longer on the needs of a family but, rather, on the capacity of a power machine to till the earth. Man's relation to the soil was profoundly changed. Formerly man had been part of nature; now he was the exploiter of nature. Nowhere else in the world did farmers develop any analogous agricultural implement. Is it coincidence that modern technology, with its ruthlessness toward nature, has so largely been produced by descendants of these peasants of northern Europe?

This same exploitive attitude appears slightly before A.D. 830 in Western illustrated calendars. In older calendars the months were shown as passive personifications. The new Frankish calendars, which set the style for the Middle Ages, are very different: they show men coercing the world around them—plowing, harvesting, chopping trees, butchering pigs. Man and nature are two things, and man is master.

These novelties seem to be in harmony with larger intellectual patterns. What people do about their ecology depends on what they think about themselves in relation to things around them. Human ecology is deeply conditioned by beliefs about our nature and destiny—that is, by religion. To Western eyes this is very evident in, say, India or Ceylon. It is equally true of ourselves and of our medieval ancestors.

The victory of Christianity over paganism was the greatest psychic revolution in the history of our culture. It has become fashionable today to say that, for better or worse, we live in "the post-Christian age." Certainly the forms of our thinking and language have largely ceased to be Christian, but to my eye the substance often remains amazingly akin to that of the past. Our daily habits of action, for example, are dominated by an implicit faith in perpetual progress which was unknown either to Greco-Roman antiquity or to the Orient. It is rooted in, and is indefensible apart from, Judeo-Christian teleology. The fact that Communists share it merely helps to show what can be demonstrated on many other grounds: that Marxism, like Islam, is a Judeo-Christian heresy. We continue today to live, as we have lived for about 1700 years, very largely in a context of Christian axioms.

What did Christianity tell people about their relations with the environment?

While many of the world's mythologies provide stories of creation, Greco-Roman mythology was singularly incoherent in this respect. Like Aristotle, the intellectuals of the ancient West denied that the visible world had had a beginning. Indeed, the idea of a beginning was impossible in the framework of their cyclical notion of time. In sharp contrast, Christianity inherited from Judaism not only a concept of time as nonrepetitive and linear but also a striking story of creation. By gradual stages a loving and all-powerful God had created light and darkness, the heavenly bodies, the earth and all its plants, animals, birds, and fishes. Finally, God had created Adam and, as an afterthought, Eve to keep man from being lonely. Man named all the animals, thus establishing his dominance over them. God planned all of this explicitly for man's benefit and rule: no item in the physical creation had any purpose save to serve man's purposes. And, although man's body is made of clay, he is not simply part of nature: he is made in God's image.

Especially in its Western form, Christianity is the most anthropocentric religion the world has seen. As early as the 2nd century both Tertullian and Saint Irenaeus of Lyons were insisting that when God shaped Adam he was foreshadowing the image of the incarnate Christ, the Second Adam. Man shares, in great measure, God's transcendence of nature. Christianity, in absolute contrast to ancient paganism and Asia's religions (except, perhaps, Zoroastrianism), not only established a dualism of man and nature but also insisted that it is God's will that man exploit nature for his proper ends.

At the level of the common people this worked out in an interesting way. In Antiquity every tree, every spring, every stream, every hill had its own *genius loci*, its guardian spirit. These spirits were accessible to men, but were very unlike men; centaurs, fauns, and mermaids show their ambivalence. Before one cut a tree, mined a mountain, or dammed a brook, it was important to placate the spirit in charge of that particular situation, and to keep it placated. By destroying pagan animism, Christianity made it possible to exploit nature in a mood of indifference to the feelings of natural objects.

It is often said that for animism the Church substituted the cult of saints. True; but the cult of saints is functionally quite different from animism. The saint is not *in* natural objects; he may have special shrines, but his citizenship is in heaven. Moreover, a saint is entirely a man; he can be approached in human terms. In addition to saints, Christianity of course also had angels and demons inherited from Judaism and perhaps, at one remove, from Zoroastrianism. But these were all as mobile as the saints themselves. The spirits *in* natural objects, which formerly had protected nature from man, evaporated. Man's effective monopoly on spirit in this world was confirmed, and the old inhibitions to the exploitation of nature crumbled.

When one speaks in such sweeping terms, a note of caution is in order. Christianity is a complex faith, and its consequences differ in differing contexts. What I have said may well apply to the medieval West, where in fact technology made spectacular advances. But the Greek East, a highly civilized realm of equal Christian devotion, seems to have produced no marked technological innovation after the late 7th century, when Greek fire was invented. The key to the contrast may perhaps be found in a difference in the tonality of piety and thought which students of comparative theology find between the Greek and the Latin Churches. The Greeks believed that sin was intellectual blindness, and that salvation was found in illumination, orthodoxy—that is, clear thinking. The Latins, on the other hand, felt that sin was moral evil, and that salvation was to be found in right conduct. Eastern theology has been intellectualist. Western theology has been voluntarist. The Greek saint contemplates; the Western saint acts. The implications of Christianity for the conquest of nature would emerge more easily in the Western atmosphere.

The Christian dogma of creation, which is found in the first clause of all the Creeds, has another meaning for our comprehension of today's ecologic crisis. By revelation, God had given man the Bible, the Book of Scripture. But since God had made nature, nature also must reveal the divine mentality. The religious study of nature for the better understanding of God was known as natural theology. In the early Church, and always in the Greek East, nature was conceived primarily as a symbolic system through which God speaks to men: the ant is a sermon to sluggards; rising flames are the symbol of the soul's aspiration. This view of nature was essentially artistic rather than scientific. While Byzantium preserved and copied great numbers of ancient Greek scientific texts, science as we conceive it could scarcely flourish in such an ambience.

However, in the Latin West by the early 13th century natural theology was following a very different bent. It was ceasing to be the decoding of the physical symbols of God's communication with man and was becoming the effort to understand God's mind by discovering how his creation operates. The rainbow was no longer simply a symbol of hope first sent to Noah after the Deluge: Robert Grosseteste, Friar Roger Bacon, and Theodoric of Freiberg produced startlingly sophisticated work on the optics of the rainbow, but they did it as a venture in religious understanding. From the 13th century onward, up to and including Leibnitz and Newton, every major scientist, in effect, explained his motivations in religious terms. Indeed, if Galileo had not been so expert an amateur theologian he would have got into far less trouble: the professionals resented his intrusion. And Newton seems to have regarded himself more as a theologian than as a scientist. It was not until the late 18th century that the hypothesis of God became unnecessary to many scientists.

It is often hard for the historian to judge, when men explain why they are doing what they want to do, whether they are offering real reasons or merely culturally acceptable reasons. The consistency with which scientists during the long formative centuries of Western science said that the task and the reward of the scientist was "to think God's thoughts after him" leads one to believe that this was their real motivation. If so, then modern Western science was cast in a matrix of Christian theology. The dynamism of religious devotion, shaped by the Judeo-Christian dogma of creation, gave it impetus.

An Alternative Christian View

We would seem to be headed toward conclusions unpalatable to many Christians. Since both *science* and *technology* are blessed words in our contemporary vocabulary, some may be happy at the notions, first, that, viewed historically, modern science is an extrapolation of natural theology and, second, that modern technology is at least partly to be explained as an Occidental, voluntarist realization of the Christian dogma of man's transcendence of, and rightful mastery over, nature. But, as we now recognize, somewhat over a century ago science and technology—hitherto quite separate activities—joined to give mankind powers which, to judge by many of the ecologic effects, are out of control. If so, Christianity bears a huge burden of guilt.

I personally doubt that disastrous ecologic backlash can be avoided simply by applying to our problems more science and more technology. Our science and technology have grown out of Christian attitudes toward man's relation to nature which are almost universally held not only by Christians and neo-Christians but also by those who fondly regard themselves as post-Christians. Despite Copernicus, all the cosmos rotates around our little globe. Despite Darwin, we are *not*, in our hearts, part of the natural process. We are superior to nature, contemptuous of it, willing to use it for our slightest whim. The newly elected Governor of California, like myself a churchman but less troubled than I, spoke for the Christian tradition when he said (as is alleged), "when you've seen one redwood tree, you've seen them all." To a Christian a tree can be no more than a physical fact. The whole concept of the sacred grove is alien to Christianity and to the ethos of the West. For nearly 2 millennia Christian missionaries have been chopping down sacred groves, which are idolatrous because they assume spirit in nature.

What we do about ecology depends on our ideas of the man-nature relationship. More science and more technology are not going to get us out of the present ecologic crisis until we find a new religion, or rethink our old one. The beatniks, who are the basic revolutionaries of our time, show a sound instinct in their affinity for Zen Buddhism, which conceives of the man-nature relationship as very nearly the mirror image of the Christian view. Zen, however, is as deeply conditioned by Asian history as Christianity is by the experience of the West, and I am dubious of its viability among us.

Possibly we should ponder the greatest radical in Christian history since Christ: Saint Francis of Assisi. The prime miracle of Saint Francis is the fact that he did not end at the stake, as many of his left-wing followers did. He was so clearly heretical that a General of the Franciscan Order, Saint Bonaventura, a great and perceptive Christian, tried to suppress the early accounts of Franciscanism. The key to an understanding of Francis is his belief in the virtue of humility—not merely for the individual but for man as a species. Francis tried to depose man from his monarchy over creation and set up a democracy of all God's creatures. With him the ant is no longer simply a homily for the lazy, flames a sign of the thrust of the soul toward union with God; now they are Brother Ant and Sister Fire, praising the Creator in their own ways as Brother Man does in his.

Later commentators have said that Francis preached to the birds as a rebuke to men who would not listen. The records do not read so: he urged the little birds to praise God, and in spiritual ecstasy they flapped their wings and chirped rejoicing. Legends of saints, especially the Irish saints, had long told of their dealings with animals but always, I believe, to show their human dominance over creatures. With Francis it is different. The land around Gubbio in the Apennines was being ravaged by a fierce wolf. Saint Francis, says the legend, talked to the wolf and persuaded him of the error of his ways. The wolf repented, died in the odor of sanctity, and was buried in consecrated ground.

What Sir Steven Ruciman calls "the Franciscan doctrine of the animal soul" was quickly stamped out. Quite possibly it was in part inspired, consciously or unconsciously, by the belief in reincarnation held by the Cathar heretics who at that time teemed in Italy and southern France, and who presumably had got it originally from India. It is significant that at just the same moment, about 1200, traces of metempsychosis are found also in western Judaism, in the Provençal *Cabbala*. But Francis held neither to transmigration of souls nor to pantheism. His view of nature and of man rested on a unique sort of pan-psychism of all things animate and inanimate, designed for the glorification of their transcendent Creator, who, in the ultimate gesture of cosmic humility, assumed flesh, lay helpless in a manger, and hung dying on a scaffold.

I am not suggesting that many contemporary Americans who are concerned about our ecologic crisis will be either able or willing to counsel with wolves or exhort birds. However, the present increasing disruption of the global environment is the product of a dynamic technology and science which were originating in the Western medieval world against which Saint Francis was rebelling in so original a way. Their growth cannot be understood historically apart from distinctive attitudes toward nature which are deeply grounded in Christian dogma. The fact that most people do not think of these attitudes as Christian is irrelevant. No new set of basic values has been accepted in our society to displace those of Christianity. Hence we shall continue to have a worsening ecologic crisis until we reject the Christian axiom that nature has no reason for existence save to serve man.

The greatest spiritual revolutionary in Western history, Saint Francis, proposed what he thought was an alternative Christian view of nature and man's relation to it: he tried to substitute the idea of the equality of all creatures, including man, for the idea of man's limitless rule of creation. He failed. Both our present science and our present technology are so tinctured with orthodox Christian arrogance toward nature that no solution for our ecologic crisis can be expected from them alone. Since the roots of our trouble are so largely religious, the remedy must also be essentially religious, whether we call it that or not. We must rethink and refeel our nature and destiny. The profoundly religious, but heretical, sense of the primitive Franciscans for the spiritual autonomy of all parts of nature may point a direction. I propose Francis as a patron saint for ecologists.

5B1. Subduing the Earth

Genesis 1, Early Modern Science, and the Exploitation of Nature

By Peter Harrison

In a short paper which appeared thirty years ago in the journal *Science,* historian Lynn White, Jr., suggested that in "the orthodox Christian arrogance toward nature" may be found the ideological source of our contemporary environmental woes. The Christian doctrine of the creation sets the human being apart from nature, advocates human control of nature, and implies that the natural world was created solely for our use. The biblical text that best exemplifies this view is Gen. 1:28: "And God said to them 'Be fruitful and multiply, and fill the earth and subdue it; and have dominion over the fish of the sea and over the birds of the air and over every living thing that moves upon the earth.'" In the Christian Middle Ages, according to White, we already encounter evidence of attempts at the technological mastery of nature, and of those incipient exploitative tendencies that come to full flower in scientific and technological revolutions of later eras. All of this is attributed to the influence of Judeo-Christian conceptions of creation. Christianity, White concludes, "bears a huge burden of guilt for environmental deterioration."[1]

White's views have attracted considerable criticism. Historians have pointed out that the exploitation of nature is not unique to the West; biblical scholars have maintained that the relevant passages of the Judeo-Christian scriptures do not sustain the interpretation placed on them by White and his followers; social scientists have claimed that no correlation presently obtains between Christian belief and indifference to the fortunes of the environment. Moreover, since the publication of White's article, more nuanced accounts of the ideological sources of Western attitudes toward nature have appeared. In the influential *Man's Responsibility for Nature* (1974), John Passmore identified two distinct emphases within the Christian tradition, despotism and stewardship, suggesting that the counterproductive attempt to dominate nature—"man as despot"—owes more to Greek conceptions

---

1   Lynn White. Jr., "The Historical Roots of Our Ecological Crisis," *Science* 155 (1967): 1203–7. Major discussions of the thesis include Ian Barbour, ed., *Western Man and Environmental Ethics: Attitudes towards Nature and Technology* (Reading, Mass., Addison-Wesley, 1973): Donald Gowan and Millard Shumaker, *Subduing the Earth: An Exchange of Views* (Kingston: United Church of Canada, 1980), esp. the bibliography; Robin Aufield, *The Ethics of Environmental Concern* (Oxford: Blackwell, 1983); David Spring and Eileen Spring, eds., *Ecology and Religion in History* (New York: Harper & Row, 1974); Carl Mitcham and Jim Grote, eds., *Theology and Technology: Essays in Christian Analysis and Exegesis* (New York: University Press of America, 1984); Jeremy Cohen, *"Be Fertile and Increase, Fill the Earth and Master It": The Ancient and Medieval Career of a Biblical Text* (Ithaca, N.Y.: Cornell University Press, 1989), pp. 15–18, and Elspeth Whitney, "Lynn White, Ecotheology, and History," *Environmental Ethics* 15 (1993): 151–69.

Peter Harrison, "Subduing the Earth: Genesis 1, Early Modern Science, and the Exploitation of Nature," *Journal of Religion*, vol. 79, no. 1, pp. 86–109. Copyright © 1999 by University of Chicago Press. Reprinted with permission.

than to the biblical tradition.[2] But despite these developments, the idea that the Christian doctrine of creation provided the ideological basis for the exploitation of the nature has proven tenacious. White himself saw no reason to resile from his original observations, and his views, despite their never having been developed to any great degree, continue to attract adherents. The presumed historical link between the Christian doctrine of creation and the Western attitude toward nature has been endlessly rehearsed in the burgeoning literature on environmental degradation and its causes. In a further development, many within the Christian tradition itself have endorsed aspects of the White thesis, calling for a radical revision of those traditional Christian doctrines that are supposed to have inspired ecological irresponsibility and chauvinism toward the natural world.

In this article I shall examine some of the ways in which the creation narratives of Genesis were used in the medieval and early modern periods, with a view to showing that "the roots of our environmental crisis" are somewhat more complex than either White or his critics imagined.[3] As we shall see, while the biblical imperative "have dominion" played an important role in the rise of modern science and is undoubtedly implicated in what appears to be the "exploitation" of nature, the same imperative, when linked to the human fall, also promoted the goal of the restoration of the earth. "Despot" and "steward" thus turn out to be twin aspects of single role, rather than opposing traditions. In addition, I will suggest that the supposed anthropocentrism of the Western tradition has little to do with environmental degradation, falling into decline at precisely that historical moment that witnesses the beginnings of the large-scale exploitation of nature. There is, therefore, a need to revise standard accounts of the religious origins of Western attitudes toward nature and to call into question the fundamental premise of those new, ecologically sensitive theologies that too easily concede that the ecological crisis is to be attributed in part to the Christian doctrine of creation.

I

Before proceeding to the history of interpretation of Genesis 1 in medieval and early modern periods, it is worth dwelling briefly on a common but misplaced line of argument in this general discussion. Some of the most vocal attacks on the White thesis have come from the sphere of biblical criticism. A number of biblical scholars have patiently tried to explain that when we examine such Hebrew terms as "have dominion" and "subdue," we find that they do not really mean "have dominion" and "subdue." James Barr, for example, informs us that the verb *rada*—"have dominion"—is not a particularly strong expression and was used to refer to Solomon's peaceful rule; *kabash,* "subdue," refers simply to "the

---

2   John Passmore, *Man's Responsibility for Nature* (London: Duckworth, 1974), pt. I. See also Clarence Glacken, *Traces on the Rhodian Shore: Nature and Culture in Western Thought from Ancient Tunes to the End of the Eighteenth Century* (Berkeley: University of California Press, 1973).

3   The need for such a study has already been pointed out by Jeremy Cohen, "The Bible, Man, and Nature, in the History of Western Thought: A Call for Reassessment." *Journal of Religion* 65 (1985), 155–72. To a degree, this need has been admirably met by Cohen's *"Be Fertile and Increase."* However, his study, comprehensive as it is, deals with only the ancient and medieval periods.

'working' or 'tilling' of the ground in the J story."[4] Lloyd Steffen follows suit, pointing out that while it is true that one of the meanings of the word "dominion" (*rada*) is "to tread down," what the term denotes in the Genesis context is "the ideal of just and peaceful governance." Dominion, he concludes, "is not a domination concept."[5]

Other biblical scholars have accused White of being ignorant of findings of source criticism. The creation stories in Genesis, we are told, have their origins in two distinct sources—the priestly account, P, and the Yahwist, J—and these sources ought not to be confused. Had not Lynn White been "critically illiterate," Richard Hiers observes, he would not have conflated the P and J creation stories, "thereby obscuring and omitting significant elements."[6] J. Baird Calicott complains similarly that White mistakenly thinks of Genesis "as a composite whole," and that he jumps carelessly between J and P to wrest his preferred interpretation from the text.[7]

Finally, a number of critics have pointed out that the bible does not present a single perspective on the question of the human relation to the natural world. There are, Ian Barbour points out, "diverse strands in the Bible" regarding this issue.[8] If Genesis contains a dominion concept, it also puts forward one of stewardship. Gabriel Fackre thus suggests that Genesis teaches "stewardship over the earth before a higher claimant." Human beings, he adds, are "called to tend the earth in responsibility to its Creator."[9] John Passmore speaks similarly of a minority view within the Western tradition, which regards the human being as steward rather than a despot.[10] Indeed White himself has remarked that the most common complaint he received regarding his thesis was that he had ignored the fact that human dominion granted by God was intended to make human beings stewards of his creation rather than its despoilers.[11]

---

4   James Barr. "The Ecological Controversy and the Old Testament," *Bulletin of the John Rylands Library* 55 (1972): 9–32, esp. p. 22.

5   Lloyd H. Steffen, "In Defence of Dominion," *Environmental Ethics* 14 (1992): 63–80. For similar analyses, see Aufield, pp. 27–32; Claus Westerman. *Creation* (London: SPCK, 1974), pp. 52 and 82, and *Genesis 1–11: A Commentary,* trans. J. Scullion (Minneapolis: Augsburg, 1984), p. 159; Susan Bratton, "Christian Ecotheology and the Old Testament." *Environmental Ethics* 6 (1984): 195–209; George Coats, "God and Death: Power and Obedience in the Primeval History." *Interpretation* 29 (1975); 227–39; Gowan and Shumaker, pp. 16–17, 22. An exception to these awkward attempts to avoid the natural sense of the passages in question is Wilhelm Fudpucker, who with refreshing honesty suggests that the biblical injunction "subdue the earth" should be translated with its full force, "to tread down," "to conquer," "to trample", see his "Through Christian Technology to Technological Christianity," in Mitcham and Grote, eds., pp. 53–69. See also John Black, *The Dominion of Man* (Edinburgh: Edinburgh University Press, 1970), p. 37; A. S. Kapelrud, "Die Theorie der Schöpfung im Alten Testament," *Zeitschrift für die alttestamentliche Wissenschaft* 91 (1979): 159–69, Hans Wulff, *Anthropology of the Old Testament* (London: SCM. 1974), pp. 226–27.

6   Richard H. Hiers, "Ecology, Biblical Theology, and Methodology: Biblical Perspectives on the Environment." *Zygon* 19 (1984): 43–59, esp. 45. Also, on J. and P. see Black, pp. 40–41.

7   J. Baird Calicott, "Genesis Revisited: Murian Musings on the Lynn White, Jr. Debate," *Environmental History Review* 14 (1990): 65–90.

8   Barbour, ed., p. 6.

9   Gabriel Fackre, "Ecology and Theology," in Barbour, ed., p. 122.

10   Passmore, chap. 2. Passmore notes, however, that there is "very little" support for this interpretation within the Christian tradition. The "stewardship" tradition was originally identified by Black, pp. 44–57.

11   Lynn White, Jr., "Continuing the Conversation," in Barbour, ed., p. 60.

What such criticisms fail to take into consideration, however, is the fact that the original meaning of the text, or the true meaning of the text, or the meaning of the text as established by current methods of biblical criticism, is at best tangentially related to the issue of how the text might have informed attitudes toward nature and environmental practices. White's thesis is not concerned with the meaning of the text as such, with how it was understood by the community in which it first appeared, or with what modern biblical scholars have made of it, but rather with what the text was taken to mean at certain periods of history, how it motivated specific activities, and how it came to sanction a particular attitude toward the natural world. In other words, it is the reception of the text, and not its presumed meaning, which is at issue here. White's thesis does not therefore lie within the ambit of biblical criticism or hermeneutics but in the sphere of history.[12] Thus it is not clear that contemporary understandings of the meaning of the Genesis accounts of the creation have a direct bearing on the question of how such texts were used in the past, nor on what practices they might have encouraged. In order to evaluate claims about a connection between biblical doctrines and attitudes toward nature, we need to abandon the quest for definitive meaning and attend to the history of interpretation of the relevant texts.[13]

II

For the first fifteen hundred years of the Christian era there is little in the history of interpretation of Genesis to support White's major contentions. Patristic and medieval accounts of human dominion are not primarily concerned with the exploitation of the natural world. A common patristic reading of "dominion over the beasts," for example, relies upon the ancient conception of the human being as a microcosm of the world and internalizes the idea of dominion, directing it inward to the faculties of the human soul. Origen, the third-century church father who pioneered the allegorical reading of scripture, pointed out that the mind is "another world in miniature" and that it contains all manner

---

12   Thus, attempts to refute the White thesis on the basis of contemporary social scientific studies of religious belief and attitudes to the environment are also misplaced. For examples of such studies, see Michelle Wokomir et al., "Substantive Religious Belief and Environmentalism," *Social Science Quarterly* 78 (1997): 96–108; Douglas Eckberg and T. Jean Blocker, "Varieties of Religious Involvement and Environmental Concerns: Testing the Lynn White Thesis," *Journal for the Scientific Study of Religion* 28 (1989): 509–17.

13   Some of White's critics seem to concede this point. Barr candidly admits "it is of course possible to argue that the Genesis account, of creation has had an influence not through its own original meaning but through interpretations which have been placed upon it. ... This may or may not be so; I have not been able to carry out a study of the ways in which Genesis in this regard has been used over a period of many centuries" (Barr. p. 23). Also. Whitney (n. 1 above) states that "White's claim that the Bible had inspired the development of Western technology and control of nature rested not on the biblical text per se or on any 'timeless' theological explication of it. ... The crucial question, therefore was not so much what the writers of the Old and New Testaments had meant about technology, or even bow their world might be construed by modern readers, but how the Bible had been interpreted in the Middle Ages and after" (p. 162). Compare Odil Steck, *World and Environment* (Nashville, Tenn.: Abingdon, 1980), p. 198; Roderick Nash. *The Rights of Nature* (Madison: University of Wisconsin Press, 1988). p. 89.

of living things.[14] The allegorical reading of the creation of the animals thus construed them as "the impulses and thoughts of our mind which are brought forth from the depths of our heart."[15] Accordingly, the dominion over nature referred to in Genesis was frequently interpreted by the church fathers to mean dominion over the rebellious beasts within. "The saints and all who preserve the blessing of God in themselves exercise dominion over these things," wrote Origen, "but on the other hand, the same things which are brought forth by the vices of the flesh and the pleasures of the body hold dominion over sinners."[16] Jerome similarly identified various beasts with the "irascible and concupiscible passions," while John Chrysostom advocated "bringing the beast under control" by "banishing the flood of unworthy passions."[17] Augustine thought that the beasts "signify the affections of the soul." The unruly impulses of the body are thus "animals" that "serve reason when they are restrained from their deadly ways."[18] The imperative force of the biblical injunction "have dominion" thus became, during the patristic period, a powerful incentive to bring rebellious carnal impulses under the control of reason.

This allegorical approach to texts, which became universal practice during the Middle Ages, also informed the structures of knowledge of the natural world. Knowledge of things was not pursued in order to bring nature under human control but, rather, to shed light on the meanings of nature and of the sacred page. Nature and scripture were both books, and their elucidation called for an interpretive science. Living things, it was assumed, had been designed in part to serve for the physical needs of human beings but equally to serve a spiritual function as well. In this latter role, natural objects symbolized eternal verities, or taught important moral lessons. Nature, in this scheme of things, was to be known in order to determine its moral and spiritual meanings and not so that it might be materially exploited.

No work embodies this approach to nature better than the *Physiologus*—a work on animals, plants, and stones, produced in Alexandria at some time between the second and fifth centuries. The *Physiologus* sets out the moral and theological significance of numerous natural objects. Throughout the Middle Ages it was to enjoy a popularity second only to the Bible itself. Indeed in the jaundiced judgments of previous generation of scholars, this was the work that substituted fanciful fables for the measured and rational judgments of Aristotelian natural history, eclipsing for a thousand years

---

14 Origen, *Homilies on Leviticus* 5.2, in *Fathers of the Church* (hereafter *FC*) (Washington, D.C.: Catholic University of America Press, 1947–), 83:91–92. For other readings suggesting the human microcosm, see Gregory, *Homiliae in Evangelium* 29 in *Patrologia cursus completus, series Latina* (hereafter *PL*) (Paris 1958–). ed. J. P. Migne, 76:1212; Ambrose, *Hexameron* 6.2.3. Gregory of Nyssa, *De hominis opificio* 4.1. Also see Patricia Cox, "Origen and the Bestial Soul," *Vigiliae Christianiae* 36 (1982): 115–40, esp. 123.

15 Origen, *Homilies on Genesis* 1.11 (*FC* 71:60). See also the fragment attributed to Origen, D. Glaue, ed., *Ein Bruchstück des Origenes über Genesis 1. 28* (Giessen: Alfred Töpelmann, 1928), pp. 8–10.

16 Origen. *Homilies on Genesis* 1.16 (*FC* 71:69).

17 Jerome, *Commentariorum in Hiezechielem* 1.1.6/8, Corpus Christianorum Series Latina, vol. 75 (Turnholti: Brepols, 1975), pp. 11 ff. Jerome, *Homilies* 7.30. John Chrysostom. *Homilies on Genesis* 8.14 (*FC* 74:113). Compare Philo, *De plantatione* 11.43, *De opificio mundi* 51.146, 53.151.

18 Augustine, *Confessions* 13.21, trans. Henry Chadwick (Oxford: Oxford University Press, 1991). p. 291.

the systematic scientific approach of the Greek philosopher.[19] Yet the fables of the *Physiologus* helped created a rich symbolic world in which natural objects came to be invested with profound and mystical meanings. If this was not a scientific view of nature, it was nonetheless one which found in the cosmos a moral and theological order and located human beings at its centre.

In one sense, the *Physiologus* might be said to present a utilitarian approach to the natural world. However, the utilities of living things are seen to reside in their symbolic and moral functions. The fox, to take a single example, is described thus:

> The fox is an entirely deceitful animal who plays tricks. If he is hungry and finds nothing to eat, he seeks out a rubbish pit. Then, throwing himself on his back, he stares upwards, draws in his breath, and thoroughly bloats himself up. Now the birds, thinking the fox dead, descend upon him to devour him. But he stretches out and seizes them, and the birds themselves die a miserable death.

> The fox is a figure of the devil. To those who live according to the flesh he pretends to be dead. Although he may hold sinners in his gullet, to spiritual men and those perfected in faith, however, he is dead and reduced to nothing.[20]

The purpose of the fox is to teach an important lesson, to inspire the faithful, and to give pause to the apostate. Nature had not been created solely, or even primarily, to cater for the material needs of the human race, but to serve spiritual and moral requirements as well. The use of creatures, in this scheme of things, requires knowledge of their meanings. The *Physiologus* promotes an anthropocentric conception of nature, but it is a conception that takes a passive, interpretive view of the world, rather than one that actively seeks its material exploitation. The enormously popular bestiaries of the later Middle Ages were all based on the *Physiologus*.[21] These books of birds and beasts reinforced the symbolic and moral functions of the things of nature.

With the thirteenth-century translation of the biological works of Aristotle into Latin, a new source of knowledge of the natural world arrived in the West. If the monasteries tended to persist with the emblematic approach of the bestiary, the new schools turned to the writings of the Greek philosopher, producing encyclopedic works which, collating a wide variety of sources, contained all

---

19   Patricia Cox. "The *Physiologus*: A *Poiesis* of Nature." *Church History* 52 (1983): 433–43, esp. 433.

20   *Physiologus* 17, trans. Michael Curley (Austin: University of Texas Press, 1979), pp. 27–28.

21   For the story of the fox in twelfth- and thirteenth-century bestiaries, see, e.g., *Bestiary,* trans. Richard Barber (Woodbridge: Boydell, 1993), p. 65, *The Book of Beasts,* trans. T. H. White (London: Cape, 1954), pp. 53–54. For general studies of the bestiaries, see M. R. James, *The Bestiary* (Oxford: Roxburghe Club, 1928): Florence McCulloch, *Medieval Latin and French Bestiaries* (Chapel Hill: University of North Carolina Press, 1962); W. B. Clark and M. T. McMunn, eds., *The Bestiary and Its Legacy* (Philadelphia: University of Pennsylvania Press, 1989).

extant knowledge of natural things.[22] The rediscovery of ancient Greek knowledge during the course of the twelfth and thirteenth centuries thus inspired a more direct engagement with the empirical world, adding a new dimension, the idea of dominion over nature. Yet we still do not encounter an explicit ideology of material exploitation of the world. Rather, the new emphasis is on the intellectual mastery of the knowledge of living things. Adam, it was believed, had once enjoyed a perfect knowledge of nature, a knowledge evidenced in his naming of the creatures (Gen. 2:20). With the fall, the creatures rebelled, and antipathies developed among them and between them and the erstwhile masters. The creatures were now to be reunited in the human mind. The thirteenth-century Franciscan Bonaventure wrote that Adam in the state of innocence "possessed knowledge of created things and was raised through their representation to God and to his praise, reverence and love." With the fall, Adam and his progeny had become alienated from God and had lost that knowledge. For Bonaventure, the reaccumulation of this lost knowledge was "the goal of the creatures and the way they are led back to God."[23] To know the things of nature was thus to reorder them mentally. Honorius Augustodunensis, author of the popular medieval digest of cosmology and geography *Imago mundi,* had written something similar in the twelfth century. Man, he claimed, is the supreme animal in which God willed all things to be reunited.[24] Knowledge of the creatures was thus another way of restoring, in a fashion, the original dominion that the human race had once enjoyed. Two of the dominant senses of dominion that we encounter in the patristic period and the Middle Ages are thus to do with the realm of the human mind. Both rely to a degree on the idea of the human microcosm. Thomas Aquinas is typical of the Middle Ages in claiming that human dominion over things is intimately related to the fact that the human individual "contains all things."[25]

Having said this, it must be conceded that the modification of nature, oftentimes on a large scale, undoubtedly took place during the Middle Ages. The pious spiritual works performed by medieval monastic communities, for example, were invariably accompanied by more mundane pursuits, for the monasteries in which these acts of contemplation were to occur, of necessity, had also to cater for bodily needs. This in turn required agriculture and husbandry and the transformation of woods and swamps into fields and pastures. William of Malmesbury thus lauded the improvements made to the natural world by the industry of the monks of Thorney:

---

22   Michel de Boüard. "Encyclopédies médiévales: Sur la connaissance de la nature et du monde au Moyen Age," *Revue des questions historiques,* ser. 3, 16 (1930): 258–304, esp. 267. n. 2. Willene Clark. *The Medieval Book of Birds: Hugh of Fouilloy's Aviarum* (Birmingham, N.Y.: Medieval and Renaissance Texts and Studies, 1992), introduction, p 23.

23   Bonaventure. *Hexameron* 13, quoted in J. McEvoy. "Microcosm and Macrocosm in the Writings of St. Bonaventure," *Commissio Internationalis Bonaventurianae S. Bonaventura: Volumen Commemoratrum ... Cura et Studio Commissionis Internationalis Bonventurianae* (Rome: Padre di Editori di Quaracci, 1972–74), p. 330.

24   Honorius Augustodunensis, *Hexaemeron* 3 (*PL* 172:258D–259A), *De animae exsilio et patria* 13 (*PL* 172:1246B). Compare Hugh of St. Victor. *De arca Noe morali,* Prologus (*PL* 176:619). *In ecclesiasten homiliae* (*PL* 174:277D), *Didascalicon* 2.1, trans. J. Taylor (New York: Columbia University Press. 1961), p. 61.

25   Thomas Aquinas. *Summa theologiae* 1a.96.2. Blackfriars edition (London: Eyre & Spottiswoode, 1964–76).

In the middle of wild swampland where the trees are intertwined in an inextricable thicket, there is a plain with very green vegetation which attracts the eye by reason of its fertility; no obstacle impedes the walker. Not a particle of the soil is left to lie fallow; here the earth bears fruit trees, there grapevines cover the ground or are held on high trellises. In this place cultivation rivals nature; what the latter has forgotten the former brings forth. What can I say of the beauty of the buildings whose unshakeable foundations have been built into the marshes. … This is an image of Paradise; it makes one think already of heaven.[26]

Reference to the reconstruction of a paradise on earth seems to suggest that here we have a clear instance of a religiously motivated attempt to conquer nature. Yet this was not an engagement with natural world in order to assert dominion or reap material gain; neither was it informed by a callous disregard for the earth. It was otherworldly preoccupations that motivated this activity. Malmesbury thus continues: "This incomparable solitude has been granted the monks so that they may grow more closely attached to the higher realities for being the more detached from those of mortal life."[27] Control of nature was exercised in this attenuated fashion to promote the concerns of the other world and thus, paradoxically, to further a detachment from material nature.

White himself has pointed to other examples of medieval attempts to master nature that occur quite independent of religious communities. The introduction of the heavy plough into northern Europe made possible the large-scale cultivation of land and lifted agricultural production above the level of subsistence farming. This technological innovation thus revolutionized the relationship between human beings and the land that they inhabited, yielding up food surpluses and facilitating the development of towns. According to White, this single agricultural advance meant that whereas "once man had been a part of nature; now he became her exploiter."[28] In addition, the medieval deployment of an impressive array of machines—water wheels, windmills, cranks and con-rods, fly-wheels, and treadles—are for White symptomatic of "the emergence of a conscious and generalised lust for natural energy and its application to human purposes."[29] Yet in none of this do we encounter the explicit articulation of an attitude of indifference to, or hostility toward, nature. Indeed, there seems to be no compelling reason to view these developments as anything more than particular expressions of

---

26   William of Malmesbury, *De gestis pontificum Angliae,* in *PL* 175:1612–13, quoted in Jean Leclercq. *The Love of Learning and the Desire for God* (New York: Fordham University Press, 1074). p. 165.

27   Leclercq, p. 165. Leclerq thus suggests that "the cloister is the 'true paradise'" and that the surrounding countryside merely "shares in its dignity" (ibid.). Other monastic concerns, too, called for the control of nature. Leclercq informs us that a flock of sheep was required to provide the parchment for a single copy of a work by Cicero or Seneca. In addition, the leather to bind such works required the hunting of wild beasts—deer, roebuck, boar (p. 155).

28   Lynn White. Jr., *Medieval Technology and Social Change* (Oxford: Oxford University Press. 1964). p. 56.

29   Ibid., p. 129. We also witness in the later Middle Ages the widespread practice of forest clearing by fire or by axe. Glacken (n. 2 above) refers to the period of the eleventh to the thirteenth century as "the great age of forest clearance" (p. 330). For medieval modifications of nature generally, see pp. 318–51.

the universal tendency of all cultures to seek efficient means to provide for basic human needs. Such activities require no religious ideology to motivate them, nor do they need any other justification than that human beings require food and shelter, and when these are met, further creature comforts as well. The medieval West, in other words, shares with every culture a concern to feed and clothe itself. These imperatives frequently lead to the depletion of natural resources and ecological change. While the modes of exploitation may differ, the underlying impulse is universal.[30]

What is lacking in this analysis, then, is the identification of a *religiously* motivated ideology of exploitation, explicitly informed by aspects of the Christian doctrine of creation. As I have already suggested, the absence of the obvious candidate here—the biblical conception of dominion—was owing to the fact that the literal force of the imperative "have dominion" was dissipated by moral interpretations. It is telling, in this connection, that the one extensive study that has been carried out on the history of the interpretation of the crucial text Gen. 1:28 ("be fruitful and multiply, and fill the earth, and subdue it; and have dominion") fails to support the view that it was allied with exploitative material practices during the Middle Ages. Jeremy Cohen, author of this survey, concludes that "the primary meaning of Gen. 1.28 during the period we have studied [ancient and medieval times] [is] an assurance of divine commitment and election, and a corresponding challenge to overcome the ostensive contradiction between the terrestrial and the heavenly inherent in every human being." In the Middle Ages, Cohen continues, the Genesis text that granted human dominion over nature "touched only secondarily on conquering the natural order."[31]

While dominion is interpreted psychologically, and while much of nature's utility is perceived to lie in its symbolic aspects, the goal of physical domination of the world, as an end in itself, fails to take hold. For the Middle Ages, as literal readings of the text "have dominion"—the body of the text as Origen would have it—tend to be subordinated to spiritual readings that referred the reader to the inward disciplines of self-control, so religious motivations for the material domination of nature are secondary to the pursuit of a spiritual dominion of the will over the wild and wayward impulses of the body. Undeniably, the conquest of nature is well in evidence during the Middle Ages, but for the most part this is to be attributed to pragmatic rather than ideological concerns.

However, this state of affairs was to change. Had Cohen extended his labors into the early modern period, a somewhat different picture of the influence of that text would have emerged. In the seventeenth century we find practitioners of the new sciences, preachers of the virtues of agriculture and husbandry, advocates of colonization, and even gardeners explicitly legitimating their engagement with nature by appeals to the text of Genesis. The rise of modern science, the mastery of the world that it enabled, and the catastrophic consequences for the natural environment that ensued, were intimately related to new readings of the seminal Genesis text, "Have dominion."

---

30   Thus, some of White's critics have observed that ecological problems are not restricted to the West. See. e.g., Lewis Moncrief, "The Cultural Basis of Our Environmental Crisis," *Science* 170 (1970): 508–12; Keith Thomas, *Man and the Natural World* (Ringwood: Penguin, 1984), pp. 23–24.

31   Cohen, "Be Fertile and Increase" (n. 1 above), p. 313.

III

While the themes of moral and intellectual dominion have not entirely disappeared in the seventeenth century, "dominion over the earth" is now read by most commentators as having to do with the exercise of control not in the mind, but in the natural world. A variety of interrelated factors can be suggested to account for this shift: the demise of the rich, arcane conception of the microcosm in which features of the natural world had been mapped onto the human psyche; the "death of nature," which saw the replacement of Aristotelian vitalism with a mechanical world view; the collapse of the "symbolist mentality" of the Middle Ages and the radical contraction of sacramentalism, which resulted in a denial of the transcendental significance of the things of nature; the appearance on the religious landscape of this-worldly Protestantism with its attendant work ethic; and finally, the new hermeneutics of modernity, which looks to the literal sense as the true meaning of a text.[32] It is this last factor in particular which brings about new readings of the biblical imperative "have dominion."[33]

The literal approach to texts that, from the sixteenth century onward, becomes a hallmark of modern hermeneutics, meant that natural objects were no longer to be treated as symbols. The fundamental presupposition of allegorical interpretation was that natural objects could function, like words, as signs. A word in scripture would refer to an object, and the object in turn would refer to some theological or moral truth. Irenaeus had written that "earthly things should be types of the celestial." Origen agreed that "this visible world teaches us about that which is invisible, and ... this earthly scene contains patterns of things heavenly."[34] The disintegration of this symbolist mentality, to which the Protestant insistence that only words and not things have referential functions was a major contributing factor, meant that practical uses would now have to be sought for natural objects that had hitherto served merely symbolic functions. In part, then, "scientific" modes of explanation, along with the search for the practical uses of the things of nature, came into being in order to fill the vacuum left by the demise of traditional medieval systems of representation.[35]

Now the injunction to exercise dominion over birds and beasts was taken quite literally to refer to the actual exercise of power over the things of nature, its sense no longer being distributed across

---

32   For discussions of some of these themes, see Carolyn Merchant. *The Death of Nature: Women, Ecology, and the Scientific Revolution* (New York: Harper & Row, 1990); John Brooke. *Science and Religion: Some Historical Perspectives* (Cambridge: Cambridge University Press, 1991), pp. 82–116; Thomas. pp. 22–24; David Lindberg and Ronald Numbers, eds., *God and Nature: Historical Essays on the Encounter between Christianity and Science* (Berkeley: University of California Press, 1986).

33   Much of the impetus for the literal reading of texts came from the Protestant reformers. See. e.g., Martin Luther. "The Babylonian Captivity of the Church," in *Three Treatises* (Philadelphia: Fortress Press, 1970), pp. 146, 241; John Calvin, *Institutes* 2.5, trans. H. Beveridge, 2 vols. (London: Clark, 1953); Alister McGrath. *The Intellectual Origins of the European Reformation* (Oxford: Blackwell, 1987), p. 186; Pierre Fraenkel, *Testimonia Patrum: The Function of the Patristic Argument in the Theology of Philip Melanchthon* (Geneva: Droz, 1961), pp. 70–93; Hans Frei, *The Eclipse of Biblical Narrative* (New Haven, Conn.: Yale University Press, 1974), p. 37.

34   Irenaeus, *Against Heresies* 4.19, in *Ante-Nicene Fathers* (Edinburgh: T. & T. Clark, 1989), 5:439; Origen. *The Song of Songs, Commentary and Homilies,* trans. R. P. Lawson (London: Longmans, Green, 1957), p. 218.

35   For a more detailed discussion of this general theme, see Peter Harrison, *The Bible, Protestantism, and the Rise of Natural Science* (Cambridge: Cambridge University Press, 1998), esp. pp. 107–20.

allegorical, anagogical, or tropological readings. The beasts of Genesis did not represent impulses of the mind, which needed to be bridled by reason, nor was the desired control of living things to be achieved merely through systematically ordering them in the mind. Adam had once literally been lord of all the creatures, and this was the kind of dominion sought by his seventeenth-century imitators. With the turn away from allegorical interpretation, the things of nature lost their referential functions, and the dominion over nature spoken of in the book of Genesis took on an unprecedented literal significance.[36]

There are numerous examples that serve to show how this new impulse of dominion was incorporated into the rhetoric of scientific progress in the seventeenth century. Francis Bacon, who first set out the method of the empirical sciences, famously observed that only "by digging further and further into the mine of natural knowledge" could the human race extend "the narrow limits of man's dominion over the universe" to their "promised bounds."[37] Genesis taught that dominion had been lost as a result of the Fall but now, through science and industry, that dominion could be restored: "For man by the fall fell at the same time from this state of innocency and from his dominion over creation. Both of these losses however can even in this life be in some part repaired; the former by religion and faith, the latter by arts and sciences. For creation was not by the curse made altogether and forever a rebel, but ... is now by various labours ... at length and in some measure subdued to the supplying of man with bread; that is to the uses of human life."[38] The Baconian program of dominion over nature was subsequently adopted by the Royal Society, First historian of the society, Thomas Sprat, stated as one of the group's objectives a reestablishment of "Dominion over *Things*."[39] In an address delivered to that same august body, Platonist and religious writer Joseph Glanvill announced that the new philosophy had provided "ways of *captivating Nature,* and making her *subserve* our *purposes* and *designments*" leading to the restoration of "the *Empire of Man* over *Nature*."[40] Nature, he was to remark elsewhere, was to be "master'd, managed, and used in the Services of Humane life."[41] Such services might include "the accelerating and *bettering of Fruita, emptying Mines, drayning Fens* and *Marshes*." "*Lands,*" he concluded, "may be *advanced* to scarce credible degrees of *improvement,*

---

36 On the exposition of Genesis during the early modern period, see Arnold Williams, *The Common Expositor: An Account of the Commentaries on Genesis, 1527–1633* (Chapel Hill: University of North Carolina Press, 1948); Joseph Duncan, *Milton's Earthly Paradise* (Minneapolis: University of Minnesota Press, 1972), chap. 5.

37 Quoted in Merchant, p. 170; on Bacon and dominion generally, see pp. 164–90. Compare William Leiss, *The Domination of Nature* (New York: George Braziller, 1972), pp. 45–71. On the continent, Descartes offered the similar remark that through science we can "thus make ourselves, as it were, the lords and masters of nature" (*Discourse on Method,* vol. 6, in *The Philosophical Writings of Descartes* trans. J. Cottingham, R. Stoothoff, and D. Murdoch [Cambridge: Cambridge University Press, 1984–], 1:142–43).

38 Francis Bacon, *Novum Organum* 2.52, in *Works,* 14 vols., ed. James Spedding, Robert Leslie Ellis, and Douglas Denon Heath (London: Longman, 1857–74), 4:247–48.

39 Thomas Sprat, *History of the Royal Society* (London, 1667), p. 62.

40 Joseph Glanvill, *Scepsis Scientifica* (London, 1665), sig. b3v.

41 Joseph Glanvill, *Plus Ultra* (London: 1668), p. 87. cf. p. 104.

and innumerable other *advantages* may be obtained by an *industry* directed by *Philosophy* and *Mechanicks*.[42]

The notion that it was the new natural philosophy that would promote the control of nature also had its inspiration in the Genesis text. During the periods of the Renaissance and the scientific revolution there was a renewed interest in the encyclopedic knowledge that Adam had possessed before his fall. Educational reformer John Webster, to take a single example, pointed out in his attack on the English universities that Adam understood the "internal natures" of all creatures and that "the imposition of names was adequately agreeing to their natures." While this knowledge had been lost at the Fall, it was the proper role of the universities to promote the regaining of this Adamic wisdom, "to know nature's power in the causes and effects" and "to make use of them for the general good and benefit of mankind, especially for the conservation of and restauration of the health of man, and of those creatures which are usefull for him."[43] Some of the leading scientists of the seventeenth century actually saw their task as the revival of an ancient science. Adam, it was thought, had subscribed to the heliocentric hypothesis, to corpuscular philosophy, and possibly even the theory of gravitation.[44] Dominion over the earth was to be established through a regaining of the knowledge once possessed by Adam in Eden. At this time, then, Adam's encyclopedic knowledge was sought not in order to reunite all of the creatures in the human mind and thereby find the way back to the deity, as had been the case in the Middle Ages but, rather, to revisit Adam's literal dominion.

Knowledge alone would not suffice for the domination of nature, however. Work was required. The emergence of the Protestant work ethic, commonly associated with Calvinist notions of election, also gained support from literal readings of Genesis. What made this possible was the fact that the Garden of Eden was now seen to be an actual garden, in which Adam had literally carried out agricultural work.[45] Eden was not an allegory of the human soul, and the fruits that Adam had cultivated were not the fruits of the spirit. Neither was paradise to be located in the incorruptible regions of the heavens. Thus Adam's work was not the pious contemplation of higher spiritual realities but a physical engagement with material things.[46] According to Bishop Lancelot Andrewes, one of the translators of

---

42   Glanvill, *Scepsis Scienlifica*, sigs. b4r–v.

43   John Webster, *Academiarum Examen* (London, 1654), pp. 29, 19. On Adam's knowledge, see also Francis Bacon, *The Advancement of Learning* (Oxford: Clarendon. 1974), p. 6; William Coles. *Adam in Eden* (London: 1657), preface; Henry Cornelius Agrippa, *Three Books of Occult Philosophy* (London: 1651), p. 153; Thomas Browne, *Religio Medici* (Oxford: Clarendon. 1982). 2.2. p. 65; Lancelot Andrewes, *Apospasmatia Sacra* (London, 1657), pp. 208–12; Robert South, *Sermons,* in *English Prose,* ed. W. Peacock, 5 vols. (Oxford: Oxford University Press, 1949). 2:208; John Salkeld, *Treatise of Paradise* (London. 1617), pp. 185–96: George Walker, *The History of the Creation* (London, 1641), p. 193.

44   See. e.g., Henry More, *A Collection of Several Philosophical Writings,* 2d ed. (London, 1662), pp. xviii–xix; Richard Bentley, *The Works of Richard Bentley D.D.,* 3 vols. (London, 1838). 3:74: Frank Manuel, *The Religion of Isaac Newton* (Oxford: Clarendon, 1974). p. 23: J. E. McGuire and P. M. Rattansi, "Newton and the Pipes of Pan," *Notes and Records of the Royal Society of London* 21 (1966): 108–43.

45   Duncan, pp. 152–54.

46   For such allegorical readings of paradise, see Alexander Neckham, *De naturis rerum* 2.49: Guibert of Nogent, *Moralium Geneseos* 1.1.21–24; Bartholomew Anglicus, *De proprietatibs rerum* 15:111, 158. For seventeenth-century criticism of these readings, see Salkeld, p. 4. See also Williams (n. 36 above), p. 110.

the Authorized Version, God made man "to labour, not to be idle." It was for this reason that Adam "was put into the garden of Eden that he might dresse it and keep it."[47] English jurist Matthew Hale (whom, incidentally, John Passmore regards as the sole seventeenth-century exemplar of the "stewardship tradition") insisted that the paradise that God had created was one that by its very nature needed to be worked.[48] Adam's original vocation, Richard Neve thought, sanctified agriculture, and tilling the earth was thus "the most *Ancient*, most Noble, and most Useful of all the Practical *Sciences*"—a science without which, moreover, the earth would quickly degenerate into a wilderness.[49] In his commentary on the first three chapters of Genesis, John White wrote that when God ordered Adam to subdue the earth, he intended him "by Culture and Husbandry, to Manure and make it fit to yield fruits and provision."[50] Other commentators agreed that, "subduing the earth" was to be understood to mean "plowing, tilling, and making use of it."[51] Such readings suggest that labor came to be more than just a means of providing human sustenance. Work was now regarded as a sanctified activity, an intrinsic good. By implication, working the earth and transforming the natural landscape were no longer simply means to an end, but ends in themselves.

A final incentive for this energetic engagement with the material world came with the linkage of the imperative "have dominion" to justifications of property ownership and colonization. In his *Second Treatise of Government* (1689), John Locke set out the view that in the state of nature, all land had been common. Land became private property when it was improved by clearing, planting, cultivation, or stocking with animals. The justification for this influential understanding of the basis of property ownership came from the biblical story of creation: for inasmuch as "God and his reason commanded him to subdue the earth, i.e. improve it for the benefit of life ... he that in obedience to this command of God, subdued, tilled, and sowed any part of, thereby annexed to it something that was his property."[52] Logically, it followed that those who occupied lands, yet had done nothing to bring them under control, could legitimately be dispossessed of them. Such notions were to play an important role in the justification of overseas plantations and colonies. Richard Eburne explained in *A Plaine Pathway to Plantations* (1624) that colonization was to be justified on account of "God's expresse commandment *to Adam, Genesis* 1.28. that hee should *fill the earth, and subdue it.*"[53] George Walker reasoned similarly that those parts of the world "which are not replenished with men able to

47   Andrewes. p. 104.

48   Matthew Hale. *The Primitive Origination of Mankind* (London, 1677), p. 317.

49   Richard Neve [T. Snow, pseudonym], *Apopiroscipy* (London, 1702), chap. 2, p. 3.

50   John White. *A Commentary upon the First Three Chapters of the First Book of Moses Called Genesis* (London, 1656), bk. 1, pp. 113–14.

51   George Hughes, *An Analytical Exposition of the First Book of Moses* (London, 1672), p 11 Compare John Pettus, *Volatiles from the History of Adam and Eve* (London, 1674), p. 83.

52   John Locke, *Two Treatises*, in *Works*, 10th ed., 10 vols. (London, 1801), 5:354, 356, 362.

53   Richard Eburne, *A Plaine Pathway to Plantation* (London, 1624). sig. B2v, pp. 16–18 (emphasis in original). Also see Christopher Hill, *The English Bible and the Seventeenth-Century Revolution* (Ringwood: Penguin. 1994), p. 136.

subdue the Earth and till it," are open to those who could properly exploit them."[54] Later in the century, clergy man and naturalist John Ray pointed out that the author of nature "is well pleased with the Industry of Man in adorning the Earth with beautiful Cities and Castles, with pleasant Villages and Country Houses, with regular Gardens and Orchards and Plantations." In this respect, he pointed out, Europe differed markedly from "a rude and unpolished America, peopled with slothful and naked Indians," hinting darkly that the conquest of America was in keeping with the biblical injunction to subdue the earth.[55] Developing conceptions of private property, along with commercial incentives for colonization, thus played their role in the modern conquest of nature, and these factors, too, found their ideological justification in seventeenth- and eighteenth-century readings of Genesis.[56]

In the rhetoric of seventeenth-century scientists and exegetes, then, we encounter new and momentous applications of the biblical imperatives "subdue" and "have dominion." It is difficult to escape the conclusion that the Genesis creation narratives provided the program for not only the investigation of nature but its exploitation as well.[57] Stripped of their allegorical and moral connotations, these passages were taken to refer unambiguously to the physical world and its living occupants. Whatever the ecological practices of medieval societies had been, at no time in the West prior to this do we encounter so explicit an ideology of the subordination of nature. White was correct to assign an important role to the creation story in the development of modern science and technology but mistaken in locating that effect earlier than the seventeenth century.[58]

IV

This may seem to lend support to the general thesis that the biblical account of the creation played an important role in the development of an exploitative attitude toward the natural world. However, the situation is more complex than this. When we attend closely to the seventeenth-century contexts in which the biblical imperative "have dominion" is used to justify the technological mastery of the natural world, we find that dominion is almost invariably associated with the Fall. Many writers allude to the fact the human rule over the earth had been lost through human disobedience to God.

---

54   Walker (n. 43 above), p. 222 (emphasis in original).

55   John Ray, *The Wisdom of God Manifested in the Works of Creation* (London. 1691), pp. 117–18.

56   Thus Karl Marx's claim that it was the coming of private property that led Christians to exploit nature is not necessarily inconsistent with the thesis of theological motivation. See Marx, *Grundrisse,* ed. David McLellan (St. Albans: Paladin, 1973), pp. 94–95. On the theological justifications of capitalism generally, see William Coleman, "Providence, Capitalism, and Environmental Degradation: English Apologists in an Era of Economic Revolution," *Journal of the History of Ideas* 37 (1976): 27–44.

57   In this connection, Bono has recently argued that the Genesis accounts of the Fall and Babel became for the early modern period a "master narrative" that eventually gave rise to scientific practices. See James Bono, *The Word of God and the Languages of Man: Interpreting Nature in Early Modern Science and Medicine* (Madison: University of Wisconsin Press, 1995), vol. 1.

58   Compare Glacken: "It is in the thought of this period [i.e., the seventeenth century] that there begins a unique formulation in Western thought, marking itself off from the other great traditions, such as the Indian and the Chinese. ... The religious idea that man has dominion over the earth, that he completes the creation, becomes sharper and more explicit by the seventeenth century" (Glacken [n. 2 above], pp. 494–95).

The dominion that plays so crucial a role in much seventeenth-century scientific discourse is thus a *recovered* dominion or a *restored* dominion, a pale imitation of that original sovereignty that had been granted to the human race. Loss of dominion, moreover, was not the only misfortune to have followed upon the lapse of our first parents: "Cursed it the ground because of you," the Lord says to Adam, "in toil you shall eat of it all the days of your life; thorns and thistles it shall bring forth to you; and you shall eat the plants of the field" (Gen. 4:17b–18). As a consequence of the human fall, the natural world, too, it was thought, fell from its original perfection. The whole creation, Saint Paul had written, now "groans in travail" (Rom. 8:22).

For seventeenth-century commentators, the consequences of the divine curse were pervasive. The fallen world inhabited by Adam's descendants was not the earth in its natural state, but an earth suffering under a curse on account of human transgression. The infertility of the ground, the ferocity of savage beasts, the existence of weeds, thorns, and thistles, of ugly toads and venomous serpents, all of these were painful reminders of the irretrievable loss of the paradisal earth. Even the surface of the globe itself, once a smooth and perfect sphere, had been transformed into hideous vistas of bogs, valleys, ravines, hills, and mountains. In its original, pristine state, the whole earth had been an ordered garden, now it was an untamed and unkempt wilderness, inhabited by a menagerie of mostly unmanageable beasts.[59]

Viewed in this context, early modern discourse about human dominion is not an assertion of a human tyranny over a hapless earth, nor does it exemplify an arrogant indifference to the natural world. Rather, dominion is held out as the means by which the earth can be restored to its prelapsarian order and perfection. It is for this reason that the seventeenth-century discourse of dominion is almost invariably accompanied by a rhetoric of restoration. John Pettus, for example, speaks of "subduing the earth" and "conquering those extravagancies of nature," but his aim is "the replenishment of the first creation." The "extravagancies" to which he refers are those of a nature gone wild and unchecked. Agriculture, which required a clearing of the native vegetation, a levelling of land, and a draining of swamps, was the activity that lay at the vanguard of these projects of restoration. Metaphysical poet Thomas Traherne wrote that the earth "had been a Wilderness overgrown with Thorns, and Wild Beasts, and Serpents: Which now by the Labor of many hands, is reduced to the Beauty and Order of *Eden*."[60] According to Timothy Nourse, agricultural activities heal the land of "the Original Curse of Thorns and Bryers" thus effecting "the *Restauration of Nature,* which may be looked upon as a *New Creation* of things."[61] In a similar vein, Richard Burton was to write of his ideal estate, "I will have no bogs, fens, marshes, vast woods, deserts, heaths … I will not have a barren acre in all my territories, not

---

59   For typical accounts of the mutations of the earth and its creatures that resulted from the fall, see Walker, pp. 23–25; Jean-François Senault, *Man Becom Guilty, Or the Corruption of Nature by Sinne, According to St. Augustin's Sense* (London, 1650). pp. 319–90: Richard Franck, *A Philosophical Treatise* (London, 1687), pp. 124–70.

60   Thomas Traherne, *Christian Ethicks* (London, 1675), p. 103.

61   Pettus (n. 51 above), p. 83. Timothy Nourse, *Campania Foelix* (London, 1700), p. 2.

so much as the tops of the mountains: where nature fails, it shall be supplied by art."[62] Human artifice compensates for the defects of nature, and fittingly so, for these defects represent the consequences of human sin. It is our business, wrote John Donne, "To rectifie nature to what she was."[63] Bacon himself wrote that the endeavour "to establish and extend the power and dominion of the human race itself over the universe" was undertaken with a view to enabling the human race to "recover the light over nature which belongs to it by divine bequest."[64] Dominion, then, was not exercised so that humanity could leave its mark upon the earth. On the contrary, it was to erase those scars that embodied the physical legacy of a moral fall. These measures were intended to improve the earth, to reinstate a paradise on earth, and provide an anticipation of heaven. "A skilful and industrious improvement of the creatures," observed one writer, would lead to "a fuller taste of Christ and Heaven."[65] The rhetoric of dominion and subjection that we encounter in this period does not therefore betray an indifference to the fortunes of nature but a concern to restore it to its original perfection.

The seventeenth century furnishes us with further evidence that challenges standard accounts of "Christian attitudes towards nature." Many such accounts refer to a connection between anthropocentrism and environmental exploitation. White, for example, maintained that "Christianity is the most anthropocentric religion the world has seen."[66] While this may be the case, it is by no means clear that anthropocentrism inevitably leads to an aggressive violation of the integrity of nature. As it turns out, the link between anthropocentrism and the early modern exploitation of the natural world is quite different from what we might expect, for the first serious challenges to anthropocentrism in the West come in the seventeenth century.[67] Many divines and scientists who unambiguously subscribed to a Christian doctrine of creation questioned the prevailing view that the whole of the created order had been brought into existence to serve human beings. Robert Boyle, one of the fathers of modern chemistry, described the idea as "erroneous." William Derham thought it a vulgar error. Fellow physico-theologian John Ray agreed that it was "vulgarly received" that "all this visible world was created for Man," but that "Wise Men now think otherwise." Thomas Burnet, who advocated a kind of seventeenth-century creation science, regarded as absurd the belief that the earth and the myriad celestial bodies were designed for use by "the meanest of all the Intelligent Creatures." Anthropocentrism was an opinion, wrote Archbishop William King, attended with "inextricable difficulties."[68]

---

62   Quoted in John Hale, *The Civilization of Europe in the Renaissance* (New York: Touchstone, 1995), p. 511.

63   John Donne, "To Sr Edward Herbert. At Julyers," lines 33–34.

64   Bacon, *Novum Organum* (n. 38 above). 1.129.

65   John Flavell, *Husbandry Spiritualized* (London, 1669), sig. A2v.

66   Lynn White, in Barbour, ed. (n. 1 above), p. 25.

67   Some pagan writers of the patristic period—most notably Celsus and, later, Porphyry—took issue with the anthropocentric stances of Stoicism and Christianity. See, e.g., Origen, *Against Celsus* 4; Porphyry, *De abstinentia* 3.20, and passim.

68   Robert Boyle, *A Disquisition about the Final Causes of Things* (London, 1688), p. 10; William Derham, *Astro-Theology; Or, a Demonstration of the Being and Attributes of God from a Survey of the Heavens* (London, 1715), p. 39; Ray (n. 55 above), pp. 127–28; Thomas Burnet, *The Sacred Theory of the Earth* (1690–91), 2.11 (London: Centaur Press, 1965), p. 218; William King, *An Essay on the Origin of Evil* (London, 1731), p. 91. Also see Henry More. *An Antidote against Atheism*, 2d ed. (London, 1662), appendix, p. 178; Jean d'Espagnet, *Enchyridion physicae restitutae* (London, 1651). p 162; Pierre Charron, *On Wisdom* (London, 1697), pp. 365–66.

We do not need to search far to discover the reasons for this challenge. The Copernican hypothesis that had displaced the earth from the center of the cosmos gained increasing support during the course of the seventeenth century. Many critics of anthropocentrism were Copernicans, and some explicitly identified their heliocentric commitments as the reason for their rejection of anthropocentrism. The expansion of the universe that came with the invention of the telescope also called into question the privileged place of the human race. The new astronomy, complained one of its critics, had made the earth "a despicable Spot, a Speck, a Point in comparison of the Vast and Spacious Conjeries of the Sun and Fixed Lights."[69] Such an insignificant planet could hardly serve as the home of the creature that was supposedly the pinnacle of the material creation. The passing of the microcosmic conception of the human being as the one creature in which all others were comprehended further eroded the prestige of the human animal. Added to this, the criticism of explanation in terms of final causes, articulated by such influential figures as Bacon and Descartes, removed human needs and purposes from the sphere of scientific explanation.

It is not unreasonable to conclude that during the course of the seventeenth century active engagement with the natural world increased as anthropocentric convictions waned. This development is not as surprising as it may at first seem. Francis Bacon's notorious advocacy of wresting natures secrets from her by force was premised on the view that nature is not a pliant servant, transparent to the intellect and designed to cater for human needs. It is because nature does not readily acquiesce in its own exploitation that force is called for. Nature, wrote Bacon, is to be interrogated and subjected to "trials and vexations of art."[70] A number of his contemporaries agreed. According to Galileo, nature does not care "a whit whether her abstruse reasons and methods of operation are understandable to men." Robert Hooke thought that nature seemed "to use som kind of art in indeavouring to avoid our discovery." Thus nature was to be investigated when "she seems to be put to her shifts, to make many doublings and turnings."[71] It had been a central assumption of Aristotelianism, by way of contrast, that the interpretation of nature could be based on commonsense observations of everyday phenomena. Accordingly, Aristotle and his medieval successors had erroneously concluded that heavy objects will fall faster than light ones, that objects in motion will naturally tend to come to rest, that the apparently circular motions of celestial objects were based on principles fundamentally different from those of terrestrial mechanics. The Aristotelian approach to knowledge of nature thus meshed neatly with the anthropocentric presumption. For seventeenth-century investigators, however, it was precisely because nature had not been framed solely with human utility in mind that an aggressive stance

---

69 John Edwards, *Brief Remarks upon Mr. Whiston's New Theory of the Earth* (London, 1697), "Epistle Dedicatory," pp. 23–26. Edwards believed that the Copernican hypothesis was a passing fad. On the connection between final causes and cosmology, also see John Witty, *An Essay towards a Vindication of the Vulgar Exposition of the Mosaic History of the World,* 2 vols. (London, 1705), 1:105, 108–9. Also see Boyle, preface, pp. 32–33, for a comparison of the Cartesian and Epicurean denials of final causes.

70 Francis Bacon, *De dignitate,* in *Works,* 4:298. Compare *Novum Organum* 1.98, in *Works,* 4:94.

71 Galileo, *Letter to the Grand Duchess Christina,* in *Discoveries and Opinions of Galileo,* trans. Stillman Drake (New York: Anchor, 1957), p 183; cf. pp. 187, 199; Robert Hooke, *Micrographia* (London, 1665), preface.

toward it was considered necessary. Robert Boyle thus thought it a mistake to claim that all things in the visible world had been created for the use of human beings, yet he allowed that all things had potential uses that could be determined only through systematic investigation.[72]

Growing uncertainties about how human interests fitted into the cosmic scheme of things thus combined with the ancient narrative of the expulsion from the garden, now read exclusively in its literal sense, to relocate early modern individuals into an apparently hostile environment in which they must make their own way and painstakingly accumulate knowledge from a world reluctant to yield up its secrets. Whatever the past glories of Eden, whatever easy assumptions of the superiority of the human race had been made in the previous periods of history, the present world was no longer regarded as the place over which human beings exercised a natural superiority, nor did the earth compliantly satisfy intellectual curiosity and provide for the material comforts of its human tenants. It was not arrogance, but modesty, that motivated the first of the modern scientists, and their program was not the violation of nature but the restoration of the earth to a paradise in which all creatures could take their proper place.

V

All of this suggests that some prevalent ideas about the relationship between the Christian doctrine of creation and Western attitudes toward nature require significant revision in a number of areas. First, if White was fundamentally correct to identify in specific Christian ideas and in particular biblical texts powerful determinants of Western attitudes toward the natural world, he was, for all that, mistaken in attributing to these an influence that predated the rise of science in the early modern period. Whatever evidence there may be of human impact on the natural landscape during the Middle Ages, only in the early modern period do we encounter the explicit connection between the exploitation of nature and the Genesis creation narratives.

Second, the common assumption that anthropocentrism is one of the engines that drives the exploitation of nature now seems questionable. For the Middle Ages, the centrality of the human being in the cosmos was unquestioned. For the moderns, it was precisely the loss of this centrality that motivated the quest to conquer an obstinate and uncooperative earth. From the perspective of Francis Bacon and his generation, if the natural world were genuinely to function as a willing vassal for its human masters, its active exploitation would have been unnecessary. Were nature truly

---

72   Boyle, p. 10, cf. pp. 230–31. The rise of theological voluntarism is also a relevant consideration here. If the laws of nature rested upon the divine will, rather than the divine reason, the basis of the regularities of nature could only be discovered through empirical investigation and not merely through the exercise of human reason alone. See Richard Westfall, *Science and Religion in Seventeenth-Century England* (New Haven, Conn.: Yale University Press, 1958), pp. 5–7, Richard Greaves, "Puritanism and Science," *Journal of the History of Ideas* 30 (1969): 345–68; R. Hooykaas. *Religion and the Rise of Modern Science* (Grand Rapids, Mich.: Eerdmans, 1972), pp. 98–114; Eugene Klaaren, *Religious Origins of Modern Science* (Grand Rapids, Mich.: Eerdmans, 1977), pp. 32–52.

submissive—as once it had been in Eden—it would already cater to all human needs. Thus doubts about the cosmic status of human beings motivated the investigation of nature in the search for hitherto hidden utilities. Such considerations furthered the cause of the scientific enterprise and indirectly contributed to environmental degradation.

Third, the role played by the narratives of creation and fall in the seventeenth-century discourses of the domination of nature suggests that the long-standing distinction between the traditions of "stewardship" and "despotism" in the Western tradition might have outlived its usefulness. The key to resolving the apparent tension between the views of the human being as steward or despot—the opposing perspectives of our relation to the natural world supposedly inherent in the Judeo-Christian tradition—lies in the conception of nature to which our early modern counterparts subscribed. For them, the world in its virgin state, untouched by human industry, was not the "natural" world but a fallen and disfigured creature, a standing rebuke to human sin and idleness. Accordingly, their responsibility, as they perceived it, was not to leave the world in its fallen state but rather to manipulate it, to improve it, to experiment upon it, all with a view to restoring it to its original perfection. In carrying out such activities they sought to redeem nature from the curse to which it had been subject for centuries on account of our first father's disobedience. In an important sense, then, early modern advocates of dominion and contemporary environmentalists share a common concern—to preserve or restore the natural condition of the earth, with the crucial difference between them residing in their respective views of what that "natural condition" is believed to be. What is certain is that, during this period of history at least, the impulses of dominion and stewardship were directed toward a common goal.

Finally, and following on directly from the previous point, it might be said that in these early modern understandings of creation and fall are the resources for an ecologically sensitive theology. It is intriguing, then, that so many advocates of ecotheology have tended to regard traditional theology as the problem rather than the solution.[73] Thomas Berry, one of the leading Catholic thinkers in this field, thus observes that our environmental problems are to be attributed at least in part to "our identification of the divine as transcendent to the natural world." What is required instead, he suggests, is "a new type of religious orientation."[74] Sally McFague, who has sought to articulate new models of

---

73   See, e.g., H. Paul Santmire, *The Travail of Nature: The Ambiguous Ecological Promise of Christian Theology* (Philadelphia: Fortress Press, 1985), pp. 146–47, "Healing the Protestant Mind: Beyond the Theology of Human Dominion," in *After Natures Revolt: Eco-Justice and Theology,* ed. D. Hessel (Philadelphia; Fortress Press. 1992), pp. 62–63; William French, "Subject-Centered and Creation-Centered Paradigms in Recent Catholic Thought," *Journal of Religion* 70 (1990): 48–72; Gustaf Wingren, *The Flight from Creation* (Minneapolis: Augsburg, 1971); Frederick Elder, *Crisis in Eden: A Religious Study of Man and Environment* (Nashville, Tenn.: Abingdon, 1970); Sean McDonagh, *To Care for the Earth: A Call to a New Theology* (Santa Fe, N.M.: Bear, 1987); John Carmody, *Ecology and Religion: Toward a New Christian Theology of Nature* (New York: Paulist, 1983); Rosemary Ruether, *Sexism and God-Talk: Toward a Feminist Theology* (Boston: Beacon, 1983): Roderick Nash. *Wilderness and the American Mind* (New Haven. Conn.: Yale University Press, 1970), and *The Rights of Nature* (n. 13 above). chap. 4: John Cobb. *Is It Too Late? A Theology of Ecology* (Beverly Hills, Calif.: Bruce, 1972); Matthew Fox, *The Coming of the Cosmic Christ* (San Francisco: Harper, 1988).
74   Thomas Berry, *The Dream of the Earth* (San Francisco: Sierra Books, 1988), pp. 113–15, 87. Intriguingly, White also spoke of a religious solution to our environmental problems, suggesting the revival of the theology of Saint Francis of Assisi, and proposing him as the patron saint of ecologists. See Barbour, ed., p. 30.

God more congruent with contemporary ecological sensitivities, has likewise criticized the theological stance according to which God is "distant from the world and relates only to the human world." It is this "image of sovereignty" that "supports attitudes of control and use toward the nonhuman world."[75] Perhaps most directly relevant of all for our present discussion is Matthew Fox, who in *Original Blessing* (1983) blames "Augustinian Fall-redemption theology" for what he identifies as an openly antagonistic approach to the natural world.[76] In light of the history of various readings of the creation and fall, it seems that such analyses concede too easily the agenda of White and his successors and prematurely abandon traditional Christian understandings of God's relation to the world. While it is tempting to speculate about simple connections between such ideas as divine transcendence or human dominion on the one hand, and attitudes of arrogance toward the natural order on the other, and while such links may seem to have a prima facie plausibility, history bears out the fact that the real situation is rather more complex.

The brief account of some of the dominant early modern readings of the Genesis text that I have provided is admittedly far from complete. Yet it serves to show the inadequacy of commonly held views about the relationship between Christianity and the exploitation of nature. I hope also to have shown that the religious convictions of previous eras are perhaps not as irrelevant to our present predicament as is often claimed. However ecologically naive our seventeenth-century forebears might now appear, and however misguided their efforts to "improve" the natural world, their program of retrieving a nature that had fallen into ruin on account of human transgressions seems not entirely inappropriate for the late twentieth century.

---

75 Sally McFague. *Models of God: Theology for an Ecological, Nuclear Age* (Philadelphia: Fortress Press, 1987), p. 68.
76 Matthew Fox, *Original Blessing* (Santa Fe, N.M.: Bear, 1983), pp. 10–11.

5B2. China's Environmental Crisis and Confucianism

Proposing a Confucian Green Theory to Save the Environment

By Joel Jay Kassiola

> *The Master said: "Both keeping past teachings alive and understanding the present—someone able to do this is worthy of being a teacher."*
>
> —Confucius, *Analects,* 2.11; Slingerland 2003:11[1]

Introduction: Why Non-Western Political Theory and Confucianism Now

The goal of this [reading] is to explain how consideration of Confucius's philosophy and the two-and-a-half millennia and evolving tradition of commentary and development of Confucian thought can advance environmental political thinking and policy. I will maintain that Confucianism can provide an intellectual framework for changing China's and the world's current unsustainable path to more effective environmental thought and decision-making. This objective may provoke fundamental skepticism that needs to be addressed at the outset: why prescribe an ancient Chinese philosopher who is not part of modern Western thought nor associated with the environment? Why deviate from the longstanding practice of Western exclusivity regarding the environment and examine Confucius's and his followers' thought regarding this important topic?

In order to address these questions, I recommend that we note the recent creation and growth of a new subfield within political theory and political science that is labeled as "Comparative Political Theory" or "Non-Western Political Theory" and consider its potential importance to the mission of achieving a sustainable and just social order.

This line of new thinking argues that the advent of globalization in the twentieth century and its intensification in the twenty-first have made it clear that the core assumptions in the Western thinkers from Plato to Rawls are misguided and narrow.[2]

The editors of these first books in the new academic field provide insight into the justification for this discussion of the contribution Confucianism can make to thinking about the environmental crisis in China and the world. One of them, while recognizing the value of traditional Western political

Joel Kassiola, "China's Environmental Crisis and Confucianism: Proposing a Confucian Green Theory to Save the Environment," *Chinese Environmental Governance: Dynamics, Challenges, and Prospects in a Changing Society*, ed. Bingqiang Ren and Huisheng Shou, pp. 227-242. Copyright © 2013 by Palgrave Macmillan. Reprinted with permission.

theory, quickly adds: "... in the age of rapid globalization, confinement to this [Western] canon is no longer adequate or justifiable. In our time, when the winds of trade spread not only goods but also ideas and cultural traditions around the globe, confinement to the Western tradition amounts to a parochial self-enclosure incompatible with university studies" (Dallmayr 2010:ix). Another leader of this emerging academic subfield argues as follows, again providing a rationale for this [reading's] claim of the value of considering Confucianism in the face of our environmental crisis.

> There is mounting evidence which suggests that the claims of universality made by modern western political philosophy are being questioned by other cultures, or at least by the significant representatives of these cultures. Indeed, in the West itself the claims of modern western philosophy are being questioned by those who challenge the assumptions underlying modernity. Such critical inquiry makes the comparative study of political philosophies both opportune and intellectually satisfying.
>
> (Parel 2003:11)

If the globalized world today has become Marshall McLuhan's "global village" with global telecommunications, culture, environment, and economic interdependence, then *all* political thinkers and cultural traditions should be considered as sources of political insight and direction within a comparative discussion and assessment as China and the world confront our many contemporary and interconnected problems, foremost of which is the crisis of the Earth's environment. Therefore, widening the net of intellectual resources beyond the standard Western political canon seems strongly advisable for the desirable and effective environmental political theory of the future. This is especially true when the theorists are non-Western and ancient, like Confucius, whose thought may be viewed as a powerful antidote to the root cause of the environmental crisis: modernity and its values, constituting the currently hegemonic worldview understood as a complex set of ideas and social institutions.

The founders of the new subfield of Comparative Political Theory make it clear that the driving force for their innovative approach is to criticize and offer superior alternatives to the dominant modern social order and its underlying philosophy as "a neutralizing antidote to the 'baleful' power and influence of uncontested modern western political philosophy" (Parel 2003:28).[3] The merit of including Confucius and the tradition of Confucian thought in such an enterprise seems clear. Although Confucius pronounced his views thousands of years ago during a period of distinctly non-Western Chinese culture, the ongoing tradition of Confucian philosophy may be viewed as both a powerful critique of and an alternative to modernity, especially regarding the latter's essential belief in the separation and superiority of humanity to nonhuman nature, or anthropocentrism.[4] In addition, Confucianism can provide a system of ideas that can become important to the crucial but difficult process of environmental movement in the past 40 years: creating a substitute and superior worldview to the "baleful" hegemonic modernity. Confucius's profound insight about the value of the past to our understanding of the present (see epigraph), while in conflict with modernity's "contempocentric" (Speth 2008:xvii) preoccupations, becomes, I submit, an instructive alternative teaching for today in China and beyond.

Another virtue of Comparative Political Theory and analyses across time and space comparing Western and non-Western perspectives is how similarities and differences between philosophies expose presuppositions that are uncritically accepted or taken-for-granted in the modern Western view of humanity, politics, and society, particularly concerning the important relationship between nature and humanity. This comparative process, illustrated below, can improve understanding of one's own philosophy as well as the philosophy of the other tradition as a result of the comparative analytical project.

Yet, even if we accept the reasoning of Comparative Political Theory, why select Confucius and the millennia-long Confucian philosophical tradition built upon his thought? As I have argued elsewhere (Kassiola 2010:195–218), there are special qualities and beliefs in Confucian thought that make it particularly relevant and valuable—perhaps uniquely so—at the present time of dangerous environmental threats to all inhabitants of our planet. It is the aim of this [reading] to defend this wide-ranging claim and to demonstrate the value of non-Western comparative environmental political theory, particularly Confucianism, and to stimulate others to conduct further similar inquiry.

Some Preliminary Points about Confucianism

Let us envision an alternative social order and social values to the hegemonic and unsustainable modern society that will, instead, respect the environmental limits of our finite planet. Such a postmodern sustainable society must reflect, in my view, an appreciation of the importance of morality; the central characteristic of the proposed new social order should be one whereby human beings alone are not viewed as the ultimate value as they are in anthropocentric modernity. In contrast, the Confucian social order, in its later neo-Confucian form, addresses not only the human condition but the realm of all other components of nonhuman nature, and importantly, the universe as a whole. Therefore, I advocate a Confucian Green Theory for the twenty-first century based upon the Neo-Confucian "continuity of being" (Tu 1985:35–50) theory; an "anthropocosmic" or alternatively termed, "cosmoanthropic" triad or trinity among Heaven, humanity, and the Earth (Tu 1989; Tu 1993, 1998 and Ro 1998:171).

The second term, "cosmoanthropic," seems to me to be an improvement on Tu's suggested "anthropocosmic" word as both terms attempt to show how the Confucian theory overcomes the anthropocentrism of Western modernity. This is so, I believe, because the term suggested by Ro puts the reference to the cosmos first and humanity as part of the larger universe, while the term suggested by Tu Wei-ming, "anthropocosmic," places humanity first and at the center of the universe with the highest value. In opposition to Tu, Young-chan Ro calls for a "cosmological anthropology rather than an anthropological cosmology; human beings must be understood in light of the universe rather than the human rationality or logos being imposed on the universe" (Ro 1998:186).

Confucianism is in stark contrast to modernity with regard to our current veneration of the "new and improved" and its corresponding downgrading of the "old," as expressed by Confucius's counterpoint in *Analects* 2.11 (see epigraph). The vital link between the old and the new, past and present, with lessons to be learned from the past, is a foundational belief in Confucian thought. Confucius himself looked back thousands of years prior to his own time of the sixth and fifth centuries BCE to the legendary Sage Kings of Chinese history and their ideal rule in the third millennium BCE (Yao, Shun, and Yu) as well as the "Golden Age" of the Early or Western Chou Dynasty (1111–771 BCE) led by Confucius's and China's cultural heroes: King Wen, King Wu, and the Duke of Chou (Ebrey 1999; Slingerland 2003:248–255).

These figures were the creators and rulers of the longest-lasting and most successful Dynasty in Chinese history in the Early (or Western—in geographic terms) praiseworthy stage of the Chou Dynasty, the one that Confucius referred to because it embodied Confucius's social, political, and ethical ideals. We should structure the present social order, according to Confucius, based upon understanding of the past—both good and bad. The latter could include the corruption of rulers and the resulting social disorder leading to the demise of the Shang Dynasty (1751–1112 BCE) and the moral decay and full of internal discord of his own Eastern Chou Dynasty (771–221 BCE) broken down into two distinct periods, known as "The Spring and Autumn" period (722–481 BCE), which would eventually precipitate the violent and destructive "Warring States" period (480–222 BCE) that brought down Confucius's ideal Chou Dynasty in 222 BCE some 250 years after his death following hundreds of years of violence among the States despite Confucius's own valiant efforts to save it (Chan 1963:xv).

A different translation of the *Analects* 2.11 passage (see epigraph) shows the dependent relationship of the new upon the old, and, therefore, the ineradicable value of the old, according to Confucius: "The Master said: 'A man is worthy of a teacher who gets to know what is new by keeping fresh in his mind what he is already familiar with.'" (Lau 1979:64). Therefore, according to this translation, we come to know the new by retaining and utilizing humanity's past thoughts and actions, according to Confucius, who used the Western Chou Dynasty and its Sage leaders as prescriptive models for his own philosophy and recommendations to others on how to live.

Another important preliminary point about Confucian thought concerns his "bell clapper" role. This salient aspect of Confucianism for contemporary society refers to his sounding the alarm for societal transformation amidst a violent and morally decadent society in crisis. The society in upheaval in the sixth century BCE China that Confucius was born into is expressed in *Analects* 3.24:

> After emerging from the audience [with the Master] the border official remarked,
> "You disciples, why should you be concerned about your Master's loss of office?

The world has been without the Way [*Tao*] for a long time now, and Heaven [*T'ien*] intends to use your Master like a wooden clapper for a bell [to awaken people]."

(Slingerland 2003:27; Chan 1963:25)

Translator Slingerland adds about this passage the following important note: "… the border official's point is thus that Heaven has deliberately caused Confucius to lose his official position [in the State of Lu] so that he might wander throughout the realm spreading the teachings of the Way and waking up the fallen world" (Slingerland 2003:27–28). *It is this crucial "bell clapper" role of sounding the alarm and "waking up the fallen world" of Confucius's time that inspire this [reading], which seeks to draw an analogy between our own "fallen world" and the alarming environmental crisis requiring transformational change and Confucius's tumultuous time and his transformational role.* (The important Confucian concept of *T'ien* or Heaven shall be discussed subsequently.).

The Eastern or Later Chou Dynasty, which Confucius was born into and formed the social context for his thought, was on its way to full-blown civil war by the time of Confucius's death with the onset of the Warring States period in Chinese history (480–222 BCE), which terminated the 800-year reign of the Chou Dynasty.

We can find similarities between Confucius's time of upheaval during the sixth and fifth centuries BCE in China, which was characterized by social corruption, disorder, a crisis of values, and violence caused by venal and decadent kings and their courts, and our modern Western consumer society (now global, including China) plagued by an environmental crisis brought on by erroneous and corrupt social values and institutions that resist and obstruct the necessary societal transformation.

Today, the world is beset by value crises and multiple wars within and between different States with the possibility of even more warfare over material resources (like oil or water) as they become scarcer, plus rampant corruption among political leaders throughout the world (including the United States). These phenomena occur in both developed and developing nations with social unrest, value disharmony, and conflict. Decadent and environmentally degrading and unsustainable luxurious consumption echoes Confucius's chaotic time in China during the Spring and Autumn, and Warring States periods of the Later Chou Dynasty. Furthermore, our current disorganized and violent global society faces lethal threats to its existence in the form of environmental challenges from climate change, desertification, water scarcity and pollution, air pollution, soil erosion, and so on (Speth 2008:17–45).

How our own declining global order will meet its own violent demise, whether from military conflict, like Confucius's own Chou Dynasty, or from an anthropogenic environmental catastrophe, remains to be seen. I propose that we follow Confucius's example of sounding the warning alarm to his own declining society for the need for transformation and moral improvement so many centuries ago. By examining the philosophical tradition that built Confucius's ideas, we can learn about ways to avert an environmental disaster and lead a more moral and satisfying life by creating a sustainable and just postmodern social order. As Comparative Political Theory maintains about different cultural traditions, and as I maintain about Confucius's different temporal period, comparison of disparate political philosophical traditions in space and time not only achieves the benefit of insights from the "other" tradition (in this case Chinese Confucianism) but also provides us with a deeper understanding of our own present tradition as well.

From this point of view, by engaging in comparative political analysis of both Confucianism and Modernism, we are fulfilling the ultimate Confucian goal of self-cultivation leading to self-transformation and self-realization—the highest Confucian value—or actualizing our potential humanity given to us by Heaven (Tu 1985). For Confucians, humans need to ethically cultivate themselves by seeking knowledge—learning—endlessly, ceasing only with death, as a means to realizing our Heavenly-endowed humanity *(jen).* The upshot is to try to understand the world and develop continuously in order to improve both ourselves and the world. The similarity of these Confucian ideas to the origin of Western political theory of Socrates and Plato with their philosophical watchword of: "The unexamined life is not worth living" is striking and substantiates the comparativists' approach to studying different cultural traditions and its payoff.

As I see it, for contemporary humanity as a whole, and China specifically, analogous to Confucius's own tumultuous time, the environmental crisis is like Confucius's "bell-tolling," signaling the need for societal transformation. The alarming "message" we are receiving from the environment constitutes a warning to modern societies and those societies aspiring to become modern and endlessly consumption-based, that "business as usual" or the uncritical modern values and institutions of contemporary consumer society cannot and should not (were it, *per impossible,* be able) to continue and must be transformed quickly. To that end, let us compare critically the fundamental assumptions of Modernism and Confucianism, and then consider later neo Confucian thought (beginning in the eleventh century CE during the Sung Dynasty [960–1279 CE]), especially its cosmology with its unique vision of relationships and interactions among Heaven, humanity, and the Earth (nonhuman nature).

Modernism and Confucianism: A Critical Comparison

What I propose to do in this section of the [reading] is to sketch (because of space limitations) a broad outline of the major differences between Modernism and Confucianism. I realize that whole books have been written on the nature of each worldview's content and values, and furthermore, that other interpretations are possible. Uppermost in my mind is the urgent need for an alternative social order that has, thus far, eluded environmentally focused critics of the modernist status quo that I think justifies the approach taken here.

James Gustave Speth, a veteran of decades in the American environmental movement has written: "... today's environmental policy and politics offer too weak a medicine, the proper perspective on environmental business as usual must be critical and must offer proposals for deeper change ... The issues require a fresh conceptualization and a new way of thinking, even a new vocabulary"

(Speth 2008:xiii–xiv). This "fresh conceptualization" view holds that a more positive argument than "the doom and gloom" approach of the past 40 years of the environmental movement that has not succeeded in convincing citizens and policymakers in contemporary consumer societies to give up their (impossible) idea of a ceaselessly growing materially affluent way of life (whether realized or not) that is so damaging to other realms of life: the environment, morality, politics, the family, and so on.

The practical focus of Confucius and his followers sought realizable solutions for how to live within the actual social reality of a particular time. His principle of timeliness (*shih*) emphasized how changing social conditions drive the appropriateness of specific human actions (see Confucius's *Analects* 8.13; Slingerland 2003:82). This teaching of Confucius can be especially useful to us despite the passage of so much time since Confucius's day. The reasons for this powerful parallel with a non-Western cultural tradition in ancient times, I believe, lies in the remarkable equivalences regarding the troubled nature of our respective societies.

In modern society, we suffer from moral decay and political violence. In addition to these fatal threats that eventually brought down Confucius's Chou Dynasty, we have added, ominously, a dangerous global environmental crisis. In *Analects* 14.1 Confucius considers whether refraining from "... competitiveness, boastfulness, envy, and greed" can be considered goodness (Confucius' *Analects* 14.1; Slingerland 2003:153). Despite the many centuries since Confucius's life in China, who would deny the applicability of these very same vices today, especially as they express themselves—with social support and even instigation—in our competitive materialistic consumer society?

The current time does indeed appear "ripe" for societal transformation, and China can be a world model and leader by using its Confucian heritage in constructing the needed alternative social order. In fact, it might be humanity's last great opportunity for such a transformation before some enormous disaster, like the extreme consequences of climate change, befalls the planet.

With that goal in mind, I would like to present a sample comparison between the profound philosophical building blocks of Modernism and Confucianism by the means of a chart. Of course, each of these values and doctrines can be elaborated upon at length. Nonetheless, my hope is that the summary chart of the doctrinal comparisons between Modernism and Confucianism will suffice as a starting point for the readers of this [reading] and constitute an agenda for future thinking and research (Table 5.1).

I hope this analytical skeleton will give readers a general idea of the breadth and depth of the many points of opposition between Modernism and Confucianism. Each of these factors is an important component of a society's paradigm or view of the world, and together show the profundity and comprehensiveness of the differences between the modern and the Confucian traditions. Furthermore, by this fecund contrast with Confucianism, if the modern social order is unsustainable because of environmental limits and its normative deficiencies, then the Confucian model stands ready to inspire and shape the necessary reconstruction of modern social life through the rediscovery and reinterpretation of the Confucian Way: life based upon different political, moral, spiritual, and social truths.

Table 5.1 A Critical Comparison of Modernism and Confucianism

Modernism's Fundamental Beliefs	Confucianism's Fundamental Beliefs
A. Anthropocentrism Humanity's domination of nature; separation/alienation of humanity from nature with humanity superior; loss of sacred view of the Earth and nonhuman nature; humanity is the center of the universe; nonhuman nature is the means for human ends.	1. Cosmoanthropism [Anthropocosmism] A cosmic trinity with Heaven, humanity, and the Earth interrelated and unified; sacredness of the Earth reinforced through reaction by Heaven; the unity of heaven and humanity; and humanity and the Earth.
B. Individualism The isolated individual human being is the most important unit of analysis, and a real entity; denial of society as an independent super-individual (see Margaret Thatcher's denial of society); individuals not related to each other or nonhuman nature except self-interestedly.	2. Social definition of humanity Humans are essentially social-relational emphasizing key relationships: parental, spousal, sibling, friend, and ruler relationships. No conflict between self and society since the two are related and that the individual self is realized through social development
C. Materialism/Consumerism Human happiness is achieved through material acquisitions, endlessly and limitlessly; importance of public image and external goods are emphasized; seeking wealth is top goal.	3. Non-materialism Interior moral development is most important; materially rich life and wealth-seeking are subordinated to nonmaterial pursuit of self-cultivation, self-transformation, and self-realization.
D. Dualistic view of the world Oppositions between competing pairs emphasized; for example, self vs. society, matter vs. spirit, culture vs. nature, etc.	4. Continuity of being No such modern dualisms but part of unified world.
E. Economism Economics and economic values are most important; economic values overrule nonmaterial and other internal values; supercedes other fields like politics and religion.	5. Materially simple but non-materially rich life Nonmaterial values and life prioritized, such as: loyalty, courage, benevolence, etc.
F. Value skepticism/Value relativism/Value subjectivism Skeptical of all normative discourse: politics, morality, aesthetics and theology; denies normative discourse rationality; values can only be grounded in different cultures, individuals, or paradigms.	6. Value objectivism/Value realism Supports existence of the Good, which can be known by humanity; considers normative discourse rational.

G. Political reductionism/The nature of politics	7. Moralism
Separates politics from ethics; reduces politics to self-focused materialist ends.	Robust relationship between morality and politics with morality most important in society; cosmic politics seeks to achieve realization of Heavenly endowed humanity
H. Instrumental rationalism	8. Intrinsic values
Human reason emphasizes means to given ends with latter not amenable to rational discourse.	Choice of ends that are intrinsically valuable is the goal of self-cultivation and self-transformation through learning.
I. Liberalism	9. Substantive goals of the state
"Thin state," relinquishes seeking of the good; focus on procedures and procedural justice and individual rights against the state and fellow citizens.	Includes goodness; "thick state" seeking to achieve substantive values for its citizens.

Data Source: Drawn from Kassiola (2010:210–212); Kassiola (1990); and Kassiola (2003:231–234).

In this context of the alternative possibilities of Confucianism I would like to introduce perhaps the most important aspect of Confucianism's contributions to environmentalism: the cosmoanthropism of Confucianism in which Heaven plays a central role in forming the cosmoanthropic unity between humankind and the Earth. I believe that by understanding the importance of the neo-Confucian cosmology, in sharp contrast to Western modern anthropocentrism, we can make sounder judgments regarding the health of the environment and humanity based on our connection to nonhuman nature instead of our disconnection and alienation from it.

Neo-Confucian Cosmology as a Contribution to Creating a Sustainable and Desirable Postmodern Social Order by Eclipsing Modern Anthropocentrism

The first point that needs to be made regarding the purported contribution of neo-Confucian cosmology to a sustainable and desirable postmodern social order concerns the nature of modern anthropocentrism and its essential position within the modern paradigm of the world. Largely stemming from just a few chapters in the Judeo-Christian Scripture (Book of *Genesis,* Chapters 1–2) (Leiss 1974; White 2001), our modern anthropocentric view holds that humankind is divinely separated from nonhuman nature *and* is superior to it by divine commandment. According to this foundational view of Western Civilization, humans are empowered to control nonhuman nature for our own uses and interests.

If modernity is the main cause of the environmental crisis, as I believe it is, and anthropocentrism is at the core of modernity, then an alternative vision for this modern paradigmatic position will be necessary if we are to achieve a transformation of modernity and avoid an environmental catastrophe. Here is where we find the quintessential contribution to environmentalism by Confucianism in its neo-Confucian form.

It is important to recognize that neo-Confucianist cosmology is central to the overall worldview of the neo-Confucians, given that cosmology was not a major focus of Confucius in *Analects,* in which the Master was mostly concerned about ethics and religion. In contrast to our Earth-bound, modern view, the major significance of the neo-Confucian cosmoanthropic view of environmentalism is that one must define the ecological issues on Earth from a "cosmocentric" perspective of the universe. As one neo-Confucian scholar importantly puts it: "The earth has to be understood in relation to the universe. Ecology, in this sense, has to be situated within the proper context of cosmology: we cannot develop a proper ecology without a relevant cosmology" (Ro 1998:171).

Professor Tu, in an often-reprinted essay, "The Continuity of Being: Chinese Visions of Nature" (1985:35–50), subordinates the point that the difference between the Western and Chinese cosmologies is based upon the lack of creation myth like the one in the Book of *Genesis.* Importantly for this discussion he concludes: "The real issue is not the presence or absence of creation myths, but the underlying assumption of the cosmos: whether it is continuous or discontinuous with its creator … It is not a creation myth as such but the Judeo-Christian version of it that is absent in the Chinese mythology" (Tu 1985:35–36).

Therefore, it is the neo-Confucian belief in the continuity (or connection) with nonhuman nature along with the creator, Heaven (*T'ien*), that distinguishes it from the Judeo-Christian conception of the creation of the world by a discontinuous, transcendental God, a divine being who in the *Genesis* account creates the world *ex nihilo,* from nothing. It is within this fundamental difference regarding the nature of the universe that the sharp contrast between Western and Chinese cosmologies emerges. We are presented with a universe created by an external disconnected (divine) source (Judeo-Christian) versus one in which the universe exists in an ongoing continuous and endless process of creation, producing a unified cosmological theory (Confucian). As Tu puts it: "there is no temporal beginning to specify, no closure is ever contemplated" (Tu 1985:39).

In this Chinese cosmological view, the central idea of the cosmoanthropic trinity among Heaven, humanity, and the Earth, as mentioned in *The Doctrine of the Mean,* is most important:

> Only those who absolutely sincere [*ch'eng*] can fully develop their nature. If they can fully develop the nature, they can then fully develop the nature of others. If they can fully develop the nature of others, they can fully develop the nature of things. If they can fully develop the nature of things, they can assist in the transforming and nourishing process of Heaven and Earth, they can thus form a trinity with Heaven and Earth.
>
> (Chan 1963:107–108)

Translator Wing-Tsit Chan comments on this significant passage as follows: "The important point is the ultimate trinity with Heaven and Earth. It is of course another way of saying the unity of man and Heaven or Nature, a doctrine which eventually assumed the greatest importance in Neo-Confucianism" (Chan 1963:108),

Heaven, which is not a place but "the source of normativity in the universe" (Slingerland 2003:239; Eno 1990:81–82), endows both humanity and the Earth with their respective natures, and, thus, creates a triad of relationships among these cosmological entities. Implied in this cosmological theory that encompasses both humankind and the Earth, is the unity of all three cosmological components of the universe. This, in turn, creates a set of bilateral relationships between Heaven and humanity, between humanity and the Earth, and finally between Heaven and Earth. Tu puts this crucial point clearly: "To say that the cosmos is a continuum and that all of its components are internally connected is also to say that it is an organismic unity, holistically integrated at each level of complexity" (Tu 1985:39).

The remarkable passage from neo-Confucian, Chang Tsai, about Heaven being humankind's father and the Earth its mother reflects the neo-Confucian cosmological trinity and makes all humanity the "children of the universe" and connected to all "things" in it as "companions."

> Heaven is my father and Earth is my mother, and even such a small creature as
> I finds an intimate place in their midst. Therefore that which fills the universe
> I regard as my body and that which directs the universe I consider as my nature.
> All people are my brothers and sisters, and all things are my companions.
>
> (Chang Tsai 1963:497)

The sixteenth-century Confucian, Wang Yang-ming, expresses this crucial point in a famous adage: "I really form one body with Heaven, Earth and the myriad of things" taken from the following important passage for our purpose here:

> Master Wang said: "The great man regards Heaven and Earth and the myriad of
> things as one body. He regards the world, as one family and the country as one
> person. As to those who make a cleavage between objects and distinguish between
> the self and others, they are small men. That the great man can regard Heaven,
> Earth and the myriad of things as one body is not because he deliberately wants
> to do so, but because it is natural to the humane nature of his mind that he do
> so ... Everything from ruler, minister, husband, wife, and friends to mountains,
> rivers, spiritual beings, birds, animals, and plants should be truly loved in order to
> realize my humanity that forms one body with them, and then my clear character
> will be completely manifested, and I really form one body with Heaven, Earth,
> and the myriad of things."
>
> (Wang Yang-ming 1963:659, 661)

The Chinese civilization is deeply characterized by respect for one's ancestors and the duty of filial piety *(xiao)* as Confucius emphasized throughout the *Analects* (according to Slingerland 2003:238, see *Analects*: 1.2, 2.5, 2.7–2.8, and 19.18). Slingerland (2003:238) describes this Confucian value as follows: "The virtue of being a dutiful and respectful son or daughter, considered by Confucius to be the key to other virtues developed in later life." Therefore, a filial relationship between Heaven and Earth and all the Earthly inhabitants is of utmost importance. Consider the environmental consequences wherein humankind is duty-bound to honor, respect, and take care of its cosmic mother, the Earth. The contrast is stark here between this neo-Confucian filial view toward the Earth and the West's hierarchical anthropocentric view of domination and exploitation of the Earth as humans see fit.

The neo-Confucian cosmology engenders respect, even reverence, for the Earth as a creation of Heaven (and, of course, Heaven, as well), plus for all the "myriad things" on Earth as our "companions" that including fellow humans, birds, animals, plants, and (puzzlingly to the Westerner) even "tiles and stones." Wang Yang-ming writes that identifying with humans, birds, animals, and plants shows one body is formed understandably among living creatures. He adds, which to the Western mind would seem cryptic, "Yet even when he [humanity] sees tiles and stones shattered and crushed he cannot help a feeling a regret. This shows that his humanity forms one body with tiles and stones" (Wang Yang-ming 1963:660). This Confucian cosmoanthropic unity of the "continuity of being" to include such things as "tiles and stones" is perhaps beyond the Western modern's ken, as it is drawn from an incommensurable cosmology that unites the range of entities from stones to Heaven, including humankind and all other living creatures and myriad things.

The factor that controls all these different members of the grand cosmic unity from Heaven to Earth to humanity to plants, animals, stones, and tiles, "the myriad things," is the rich Chinese concept of *ch'i* (see Chan 1963:495–517, 784, where Chan translates this important Chinese ontological term as "material force"). Chan goes on to explain this concept at the start of the neo-Confucian philosophy in the eleventh century CE: *"ch'i* denotes the psychophysiological power associated with look and breath. As such it is translated as 'vital force' or 'vital power ...'" (Chan 1963:495–517, 784). Tu comments on this comments as follows: "The continuous presence of *ch'i* in all modalities of being makes everything flow together as the unfolding of a single process ... the motif of wholeness is directly derived from the idea of continuity as all-encompassing" (Tu 1985:38). Space limitations do not permit a discussion of the Confucian philosophy of *ch'i* and its two well-known components of *yin* and *yang*. However, I do want to, at least, summarize the implications of this cosmoanthropic theory of Confucianism.

Summary of the Implications of Confucius's Cosmoanthropic Theory

1. Nonhuman nature (or the Earth) is *not* humanity's subordinate or means to be exploited for humanity's goals or values. There is no domination of nature in (neo-)Confocian cosmology or morality. And, furthermore, because under Confucian cosmoanthropism, both humankind and the Earth are equally endowed by Heaven, both entities are equivalent components of the cosmic trinity with Heaven.

2. Since the Earth (or nonhuman) nature is Heavenly endowed, humankind must treat nature with respect and care since all Earthy entities are united "companions" under Heaven.

3. Humans are neither the center of nor the lords of the universe but equal partners with the other members of the Confucian cosmological trinity: Heaven and Earth. It seems odd for us to equate Heaven with humanity but that is one of the important teachings of the Confucian cosmology. This follows from the belief that Heaven's endowment to humanity is only in potential and it remains humans' responsibility to cultivate and transform ourselves to fully realize Heaven's endowment. Confucians emphasize this as "learning to be human." In this self-fulfillment process, Heaven and humankind are co-creators of the universe—and need each other: Heaven needs humanity to realize its potential ("The Master said, 'Human beings can broaden the Way—it is not the Way that broadens human beings.'" *Analects* 15.29; Slingerland 2003:185), and humanity needs Heaven for the initial potential to be actualized through its self-cultivation and self-transformational learning process, which is endless. Humanity is a full and equal participant in the cosmoanthropic process envisioned by Confucianism. Translator Slingerland comments on this point: "As Cai Mo [Fourth century CE commentator on the *Analects*] explains, 'The Way is silent and without action, and requires human beings in order to be put into practice;' and, 'The Way thus is transcendent,' in the sense that it continues to exist even when it is not being actively manifested in the world, but it requires human beings to be fully realized" (2003:185–186).

4. The Earth is sacred; it is endowed by the same Heaven as humanity is endowed by. Thus, we must treat it as such, with respect and care that is deserving of Heaven.

In sum, while Confucians emphasize unity between Heaven and humanity, Confucian Greens, interpreting Confucianism for an environmentally based transformation of modernity, can stress the unity between humankind and the Earth as an effective antidote to the alienating separation from the Earth of humanity by Modernism's anthropocentric worldview. *In this cosmoanthropic trinity of Confucianism, I believe contemporary humanity can find a compelling alternative conceptual framework for constructing an environmentally sustainable and morally just new world that is not based upon the misguided anthropocentrism of modernity.*

I do not pretend that this necessarily brief presentation of the Confucian and neo-Confucian cosmological theory with its central vision of a cosmoanthropic trinity among Heaven, humanity, and the Earth is anything close to the richness of details required for a full discussion (for example, it omits how the philosophies of *ch'i* and *yin/yang* provide an ontological theory of the matter or material force that all "things" in the world share), but I hope it is sufficient to demonstrate a clear contrast to the hegemonic modern anthropocentrism of the West. In this manner, I suggest how Confucianism can provide conceptual resources for understanding today's environmental crisis and help us create another path. With this accomplishment, we can truly learn from Confucius and Confucianism, and, perhaps, thereby, save the planet, ourselves, and all the "myriad things" on Earth that are our "companions."

Notes

1. Conventional notation for the *Analects* is by book and chapter such that "2.11" means: Book 2, Chapter 11. Hereafter all references to the *Analects* will follow this standard notational convention with the specific translation noted as well.

2. For recent works within this new scholarly emphasis within political theory that seek to transcend and expand previous European and American domination of the field, see Parel and Keith 2003; Dallmayr 2010; and, Freeden and Vincent 2013.

3. The word in single quotes comes from the *Oxford Dictionary's* description of the Upas tree [...]: "a fabulous Javanese tree so poisonous as to destroy life for many miles around." Metaphorically, it stands for an entity that has a "baleful power or influence;" see p. 27 of Parel 2003 for this description of the Upas tree.

4. On anthropocentrism, the central doctrine of modernity, see any text on environmental ethics, for example, Baxter 2012: 355–358.

References

Baxter, William F. 2012. "People or Penguins: The Case for Optimal Pollution," In Barbara Mackinnon (ed.) *Ethics: Theory and Contemporary Issues, Seventh Edition with Readings.* Boston: Wadsworth Publishers, pp. 355–358.

Chan, Wing-Tsit. (trans. and compiled). 1963. *A Source Book in Chinese Philosophy.* Princeton: Princeton University Press.

Chang, Tsai. 1963. "The Western Inscription." In Chan, Wing-Tsit, (trans. and compiled). *A Source Book in Chinese Philosophy.* Princeton: Princeton University Press, pp. 497–517.

Dallmayr, Fred, (ed.) 2010. *Comparative Political Theory: An Introduction.* New York: Palgrave Macmillan.

Ebrey, Particia Buckley. 1999. *The Cambridge Illustrated History of China.* Cambridge: Cambridge University Press.

Eno, Robert. 1990. *The Confucian Creation of Heaven: Philosophy and the Defense of Ritual Mastery.* Albany: State University of New York Press.

Freeden, Michael and Andrew Vincent (eds.) 2013. *Comparative Political Thought: Theorizing Practices.* London: Routledge.

Kassiola, Joel J. 1990. *The Death of Industrial Civilization: The Limits to Economic Growth and the Repoliticization of Advanced Industrial Society.* Albany: State University of New York Press.

Kassiola, Joel J. (ed.) 2003. *Explorations in Environmental Political Theory: Thinking About What We Value.* Armonk: M. E. Sharpe.

Kassiola, Joel Jay. 2010. "Confucianizing Modernity and 'Modernizing Confucianism': Environmentalism and the Need for a Confucian Positive Argument for Social Change." In Joel Jay Kassiola and Sujian Guo (eds.) *China's Environmental Crisis: Domestic and Global Political Impacts and Responses*. New York: Palgrave Macmillan, pp. 195–218.

Lau, D. C. 1979. trans. Confucius, *Analects*. New York: Penguin Books.

Leiss, William. 1974. *The Domination of Nature*. Boston: Beacon Press.

Parel, Anthony J. 2003. "The Comparative Study of Political Philosophy." In Anthony J. Parel, and Ronald C. Keith (eds.) *Comparative Political Philosophy: Studies Under the Upas Tree*. Lanham, MD: Lexington Books, pp. 11–28.

Parel, Anthony J. and Ronald C. Keith (eds.) 2003. *Comparative Political Philosophy: Studies Under the Upas Tree*. Lanham: Lexington Books.

Ro, Young-chan. 1998. "Ecological Implications of Yi Yulgok's Cosmology." In Tucker, Mary Evelyn and John Berthong (eds.) *Confucianism and Ecology: The Interrelation of Heaven, Earth and Humanity*. Cambridge: Harvard Center for the Study of World Religions, pp. 169–186.

Slingerland, Edward, (trans.) 2003. Confucius, *Analects with Selections from Traditional Commentaries*. Indianapolis: Hackett Publishing Company.

Speth, James Gustave. 2008. *The Bridge at the Edge of the World: Capitalism, the Environment, and Crossing from Crisis to Sustainability*. New Haven: Yale University Press.

Tu, Wei-ming. 1985. "The Continuity of Being: Chinese Visions of Nature." In Wei-ming Tu (ed.) *Confucian Thought: Selfhood as Creative Transformation*. Albany: State University of New York Press, pp. 35–50.

Tu, Wei-ming. 1985. *Confucian Thought: Selfhood as Creative Transformation*. Albany: State University of New York Press.

Tu, Wei-ming. 1989. *Centrality and Commonality: An Essay on Confucian Religiousness*. New York: State University of New York Press.

Tu, Wei-ming. 1998. *Humanity and Self-Cultivation: Essays in Confucian Thought*. Boston: Cheng and Tsui Company.

Tu, Wei-Ming. 1993. Way, *Learning, and Politics: Essays on the Confucian Intellectual*. Albany: State University of New York Press.

Wang, Yang-Ming. 1963. "Inquiry on the Great Learning." In Chan, Wing-Tsit (trans. and compiled). *A Source Book in Chinese Philosophy*. Princeton: Princeton University Press, pp. 659–691.

White, Lynn. 2001. "The Historical Roots of Our Ecological Crisis." In Pojman, Louis P. (ed.) *Environmental Ethics: Readings in Theory and Application*. Belmont: Wadsworth Publishers, pp. 13–18.

CHAPTER 6

The Expansion of Our Anthropocentric Environmental Ethical Boundaries with Breakthrough Nonanthropocentric Worldviews: Aldo Leopold's Ecocentrism, Peter Singer's Zoocentrism, Paul Taylor's Biocentrism, and Their Critics

6A1. The Land Ethic

By Aldo Leopold

When god-like Odysseus returned from the wars in Troy, he hanged all on one rope a dozen slave-girls of his household whom he suspected of misbehavior during his absence.

This hanging involved no question of propriety. The girls were property. The disposal of property was then, as now, a matter of expediency, not of right and wrong.

Concepts of right and wrong were not lacking from Odysseus' Greece: witness the fidelity of his wife through the long years before at last his black-prowed galleys clove the wine-dark seas for home. The ethical structure of that day covered wives, but had not yet been extended to human chattels. During the three thousand years which have since elapsed, ethical criteria have been extended to many fields of conduct, with corresponding shrinkages in those judged by expediency only.

The Ethical Sequence

This extension of ethics, so far studied only by philosophers, is actually a process in ecological evolution. Its sequences may be described in ecological as well as in philosophical terms. An ethic, ecologically, is a limitation on freedom of action in the struggle for existence. An ethic, philosophically, is a differentiation of social from anti-social conduct. These are two definitions of one thing. The thing has its origin in the tendency of interdependent individuals or groups to evolve modes of co-operation. The ecologist calls these symbioses. Politics and economics are advanced symbioses in which the original free-for-all competition has been replaced, in part, by co-operative mechanisms with an ethical content.

The complexity of co-operative mechanisms has increased with population density, and with the efficiency of tools. It was simpler, for example, to define the anti-social uses of sticks and stones in the days of the mastodons than of bullets and billboards in the age of motors.

The first ethics dealt with the relation between individuals; the Mosaic Decalogue is an example. Later accretions dealt with the relation between the individual and society. The Golden Rule tries to integrate the individual to society; democracy to integrate social organization to the individual.

There is as yet no ethic dealing with man's relation to land and to the animals and plants which grow upon it. Land, like Odysseus' slave-girls, is still property. The land-relation is still strictly economic, entailing privileges but not obligations.

The extension of ethics to this third element in human environment is, if I read the evidence correctly, an evolutionary possibility and an ecological necessity. It is the third step in a sequence. The first two have already been taken. Individual thinkers since the days of Ezekiel and Isaiah have asserted that the despoliation of land is not only inexpedient but wrong. Society, however, has not yet affirmed their belief. I regard the present conservation movement as the embryo of such an affirmation.

An ethic may be regarded as a mode of guidance for meeting ecological situations so new or intricate, or involving such deferred reactions, that the path of social expediency is not discernible to the average individual. Animal instincts are modes of guidance for the individual in meeting such situations. Ethics are possibly a kind of community instinct in-the-making.

The Community Concept

All ethics so far evolved rest upon a single premise: that the individual is a member of a community of interdependent parts. His instincts prompt him to compete for his place in that community, but his ethics prompt him also to co-operate (perhaps in order that there may be a place to compete for).

The land ethic simply enlarges the boundaries of the community to include soils, waters, plants, and animals, or collectively: the land.

This sounds simple: do we not already sing our love for and obligation to the land of the free and the home of the brave? Yes, but just what and whom do we love? Certainly not the soil, which we are sending helter-skelter downriver. Certainly not the waters, which we assume have no function except to turn turbines, float barges, and carry off sewage. Certainly not the plants, of which we exterminate whole communities without batting an eye. Certainly not the animals, of which we have already extirpated many of the largest and most beautiful species. A land ethic of course cannot prevent the alteration, management, and use of these 'resources,' but it does affirm their right to continued existence, and, at least in spots, their continued existence in a natural state.

In short, a land ethic changes the role of *Homo sapiens* from conqueror of the land-community to plain member and citizen of it. It implies respect for his fellow-members, and also respect for the community as such.

In human history, we have learned (I hope) that the conqueror role is eventually self-defeating. Why? Because it is implicit in such a role that the conqueror knows, *ex cathedra,* just what makes the community clock tick, and just what and who is valuable, and what and who is worthless, in community life. It always turns out that he knows neither, and this is why his conquests eventually defeat themselves.

In the biotic community, a parallel situation exists. Abraham knew exactly what the land was for: it was to drip milk and honey into Abraham's mouth. At the present moment, the assurance with which we regard this assumption is inverse to the degree of our education.

The ordinary citizen today assumes that science knows what makes the community clock tick; the scientist is equally sure that he does not. He knows that the biotic mechanism is so complex that its workings may never be fully understood.

That man is, in fact, only a member of a biotic team is shown by an ecological interpretation of history. Many historical events, hitherto explained solely in terms of human enterprise, were actually biotic interactions between people and land. The characteristics of the land determined the facts quite as potently as the characteristics of the men who lived on it.

Consider, for example, the settlement of the Mississippi valley. In the years following the Revolution, three groups were contending for its control: the native Indian, the French and English traders, and the American settlers. Historians wonder what would have happened if the English at Detroit had thrown a little more weight into the Indian side of those tipsy scales which decided the outcome of the colonial migration into the cane-lands of Kentucky. It is time now to ponder the fact that the cane-lands, when subjected to the particular mixture of forces represented by the cow, plow, fire, and axe of the pioneer, became bluegrass. What if the plant succession inherent in this dark and bloody ground had, under the impact of these forces, given us some worthless sedge, shrub, or weed? Would Boone and Kenton have held out? Would there have been any overflow into Ohio, Indiana, Illinois, and Missouri? Any Louisiana Purchase? Any transcontinental union of new states? Any Civil War?

Kentucky was one sentence in the drama of history. We are commonly told what the human actors in this drama tried to do, but we are seldom told that their success, or the lack of it, hung in large degree on the reaction of particular soils to the impact of the particular forces exerted by their occupancy. In the case of Kentucky, we do not even know where the bluegrass came from—whether it is a native species, or a stowaway from Europe.

Contrast the cane-lands with what hindsight tells us about the Southwest, where the pioneers were equally brave, resourceful, and persevering. The impact of occupancy here brought no bluegrass, or other plant fitted to withstand the bumps and buffetings of hard use. This region, when grazed by livestock, reverted through a series of more and more worthless grasses, shrubs, and weeds to a condition of unstable equilibrium. Each recession of plant types bred erosion; each increment to erosion bred a further recession of plants. The result today is a progressive and mutual deterioration, not only of plants and soils, but of the animal community subsisting thereon. The early settlers did not expect this: on the ciénegas of New Mexico some even cut ditches to hasten it. So subtle has been its progress that few residents of the region are aware of it. It is quite invisible to the tourist who finds this wrecked landscape colorful and charming (as indeed it is, but it bears scant resemblance to what it was in 1848).

This same landscape was 'developed' once before, but with quite different results. The Pueblo Indians settled the Southwest in pre-Columbian times, but they happened *not* to be equipped with range livestock. Their civilization expired, but not because their land expired.

In India, regions devoid of any sod-forming grass have been settled, apparently without wrecking the land, by the simple expedient of carrying the grass to the cow, rather than vice versa. (Was this the result of some deep wisdom, or was it just good luck? I do not know.)

In short, the plant succession steered the course of history; the pioneer simply demonstrated, for good or ill, what successions inhered in the land. Is history taught in this spirit? It will be, once the concept of land as a community really penetrates our intellectual life.

The Ecological Conscience

Conservation is a state of harmony between men and land. Despite nearly a century of propaganda, conservation still proceeds at a snail's pace; progress still consists largely of letterhead pieties and convention oratory. On the back forty we still slip two steps backward for each forward stride.

The usual answer to this dilemma is 'more conservation education.' No one will debate this, but is it certain that only the *volume* of education needs stepping up? Is something lacking in the *content* as well?

It is difficult to give a fair summary of its content in brief form, but, as I understand it, the content is substantially this: obey the law, vote right, join some organizations, and practice what conservation is profitable on your own land; the government will do the rest.

Is not this formula too easy to accomplish anything worth-while? It defines no right or wrong, assigns no obligation, calls for no sacrifice, implies no change in the current philosophy of values. In respect of land-use, it urges only enlightened self-interest. Just how far will such education take us? An example will perhaps yield a partial answer.

By 1930 it had become clear to all except the ecologically blind that southwestern Wisconsin's topsoil was slipping seaward. In 1933 the farmers were told that if they would adopt certain remedial practices for five years, the public would donate CCC labor to install them, plus the necessary machinery and materials. The offer was widely accepted, but the practices were widely forgotten when the five-year contract period was up. The farmers continued only those practices that yielded an immediate and visible economic gain for themselves.

This led to the idea that maybe farmers would learn more quickly if they themselves wrote the rules. Accordingly the Wisconsin Legislature in 1937 passed the Soil Conservation District Law. This said to farmers, in effect: *We, the public, will furnish you free technical service and loan you specialized machinery, if you will write your own rules for land-use. Each county may write its own rules, and these will have the force of law.* Nearly all the counties promptly organized to accept the proffered help, but after a decade of operation, *no county has yet written a single rule.* There has been visible progress in such practices as strip-cropping, pasture renovation, and soil liming, but none in fencing woodlots against grazing, and none in excluding plow and cow from steep slopes. The farmers, in short, have selected those remedial practices which were profitable anyhow, and ignored those which were profitable to the community, but not clearly profitable to themselves.

When one asks why no rules have been written, one is told that the community is not yet ready to support them; education must precede rules. But the education actually in progress makes no mention of obligations to land over and above those dictated by self-interest. The net result is that we have more education but less soil, fewer healthy woods, and as many floods as in 1937.

The puzzling aspect of such situations is that the existence of obligations over and above self-interest is taken for granted in such rural community enterprises as the betterment of roads, schools, churches, and baseball teams. Their existence is not taken for granted, nor as yet seriously discussed, in bettering the behavior of the water that falls on the land, or in the preserving of the beauty or diversity of the farm landscape. Land-use ethics are still governed wholly by economic self-interest, just as social ethics were a century ago.

To sum up: we asked the farmer to do what he conveniently could to save his soil, and he has done just that, and only that. The farmer who clears the woods off a 75 percent slope, turns his cows into the clearing, and dumps its rainfall, rocks, and soil into the community creek, is still (if otherwise decent) a respected member of society. If he puts lime on his fields and plants his crops on contour, he is still entitled to all the privileges and emoluments of his Soil Conservation District. The District is a beautiful piece of social machinery, but it is coughing along on two cylinders because we have been too timid, and too anxious for quick success, to tell the farmer the true magnitude of his obligations. Obligations have no meaning without conscience, and the problem we face is the extension of the social conscience from people to land.

No important change in ethics was ever accomplished without an internal change in our intellectual emphasis, loyalties, affections, and convictions. The proof that conservation has not yet touched these foundations of conduct lies in the fact that philosophy and religion have not yet heard of it. In our attempt to make conservation easy, we have made it trivial.

Substitutes for a Land Ethic

When the logic of history hungers for bread and we hand out a stone, we are at pains to explain how much the stone resembles bread. I now describe some of the stones which serve in lieu of a land ethic.

One basic weakness in a conservation system based wholly on economic motives is that most members of the land community have no economic value. Wildflowers and songbirds are examples. Of the 22,000 higher plants and animals native to Wisconsin, it is doubtful whether more than 5 percent can be sold, fed, eaten, or otherwise put to economic use. Yet these creatures are members of the biotic community, and if (as I believe) its stability depends on its integrity, they are entitled to continuance.

When one of these non-economic categories is threatened, and if we happen to love it, we invent subterfuges to give it economic importance. At the beginning of the century songbirds were supposed to be disappearing. Ornithologists jumped to the rescue with some distinctly shaky evidence to the effect that insects would eat us up if birds failed to control them. The evidence had to be economic in order to be valid.

It is painful to read these circumlocutions today. We have no land ethic yet, but we have at least drawn nearer the point of admitting that birds should continue as a matter of biotic right, regardless of the presence or absence of economic advantage to us.

A parallel situation exists in respect of predatory mammals, raptorial birds, and fish-eating birds. Time was when biologists somewhat overworked the evidence that these creatures preserve the health of game by killing weaklings, or that they control rodents for the farmer, or that they prey only on 'worthless' species. Here again, the evidence had to be economic in order to be valid. It is only in recent years that we hear the more honest argument that predators are members of the community, and that no special interest has the right to exterminate them for the sake of a benefit, real or fancied, to itself. Unfortunately this enlightened view is still in the talk stage. In the field the extermination of predators goes merrily on: witness the impending erasure of the timber wolf by fiat of Congress, the Conservation Bureaus, and many state legislatures.

Some species of trees have been 'read out of the party' by economics-minded foresters because they grow too slowly, or have too low a sale value to pay as timber crops: white cedar, tamarack, cypress, beech, and hemlock are examples. In Europe, where forestry is ecologically more advanced, the non-commercial tree species are recognized as members of the native forest community, to be preserved as such, within reason. Moreover some (like beech) have been found to have a valuable function in building up soil fertility. The interdependence of the forest and its constituent tree species, ground flora, and fauna is taken for granted.

Lack of economic value is sometimes a character not only of species or groups, but of entire biotic communities: marshes, bogs, dunes, and 'deserts' are examples. Our formula in such cases is to relegate their conservation to government as refuges, monuments, or parks. The difficulty is that these communities are usually interspersed with more valuable private lands; the government cannot possibly own or control such scattered parcels. The net effect is that we have relegated some of them to ultimate extinction over large areas. If the private owner were ecologically minded, he would be proud to be the custodian of a reasonable proportion of such areas, which add diversity and beauty to his farm and to his community.

In some instances, the assumed lack of profit in these 'waste' areas has proved to be wrong, but only after most of them had been done away with. The present scramble to reflood muskrat marshes is a case in point.

There is a clear tendency in American conservation to relegate to government all necessary jobs that private land-owners fail to perform. Government ownership, operation, subsidy, or regulation is now widely prevalent in forestry, range management, soil and watershed management, park and wilderness conservation, fisheries management, and migratory bird management, with more to come. Most of this growth in governmental conservation is proper and logical, some of it is inevitable. That I imply no disapproval of it is implicit in the fact that I have spent most of my life working for it. Nevertheless the question arises: What is the ultimate magnitude of the enterprise? Will the tax base carry its eventual ramifications? At what point will governmental conservation, like the mastodon, become handicapped by its own dimensions? The answer, if there is any, seems to be in a land ethic, or some other force which assigns more obligation to the private landowner.

Industrial landowners and users, especially lumbermen and stockmen, are inclined to wail long and loudly about the extension of government ownership and regulation to land, but (with notable exceptions) they show little disposition to develop the only visible alternative: the voluntary practice of conservation on their own lands.

When the private landowner is asked to perform some unprofitable act for the good of the community, he today assents only with outstretched palm. If the act costs him cash this is fair and proper, but when it costs only forethought, open-mindedness, or time, the issue is at least debatable. The overwhelming growth of land-use subsidies in recent years must be ascribed, in large part, to the government's own agencies for conservation education: the land bureaus, the agricultural colleges, and the extension services. As far as I can detect, no ethical obligation toward land is taught in these institutions.

To sum up: a system of conservation based solely on economic self-interest is hopelessly lopsided. It tends to ignore, and thus eventually to eliminate, many elements in the land community that lack commercial value, but that are (as far as we know) essential to its healthy functioning. It assumes, falsely, I think, that the economic parts of the biotic clock will function without the uneconomic parts. It tends to relegate to government many functions eventually too large, too complex, or too widely dispersed to be performed by government.

An ethical obligation on the part of the private owner is the only visible remedy for these situations.

The Land Pyramid

An ethic to supplement and guide the economic relation to land presupposes the existence of some mental image of land as a biotic mechanism. We can be ethical only in relation to something we can see, feel, understand, love, or otherwise have faith in.

The image commonly employed in conservation education is 'the balance of nature.' For reasons too lengthy to detail here, this figure of speech fails to describe accurately what little we know about the land mechanism. A much truer image is the one employed in ecology: the biotic pyramid. I shall first sketch the pyramid as a symbol of land, and later develop some of its implications in terms of land-use.

The Land Ethic

Plants absorb energy from the sun. This energy flows through a circuit called the biota, which may be represented by a pyramid consisting of layers. The bottom layer is the soil. A plant layer rests on the soil, an insect layer on the plants, a bird and rodent layer on the insects, and so on up through various animal groups to the apex layer, which consists of the larger carnivores.

The species of a layer are alike not in where they came from, or in what they look like, but rather in what they eat. Each successive layer depends on those below it for food and often for other services, and each in turn furnishes food and services to those above. Proceeding upward, each successive layer decreases in numerical abundance. Thus, for every carnivore there are hundreds of his prey, thousands of their prey, millions of insects, uncountable plants. The pyramidal form of the system reflects this numerical progression from apex to base, Man shares an intermediate layer with the bears, raccoons, and squirrels which eat both meat and vegetables.

The lines of dependency for food and other services are called food chains. Thus soil-oak-deer-Indian is a chain that has now been largely converted to soil-corn-cow-farmer. Each species, including ourselves, is a link in many chains. The deer eats a hundred plants other than oak, and the cow a hundred plants other than corn. Both, then, are links in a hundred chains. The pyramid is a tangle of chains so complex as to seem disorderly, yet the stability of the system proves it to be a highly organized structure. Its functioning depends on the co-operation and competition of its diverse parts.

In the beginning, the pyramid of life was low and squat; the food chains short and simple. Evolution has added layer after layer, link after link. Man is one of thousands of accretions to the height and complexity of the pyramid. Science has given us many doubts, but it has given us at least one certainty: the trend of evolution is to elaborate and diversify the biota.

Land, then, is not merely soil; it is a fountain of energy flowing through a circuit of soils, plants, and animals. Food chains are the living channels which conduct energy upward; death and decay return it to the soil. The circuit is not closed; some energy is dissipated in decay, some is added by absorption from the air, some is stored in soils, peats, and long-lived forests; but it is a sustained circuit, like a slowly augmented revolving fund of life. There is always a net loss by downhill wash, but this is normally small and offset by the decay of rocks. It is deposited in the ocean and, in the course of geological time, raised to form new lands and new pyramids.

The velocity and character of the upward flow of energy depend on the complex structure of the plant and animal community, much as the upward flow of sap in a tree depends on its complex cellular organization. Without this complexity, normal circulation would presumably not occur. Structure means the characteristic numbers, as well as the characteristic kinds and functions, of the component species. This interdependence between the complex structure of the land and its smooth functioning as an energy unit is one of its basic attributes.

When a change occurs in one part of the circuit, many other parts must adjust themselves to it. Change does not necessarily obstruct or divert the flow of energy; evolution is a long series of self-induced changes, the net result of which has been to elaborate the flow mechanism and to lengthen the circuit. Evolutionary changes, however, are usually slow and local. Man's invention of tools has enabled him to make changes of unprecedented violence, rapidity, and scope.

One change is in the composition of floras and faunas. The larger predators are lopped off the apex of the pyramid; food chains, for the first time in history, become shorter rather than longer. Domesticated species from other lands are substituted for wild ones, and wild ones are moved to new habitats. In this world-wide pooling of faunas and floras, some species get out of bounds as pests and diseases, others are extinguished. Such effects are seldom intended or foreseen; they represent unpredicted and often untraceable readjustments in the structure. Agricultural science is largely a race between the emergence of new pests and the emergence of new techniques for their control.

Another change touches the flow of energy through plants and animals and its return to the soil. Fertility is the ability of soil to receive, store, and release energy. Agriculture, by overdrafts on the soil, or by too radical a substitution of domestic for native species in the superstructure, may derange the channels of flow or deplete storage. Soils depleted of their storage, or of the organic matter which anchors it, wash away faster than they form. This is erosion.

Waters, like soil, are part of the energy circuit. Industry, by polluting waters or obstructing them with dams, may exclude the plants and animals necessary to keep energy in circulation.

Transportation brings about another basic change: the plants or animals grown in one region are now consumed and returned to the soil in another. Transportation taps the energy stored in rocks, and in the air, and uses it elsewhere; thus we fertilize the garden with nitrogen gleaned by the guano birds from the fishes of seas on the other side of the Equator. Thus the formerly localized and self-contained circuits are pooled on a world-wide scale.

The process of altering the pyramid for human occupation releases stored energy, and this often gives rise, during the pioneering period, to a deceptive exuberance of plant and animal life, both wild and tame. These releases of biotic capital tend to becloud or postpone the penalties of violence.

This thumbnail sketch of land as an energy circuit conveys three basic ideas:

1. That land is not merely soil.
2. That the native plants and animals kept the energy circuit open; others may or may not.
3. That man-made changes are of a different order than evolutionary changes, and have effects more comprehensive than is intended or foreseen.

These ideas, collectively, raise two basic issues: Can the land adjust itself to the new order? Can the desired alterations be accomplished with less violence?

Biotas seem to differ in their capacity to sustain violent conversion. Western Europe, for example, carries a far different pyramid than Caesar found there. Some large animals are lost; swampy forests have become meadows or plow-land; many new plants and animals are introduced, some of which escape as pests; the remaining natives are greatly changed in distribution and abundance. Yet the soil is still there and, with the help of imported nutrients, still fertile; the waters flow normally; the new structure seems to function and to persist. There is no visible stoppage or derangement of the circuit.

Western Europe, then, has a resistant biota. Its inner processes are tough, elastic, resistant to strain. No matter how violent the alterations, the pyramid, so far, has developed some new *modus vivendi* which preserves its habitability for man, and for most of the other natives.

Japan seems to present another instance of radical conversion without disorganization.

Most other civilized regions, and some as yet barely touched by civilization, display various stages of disorganization, varying from initial symptoms to advanced wastage. In Asia Minor and North Africa diagnosis is confused by climatic changes, which may have been either the cause or the effect of advanced wastage. In the United States the degree of disorganization varies locally; it is worst in the Southwest, the Ozarks, and parts of the South, and least in New England and the Northwest. Better land-uses may still arrest it in the less advanced regions. In parts of Mexico, South America, South Africa, and Australia a violent and accelerating wastage is in progress, but I cannot assess the prospects.

This almost world-wide display of disorganization in the land seems to be similar to disease in an animal, except that it never culminates in complete disorganization or death. The land recovers, but at some reduced level of complexity, and with a reduced carrying capacity for people, plants, and animals. Many biotas currently regarded as 'lands of opportunity' are in fact already subsisting on exploitative agriculture, i.e. they have already exceeded their sustained carrying capacity. Most of South America is overpopulated in this sense.

In arid regions we attempt to offset the process of wastage by reclamation, but it is only too evident that the prospective longevity of reclamation projects is often short. In our own West, the best of them may not last a century.

The combined evidence of history and ecology seems to support one general deduction: the less violent the man-made changes, the greater the probability of successful readjustment in the pyramid. Violence, in turn, varies with human population density; a dense population requires a more violent conversion. In this respect, North America has a better chance for permanence than Europe, if she can contrive to limit her density.

This deduction runs counter to our current philosophy, which assumes that because a small increase in density enriched human life, that an indefinite increase will enrich it indefinitely. Ecology knows of no density relationship that holds for indefinitely wide limits. All gains from density are subject to a law of diminishing returns.

Whatever may be the equation for men and land, it is improbable that we as yet know all its terms. Recent discoveries in mineral and vitamin nutrition reveal unsuspected dependencies in the up-circuit: incredibly minute quantities of certain substances determine the value of soils to plants, of plants to animals. What of the down-circuit? What of the vanishing species, the preservation of which we now regard as an esthetic luxury? They helped build the soil; in what unsuspected ways may they be essential to its maintenance? Professor Weaver proposes that we use prairie flowers to reflocculate the wasting soils of the dust bowl; who knows for what purpose cranes and condors, otters and grizzlies may some day be used?

Land Health and the A-B Cleavage

A land ethic, then, reflects the existence of an ecological conscience, and this in turn reflects a conviction of individual responsibility for the health of the land. Health is the capacity of the land for self-renewal. Conservation is our effort to understand and preserve this capacity.

Conservationists are notorious for their dissensions. Superficially these seem to add up to mere confusion, but a more careful scrutiny reveals a single plane of cleavage common to many specialized fields. In each field one group (A) regards the land as soil, and its function as commodity-production; another group (B) regards the land as a biota, and its function as something broader. How much broader is admittedly in a state of doubt and confusion.

In my own field, forestry, group A is quite content to grow trees like cabbages, with cellulose as the basic forest commodity. It feels no inhibition against violence; its ideology is agronomic. Group B, on the other hand, sees forestry as fundamentally different from agronomy because it employs natural species, and manages a natural environment rather than creating an artificial one. Group B prefers natural reproduction on principle. It worries on biotic as well as economic grounds about the loss of species like chestnut, and the threatened loss of the white pines. It worries about a whole series of secondary forest functions: wildlife, recreation, watersheds, wilderness areas. To my mind, Group B feels the stirrings of an ecological conscience.

In the wildlife field, a parallel cleavage exists. For Group A the basic commodities are sport and meat; the yardsticks of production are ciphers of take in pheasants and trout. Artificial propagation is acceptable as a permanent as well as a temporary recourse—if its unit costs permit. Group B, on the other hand, worries about a whole series of biotic side-issues. What is the cost in predators of producing a game crop? Should we have further recourse to exotics? How can management restore the shrinking species, like prairie grouse, already hopeless as shootable game? How can management restore the threatened rarities, like trumpeter swan and whooping crane? Can management principles be extended to wildflowers? Here again it is clear to me that we have the same A-B cleavage as in forestry.

In the larger field of agriculture I am less competent to speak, but there seem to be somewhat parallel cleavages. Scientific agriculture was actively developing before ecology was born, hence a slower penetration of ecological concepts might be expected. Moreover the farmer, by the very nature of his techniques, must modify the biota more radically than the forester or the wildlife manager. Nevertheless, there are many discontents in agriculture which seem to add up to a new vision of 'biotic farming.'

Perhaps the most important of these is the new evidence that poundage or tonnage is no measure of the food-value of farm crops; the products of fertile soil may be qualitatively as well as quantitatively superior. We can bolster poundage from depleted soils by pouring on imported fertility, but we are not necessarily bolstering food-value. The possible ultimate ramifications of this idea are so immense that I must leave their exposition to abler pens.

The discontent that labels itself 'organic farming,' while bearing some of the earmarks of a cult, is nevertheless biotic in its direction, particularly in its insistence on the importance of soil flora and fauna.

The ecological fundamentals of agriculture are just as poorly known to the public as in other fields of land-use. For example, few educated people realize that the marvelous advances in technique made during recent decades are improvements in the pump, rather than the well. Acre for acre, they have barely sufficed to offset the sinking level of fertility.

In all of these cleavages, we see repeated the same basic paradoxes: man the conqueror *versus* man the biotic citizen; science the sharpener of his sword *versus* science the searchlight on his universe; land the slave and servant *versus* land the collective organism. Robinson's injunction to Tristram may well be applied, at this juncture, to *Homo sapiens* as a species in geological time:

> Whether you will or not
> You are a King, Tristram, for you are one
> Of the time-tested few that leave the world,
> When they are gone, not the same place it was.
> Mark what you leave.

The Outlook

It is inconceivable to me that an ethical relation to land can exist without love, respect, and admiration for land, and a high regard for its value. By value, I of course mean something far broader than mere economic value; I mean value in the philosophical sense.

Perhaps the most serious obstacle impeding the evolution of a land ethic is the fact that our educational and economic system is headed away from, rather than toward, an intense consciousness of land. Your true modern is separated from the land by many middlemen, and by innumerable physical gadgets. He has no vital relation to it; to him it is the space between cities on which crops grow. Turn him loose for a day on the land, and if the spot does not happen to be a golf links or a 'scenic' area, he is bored stiff. If crops could be raised by hydroponics instead of farming, it would suit him very well. Synthetic substitutes for wood, leather, wool, and other natural land products suit him better than the originals. In short, land is something he has 'outgrown.'

Almost equally serious as an obstacle to a land ethic is the attitude of the farmer for whom the land is still an adversary, or a taskmaster that keeps him in slavery. Theoretically, the mechanization of farming ought to cut the farmer's chains, but whether it really does is debatable.

One of the requisites for an ecological comprehension of land is an understanding of ecology, and this is by no means co-extensive with 'education'; in fact, much higher education seems deliberately to avoid ecological concepts. An understanding of ecology does not necessarily originate in courses bearing ecological labels; it is quite as likely to be labeled geography, botany, agronomy, history, or economics. This is as it should be, but whatever the label, ecological training is scarce.

The case for a land ethic would appear hopeless but for the minority which is in obvious revolt against these 'modern' trends.

The 'key-log' which must be moved to release the evolutionary process for an ethic is simply this: quit thinking about decent land-use as solely an economic problem. Examine each question in terms of what is ethically and esthetically right, as well as what is economically expedient. A thing is right when it tends to preserve the integrity, stability, and beauty of the biotic community. It is wrong when it tends otherwise.

It of course goes without saying that economic feasibility limits the tether of what can or cannot be done for land. It always has and it always will. The fallacy the economic determinists have tied around our collective neck, and which we now need to cast off, is the belief that economics determines *all* land-use. This is simply not true. An innumerable host of actions and attitudes, comprising perhaps the bulk of all land relations, is determined by the land-users' tastes and predilections, rather than by his purse. The bulk of all land relations hinges on investments of time, forethought, skill, and faith rather than on investments of cash. As a land-user thinketh, so is he.

I have purposely presented the land ethic as a product of social evolution because nothing so important as an ethic is ever 'written.' Only the most superficial student of history supposes that

Moses 'wrote' the Decalogue; it evolved in the minds of a thinking community, and Moses wrote a tentative summary of it for a 'seminar.' I say tentative because evolution never stops.

The evolution of a land ethic is an intellectual as well as emotional process. Conservation is paved with good intentions which prove to be futile, or even dangerous, because they are devoid of critical understanding either of the land, or of economic land-use. I think it is a truism that as the ethical frontier advances from the individual to the community, its intellectual content increases.

The mechanism of operation is the same for any ethic: social approbation for right actions: social disapproval for wrong actions.

By and large, our present problem is one of attitudes and implements. We are remodeling the Alhambra with a steam-shovel, and we are proud of our yardage. We shall hardly relinquish the shovel, which after all has many good points, but we are in need of gentler and more objective criteria for its successful use.

6B1. Acts of Objectification and The Repudiation of Dominance

Leopold, Ecofeminism, and the Ecological Narrative

By Chaone Mallory

Introduction: Leopold and the Foundations of Environmental Ethics

As an environmental figure, the name of Aldo Leopold is well-known in such diverse fields as forestry, wildlife ecology, outdoor recreation studies, and environmental philosophy, and the influence of his ideas in the environmental movement is even more widespread. A prolific, and all agree, eloquent writer, his works have had a tremendous impact on the genesis and continued development of what is now called environmental ethics. As the author of "The Land Ethic," Leopold (1949) is widely recognized as one of the first contemporary environmental writers to actively and directly advocate a different understanding of the relationship between human beings and the natural world, an understanding not predicated on utility and "wise use"[1] but centered instead on a more humble awareness that the biota is an integral whole in which humanity participates as "plain member and citizen."

Leopold's essays, books, and other contributions to the fields of forestry and game management (now called wildlife ecology) have been instrumental in forging cross-disciplinary links between the science of ecology and the ethics and aesthetics of philosophy. As such, Leopold has been a deeply inspirational figure to generations of environmentalists. However those with environmental sensibilities are not united in their untempered enthusiasm for all that Leopold has said and done. One particularly controversial aspect of Leopold's writings has centered around his self-avowed love of hunting. Many have rightfully questioned the propriety and consistency of a position such as Leopold's, in which a fierce attitude of protectionism for wildlife and wildlife habitat is coupled with—indeed apparently *gotten* from—the enjoyment derived from the hunting experience. Nowhere else in Leopold's writings are intimate descriptions of the land detailed to such a high degree than in journal sections written while reflecting on awarenesses gained during hunting excursions. No other passages describe as clearly and articulately the close relationship between the different parts of the biota—trees, soils, scents, wind, fallen leaves, waters; and no place in the writings of Leopold does he more effectively convey that in order to have a proper ethic toward the land one must have an active and participatory relationship with it.

Chaone Mallory, "Acts of Objectification and the Repudiation of Dominance: Leopold, Ecofeminism, and the Ecological Narrative," *Ethics and the Environment*, vol. 6, no. 2, pp. 59-89. Copyright © 2001 by Indiana University Press. Reprinted with permission.

There are two kinds of hunting: ordinary hunting, and ruffed-grouse hunting. There are two places to hunt grouse: ordinary places, and Adams County. There are two times to hunt in Adams: ordinary times and when the tamaracks are smoky gold. ... The tamaracks change from green to yellow when the first frosts have brought woodcock, fox sparrows, and juncos out of the north. Troops of robins are stripping the last white berries from the dogwood thickets, leaving the empty stems as a pink haze against the hill. The creekside alders have shed their leaves, exposing here and there an eyeful of holly. Brambles are aglow, lighting your footsteps grouseward. (Leopold 1949, 54–55)

This passage is but one example of the depth and intensity of Leopold's prose, unrivaled in its descriptive ability, evoking a keen image of the features of the natural environment, and a true sense of the felt meaning, importance, and necessity of contact with the natural world. None dispute that Aldo Leopold's Land Ethic contains much ecological wisdom and insight and that his work as a whole has made an important contribution to environmental discourse and the dissemination of ecological ideas into popular consciousness. Leopold enabled future generations of environmental philosophers to expand upon his notion that "the land" encompasses much more than mere inert earth but includes "soils, waters, plants, and animals" and is not a commodity that we own but a "community to which we belong" (204, viii). And, perhaps most important, Leopold's work makes us aware that an ethical stance toward natural creatures and environments is necessary in order to change "the role of *Homo sapiens* from conqueror of the land-community to plain member and citizen of it" (204). Furthermore, Leopold was one of the first scientists to recognize and publicly affirm that environmental problems must be addressed as questions for ethics and philosophy as well as science and technology, and that a precondition for solving our environmental problems is a change in our attitudes and values. And finally, the impact of Leopold's thinking has been particularly potent among environmental professionals and scientists, who see him as "one of their own" and are able to readily relate to his supplications to treat the land as though it has value of an intrinsic sort.

Leopold, Hunting, and Environmental Philosophy

It is because Leopold enjoys such strong approval and even adulation from a wide range of environmental audiences that the legacy of Leopold may present a problem for those interested in the very project Leopold advances: the repudiation of an attitude of anthropocentric superiority and the cultivation of respect for the moral standing of natural entities.[2] In what follows I develop the thesis that it is important for those involved on a theoretical level in the project of environmental ethics to be aware that the ideas of Leopold have been heavily influenced by his life-long love of sport hunting. And I argue that in order for one to participate in hunting one must have accepted a principle of human domination over the nonhuman world, a principle antithetical to those strains of environmental ethics—most notably ecofeminism—which affirm that humans and members of the more-than-human world possess comparable moral worth.

J. Baird Callicott (1989) has argued in his piece, "Animal Liberation: A Triangular Affair" that there is no moral inconsistency evinced by the fact of Leopold's unregenerate hunting[3] because the Land Ethic is "holistic." But I contend that the ideas of Leopold nonetheless insidiously, although certainly unintentionally, convey an attitude that the natural world is a noble and ennobling object for human enjoyment and exploitation. What I am suggesting here is that through the many, *favorably* portrayed depictions of hunting a more subtle but equally as powerful message is being fashioned, one that is likely to be received by Leopold's readers on a much more visceral and thus less critical level. I develop this idea in more detail later. Also, I establish (with the support of authors who have examined the ethics of hunting) that the point of the "good sportsmanship," which Leopold advocates is not to convey respect for one's prey as is commonly argued by defenders of hunting, but rather serves to refine one's skills in a "gentlemanly" fashion. This marks hunting as largely an elite activity practiced mainly by those with privileged cultural and economic status, a status possessed by Leopold as well as the majority of hunters in North America. Ecofeminists have effectively pointed out the ways in which gender, class, racial, and environmental oppression are intertwined;[4] thus I believe that analyzing Leopold's teachings from this perspective exposes the ways in which hunting and justifications of hunting promote the discourses of dominance upon which ecological degradation depends. I also believe that, though it goes unrecognized by the many who have written on Leopold, he has in at least one instance linked nature to the feminine—it is significant, I think, that Leopold makes it a she-wolf who is shot in the famous essay, "Thinking Like a Mountain" (1949). This resonates with the claims of ecofeminist writers like Carolyn Merchant, Val Plumwood, and Susan Griffin, who say that women have been linked to nature and nature has been personified as female because in a patriarchal and phallogocentric world both women and nature must be posited as "other" in order to justify their domination. Thus my contention is that what knowledge and understanding of the biota that Leopold has (and indeed it is extensive for a person of his time, when the empirical and normative implications of the science of ecology had barely been heard of) is founded on a privileged perspective—the privileged insider's point-of-view of the hunter peeking through the peephole of the thicket, casting nature (in the form of the quarry) as the objectified other.

This, then, is my general position: while the particular insights of Aldo Leopold have, on one level, proven to be very useful in getting the debate about environmental ethics "on the table" and into scientific and philosophical discourse, environmental philosophers, ethicists, and professionals should exercise great caution in relying too heavily on the works of Leopold as a source of conceptual guidance, because the work of this "seminal figure" is impregnated with ideas which may be reinforcing of the very notions that have been revealed by feminist and nonfeminist environmental ethicists[5] as damaging to a harmonious nature/culture relationship.

In order to establish my claim, the claim that Aldo Leopold's role as model for contemporary ecologists and environmental ethicists is at least morally ambivalent, I first examine the issue of hunting itself. By doing so I intend to show that in order to have participated in the act of hunting a person[6] must first have accepted and endorsed anthropocentrism to a degree that is incompatible with the sort of large-scale reform of attitudes toward nature which environmental ethicists[7] hope to bring about. In a related fashion, I will simultaneously connect the act of hunting to the kind of objectification of the "other" that ecofeminists claim links the oppression of women with the domination of nature.

Hunting and Morality

Hunting is to be here understood as the seeking out of an animal in its (more or less) natural habitat for the intent and purpose of taking its life. When hunting is done for sport, and not for subsistence, it is done for the sake of the "experience" obtained. The experience many, if not the majority, of hunters seem to agree[8] is not to be understood as merely the act of killing an animal and watching it die and then harvesting the meat. Rather, it includes "communing" with nature; getting close enough to other creatures to anticipate their patterns and habits, keenly observing wind, weather, and terrain and knowing what these things indicate about the interactions between the biotic and abiotic components of the land. Indeed, the Spanish philosopher José Ortega y Gasset (1972) writes in his *Meditations on Hunting*, "One does not hunt in order to kill. One kills in order to have hunted" (121). Leopold frequently wrote of the joys of hunting, and forcefully expressed his disdain for those who were overly-enamored of utilizing the latest in technology to enhance their hunting prowess. Leopold considered the overuse of new-fangled gadgetry and failure to adhere to a self-imposed code of ethics to be "slob hunting," and it had no place in the Leopoldian schema of appreciation of things "natural, wild and free."

> [C]onsider the duck-hunter, sitting in a steel boat behind composition decoys. A put-put motor has brought him to the blind without exercise. Canned heat stands by to warm him in case of a chilling wind. He talks to the passing flocks on a factory caller, in what he hopes are seductive tones; home lessons from a phonograph record have taught him how. The decoys work despite the caller ... [h]e opens up at 70 yards, for his polychoke is set for infinity, and the advertisements have told him that Super-Z shells, and plenty of them, have a long reach. The flock flares. A couple of cripples scale off to die elsewhere. Is this sportsman absorbing cultural value? Or is he just feeding minks? The next blind opens up at 75 yards; how else is a fellow to get some shooting? This is duck shooting, current model. It is typical of all public grounds, and of many clubs. Where is the go-light idea, the one bullet tradition? (Leopold 1949, 180–181)

But it is important to understand the reasons *why* Aldo Leopold found such styles of hunting deplorable. According to him the reason for hunting was to obtain the trophy, whether it be a bird's egg, a mess of trout, a basket of mushrooms, the photograph of a beat; the pressed specimen of a wild flower, or a note tucked into the cairn on a mountain peak ... It attests that its owner has been somewhere and done something—that he has exercised skill, persistence, or discrimination in the age-old feat of *overcoming, outwitting, or reducing to possession.* These connotations which attach to the trophy usually far exceed its physical value ... Very intensive management of game or fish lowers the unit value of the trophy by artificializing it. (Leopold 1949, 169; emphasis added)

To Leopold, hunting was a potential means of cultivating high moral character although again, it was not for the sake of the animal that he was concerned with such things. In *Sand County Almanac* he rails against deer hunters who shoot and abandon the carcasses of does in their quest for an acceptable buck, stating in tones reminiscent of Kant that "such deer-hunting is not only without social value, but constitutes actual training for ethical depravity *elsewhere*" (Leopold 1949, 179). What this suggests, of course, is that the animal itself possesses no intrinsic worth, but rather its being constitutes a testing ground for human moral development. Hunting, Leopold asserted, aids in the development of the sorts of "cultural values" necessary to properly appreciate wild things. For Leopold, the virtues of the hunt (and hunter) were many:

Is it impious to weigh goose music and art in the same scales? I think not, because the true hunter is merely a non-creative artist. Who painted the first picture on a bone in the caves of France? A hunter. Who alone in our modern life so thrills to the sight of living beauty that he will endure hunger and thirst and cold to feed his eye upon it? The hunter. Who wrote the greatest hunter's poem about the sheer wonder of the wind, the hail, and the snow, the stars, the lightnings, and the clouds, the lion, the deer, and the wild goat ... Poets sing and hunters scale the mountains primarily for one and the same reason—the thrill to beauty. (Leopold 1953, 170)

Leopold claimed that, "(T)here are cultural values in the sports, customs, and experiences that renew contact with wild things. ... There is value in any experience that exercises those ethical restraints collectively called 'sportsmanship'" (1949, 177–78). He even went so far as to say that, "Hunting for sport is an improvement over hunting for food, in that there has been added to the test of skill an ethical code" (Leopold 1933, 391).

The problem with such a means of augmenting one's moral mettle (and, for that matter, "communing" with nature), however, is that it does so at the expense of another creature, a creature who undeniably has an interest in remaining alive. To persist in deliberately stalking an animal who poses little or no threat to one's person and whom one does not *need* to kill in order to be assured of being fed is to sublimate the interests of the animal to one's own for a purpose which is justifiable on strictly anthropocentric and self-serving grounds. Killing the animal becomes, in effect, entertainment, a means of escaping the pressures and rigors of civilized life. Or it is done in order to promote or enhance one's own moral development, as Leopold claims, and to refine one's skill at behaving in a manner befitting a "gentleman." Thus such an action would be, according to the traditional standpoint of an ecocentric environmental ethics, *prima facie* wrong, since these environmental ethicists[9] deny that human beings ought to be permitted to exploit the natural world for reasons such as these. To choose to hunt in the modern era is to assume an attitude of domination over the animal being sought. The hunter in his or her arrogance presumes to decide (with the help of a little luck and skill, of course) whether the animal will live or die.

To connect this even further to the project of ecocentric environmental ethics, a field of which Leopold is often considered to be a "founding father," one might remark that to hunt in the afore-mentioned manner, to hunt for the sake of the "experience" is to use the animal as a means to one's own end, to treat it as though it has only *instrumental* and not *intrinsic* worth,[10] a type of valuing that many environmental ethicists rightly identify as being at the root of our environmental troubles. When one hunts one is seeking a particular experience and using the hunted animal as a means of fulfilling one's desire for this experience.[11] Thus one is viewing the animal as an instrument to one's pleasure or satisfaction, and not considering (or is choosing to ignore) the notion that the animal has a good of its own, and a perception of the world. To do this the animal must be objectified, treated as something external to one's self, not as a co-participant in what Leopold would call the "circuit" of life. Furthermore, and most damaging to the cause of environmental ethics, a conclusion must be reached that the animal is somehow "lower" or "lesser" than oneself in order to justify sacrificing its (vital) needs to one's own (nonvital) wants.

At this point I will mention two objections that can be raised in regard to the position which I am sketching out here. Others, including moral issues related to the eating of animals, will be considered later.

In response to criticisms of their activity, hunters frequently point out that predation is natural in the wild, that death is as natural as life, and suggest that as evolutionarily driven beings we too are "entitled" to participate in the deathly dramas of nature. However, in the view of many theorists, this line of reasoning carries little moral logic. I agree with Brian Luke's observation that, "The sportsman's code, by distinguishing better from worse reasons for killing and by enjoining hunters to minimize their infliction of pain, recognizes that less violence is better than more ... it makes no sense to suggest that because some bloodshed in nature is inescapable, we might as well just wade right in and *add to it*" (Luke 1997, 41; emphasis added).

The second objection concerns the right of members of indigenous groups to continue practices which maintain their cultural integrity, even (or especially) if these practices include hunting. Although this is certainly an important point, it is beyond the scope of this paper to fully examine issues related to acts of cultural imperialism—such as the need for indigenous peoples to maintain cultural identity in the face of western hegemonization—in their entirety. For my purposes here, however, it seems sufficient to note that while non-Western or indigenous peoples may have a stronger claim of access to particular "hunting grounds" than do whites from the dominant culture, Aldo Leopold was *not* a member of a such a group, nor did he entertain ideas about "sacred game" as a matter of group identity in the same way that a modern-day member of an American Indian tribe might. I do not wish to deny that Leopold, relative to his contemporaries, colleagues, and peers, held animals and their function in the ecosystem in high regard. But this argument, if cogent, serves to show that an activity like hunting is ethically defensible if it preserves the cultural integrity and autonomy of a disenfranchised group. Leopold was *not* a member of such a group. Leopold was a member of a class of socially and economically privileged elites, graduated from one of the most exclusive universities in the nation, and had ties to German aristocracy (Meine 1988). Thus it is an ill fit to attempt to use arguments designed to defend the cultural practices of a historically oppressed or disadvantaged group to justify sport hunting as practiced by a member of the dominant group.[12]

A Defense of Leopold

Environmental philosopher J. Baird Callicott, who has written numerous essays examining the conceptual underpinnings of Leopold's Land Ethic, addresses the issue of the apparent inconsistency of Leopold's hunting. In his article, "Animal Liberation: A Triangular Affair," Callicott anticipates that some may object to the fact of Leopold's hunting on the grounds that such activities run counter to the general aims and goals of an ecocentric environmental ethic. He asks,

> What sort of reasonable and coherent moral theory would at once urge that animals (and plants and soils and waters) be included in the same class with people as beings to whom ethical consideration is owed and yet not object to some of them being slaughtered (whether painlessly or not) and eaten, others hunted, trapped, and in various other ways seemingly cruelly used? (Callicott 1989, 21)

Callicott concludes, however, that the land ethic does not prohibit sport hunting, because the land ethic is *holistic*; that is, it is not concerned with the welfare of individual plants and animals so much as it attempts to promote the "integrity, stability and beauty" of the biotic community *as a whole*. "Thus," states Callicott, "to hunt and kill a white-tailed deer in certain districts may not only be ethically permissible, it might actually be a *moral requirement*. ... Thus, the land ethic is logically coherent" (21). In the next section I argue that this view is highly problematic, as it ignores certain deeply embedded assumptions that condition the nature/culture relationship and produce ecosocial crisis.

An Ecofeminist Critique of Leopold: Domination and Dualism

Hunting and Nonhuman Others

The attitude of domination and the reinforcement of a nature/culture dualism lurking in the narrative of Aldo Leopold's life and work can be better spotted if viewed through the lens of ecofeminism. Ecofeminism is an emerging theoretical and praxis-oriented field which insists that there are important conceptual connections between the oppression of women and the domination of nature. Many ecofeminists claim that what lies at the heart of contemporary Western culture's ecodestructive practices is what Karen Warren (1990) terms the "logic of domination"—the notion that there exist some ontological entities that are "above" others, and that said superiority then entitles them to dominate and oppress those "below." Because both women and nature have historically been[13] relegated to the inferior realm of the lower, the same logic or kind of reasoning serves to justify the oppression of both. An important corollary of the ecofeminist position is that since the domination of women and nature is conceptually twinned, whatever serves to oppress one acts similarly on the other. Likewise, whatever liberates nature will relieve the oppression of women as well (Davion 1994).

Sport hunting is an inherently oppressive act. When one hunts in the manner of a Leopold or an Ortega one does so not to put food on the table (although most hunters' credos dictate that the hunter consume what he or she kills[14]) or to protect one's own right to life, but to refine one's skills and sentiments in what could be called a "gentlemanly" manner. According to Leopold,

> … there are two points about hunting that deserve special emphasis. One is that the ethics of sportsmanship is not a fixed code, but must be formulated and practiced by the individual with no referee but the Almighty. The other is that hunting generally involves the handling of dogs and horses, and the lack of this experience is one of the most serious defects of our gasoline-driven civilization. There was much truth in the old idea that any man ignorant of dogs and horses was not a gentleman. (Leopold 1953, 172)

Thus we can see that Leopold largely views hunting as an important experience which helps him to cultivate the qualities that are the mark of nobility, thereby positioning himself as a privileged elite with the right to exercise mastery over nature. Val Plumwood terms this the "colonizer identity," and states that, "The colonizer identity is positioned as an eater of Others who can never themselves be eaten, just as the unmarked gaze of the colonizer claims the power to see but not to be seen … [the colonizer] aims to make the Other over into a form that eliminates all friction, challenge, or consequence" (1996, 43).

Hunting and Holism: Reproducing Dualism

Another defense of hunting which can, and has, been mounted, in particular by Baird Callicott and Holmes Rolston[15] is that environmental ethics is concerned not with individuals *per se* but with the diversity of species and the environment which they inhabit. It is in this sense that Callicott refers to the Land Ethic as "holistic": the individual animal, plant, and so forth, is a functioning member of a greater system, and it is the system itself which constitutes the locus of moral concern. The individual is only valuable insofar as it carries the genetic coding to perpetuate the species, which in turn is evolutionarily adapted to its surroundings and helps to perpetuate the healthy functioning of the ecosystem. When the value that a natural entity such as a duck, a deer, and so forth, exhibits is conceived of in this way, it becomes quite logical to regard the individual as superfluous (granting that the species is not endangered), and if the species in question is placing environmental pressure on other populations (e.g., deer are stripping a habitat of vegetation through overgrazing), killing several individuals may even may even become the "moral requirement," Callicott claims. Thus there does indeed appear to be an insoluble tension between those who find that the suffering and erasure of perception caused to individual animals by hunting is morally unacceptable and those who say that such suffering is necessary and thus justified if done in the name of ecological sustainability: one is forced, it appears, into killing particular animals; or sparing their lives but in so doing allowing the denudation of the habitat upon which they ultimately depend. Fortunately, an ecofeminist approach can help clarify how this dilemma may be reconceived, and ultimately obviated, as I will present in the following discussion.

According to Karen Warren, Val Plumwood, and other "critical ecofeminists,"[16] one of the projects with which ecofeminism is most concerned is the exposure and elimination of "false dualisms": conceptual pairings which operate so as to perpetuate a cultural belief in a radical discontinuity between men and women, as well as humans and the more-than-human world. Such dualisms also include the dyads of mind/body, reason/emotion, and culture/nature, as well as related others. Within each of these pairings is a hierarchical ordering (Warren [1990] calls this process "normative dualism") in which the item occupying the second position is thought to be inferior to and thus eligible to be subjugated by the first. This kind of oppositional thinking contributes immensely to environmental oppression and degradation, say ecofeminists, by allowing humans, driven by patriarchal ideology, to think of themselves as operating outside of nature (since the human is defined as that which is *not* nature), and thereby entitled to exploit, oppress, and degrade it. In an article appearing in a recent issue of *Hypatia,* Ronnie Zoe Hawkins (1998) discusses at length the problematic nature of the "holistic" approach to environmental ethics in regard to the ecofeminist project of dismantling dualism. Drawing information from fields within the biological and ecological sciences, Hawkins notes how evolutionary biology points away from the notion that animals are by nature "typed," that is, fixed in a particular pattern that remains universally true across members of a given species. Hawkins argues that this amounts to a sort of essentialism, in that it makes one individual in a (nonhuman) population exchangeable for any other; while denying that there are real differences not just between species but within them. Holists, says Hawkins, claim to be taking the environment to be valuable *as a whole,* but in doing so are thus denying that specificity occurs inside animal groupings as well as human ones. But since the holist does not refute the notion that human beings "count" individually (e.g., holist philosophers would not advocate the killing of sexually active human males as a means of moderating human populations [my example, not Hawkins's]), the holist is actually embracing a normative human/nature dualism which privileges humans. Hawkins explains that,

> If the "holist" who attempts to deny nonhumans any individual standing at all is following a rationalist line that is ultimately off base biologically, the "holist" who insists that "only species count" when considering environmental concerns is likely to be—unless willing to apply the same reductionistic approach to the human species in ecological contexts—seriously guilty of adhering to a double standard, one that is yet a further manifestation of human/nature dualism. (Hawkins 1998, 169)

The problem here, as Hawkins points out, is that such holism states that either animals can be conceived of as "individuals" or as "members of a group" but never both simultaneously, or alternately, as the situation may demand. "As long as the underlying dualistic framework persists," she notes, "little has been achieved by the adoption of this sort of 'holistic' outlook, since the conceptual construct of 'the ecosystem' is simply standing in for the explicit hegemony of the human in an ongoing process of domination" (170). In the case of hunting to reduce overpopulation, the "holistic" approach of killing individuals for the sake of the herd or the habitat (or legitimating hunting on these grounds) without acknowledging the circumstances which lead to the environmentally deleterious situation merely reinforces the idea that humans and nature are separate. Thus, says Hawkins,

> Holists who justify "culling" nonhuman animals that have become superabundant in their habitats, for example, without clearly acknowledging the role of human populations in creating that superabundance through such effects as elimination of predators or compression of nonhuman populations into unsuitably small land areas, and without taking responsibility for the need to reverse such dynamics by altering our human activities, will never get to the roots of our ecological crises and hence will have no chance of resolving them. (170)

Empirical Objections to The Necessity of Hunting

An alternate, and complementary, analysis of the question of animal overpopulation and habitat deterioration has been provided by ecofeminists active in the animal liberation movement. According to research, deer overpopulation is not exclusively, or even mainly caused by loss of habitat (although this certainly remains an important factor). Rather, say these sources, hunting itself is responsible for the excess of deer now experienced regularly in several areas. This phenomenon, say such activists, did not occur before the advent of "scientific game management," (a field which Leopold, incidentally, is said to have founded) a practice designed to ensure the "maximum yield" of certain species in order to accommodate the desires of hunters. Animal liberation activist Bina Robinson explains how the process works:

> Hunting seasons cause a (temporary) population crash which results in more does breeding at a younger age and the production of more twins and triplets. This effect is aggravated by rigging hunting regulations to limit the killing to bucks, or at least mature bucks, in most areas. This leaves more food for the does during the winter and results in more fawns being born in the spring. Viola! The population is right back where it was, or even higher. In New York State, 80% of the bucks are killed every year …
>
> Does normally breed when they are one and one-half or two and and one-half years old. The stress of hunting touches off an innate herd survival mechanism that cause some to ovulate and breed when only six months old, just what the wildlife managers want. … In nature, the food supply determines how many does ovulate and how many multiple births occur. … Deer also have the ability to reabsorb embryos when food is scarce, just like rabbits, believe it or not, but it seems the stress of being hunted outweighs food considerations at least some of the time … If hunting were to stop, the deer population would maintain a reasonable balance with its food supply. (Robinson 1998)[17]

The point here, then, established both theoretically and empirically, is that a reconceiving of the so-called animal rights/environmental ethics "debate" in radically different terms than it has conventionally been presented leads us even further into an appreciation for the ways in which traditional discourses occurring both within and outside of environmental philosophy are riddled with notions of dualisms and domination. These notions must be confronted in order to achieve the aim of subverting the hegemony of our dominant anthropocentric moral frameworks. Again, it is precisely this reconceiving which an ecofeminist approach enables environmental philosophy to do, since it itself is born from the experiences of those marginalized and effaced. Therefore any presentation of the materials and quandaries faced by environmentalists without serious attention to the insights of ecofeminism is inadequate and does a disservice to the many engaged in the project of environmental repair, as the next section will continue to illustrate.

The Atavism Argument: Hunting and Gender

Neither is Leopold's hunting justifiable by observing that Leopold believes hunting to be motivated by a fundamentally atavistic drive.[18] In *Round River* Leopold implores the American public to practice conservation for the reason that "I have congenital hunting fever and three sons ... I hope to leave them good health, an education, and possibly even a competence. But what are they going to do with these things if there be no more deer in the hills, and no more quail in the coverts?" (1953, 173). In this remark there is something that should be of interest to those seeking to overcome discourses of domination. Leopold and his wife, Estella, actually had five children, two of whom were female! For what reason are they explicitly excluded from such a consideration? Are not "deer in the hills" the birthright of girls as well? Of course one does not wish to reach the uncharitable conclusion that Leopold considered his sons to be more important than his daughters, but it is clear; from this passage and others, that Leopold considered hunting to be a predominantly masculine pursuit, a holdover from our 'paleolithic' days passed on through the male line only, apparently. Although such a direct exclusion of women in what he repeatedly calls the "instinctive" pursuit of "game" is relatively rare in Leopold's writings, it is not unprecedented. At one point, readying to move to Madison from Albuquerque, Aldo writes Estella to report that there were "dozens of boys ... catching sunfish" in a nearby lake, a fact which reassures him that "there are a lot of things like that [in Wisconsin] which are going to please our boys very much" (Meine 1988, 232). As to how his girls, or women more generally, are to receive this vital and pleasurable contact with nature, Leopold leaves us with no answer.

In his field-founding work, *Game Management,* Leopold contends that "men" possess an "instinctive zest" for "physical combat." "Physical combat between men and beasts," Leopold insists, "was an economic fact." He continues:

> Since first the flight of years began, it was part and parcel of the daily business
> of getting something to eat. Gradually agriculture and commerce supplied other
> and better means of subsistence. But the *hunting instinct,* the love of weapons, the
> zest in their skillful use, did not disappear with their displacement by economic
> substitutes. Hence sport with rod and gun. (Leopold 1933, 391; emphasis added)

The problem with the atavism argument from an ecofeminist standpoint is twofold. One is that the model which Leopold uses to express the phenomena occurring in nature is founded upon a rather Hobbesian approach that asserts that all beings are fundamentally in conflict with one another. "An ethic, ecologically, is a limitation on freedom of action in the struggle for existence" (Leopold 1949, 202), as opposed to a more 'feminine' and/or ecological model of organisms cooperating and symbiotically interacting. The other is that the presumption that *Homo sapiens* evolved primarily as a hunter[19] and thus that members of the species genetically carry this 'instinctive' drive is fallacious, as it ignores the historical contributions of women as gatherers and overstates the role of hunting and the consumption of meat in human evolution. It is now widely acknowledged that in traditional societies, it was the *gathering of* botanical foodstuffs and not the hunting of meat that supplied the group with the greatest amount of calories, thereby enabling it to survive. Respected historian of science and ecofeminist philosopher Carolyn Merchant informs us that in pre-colonial New England, for instance,

> women were responsible not only for horticulture, but also for gathering nuts, berries, and probably birds' eggs. Feminist anthropologists suggest that gathering may have been the quintessential process through which human evolution originally took place. ... Male labor predominated in hunting, [which] contributed about ten percent of the Indian diet. ... Female horticulture, gathering, and fishing contributed approximately 85 percent of the total caloric intake. (Merchant 1989, 80–81)

This point deserves to be clarified further. In attempting to find a historical/evolutionary basis for hunting, some argue that predation is "natural." Comparisons are made between ourselves and other animals, especially primates, our closest genetic relatives, in order to justify hunting and meat consumption. Thus, states ecofeminist theorist Carol Adams (1996), "Some feminists have argued that the eating of animals is natural because we do not have the herbivore's double stomach or flat grinders and because chimpanzees eat meat and regard it as a treat." The flaw in such an argument, says Adams, is that it involves "selective filtering," because it fails to note that meat comprises less than 4 percent of a chimpanzee's diet. "In fact," she notes, "all primates are primarily herbivorous." Adams continues:

> It is true that chimpanzees act as if meat were a treat. When humans lived as foragers and when oil was rare, the flesh of dead animals was a good source of calories. It may be that the treat aspect of meat has to do with an ability to recognize dense sources of calories. However we no longer have a need for such dense sources of calories ... When the argument is made that eating animals is natural, the presumption is that we must continue consuming animals because this is what we require to survive, to survive in a way consonant with living unimpeded by artificial cultural constraints that deprive us of the experience of our real selves. The paradigm of carnivorous animals provides the reassurance that eating animals is natural. But how do we know what is natural when it comes to eating, both because of the social construction of reality and the fact that our history indicates a very mixed message about eating animals? Some did; the majority did not, at least to any great degree. (Adams 1996, 123–24)

Adams, in the same article, specifically denies that hunting, even so-called "relational hunting"[20] can be reconciled with an ecofeminist consciousness, because such an activity is marked by power and domination, in which "the ontologizing of animals as edible bodies creates them as *instruments of human beings; animals' lives are thus subordinated* to the human's desire to eat them even though there is, in general, no need to be eating animals" (126, emphasis added).

What the information provided by Merchant and Adams indicates is that hunting and meat consumption are not, nor were ever, essential to human survival. Therefore Leopold is mistaken about his facts at least, and perhaps can be forgiven for being a "man of his age." The larger point I have been making, though, is that sport hunting of the kind practiced by Aldo Leopold is an act of domination which is inconsistent with what is taken to be a basic claim of environmental ethics: the claim that humans are not morally superior beings who are entitled to subjugate members of the more-than-human world. This, I assert, needs to be taken into account when examining one so central to the foundations of environmental ethics as Aldo Leopold. The hunted animal is being treated as a means and not an end for reasons that do not outweigh the *prima facie* case against killing other living, sentient[21] beings. In this way the act of hunting differs substantially from say, the cultivation of vegetables and plant products.

Hunting and Vegetarianism

This is an important point, and alludes to an objection which must be addressed. In discussions such as these, hunting advocates often ask why it is not equally iniquitous to consume plants as to consume animals. "But everything needs to eat *something*" rejoins the hunters' apologist to the antihunting critic, "and you are thereby being inconsistent to your own espoused reverence for life to state that the taking of animal life is wrong while you accept and even rejoice in the destruction of defenseless, living, plants." The attempt here is to turn the vegetarian's argument into a *reductio ad absurdum,* but is itself founded on the fallacy that all ways of getting something to eat possess moral parity; that gardening and hunting are the same sort of thing. The proper response to this, in my view, consists in recognizing that unless one wants to argue that human beings are *completely* unjustified in continuing to live upon the earth (a point I presume few would want to defend), then it is necessary for humans to use and consume members of the natural world. In other words, eating is a biological necessity, and cannot be foregone, even if someone suggests that a squash plant is being held in a state of bondage by the practice of gardening (unless one is literally willing to give up one's own life). Fortunately, however, having a proper relationship with the land does not seem to require that one relinquish one's right to eat *anything;* it merely suggests that some ways of "getting a living"—eating, dwelling, working, recreating, becoming edified, and so forth—are better than others. In other words, we ought to pursue the course of action which inflicts the least amount of suffering and damage upon natural creatures and systems, and ought significantly interfere with the more-than-human world only after its interests have been given proper consideration.

In light of the foregoing discussion one may well argue that a system of monocrop farming which relies heavily on the application of toxic pesticides and petroleum-based fertilizers and puts significant stress upon the land is as indicative of an attitude of domination as is sport hunting, and I would agree. The major difference between eating animals and eating plants, however, seems to be related to the type and degree of damage done to natural systems. Farming—for instance, by utilizing organic methods[22]—*can* be conducted in a way which is compatible with the way that plant communities actually exist, whereas sport hunting requires that violence be done to a natural creature for a reason *that is unrelated to a human being's biological need to survive.* (Although one could object that most modern agri-businesses do not conduct their operations in an ecologically sound manner, it does not follow from this fact that sport hunting is morally acceptable. It simply points to the need to end farming-based environmental oppression as well.) In short, the *reasons* for interfering with natural entities and the underlying *attitude* taken toward them when doing so are of principal importance in determining whether an act is ethically permissible. Leopold appears to have hunted in order to achieve the sort of vital contact with natural systems that allow human beings to thrive and flourish. But in doing so, Leopold negated the hunted animal's concomitant entitlement to live and flourish. Although he denies that it would be as satisfying, Leopold could have chosen (and did at times choose) other ways to experience nature "first hand." The deer and the grouse, in contrast, are left with no choice as to whether or not to be shot at.

The Denial of the Other

Another potentially serious problem with the work of Aldo Leopold relates to the feminist contention that historically men, in order to establish their identities as subjective selves, have repudiated and denied the "other." As could be inferred from the earlier Plumwood analysis, the other is one to whom one stands in antagonistic opposition, not in cooperative relation.[23] The other threatens to annihilate the individuated self unless the other is overcome. Since under patriarchy it is women, who, along with nature have been posited as the other, both are seen as something to conquer and subdue.[24] Ecofeminist theorist Marti Kheel (1990) writes, "Men have historically transcended the world of contingency through exploits and projects, that is, through attempts to transform the natural world" (129). It is this desire to overcome, to dominate and transform the natural environment that many environmental philosophers, such as the ones cited here, have pointed to as being fundamental to our ecological dilemmas. Although it is claimed by many who hunt that the meaningfulness of hunting is actually in identifying with one's prey and experiencing an ultimate closeness[25] (certainly it is the vehicle through which Leopold experienced his more sublime moments), an ecofeminist perspective provides the insight that, in hunting, the "other" is in actuality being negated so that the subjective, independent male self can emerge. Elaborates Kheel:

In order to understand how the act of identification can coexist with the desire to kill a being with whom one identifies, it is important to understand the ambivalent nature of the hunt. ... The hunter is thus driven by conflicting desires to both identify with the animal and to deny that he is an animal himself. The "drama" of the hunt thus enables the hunter to experience both the yearning for a return to unity, while ensuring, through the death of the animal, that such a unification is never attained ... *animals have become objects in the eyes of these men.* In fact, Leopold openly expresses this urge to reduce animals to object status: "Critics write and hunters outwit their animals for one and the same reason-to reduce that beauty to possession." Interestingly, the original title of his famous *Sand County Almanac* was 'Great Possessions'. (Kheel 1990, 133; emphasis added)

What Kheel, in strongly de Beauvoirian tones, makes explicit in the above quote is the way in which "animal" is defined as the negation of "human" in the same sense that "woman" is defined as the negation of "man." Because both "woman" and "animal" are associated with the realm of the natural, that is, that from which human physiology and consciousness arises and that which places limitations on human existence, both are seen as something to simultaneously embrace and resist. In order to overcome the sense of limitation or restriction placed on him by biological necessity, "man" must remove himself as much as possible from the realm of what is identified as "natural"—chaotic, situated, and finite—and place himself in the world of culture—the abstract, the universal, the timeless. He typically does this through the process that Kheel identifies, by objectifying the other; thereby denying that it is a part of himself on which he depends and must interact, and then transforming or effacing it through "exploits and projects" such as hunting. "The significance of the reduction of the animal to object status," says Kheel, "is that ... [t]he feelings of yearning for union, the urge to "outwit" [the animal]—all these take precedence over the living being that will be killed. The animal is swallowed up [the other negated] in the act of merging" (133). The animal, instead of being acknowledged as a site of subjective experience, is transformed into an object or symbol designed to confirm the existence of the independent, human, male self.

Hunting and Eros

Hunting and its descriptions carry erotic undertones as well. In the act of hunting the prey is "captured" and "conquered," or as Leopold put it, "that beauty reduced to possession." These same terms and ideas can be found to express male/female interactions under patriarchy. As Susan Griffin (1978) writes in ironic metaphor in "The Hunt":

She has captured his heart. She has overcome him. He cannot tear his eyes away. He is burning with passion. He cannot live without her. He pursues her. She makes him pursue her. The faster she runs, the stronger his desire. He will overtake her. He will make her his own. He will have her. (The boy chases the doe and her yearling for nearly two hours. She keeps running despite her wounds.) ... She is wild. He is an easy target, he says. He says he is pierced. Love has shot him through, he says ... Now, he must conquer her wildness, he says, he must tame her before she drives him wild. ... (103–104)

In the above passage Griffin is drawing a comparison to the way in which the hunter is "respecting" the wildness of the animal and imagines himself to be reciprocally caught in the hunt and the way in which men often claim that women "provoke" sexual harassment and rape by "making" him "pursue" and later "possess" her. One need not, however, turn to literature or poetic philosophy to discover the cultural currency of the notion of the erotic hunt. One need only open the front page of a major newspaper where the comparison has been expressed directly. In an article appearing in the *Dallas Morning News,* a hunter is quoted as saying, "There is a [basic][26] drive within us that makes us hunt—it's like trying to explain a sex drive" (1996, 42A).

Of course, this is a comparison only; the hunter is not claiming that hunting *is* sex, only that the urge to hunt is *like* the urge for sex. But why this particular analogy? Why of all the many possible drives which could be selected—hunger, thirst, affection, and so forth—does this person choose the sex drive? Again, I would argue that in hunting one assumes an attitude of domination over the thing being pursued, just as in patriarchal cultures such as our own men as a class assume an attitude of domination over women as a class, and gratify their needs and wants at women's expense. Sexual relations are, according to feminists, an area of life where the deep social inequality between men and women manifests itself deeply. (Interestingly, males exhibiting the most egregious behavior are referred to as "sexual predators.") However, feminists such as Catharine MacKinnon (1989) have convincingly argued that there is nothing terribly unusual about the actions of men who are convicted of rape, pedophilia, and so forth, since these behaviors are in many ways encouraged by the culture at large. It is only the *degree* to which they act out their conditioning that society finds aberrant. Women are "pursued" while men are the "pursuers"; submissiveness and powerlessness are part of the cultural definition of femininity while masculinity is largely defined in accordance with aggressiveness, physical power, and the ability to do violence. These dynamics are reproduced in the hunt. As Griffin expresses in the above quote, the hunter is trying to capture, while the "game" is trying to get away, but both the hunter and the Don Juan is projecting on to the objectified other those drives which he himself is experiencing.[27] In either case, if successful, the "hunter" has made a "conquest." With the explicit recognition of this in mind, it now seems perversely logical for the hunter quoted above to have found a (probably subconscious) conceptual connection between his desire for sex and whatever sentiments motivate him to hunt.

At this point we want to ask: did Leopold eroticize hunting? Probably not, at least not in any direct way that we know of. But my claim is that the larger effect of Leopold's work on the professionals, philosophers, and students engaged in environmental ethics who draw so heavily on him is that it reproduces, keeps alive certain notions—to wit, domination and objectification—that hamper the project of environmental ethics. Ecofeminists have shown how the same reasoning that works to oppress women also works to oppress nature. Thus when women or nature are oppressed, the oppression of the other is undergirded. Given the current cultural connotations (i.e., sexuality in a context of gendered power-imbalance) attaching to the hunt, it is dangerous to allow any narrative that approves of and seems to encourage hunting to escape a careful critical analysis which brings to bear the most recent scholarship. Instead, Leopold, like other authors forming the "canon" of any field or discourse, must be subjected to the process of critical deconstruction, that we may reconstruct the narrative in such a way that our aims can be more inclusively and justly achieved.

Nature and the Feminine

A final ecofeminist insight which can be brought to bear is that Leopold, in at least one instance, feminized nature, a conceptual phenomenon related to the discourses of dominance which feed environmental degradation. In his famous essay, "Thinking Like A Mountain," Leopold writes about his remorse at killing a wolf and its pups during his days as a forest manager:

> In those days we had never heard of passing up a chance to kill a wolf. In a second we were pumping lead into the pack, but with more excitement than accuracy: how to aim a steep downhill shot is always confusing. When our rifles were empty, the old wolf was down, and a pup was dragging a leg into impassable slide-rocks.
>
> We reached the old wolf in time to watch a fierce green fire dying in her eyes. I realized then, and have known ever since, that there was something new to me in those eyes—*something known only to her and to the mountain.* (Leopold 1949, 130; emphasis added)

One possible analysis of this episode is that it is properly understood as a literal report of Aldo Leopold's own experience. Leopold expert J. Baird Callicott, however, has suggested on at least one occasion[28] that the story was contrived by Leopold as a means of capturing and conveying through narrative his own protracted epistemological transformation regarding the importance of natural predators. By validating the she-wolf's right to exist is it possible that Leopold was attempting to come to terms with the earthy, "feminine"[29] contingency of his own existence? If I am correct in suggesting that Leopold on some level intended the wolf to represent the omniscience—that is the "all knowingness"—of nature (remember he is asking us to "think like a mountain," something the wolf is already able to do), and if one accepts that nature has been fundamentally construed as feminine, then this may indicate that by hunting Leopold was paradoxically trying to both repudiate and celebrate his own dependence on the tumultuous, bountiful, inescapable natural world. Putatively, it is precisely this nature/culture interdependence which Leopold wished to affirm, as the corpus of his works attest. It is not untenable to imagine, however that Leopold, like us all, struggled internally with confronting his own (and our own) lack of ultimate control over the forces that drive the universe, and thus may have coded another meaning into the message.

Leopold: A Narrative Perspective

The encodation of meanings other than the ostensive one is a concept which can be understood if one looks at *A Sand County Almanac* (and Leopold's other writings) from a narrative perspective. Communications theorist Walter R. Fisher (1984) has suggested that works and events can be understood according to two paradigms: the rational world paradigm and the narrative paradigm. In the rational world paradigm events and authors are understood logically, that is to say, they are evaluated according to the internal consistency and strength of the inferential structures of what is *explicitly said*. All else, including the tone and vehicle of communication, the way in which the ideas are expressed and whatever "incidentals" may accompany it, is considered superfluous, not part of the argument to be rationally evaluated. According to the narrative paradigm, however, human beings are considered to be storytellers (of which Leopold is undoubtedly one of the best), and rationality is not restricted to adherence to certain learned formal logical structures. In the narrative paradigm, meaning comes from the accompanying symbolism and "dramatic stories" that an author utilizes to convey his or her message as well as from its syllogistic claims. The work is taken *en toto,* with much of it operating on a nonrational level (one might do better to say *meta*-rational), and attitudes and ideas are dispersed and absorbed according to the kind of "narrative fidelity" and "narrative probability" they evince. The point I am attempting briefly to make is that the work and words of Aldo Leopold, when examined according to the rational world paradigm, are certainly coherent and consistent; in short, logically compelling. There is nothing in his explicit and direct formulation of the more philosophical sections of the Land Ethic which would suggest an attitude of domination and exploitation of the sort that has in more recent decades been strongly linked to anthropogenic environmental harm. In fact, it was these sorts of attitudes that Leopold was attempting, with fair success, to change. However, when examined narratively, the meaning of Leopold is somewhat altered. Because Leopold's writings portray hunting so favorably, and because he himself is such a laudable figure, it is possible that persons will fail to see the connection between sport hunting and attitudes of domination. Instead his hunting may be glossed over, ignored, or written off as "natural for his time." What is happily ironic in this regard, however, is that it is Leopold's work itself which has been so influential in introducing into contemporary discourse the terms needed to conduct such a critique.

Concluding Remarks: Aldo Leopold and the Evolution of Environmental Discourse

If my thesis is correct, if it is the case that despite his recognition that conventional Western notions of "prosperity" and "progress" were in actuality impoverishing the quality of human and nonhuman life on earth, Aldo Leopold still harbored a view of nature as "other," then what does this mean for the project of environmental philosophy? What does this imply about the significance of hunting to the development of the Land Ethic? Could Leopold's profound and prophetic insights have been developed without such an activity, and if they had, would they say different things? We can't know. At a minimum, though, we can appreciate that it is the case that Leopold found hunting to place one in a position of intimate contact with the natural world, and this contact, in turn, inspired much of his fervent and eloquent entreaties to protect and preserve North America's wildlife and wildlife habitat. As much as any other single figure, Aldo Leopold is responsible for changing and enlarging our awareness regarding the biological importance and moral significance of the biota. Aldo Leopold entered into popular; professional, and academic discourse ideas which are with us still. Fifty-plus years after the publication of *A Sand County Almanac* his ideas continue to deepen the collective ecological narrative of our time. It is not my intention to suggest that Leopold's work is of *no* value because of notions it might contain. Instead I wish to draw attention to the cultural premises which his work and words are built upon, and the ones that will unavoidably provide the filters through which he will be received. As the combination of ethics and ecology has moved us from conservationism to environmentalism and now places us into the postmodern era where many traditional boundaries and thought-structures are being dissolved, we do well to examine critically the foundations of our inherited worldview. By exposing and confronting those narratives that undermine the health of the world, and by embracing those that we desperately need to 'ring true', we enable ourselves to forge a relationship between the human and land communities which is healthy and whole. We can accept the teachings of Leopold, and continue to draw upon his ideas, while incorporating the many critiques of hunting into the conversation. For, as Leopold himself understood, "Ability to see the cultural value of wilderness boils down, in the last analysis, to a question of intellectual humility" (1949, 200).

Acknowledgments

J. Baird Callicott has provided invaluable help, suggestions, and resources for the completion of this essay. It has also benefitted from suggestions by an anonymous reviewer.

Notes

1. This, of course, is the famous conservationist doctrine advocated by Gifford Pinchot, founder of the Yale School of Forestry and first chief of the U.S. Forest Service, which asserts that the natural environment consists of "resources" to be utilized for human economic benefit and thus the best methods of conservation are those which maximize utility and provide a sustained yield over the long-term. A highly anthropocentric concept, the term "Wise Use" has in recent times been seized upon by coalitions of timber, mining, and ranching industries to maintain public support for such businesses and to attempt to counter the push by nonprofit environmental organizations to raise awareness regarding environmentally destructive corporate practices. Leopold's teachings can be credited to a large extent for providing a basis for countering these kinds of approaches to natural environments.

2. My use of the term "natural entities" applies to individual members of the biotic world such as particular plants and animals, as well as processes such as hydrologic cycles, and other, more amorphous and thus disputed things like species and ecosystems. I have chosen this term in an imperfect attempt to be as inclusive as possible without erasing the very real differences among items we consider to be a part of "nature." It should be noted that while I agree, as I will continue to develop in later sections, with contemporary ecologists and philosophers such as Michael Soulé and Holmes Rolston that the natural environment is best understood not as a collection of things but rather as a series of dynamic processes, nonetheless certain entities exhibiting a high degree of individuality such as sentient animals at some levels of moral analysis are best understood as being ontologically embedded in but distinct from other features of the environment.

3. This is the subject of Leopold's second most famous book, *Round River: From the Journals of Aldo Leopold.* According to Leopold biographer Curt Meine (1988), the book is reputed not to have sold as well as its predecessor *A Sand County Almanac,* because "the unrelenting procession of hunting tales did not sit well with nonhunting conservationists" (525). Meine also claims that "no less a figure than Rachel Carson took Leopold to task" for emphasizing this activity so heavily in his work and writings.

4. The ecofeminist literature which details these interconnections and the political, social, and economic processes by which they occur is extensive; in fact it could be said that this is central to the project of ecofeminism. However, two representative sources on this matter are Vandana Shiva (1989) and Val Plumwood (1993).

5. See nn. 4 and 7.

6. My analysis of the ethical impropriety of hunting applies to human beings engaged in sport hunting only and not predators in general. That there is a significant moral difference between the activities of an animal which is biologically designed to capture and consume prey (wolves, lions, etc.) and human beings, who are certainly omnivorous, can survive quite healthily without meat-eating, and may actually have evolved as scavengers and not hunters of live prey, I take to be obvious.

7. As with ecofeminism (n. 4), the number of authors within environmental philosophy espousing a position which rejects conventional ethical notions of human superiority by virtue of the ability to "reason"—with

reason being defined narrowly as deliberate and self-reflective examination of options and conclusions—is vast. Although the umbrella of environmental ethics is large and encompasses many positions, the scope of my paper is designed primarily to address "ecocentric" environmental ethicists; that is, those who feel that human beings ought to adjust their thinking regarding the value of the natural world to recognize that nature possesses much more than value as a "resource" but is something in which the value is intrinsic or inherent. Representatives of this position include Holmes Rolston, Paul W. Taylor, Max Oelschlaeger, and J. Baird Callicott.

8. For an excellent and detailed analysis of literature which examines hunters' own thoughts and remarks regarding hunting and the inconsistencies therein, see Brian Luke (1997).

9. For example, Arne Naess (1985), founder of Deep Ecology and widely revered environmental philosopher writes that, "There is a basic intuition in deep ecology that we have no right to destroy other living beings without sufficient reason. Another is the norm that, with maturity, human beings will experience joy when other life forms experience joy, and sorrow when other life forms experience sorrow" (75).

10. Callicott (1989) defines the distinction this way: "Something is intrinsically valuable if it is valuable *in* and *for* itself—if its value is not derived from its utility, but is independent of any use or function it may have in relation to something else. In classical philosophical terminology, an intrinsically valuable entity is said to be an 'end-in-itself', not just a 'means to another's ends'" (131). As has been pointed out by an anonymous reviewer in the particular piece from which this definition is drawn, Callicott is not defending the intrinsic value of *individual* members of a species, but rather he is claiming that the species itself is intrinsically valuable, and that individual members may be expendable. However, I explain in later sections of this essay, the way in which this "holistic" position embraces a hidden dualism that is unacceptable from an ecofeminist standpoint, thereby illustrating why an ecofeminist perspective in general is needed in order to break down the so-called "debate" between environmental ethics and animal rights.

11. Part of the allure of hunting lies in the rejection of particular social modes and activities that are demanded of the individual in "normal" life. Hunters, for a time, fancy themselves as getting to "go native," to re-live an imagined human past in which human ingenuity was pitted against raw nature in a struggle to survive. Callicott (1989) writes: "Civilization has insulated and alienated us from the rigors and challenges of the natural environment. ... The land ethic, on the other hand, requires a shrinkage if at all possible, of the domestic sphere; it rejoices in a recrudescence of wilderness and a renaissance of tribal cultural experience" (34).

12. In a recent article appearing in the journal *Environmental Ethics,* a nearly identical objection, raised by an anonymous referee, is considered; interestingly, the authors' response is very similar to the one I have independently proposed here (Moriarty and Woods 1997). For an article in the same issue which argues that sport hunting is morally justified according to the tenets of the land ethic, see Charles List (1997). From an ecofeminist perspective, Greta Gaard, in a *Hypatia* article, addresses the question of hunting as a means of cultural survival through the specific case of the recent Makah whale hunt. Gaard argues that presuming that the Makah tribe must resume whale hunting to maintain cultural integrity relies on an unacceptable cultural essentialism. (Gaard 2001).

13. Conventionally this has been thought to be the case because women and nature evince such traits as "emotionality" and are "bodily" and "chaotic," which has been considered by Western culture to be a less desirable way to be than the more masculine "rational," "orderly," and "mental" or "intellectual."

14. Again, an excellent discussion of the problems inherent in so-called 'hunters' ethics' can be found in Brian Luke's piece, "A Critical Analysis of Hunters' Ethics" (1997).

15. Callicott (1989) "Animal Liberation: A Triangular Affair"; Holmes Rolston, *Environmental Ethics: Duties to and Values in the Natural World* (Philadelphia: Temple University Press 1988), 90–91.

16. This term, utilized in particular by Val Plumwood, is meant to contrast with the "essentializing ecofeminism" criticized by ecofeminists and nonecofeminists alike for drawing a link between women and nature in such a way that the similarities are assumed to be "natural" and thus unchangeable, and the exclusive privilege of biological females.

17. Carol Adams and Bina Robinson, personal correspondence, July 19, 1998 (some of Robinson's information quoted here, according to her, has been taken from *The American Hunting Myth* by Ron Baker).

18. Ortega (1973) shares such an assumption: "This is the reason men hunt. When you are fed up with the troublesome present, with being 'very twentieth century', you take your gun, whistle for your dog, go out to the mountain, and, without further ado, give yourself the pleasure during a few hours or a few days of being 'Paleolithic'" (116).

19. A considerable range of feminist authors have challenged the widely accepted belief that our hominid ancestors were frequent hunters, and that this always-imaged-as-male activity constituted the primary motor of evolution. Donna Haraway (1989) does an especially effective job of examining how such "origin stories" are particularly good at reinforcing narratives of (Western, white, male) human superiority and power-entitlement. Even Mary Zeiss Stange (1997), a controversial author who claims that hunting by women is a pro-feminist activity, devotes much of her book, *Woman the Hunter*, to disputing the culturally-prevalent notion that hunting was always a male occupation, and occurred frequently and ubiquitously in human prehistory.

20. About "relational hunting" (hunting in which there is a presumption of respect and reciprocity occurring between the hunter and the hunted), Adams (1996) has this to say: "But reciprocity involves a mutual or cooperative interchange of favors or privileges. What does the animal who dies receive in this exchange? The experience of sacrifice? How can the reciprocity of the relational hunt be verified since the other partner is both voiceless in terms of human speech and furthermore rendered voiceless through his or her death? Once the question of the willingness of the silent and silenced partner is raised, so too is the connection between the relational hunt and what I will call the 'aggressive hunt'" (127).

21. I am not here claiming that sentience—defined as the ability to experience pain—is the only or even the primary criterion for making the claim that causing an animal's death is wrong. However I believe that the matter should be approached in a pluralistic and contextualized way. In line with what I see

as an ecofeminist approach, I believe that the project of attempting to find a single, "foundational" or universal criterion upon which to rest ethical claims is unnecessarily hegemonic, and perpetuative of a modernist and nonfeminist approach to philosophy which asserts that there is only "one" correct way of viewing a quandary. In the case of natural entities who have highly developed nervous systems are highly individualized like ourselves, perhaps sentience ought to be a consideration which is given much weight. However in a different case involving organisms with a different physiology or place within the ecosystem, other ethical criteria might rise to the forefront.

22. Two long-term, ongoing projects investigating and developing methods of nonpesticide, machinery, and artificial fertilizer-dependent methods of farming which can be applied on a large enough scale to feed local communities of which I am personally aware are the Agroecology Program at the University of California, Santa Cruz, and the Center for Regenerative Studies at California Polytechnic University, Pomona.

23. Plumwood (1993) is apparently drawing on Hegel to develop her analysis, as an anonymous reviewer has helpfully pointed out.

24. See, for instance, Susan Griffin (1978); also Simone de Beauvoir (1989, 140–44).

25. Three authors who make this claim who are frequently cited by both pro- and anti-hunting theorists and activists are Paul Shepard (1973), Ted Kerasote (1993), and Spanish philosopher José Ortega y Gasset (1973). More recently, philosopher and hunter Mary Zeiss Stange (1997) has written a book critical of the ecofeminist objections to hunting, in which she claims that "the hunter serves as an agent of awareness for society at large, both by forging that most elemental conceptual connection between human and nonhuman animals, and by locating the essence of that connection in the good food that sustains life." Like Leopold (see "The Deer Swath" in *Round River* (1953, 126) in which Leopold states that the nonhunter "does not watch" nature), Stange implies that a truly deep, authentic connection with nature is the privileged experience of hunters; nonhunters are denied such a perception. "Such awareness is only available, though, to the extent that some people are actually hunting; otherwise, it is mere nostalgia … an empty metaphor" (1997, 175).

26. The word which I have here omitted is "atavistic." I have excluded it because I wish the focus of this section to be the comparison of hunting to sex, not on hunting to beliefs about human evolution.

27. Hawkins quotes Kheel as remarking that "the notion that the animal chooses to end her or his life for the benefit of the hunter has no more validity than the idea that a woman who is raped 'asked for it' or 'willingly' gave herself to the rapist" (Hawkins 1998, 170).

28. J. Baird Callicott said this in a seminar on Aldo Leopold at the University of North Texas in the Fall of 1996.

29. I am in no way suggesting here that there is a genuine, ahistorical, *essential* principle of femininity in the natural world. The association of femininity, bodily existence, and the chaos of natural forces is in my view a culturally-constructed notion which nonetheless many take to be "natural."

References

Adams, Carol J. 1996. "Ecofeminism and the Eating of Animals." In *Ecological Feminist Philosophies,* ed. Karen Warren. Bloomington: University of Indiana Press.

Callicott, J. Baird. 1989. *In Defense of the Land Ethic: Essays in Environmental Philosophy.* Albany: State University of New York Press.

The Dallas Morning News. 26 December 1996. "South Texas town is place to be for 'trophy hunters'," 42A.

Davion, Victoria. 1994. "Is Ecofeminism Feminist?" In *Ecological Feminism,* ed. Karen Warren. London: Routledge.

de Beauvoir, Simone. 1989. *The Second Sex.* New York: Vintage.

Fisher, Walter R. 1984. "Narration as a Human Communication Paradigm: The Case of Public Moral Argument," *Communication Monographs,* vol. 51.

Gaard, Greta. 2001. "Tools For a Cross-Cultural Feminist Ethics: Exploring Ethical Contexts and Contents in the Makah Whale Hunt," *Hypatia* 16 (1): 1–26.

Griffin, Susan. 1978. *Woman and Nature: The Roaring Inside Her.* San Francisco: Harper and Row.

Haraway, Donna. 1989. *Primate Visions: Gender, Race, and Nature in the World of Modern Science.* New York: Routledge.

Hawkins, Ronnie Zoe. 1998. "Ecofeminism and Nonhumans: Continuity, Difference, Dualism, and Domination," *Hypatia* 13 (1):158–97.

Kerasote, Ted. 1993. *Bloodties: Nature, Culture and the Hunt.* New York: Random House.

Kheel, Marti. 1990. "Ecofeminism and Deep Ecology: Reflections on Identity and Difference." In *Reweaving the World: The Emergence of Ecofeminism,* eds. Irene Diamond and Gloria Orenstein. San Francisco: Sierra Club Books.

Leopold, Aldo. 1933. *Game Management.* New York: Charles Scribner's Sons.

———. 1949. *A Sand County Almanac and Sketches Here and There.* New York: Oxford University Press.

———. 1953. Luna B. Leopold, ed. *Round River: From the Journals of Aldo Leopold.* New York: Oxford University Press.

List, Charles. 1997. "Is Hunting a Right Thing?" *Environmental Ethics* 19: 405–16.

Luke, Brian. 1997. "A Critical Analysis of Hunters' Ethics," *Environmental Ethics* 19: 25–44.

MacKinnon, Catharine. 1989. *Toward a Feminist Theory of the State.* Cambridge: Harvard University Press.

Meine, Curt. 1988. *Aldo Leopold: His Life and Work.* Madison: University of Wisconsin Press.

Merchant, Carolyn. *Ecological Revolutions: Nature, Gender, and Science in New England.* Chapel Hill: University of North Carolina Press.

Moriarty, Paul Veatch and Mark Woods. 1997. "Hunting = Predation," *Environmental Ethics* 19: 402–3.

Naess, Arne. 1985. "Ecosophy T." In *Deep Ecology: Living as if Nature Mattered,* eds. Bill Devall and George Sessions. Salt Lake City: Peregrine Smith Books.

Ortega y Gasset, José. 1972. *Meditations on Hunting.* New York: Charles Scribner's Sons.

Plumwood, Val. 1993. *Feminism and the Mastery of Nature.* New York: Routledge.

——— . 1996. "Being Prey," *Terra Nova* 1 (3).

Robinson, Bina. 1998. Personal correspondence.

Rolston, Holmes. 1988. *Environmental Ethics: Duties to and Values in the Natural World.* Philadelphia: Temple University Press.

Shepard, Paul. 1973. *The Tender Carnivore and the Sacred Game.* New York: Charles Scribner's Sons.

Shiva, Vandana. 1989. *Staying Alive: Women, Ecology, and Development.* London: Zed Books

Stange, Mary Zeiss. 1997. *Woman the Hunter.* Boston: Beacon Press.

Warren, Karen. 1990. "The Power and the Promise of an Ecological Feminism," *Environmental Ethics* 12: 125–43.

6A2. All Animals Are Equal

By Peter Singer

I n recent years a number of oppressed groups have campaigned vigorously for equality. The classic instance is the Black Liberation movement, which demands an end to the prejudice and discrimination that has made blacks second-class citizens. The immediate appeal of the black liberation movement and its initial, if limited, success made it a model for other oppressed groups to follow. We became familiar with liberation movements for Spanish-Americans, gay people, and a variety of other minorities. When a majority group—women—began their campaign, some thought we had come to the end of the road. Discrimination on the basis of sex, it has been said, is the last universally accepted form of discrimination, practiced without secrecy or pretense even in those liberal circles that have long prided themselves on their freedom from prejudice against racial minorities.

One should always be wary of talking of "the last remaining form of discrimination." If we have learnt anything from the liberation movements, we should have learnt how difficult it is to be aware of latent prejudice in our attitudes to particular groups until this prejudice is forcefully pointed out.

A liberation movement demands an expansion of our moral horizons and an extension or reinterpretation of the basic moral principle of equality. Practices that were previously regarded as natural and inevitable come to be seen as the result of an unjustifiable prejudice. Who can say with confidence that all his or her attitudes and practices are beyond criticism? If we wish to avoid being numbered amongst the oppressors, we must be prepared to re-think even our most fundamental attitudes. We need to consider them from the point of view of those most disadvantaged by our attitudes, and the practices that follow from these attitudes. If we can make this unaccustomed mental switch we may discover a pattern in our attitudes and practices that consistently operates so as to benefit one group—usually the one to which we ourselves belong—at the expense of another. In this way we may come to see that there is a case for a new liberation movement. My aim is to advocate that we make this mental switch in respect of our attitudes and practices towards a very large group of beings: members of species other than our own—or, as we popularly though misleadingly call them, animals. In other words, I am urging that we extend to other species the basic principle of equality that most of us recognize should be extended to all members of our own species.

All this may sound a little far-fetched, more like a parody of other liberation movements than a serious objective. In fact, in the past the idea of "The Rights of Animals" really has been used to parody the case for women's rights. When Mary Wollstonecraft, a forerunner of later feminists, published her *Vindication of the Rights of Women* in 1792, her ideas were widely regarded as absurd, and they were satirized in an anonymous publication entitled *A Vindication of the Rights of Brutes*. The author of this satire (actually Thomas Taylor, a distinguished Cambridge philosopher) tried to refute Wollstonecraft's reasonings by showing that they could be carried one stage further. If sound when applied to women, why should the arguments not be applied to dogs, cats, and horses? They seemed to hold equally well for these "brutes"; yet to hold that brutes had rights was manifestly absurd; therefore the reasoning by which this conclusion had been reached must be unsound, and if unsound when applied to brutes, it must also be unsound when applied to women, since the very same arguments had been used in each case.

One way in which we might reply to this argument is by saying that the case for equality between men and women cannot validly be extended to nonhuman animals. Women have a right to vote, for instance, because they are just as capable of making rational decisions as men are; dogs, on the other hand, are incapable of understanding the significance of voting, so they cannot have the right to vote. There are many other obvious ways in which men and women resemble each other closely, while humans and other animals differ greatly. So, it might be said, men and women are similar beings, and should have equal rights, while humans and nonhumans are different and should not have equal rights.

The thought behind this reply to Taylor's analogy is correct up to a point, but it does not go far enough. There *are* important differences between humans and other animals, and these differences must give rise to *some* differences in the rights that each have. Recognizing this obvious fact, however, is no barrier to the case for extending the basic principle of equality to nonhuman animals. The differences that exist between men and women are equally undeniable, and the supporters of Women's Liberation are aware that these differences may give rise to different rights. Many feminists hold that women have the right to an abortion on request. It does not follow that since these same people are campaigning for equality between men and women they must support the right of men to have abortions too. Since a man cannot have an abortion, it is meaningless to talk of his right to have one. Since a pig can't vote, it is meaningless to talk of its right to vote. There is no reason why either Women's Liberation or Animal Liberation should get involved in such nonsense. The extension of the basic principle of equality from one group to another does not imply that we must treat both groups in exactly the same way, or grant exactly the same rights to both groups. Whether we should do so will depend on the nature of the members of the two groups. The basic principle of equality, I shall argue, is equality of consideration; and equal consideration for different beings may lead to different treatment and different rights.

So there is a different way of replying to Taylor's attempt to parody Wollstonecraft's arguments, a way which does not deny the differences between humans and nonhumans, but goes more deeply into the question of equality, and concludes by finding nothing absurd in the idea that the basic principle of equality applies to so called "brutes." I believe that we reach this conclusion if we examine the basis on which our opposition to discrimination on grounds of race or sex ultimately rests. We will then see that we would be on shaky ground if we were to demand equality for blacks, women, and other groups of oppressed humans while denying equal consideration to nonhumans.

When we say that all human beings, whatever their race, creed or sex, are equal, what is it that we are asserting? Those who wish to defend a hierarchical, inegalitarian society have often pointed out that by whatever test we choose, it simply is not true that all humans are equal. Like it or not, we must face the fact that humans come in different shapes and sizes; they come with differing moral capacities, differing intellectual abilities, differing amounts of benevolent feeling and sensitivity to the needs of others, differing abilities to communicate effectively, and differing capacities to experience pleasure and pain. In short, if the demand for equality were based on the actual equality of all human beings, we would have to stop demanding equality. It would be an unjustifiable demand.

Still, one might cling to the view that the demand for equality among human beings is based on the actual equality of the different races and sexes. Although humans differ as individuals in various ways, there are no differences between the races and sexes *as such*. From the mere fact that a person is black, or a woman, we cannot infer anything else about that person. This, it may be said, is what is wrong with racism and sexism. The white racist claims that whites are superior to blacks, but this is false—although there are differences between individuals, some blacks are superior to some whites in all of the capacities and abilities that could conceivably be relevant. The opponent of sexism would say the same: a person's sex is no guide to his or her abilities, and this is why it is unjustifiable to discriminate on the basis of sex.

This is a possible line of objection to racial and sexual discrimination. It is not, however, the way that someone really concerned about equality would choose, because taking this line could, in some circumstances, force one to accept a most inegalitarian society. The fact that humans differ as individuals, rather than as races or sexes, is a valid reply to someone who defends a hierarchical society like, say, South Africa, in which all whites are superior in status to all blacks. The existence of individual variations that cut across the lines of race or sex, however, provides us with no defence at all against a more sophisticated opponent of equality, one who proposes that, say, the interests of those with I.Q. ratings above 100 be preferred to the interests of those with I.Q.s below 100. Would a hierarchical society of this sort really be so much better than one based on race or sex? I think not. But if we tie the moral principle of equality to the factual equality of the different races or sexes, taken as a whole, our opposition to racism and sexism does not provide us with any basis for objecting to this kind of inegalitarianism.

There is a second important reason why we ought not to base our opposition to racism and sexism on any kind of factual equality, even the limited kind which asserts that variations in capacities and abilities are spread evenly between the different races and sexes: we can have no absolute guarantee that these abilities and capacities really are distributed evenly, without regard to race or sex, among human beings. So far as actual abilities are concerned, there do seem to be certain measurable differences between both races and sexes. These differences do not, of course, appear in each case, but only when averages are taken. More important still, we do not yet know how much of these differences is really due to the different genetic endowments of the various races and sexes, and how much is due to environmental differences that are the result of past and continuing discrimination. Perhaps all of the important differences will eventually prove to be environmental rather than genetic. Anyone opposed to racism and sexism will certainly hope that this will be so, for it will make the task of ending discrimination a lot easier; nevertheless it would be dangerous to rest the case against racism and sexism on the belief that all significant differences are environmental in origin. The opponent of, say, racism who takes this line will be unable to avoid conceding that if differences in ability did after all prove to have some genetic connection with race, racism would in some way be defensible.

It would be folly for the opponent of racism to stake his whole case on a dogmatic commitment to one particular outcome of a difficult scientific issue which is still a long way from being settled. While attempts to prove that differences in certain selected abilities between races and sexes are primarily genetic in origin have certainly not been conclusive, the same must be said of attempts to prove that these differences are largely the result of environment. At this stage of the investigation we cannot be certain which view is correct, however much we may hope it is the latter.

Fortunately, there is no need to pin the case for equality to one particular outcome of this scientific investigation. The appropriate response to those who claim to have found evidence of genetically-based differences in ability between the races or sexes is not to stick to the belief that the genetic explanation must be wrong, whatever evidence to the contrary may turn up: instead we should make it quite clear that the claim to equality does not depend on intelligence, moral capacity, physical strength, or similar matters of fact. Equality is a moral ideal, not a simple assertion of fact. There is no logically compelling reason for assuming that a factual difference in ability between two people justifies any difference in the amount of consideration we give to satisfying their needs and interests. The principle of the equality of human beings is not a description of an alleged actual equality among humans: it is a prescription of how we should treat humans.

Jeremy Bentham incorporated the essential basis of moral equality into his utilitarian system of ethics in the formula: "Each to count for one and none for more than one." In other words, the interests of every being affected by an action are to be taken into account and given the same weight as the like interests of any other being. A later utilitarian, Henry Sidgwick, put the point in this way: "The good of any one individual is of no more importance, from the point of view (if I may say so) of the Universe, than the good of any other."[1] More recently, the leading figures in contemporary moral philosophy have shown a great deal of agreement in specifying as a fundamental presupposition of their moral theories some similar requirement which operates so as to give everyone's interests equal consideration—although they cannot agree on how this requirement is best formulated.[2]

It is an implication of this principle of equality that our concern for others ought not to depend on what they are like, or what abilities they possess—although precisely what this concern requires us to do may vary according to the characteristics of those affected by what we do. It is on this basis that the case against racism and the case against sexism must both ultimately rest; and it is in accordance with this principle that speciesism is also to be condemned. If possessing a higher degree of intelligence does not entitle one human to use another for his own ends, how can it entitle humans to exploit non-humans?

Many philosophers have proposed the principle of equal consideration of interests, in some form or other, as a basic moral principle; but, as we shall see in more detail shortly, not many of them have recognized that this principle applies to members of other species as well as to our own. Bentham was one of the few who did realize this. In a forward-looking passage, written at a time when black slaves in British dominions were still being treated much as we now treat nonhuman animals, Bentham wrote:

> The day *may* come when the rest of the animal creation may acquire those rights which never could have been witholden from them but by the hand of tyranny. The French have already discovered that the blackness of the skin is no reason why a human being should be abandoned without redress to the caprice of a tormentor. It may one day come to be recognized that the number of the legs, the villosity of the skin, or the termination of the *as sacrum,* are reasons equally insufficient for abandoning a sensitive being to the same fate. What else is it that should trace the insuperable line? Is it the faculty of reason, or perhaps the faculty of discourse? But a full grown horse or dog is beyond comparison a more rational, as well as a more conversable animal, than an infant of a day, or a week, or even a month, old. But suppose they were otherwise, what would it avail? The question is not, Can they reason? nor Can they *talk*? but, *Can they suffer*?[3]

In this passage Bentham points to the capacity for suffering as the vital characteristic that gives a being the right to equal consideration. The capacity for suffering—or more strictly, for suffering and/or enjoyment or happiness—is not just another characteristic like the capacity for language, or for higher mathematics. Bentham is not saying that those who try to mark "the insuperable line" that determines whether the interests of a being should be considered happen to have selected the wrong characteristic. The capacity for suffering and enjoying things is a pre-requisite for having interests at all, a condition that must be satisfied before we can speak of interests in any meaningful way. It would be nonsense to say that it was not in the interests of a stone to be kicked along the road by a schoolboy. A stone does not have interests because it cannot suffer. Nothing that we can do to it could possibly make any difference to its welfare. A mouse, on the other hand, does have an interest in not being tormented, because it will suffer if it is.

If a being suffers, there can be no moral justification for refusing to take that suffering into consideration. No matter what the nature of the being, the principle of equality requires that its suffering be counted equally with the like suffering—in so far as rough comparisons can be made—of any other being. If a being is not capable of suffering, or of experiencing enjoyment or happiness, there is nothing to be taken into account. This is why the limit of sentience (using the term as a convenient, if not strictly accurate, shorthand for the capacity to suffer or experience enjoyment or happiness) is the only defensible boundary of concern for the interests of others. To mark this boundary by some characteristic like intelligence or rationality would be to mark it in an arbitrary way. Why not choose some other characteristic, like skin color?

The racist violates the principle of equality by giving greater weight to the interests of members of his own race, when there is a clash between their interests and the interests of those of another race. Similarly the speciesist allows the interests of his own species to override the greater interests of members of other species.[4] The pattern is the same in each case. Most human beings are speciesists. I shall now very briefly describe some of the practices that show this.

For the great majority of human beings, especially in urban, industrialized societies, the most direct form of contact with members of other species is at mealtimes: we eat them. In doing so we treat them purely as means to our ends. We regard their life and well-being as subordinate to our taste for a particular kind of dish. I say "taste" deliberately—this is purely a matter of pleasing our palate. There can be no defence of eating flesh in terms of satisfying nutritional needs, since it has been established beyond doubt that we could satisfy our need for protein and other essential nutrients far more efficiently with a diet that replaced animal flesh by soy beans, or products derived from soy beans, and other high-protein vegetable products.[5]

It is not merely the act of killing that indicates what we are ready to do to other species in order to gratify our tastes. The suffering we inflict on the animals while they are alive is perhaps an even clearer indication of our speciesism than the fact that we are prepared to kill them. In order to have meat on the table at a price that people can afford, our society tolerates methods of meat production that confine sentient animals in cramped, unsuitable conditions for the entire durations of their lives. Animals are treated like machines that convert fodder into flesh, and any innovation that results in a higher "conversion ratio" is liable to be adopted. As one authority on the subject has said, "cruelty is acknowledged only when profitability ceases."[6] So hens are crowded four or five to a cage with a floor area of twenty inches by eighteen inches, or around the size of a single page of the *New York Times*. The cages have wire floors, since this reduces cleaning costs, though wire is unsuitable for the hens' feet; the floors slope, since this makes the eggs roll down for easy collection, although this makes it difficult for the hens to rest comfortably. In these conditions all the birds' natural instincts are thwarted: they cannot stretch their wings fully, walk freely, dust-bathe, scratch the ground, or build a nest. Although they have never known other conditions, observers have noticed that the birds vainly try to perform these actions. Frustrated at their inability to do so, they often develop what farmers call "vices," and peck each other to death. To prevent this, the beaks of young birds are often cut off.

This kind of treatment is not limited to poultry. Pigs are now also being reared in cages inside sheds. These animals are comparable to dogs in intelligence, and need a varied, stimulating environment if they are not to suffer from stress and boredom. Anyone who kept a dog in the way in which pigs are frequently kept would be liable to prosecution, in England at least, but because our interest in exploiting pigs is greater than our interest in exploiting dogs, we object to cruelty to dogs while consuming the produce of cruelty to pigs. Of the other animals, the condition of veal calves is perhaps worst of all, since these animals are so closely confined that they cannot even turn around or get up and lie down freely. In this way they do not develop unpalatable muscle. They are also made anaemic and kept short of roughage, to keep their flesh pale, since white veal fetches a higher price; as a result they develop a craving for iron and roughage, and have been observed to gnaw wood off the sides of their stalls, and lick greedily at any rusty hinge that is within reach.

Since, as I have said, none of these practices cater for anything more than our pleasures of taste, our practice of rearing and killing other animals in order to eat them is a clear instance of the sacrifice of the most important interests of other beings in order to satisfy trivial interests of our own. To avoid speciesism we must stop this practice, and each of us has a moral obligation to cease supporting the practice. Our custom is all the support that the meat-industry needs. The decision to cease giving it that support may be difficult, but it is no more difficult than it would have been for a white Southerner to go against the traditions of his society and free his slaves: if we do not change our dietary habits, how can we censure those slaveholders who would not change their own way of living?

The same form of discrimination may be observed in the widespread practice of experimenting on other species in order to see if certain substances are safe for human beings, or to test some psychological theory about the effect of severe punishment on learning, or to try out various new compounds just in case something turns up. People sometimes think that all this experimentation is for vital medical purposes, and so will reduce suffering overall. This comfortable belief is very wide of the mark. Drug companies test new shampoos and cosmetics that they are intending to put on the market by dropping them into the eyes of rabbits, held open by metal clips, in order to observe what damage results. Food additives, like artificial colorings and preservatives, are tested by what is known as the "LD_{50}"—a test designed to find the level of consumption at which 50% of a group of animals will die. In the process, nearly all of the animals are made very sick before some finally die, and others pull through. If the substance is relatively harmless, as it often is, huge doses have to be force-fed the animals, until in some cases sheer volume or concentration of the substance causes death.

Much of this pointless cruelty goes on in the universities. In many areas of science, non-human animals are regarded as an item of laboratory equipment, to be used and expended as desired. In psychology laboratories experimenters devise endless variations and repetitions of experiments that were of little value in the first place. To quote just one example, from the experimenter's own account in a psychology journal: at the University of Pennsylvania, Perrin S. Cohen hung six dogs in hammocks with electrodes taped to their hind feet. Electric shock of varying intensity was then administered through the electrodes. If the dog learnt to press its head against a panel on the left, the shock was turned off, but otherwise it remained on indefinitely. Three of the dogs, however, were required to wait periods varying from 2 to 7 seconds while being shocked before making the response that turned off the current. If they failed to wait, they received further shocks. Each dog was given from

26 to 46 "sessions" in the hammock, each session consisting of 80 "trials" or shocks, administered at intervals of one minute. The experimenter reported that the dogs, who were unable to move in the hammock, barked or bobbed their heads when the current was applied. The reported findings of the experiment were that there was a delay in the dogs' responses that increased proportionately to the time the dogs were required to endure the shock, but a gradual increase in the intensity of the shock had no systematic effect in the timing of the response. The experiment was funded by the National Institutes of Health, and the United States Public Health Service.[7]

In this example, and countless cases like it, the possible benefits to mankind are either non-existent or fantastically remote; while the certain losses to members of other species are very real. This is, again, a clear indication of speciesism.

In the past, argument about vivisection has often missed this point, because it has been put in absolutist terms: Would the abolitionist be prepared to let thousands die if they could be saved by experimenting on a single animal? The way to reply to this purely hypothetical question is to pose another: Would the experimenter be prepared to perform his experiment on an orphaned human infant, if that were the only way to save many lives? (I say "orphan" to avoid the complication of parental feelings, although in doing so I am being overfair to the experimenter, since the nonhuman subjects of experiments are not orphans.) If the experimenter is not prepared to use an orphaned human infant, then his readiness to use non-humans is simple discrimination, since adult apes, cats, mice and other mammals are more aware of what is happening to them, more self-directing and, so far as we can tell, at least as sensitive to pain, as any human infant. There seems to be no relevant characteristic that human infants possess that adult mammals do not have to the same or a higher degree. (Someone might try to argue that what makes it wrong to experiment on a human infant is that the infant will, in time and if left alone, develop into more than the nonhuman, but one would then, to be consistent, have to oppose abortion, since the fetus has the same potential as the infant—indeed, even contraception and abstinence might be wrong on this ground, since the egg and sperm, considered jointly, also have the same potential. In any case, this argument still gives us no reason for selecting a nonhuman, rather than a human with severe and irreversible brain damage, as the subject for our experiments.)

The experimenter, then, shows a bias in favor of his own species whenever he carries out an experiment on a nonhuman for a purpose that he would not think justified him in using a human being at an equal or lower level of sentience, awareness, ability to be self-directing, etc. No one familiar with the kind of results yielded by most experiments on animals can have the slightest doubt that if this bias were eliminated the number of experiments performed would be a minute fraction of the number performed today.

Experimenting on animals, and eating their flesh, are perhaps the two major forms of speciesism in our society. By comparison, the third and last form of speciesism is so minor as to be insignificant, but it is perhaps of some special interest to those for whom this article was written. I am referring to speciesism in contemporary philosophy.

Philosophy ought to question the basic assumptions of the age. Thinking through, critically and carefully, what most people take for granted is, I believe, the chief task of philosophy, and it is this task that makes philosophy a worthwhile activity. Regrettably, philosophy does not always live up to its historic role. Philosophers are human beings and they are subject to all the preconceptions of the society to which they belong. Sometimes they succeed in breaking free of the prevailing ideology: more often they become its most sophisticated defenders. So, in this case, philosophy as practiced in the universities today does not challenge anyone's preconceptions about our relations with other species. By their writings, those philosophers who tackle problems that touch upon the issue reveal that they make the same unquestioned assumptions as most other humans, and what they say tends to confirm the reader in his or her comfortable speciesist habits.

I could illustrate this claim by referring to the writings of philosophers in various fields—for instance, the attempts that have been made by those interested in rights to draw the boundary of the sphere of rights so that it runs parallel to the biological boundaries of the species *homo sapiens,* including infants and even mental defectives, but excluding those other beings of equal or greater capacity who are so useful to us at mealtimes and in our laboratories. I think it would be a more appropriate conclusion to this article, however, if I concentrated on the problem with which we have been centrally concerned, the problem of equality.

It is significant that the problem of equality, in moral and political philosophy, is invariably formulated in terms of human equality. The effect of this is that the question of the equality of other animals does not confront the philosopher, or student, as an issue itself—and this is already an indication of the failure of philosophy to challenge accepted beliefs. Still, philosophers have found it difficult to discuss the issue of human equality without raising, in a paragraph or two, the question of the status of other animals. The reason for this, which should be apparent from what I have said already, is that if humans are to be regarded as equal to one another, we need some sense of "equal" that does not require any actual, descriptive equality of capacities, talents or other qualities. If equality is to be related to any actual characteristics of humans, these characteristics must be some lowest common denominator, pitched so low that no human lacks them—but then the philosopher comes up against the catch that any such set of characteristics which covers *all* humans will not be possessed *only by humans.* In other words, it turns out that in the only sense in which we can truly say, as an assertion of fact, that all humans are equal, at least some members of other species are also equal—equal, that is, to each other and to humans. If, on the other hand, we regard the statement "All humans are equal" in some non-factual way, perhaps as a prescription, then, as I have already argued, it is even more difficult to exclude non-humans from the sphere of equality.

This result is not what the egalitarian philosopher originally intended to assert. Instead of accepting the radical outcome to which their own reasonings naturally point, however, most philosophers try to reconcile their beliefs in human equality and animal inequality by arguments that can only be described as devious.

As a first example, I take William Frankena's well-known article "The Concept of Social Justice."[8] Frankena opposes the idea of basing justice on merit, because he sees that this could lead to highly inegalitarian results. Instead he proposes the principle that:

> All men are to be treated as equals, not because they are equal, in any respect, but simply because they are human. They are human because they have emotions and desires, and are able to think, and hence are capable of enjoying a good life in a sense in which other animals are not.

But what is this capacity to enjoy the good life which all humans have, but no other animals? Other animals have emotions and desires, and appear to be capable of enjoying a good life. We may doubt that they can think—although the behavior of some apes, dolphins and even dogs suggests that some of them can—but what is the relevance of thinking? Frankena goes on to admit that by "the good life" he means "not so much the morally good life as the happy or satisfactory life," so thought would appear to be unnecessary for enjoying the good life; in fact to emphasize the need for thought would make difficulties for the egalitarian since only some people are capable of leading intellectually satisfying lives, or morally good lives. This makes it difficult to see what Frankena's principle of equality has to do with simply being *human*. Surely every sentient being is capable of leading a life that is happier or less miserable than some alternative life, and hence has a claim to be taken into account. In this respect the distinction between humans and non-humans is not a sharp division, but rather a continuum along which we move gradually, and with overlaps between the species, from simple capacities for enjoyment and satisfaction, or pain and suffering, to more complex ones.

Faced with a situation in which they see a need for some basis for the moral gulf that is commonly thought to separate humans and animals, but finding no concrete difference that will do the job without undermining the equality of humans, philosophers tend to waffle. They resort to high-sounding phrases like "the intrinsic dignity of the human individual";[9] they talk of the "intrinsic worth of all men" as if men (humans?) had some worth that other beings did not,[10] or they say that humans, and only humans, are "ends in themselves," while "everything other than a person can only have value for a person."[11]

This idea of a distinctive human dignity and worth has a long history; it can be traced back directly to the Renaissance humanists, for instance to Pico della Mirandola's *Oration on the Dignity of Man*. Pico and other humanists based their estimate of human dignity on the idea that man possessed the central, pivotal position in the "Great Chain of Being" that led from the lowliest forms of matter to God himself; this view of the universe, in turn, goes back to both classical and Judeo-Christian doctrines. Contemporary philosophers have cast off these metaphysical and religious shackles and freely invoke the dignity of mankind without needing to justify the idea at all. Why should we not attribute "intrinsic dignity" or "intrinsic worth" to ourselves? Fellow-humans are unlikely to reject the accolades we so generously bestow on them, and those to whom we deny the honor are unable to object. Indeed, when one thinks only of humans, it can be very liberal, very progressive, to talk of the dignity of all human beings. In so doing, we implicitly condemn slavery, racism, and other violations of human rights. We admit that we ourselves are in some fundamental sense on a par with the poorest, most ignorant members of our own species. It is only when we think of humans as no more than a small sub-group of all the beings that inhabit our planet that we may realize that in elevating our own species we are at the same time lowering the relative status of all other species.

The truth is that the appeal to the intrinsic dignity of human beings appears to solve the egalitarian's problems only as long as it goes unchallenged. Once we ask *why* it should be that all humans—including infants, mental defectives, psychopaths, Hitler, Stalin and the rest—have some kind of dignity or worth that no elephant, pig, or chimpanzee can ever achieve, we see that this question is as difficult to answer as our original request for some relevant fact that justifies the inequality of humans and other animals. In fact, these two questions are really one: talk of intrinsic dignity or moral worth only takes the problem back one step, because any satisfactory defence of the claim that all and only humans have intrinsic dignity would need to refer to some relevant capacities or characteristics that all and only humans possess. Philosophers frequently introduce ideas of dignity, respect and worth at the point at which other reasons appear to be lacking, but this is hardly good enough. Fine phrases are the last resource of those who have run out of arguments.

In case there are those who still think it may be possible to find some relevant characteristic that distinguishes all humans from all members of other species, I shall refer again, before I conclude, to the existence of some humans who quite clearly are below the level of awareness, self-consciousness, intelligence, and sentience, of many nonhumans. I am thinking of humans with severe and irreparable brain damage, and also of infant humans. To avoid the complication of the relevance of a being's potential, however, I shall henceforth concentrate on permanently retarded humans.

Philosophers who set out to find a characteristic that will distinguish humans from other animals rarely take the course of abandoning these groups of humans by lumping them in with the other animals. It is easy to see why they do not. To take this line without re-thinking our attitudes to other animals would entail that we have the right to perform painful experiments on retarded humans for trivial reasons; similarly it would follow that we had the right to rear and kill these humans for food. To most philosophers these consequences are as unacceptable as the view that we should stop treating nonhumans in this way.

Of course, when discussing the problem of equality it is possible to ignore the problem of mental defectives, or brush it aside as if somehow insignificant.[12] This is the easiest way out. What else remains? My final example of speciesism in contemporary philosophy has been selected to show what happens when a writer is prepared to face the question of human equality and animal equality without ignoring the existence of mental defectives, and without resorting to obscurantist mumbo-jumbo. Stanley Benn's clear and honest article "Egalitarianism and Equal Consideration of Interests"[13] fits this description.

Benn, after noting the usual "evident human inequalities," argues, correctly I think, for equality of consideration as the only possible basis for egalitarianism. Yet Benn, like other writers, is thinking only of "equal consideration of human interests." Benn is quite open in his defence of this restriction of equal consideration:

> Not to possess human shape *is* a disqualifying condition. However faithful or intelligent a dog may be, it would be a monstrous sentimentality to attribute to him interests that could be weighed in an equal balance with those of human beings ... if, for instance, one had to decide between feeding a hungry baby or a hungry dog, anyone who chose the dog would generally be reckoned morally defective, unable to recognize a fundamental inequality of claims.

This is what distinguishes our attitude to animals from our attitude to imbeciles. It would be odd to say that we ought to respect equally the dignity or personality of the imbecile and of the rational man ... but there is nothing odd about saying that we should respect their interests equally, that is, that we should give to the interests of each the same serious consideration as claims to considerations necessary for some standard of well being that we can recognize and endorse.

Benn's statement of the basis of the consideration we should have for imbeciles seems to me correct, but why should there be any fundamental inequality of claims between a dog and a human imbecile? Benn sees that if equal consideration depended on rationality, no reason could be given against using imbeciles for research purposes, as we now use dogs and guinea pigs. This will not do: "But of course we do distinguish imbeciles from animals in this regard," he says. That the common distinction is justifiable is something Benn does not question; his problem is how it is to be justified. The answer he gives is this:

> ... we respect the interests of men and give them priority over dogs not *insofar* as they are rational, but because rationality is the human norm. We say it is *unfair* to exploit the deficiencies of the imbecile who falls short of the norm, just as it would be unfair, and not just ordinarily dishonest, to steal from a blind man. If we do not think in this way about dogs, it is because we do not see the irrationality of the dog as a deficiency or a handicap, but as normal for the species. The characteristics, therefore, that distinguish the normal man from the normal dog make it intelligible for us to talk of other men having interests and capacities, and therefore claims, of precisely the same kind as we make on our own behalf. But although these characteristics may provide the point of the distinction between men and other species, they are not in fact the qualifying conditions for membership, or the distinguishing criteria of the class of morally

considerable persons; and this is precisely because a man does not become a member of a different species, with its own standards of normality, by reason of not possessing these characteristics.

The final sentence of this passage gives the argument away. An imbecile, Benn concedes, may have no characteristics superior to those of a dog; nevertheless this does not make the imbecile a member of "a different species" as the dog is. *Therefore* it would be "unfair" to use the imbecile for medical research as we use the dog. But why? That the imbecile is not rational is just the way things have worked out, and the same is true of the dog—neither is any more responsible for their mental level. If it is unfair to take advantage of an isolated defect, why is it fair to take advantage of a more general limitation? I find it hard to see anything in this argument except a defence of preferring the interests of members of our own species because they are members of our own species. To those who think there might be more to it, I suggest the following mental exercise. Assume that it has been proven that there is a difference in the average, or normal, intelligence quotient for two different races, say whites and blacks. Then substitute the term "white" for every occurrence of "men" and "black" for every occurrence of "dog" in the passage quoted; and substitute "high I.Q." for "rationality" and when Benn talks of "imbeciles" replace this term by "dumb whites"—that is, whites who fall well below the normal white I.Q. score. Finally, change "species" to "race." Now re-read the passage. It has become a defence of a rigid, no-exceptions division between whites and blacks, based on I.Q. scores, *not withstanding an admitted overlap* between whites and blacks in this respect. The revised passage is, of course, outrageous, and this is not only because we have made fictitious assumptions in our substitutions. The point is that in the original passage Benn was defending a rigid division in the amount of consideration due to members of different species, despite admitted cases of overlap. If the original did not, at first reading strike us as being as outrageous as the revised version does, this is largely because although we are not racists ourselves, most of us are speciesists. Like the other articles, Benn's stands as a warning of the ease with which the best minds can fall victim to a prevailing ideology.

Notes

1. *The Methods of Ethics* (7th Ed.), p. 382.

2. For example, R. M. Hare, *Freedom and Reason* (Oxford, 1963) and J. Rawls, A *Theory of Justice* (Harvard, 1972); for a brief account of the essential agreement on this issue between these and other positions, see R. M. Hare, "Rules of War and Moral Reasoning," *Philosophy and Public Affairs,* 1:2 (1972).

3. *Introduction to the Principles of Morals and Legislation,* ch. XVII.

4. I owe the term "speciesism" to Dr. Richard Ryder.

5. In order to produce 1 lb. of protein in the form of beef or veal, we must feed 21 lbs. of protein to the animal. Other forms of livestock are slightly less inefficient, but the average ratio in the U.S. is still 1:8. It has been estimated that the amount of protein lost to humans in this way is equivalent to 90% of the annual world protein deficit. For a brief account, see Frances Moore Lappé, *Diet for a Small Planet* (New York: Friends of The Earth/Ballantine, 1971) pp. 4–11.

6. Ruth Harrison, *Animal Machines* (London: Stuart, 1964). For an account of farming conditions, see my *Animal Liberation* (New York Review Company, 1975).

7. *Journal of the Experimental Analysis of Behavior,* 13:1 (1970).

8. W. Frankena, "The Concept of Social Justice" in *Social Justice,* ed. R. Brandt, (Englewood Cliffs; Prentice Hall, 1962), p. 19.

9. Frankena, "The Concept of Social Justice," p. 23.

10. H. A. Bedau, "Egalitarianism and the Idea of Equality" in *Nomos IX: Equality,* ed. J. R. Pennock and J. W. Chapman (New York: Chapman, 1967).

11. G. Vlastos, "Justice and Equality" in Brandt, *Social Justice,* p. 48.

12. For example, Bernard Williams, "The Idea of Equality" in *Philosophy, Politics and Society* (second series), ed. P. Laslett and W. Runciman (Oxford: Blackwell, 1962), p. 118; J. Rawls, A *Theory of Justice,* pp. 509–10.

13. Bedau, *Nomos IX: Equality.* The passages quoted start on p. 62.

6B2. "Animal Liberation": A Critique*

By Michael Fox

I n the past few years, philosophers have actively engaged in a (long overdue) discussion of racism and sexism. The growing body of literature on these subjects has just begun to generate a new controversey—or perhaps more accurately, to rekindle an old one—in which some of those interested in applied ethics or "current moral issues" are taking part: that of so-called animal liberation. I wish to examine here two very recent attempts to provide the cause of humane treatment for animals with a solid philosophical foundation. These are Peter Singer's *Animal Liberation: A New Ethics for Our Treatment of Animals* and Tom Regan's "The Moral Basis of Vegetarianism."[1] The authors of both works propound a doctrine of animal liberation, that is, liberation from being discriminated against and used at pleasure by human beings—Singer's treatment of the subject being both wider (supporting antivivisectionism as well as vegetarianism) and developed in more detail. They do so by advancing a case for granting moral rights to animals (the right to equal consideration of interests, the right to life).

Now, I am prepared to concede that animals may have interests, in the sense that they are capable of distinguishing between states of consciousness which are painful and those that are pleasurable or accompany physical well-being, and that they seek the latter and avoid the former as much as possible.[2] It does not seem objectionable to say that because animals are capable of pleasure as well as suffering a pleasurable existence is "in their best interest." Both Singer and Regan assert that animals' painful and pleasurable experiences are qualitatively and quantitatively the same as those of humans and that, hence, animals have a capacity to enjoy life equal to that of humans. But even leaving aside this peculiar claim (which I must confess I have no idea how to interpret or evaluate), it is very difficult to see how animals' having interests per se entails their having equal interests with human beings and, as a consequence, the associated moral rights that the latter possess. Singer and Regan, in other words, take animals' capacity to enjoy and suffer as the sole fact that is morally relevant to these alleged entailments.

---

* An earlier version of this article was presented at the Philosophy Colloquium, Queen's University, Kingston, and subsequently published as the Editor's Column in *Queen's Quarterly* 83, no. 1 (Spring 1976): 178–87, under the title "The Use and Abuse of Animals." I would like to express my appreciation to the following for advice and helpful criticism: R. Greenwood, director of the Queen's University Animal Care Service, the Office of the Dietician, Kingston General Hospital, Jonathan Mallov, and Warner Wick, editor of *Ethics*.

1 Peter Singer, *Animal Liberation: A New Ethics for Our Treatment of Animals* (New York: New York Review, 1975) (hereafter cited as S), and Tom Regan, "The Moral Basis of Vegetarianism," *Canadian Journal of Philosophy* 5, no. 2 (October 1975): 181–214 (hereafter cited as R).

2 For the purposes of this paper, I shall take "pain" and "suffering" to be equivalent in meaning. "Suffering" is probably a preferable term, since it embraces both physical and psychological distress more readily. Be this as it may; I shall assume that animals, like humans, can and do experience both kinds of distress.

Regan goes further than Singer, however, contending that animals have, in addition to the right, *ceteris paribus,* to equal consideration of interests with humans in the matter of treatment, a natural right to life, which cannot be overridden except by the most stringent utilitarian considerations. He maintains that just as no amount of human pleasure equal to or greater than a given amount of "non-trivial" (R, p. 198) animal suffering caused by man can ever neutralize the moral condemnation engendered by the infliction of that suffering, so, too, the death of an animal cannot, in general, be justified by the amount of human pleasure which is consequent upon it. His reason for saying this is that any argument which purports to show that humans have a right not to be maltreated or unjustly caused to suffer to a degree equal to or greater than the level of someone else's gain in pleasure, or that human beings have a right to life, will also hold in the case of animals (at least higher sentient animals).

I shall argue, against both of these views, that the concept of moral rights cannot be extended to include animals, and that the question of animals' rights is therefore a bogus issue. We may and ought to lie concerned about the welfare of animals and their present exploitation by man because they are sentient beings. But this concern and this simple fact neither license nor entail the postulation of animal rights.

Singer and Regan approach the question of animals' rights by focusing on a condemnation of what Singer calls "speciesism,"[3] which is defined as "a prejudice or attitude of bias toward the interests of members of one's own species and against those of members of other species" (S, p. 7). The main thesis advanced by them is that if we cannot morally justify discriminating against other human beings on grounds of race or sex (for example) then, for exactly the same sorts of reasons, we cannot morally justify discriminatory treatment of animals. Just as there are no morally relevant considerations which warrant exploiting other humans for our own ends, so there are none to warrant the exploitation of nonhumans. Just as there is no difference between human groups (such as those of different races, sexes, or intelligence levels) with respect to their capacity to suffer, so there is none between humans and animals—at least those animals with highly complex nervous systems like our own. From this standpoint humans are animals *tout court* and, as such, do not stand in any position of natural superiority. This is not, of course, to deny any significant differences between humans and animals, and neither Singer nor Regan commits himself to this absurdity. Rather, it is to deny any moral superiority on the part of *Homo sapiens.*

How can this view be sustained? It is important to note that Singer and Regan adopt the principle, first enunciated clearly by Jeremy Bentham in his *Introduction to the Principles of Morals and Legislation* (1789), that the only capacity which counts in assigning moral rights is the capacity to suffer. Color of skin, sex, rationality, intelligence, and ability to communicate are not relevant in justifying unequal treatment. And if they do not count in one instance (discrimination against other humans), then they likewise fail in every other case (including the discriminatory treatment of animals by humans). Everyone recognizes that a mature, healthy horse, cat, or pig is more intelligent than a newborn infant

---

3   A term which he borrows from Richard Ryder, author of *Victims of Science* (London: Davis-Poynter, 1975).

or a severely retarded child and communicates at least as well. Furthermore, if the ability to reason is to be attributed to any of these, it will be to the animals and not the infant. But although humans are supposed to exercise rightful dominion over all of nature because they are more intelligent, rational, capable of communicating, and so on, no one suggests that we may eat, experiment upon, hunt, or make shoes and soap out of infants and retarded children because they are less endowed in these same respects (and, indeed, less so than some animals). Nor does anyone believe that a mongoloid baby may be used as a mere means to someone else's ends because it has less potentiality for developing those capacities that are most characteristically human, though this "lesser potentiality" argument is often used as the justification for our treatment of animals—in spite of the fact that some animals have greater potentiality than many defective infants for developing or exhibiting the same valued characteristics. Now why are these things so? Singer and Regan hold that we have no answer to this question, and this merely shows the hypocrisy and logical inconsistency in our dealings with the animal kingdom.

The strategy of both authors throughout is to force the reader into the uncomfortable position of either (a) having to refute their claims—many of which are presented quite convincingly—or (b) confessing that he is a speciesist, and that since speciesism is morally indefensible and, hence, reprehensible, he must either change his behavior toward animals or be a hypocrite. Thus, Regan argues, for example, that if pain is truly an intrinsic evil—regardless of whose pain it is—if causing pain is therefore prima facie morally wrong and must always be justified, and if today's large-scale rearing and slaughtering methods do genuinely involve the unjustified infliction of (a great deal of) pain and suffering on undeserving animals, then these methods are immoral and should be prohibited. It follows that anyone who benefits from the rearing and slaughtering practices in question tacitly condones and helps sustain and encourage them and is hence in a morally untenable position.[4] For both Regan and Singer, we "are rationally compelled to regard animals as beings who count for something when we attempt to determine what we morally ought or ought not to do" (R, p. 186).

Now there is a great deal in the Singer-Regan position that merits extended discussion, and I can only hope to consider some main points here. I shall start with the question of the nature of rights itself. On this vital matter, Singer has surprisingly little to say. He accepts without reservation Bentham's line of reasoning, which may be reconstructed as follows: (1) "equal consideration of interests ... [is] a basic moral principle" (S, p. 8); (2) "the capacity for suffering and enjoyment is a *prerequisite for having interests at all*" (S, p. 9; Singer's italics); (3) this capacity is the condition that requires us to grant a right to equal consideration of interests; (4) any being which possesses this

---

4   Though I do not wish to digress too far here, it might be argued (and a Marxist surely would) that almost all the benefits which North Americans enjoy routinely, as part of their exorbitantly high standard of living relative to the rest of the world, depend upon the correlated and disproportionate suffering and deprivation caused others elsewhere in the world (e.g., in those countries which supply the raw materials that North American industry and consumerism devour at a staggering rate). From this perspective, the animal-rights debate seems considerably less urgent and a relatively "safe" area of controversy. One wonders why here (as elsewhere) there is so much concern for the plight of animals and evidently so little for that of humans.

capacity has such a right and should be treated accordingly; (5) some animals possess this capacity; (6) therefore, some animals have a right to equal consideration of interests when we decide how to treat them (i.e., when suffering and enjoyment are possible consequences of our behavior toward them). (Regan's grounds for assigning this same right to animals closely parallel those stated here and do not require independent consideration. He asserts the additional right to life, which Singer does not explicitly do, because he clearly recognizes that the Benthamite argument above entails that if animals were reared and slaughtered painlessly, and their natural needs allowed to be satisfied during their rearing period, there would be no moral objection to meat eating.) Singer and Regan both acknowledge that, as Singer points out, "the basic principle of equality does not require equal or identical *treatment*; it requires equal *consideration.* Equal consideration for different beings may lead to different treatment and different rights" (S, p. 3; Singer's italics). So it might be said that differential treatment and granting of rights can be justified by empirically determined differences among individuals or groups—but only in the light of this general moral principle. (For example, it is not society's obligation to send hopelessly brain-damaged children through elementary school, but giving them costly medical care may well be.) What is important to maintain, then, is the principle of equitable or fair treatment. Hence (known and possibly discoverable) empirical differences between races or sexes cannot by themselves justify differential treatment, for "equality is a moral idea, not an assertion of fact" (S, p. 5). Humans are, in many ways, unequal in fact. So any attempt to make equality rest on characteristics that all human beings share, both authors agree, has to seek the lowest common denominator. But this will not enable us to separate human beings from animals as beings whose interests deserve equal consideration, for the lowest common denominator will have to be nothing other than the capacity to enjoy and suffer.

There are numerous flaws in this argument. First of all, if all talk about interests (in the moral sense) is meaningful only in relation to the capacity to enjoy and suffer, then it now appears that the ethical idea of equality does rest upon an assertion of factual equality after all—namely, the fact that all human beings have this capacity. But if one factual consideration is relevant to assigning rights to beings, then others may be as well, and the question of the other capacities which beings must have to be proper subjects of morality becomes important to consider.

Singer and Regan insist that any characteristic which is used as a basis for assigning moral rights to human beings must be universal, that is, possessed by all humans without exception. This is why they fasten onto the capacity to enjoy and suffer, with the totally unsurprising result that we cannot find anything else that fits this extreme requirement. But even if we play by their rules, it can be doubted whether any characteristic is really universal in so strong a sense, the capacity to enjoy and suffer included. To begin with, as physiologists well know, there is a rare but thoroughly documented condition called "congenital universal indifference (or insensitivity) to pain,"[5] which is characterized by complete absence, throughout life, of any pain-sensing capability. But if the capacity to experience

---

5   See, for example, D. W. Baxter and J. Olszewski, "Congenital Universal Insensitivity to Pain," *Brain* 83 (1960); 381–93.

pain is missing, any rights predicated on it must vanish as well. In addition, completely anesthetized, hypnotized, or deeply comatose human beings lack the capacity in question and hence, too, any corresponding rights. If this is an unacceptable conclusion, however (as I think everyone would agree it is), it is instructive to see why. The reasons are: (1) that basic moral rights arise from other criteria than the capacity to enjoy and suffer (this capacity being a necessary but not a sufficient condition for the granting of the rights in question);[6] and (2) that what counts in establishing rights are the characteristics that a certain class of beings share in general, even if not universally.

The search for attributes that all humans, without exception, share in common and which are supposed to furnish the grounds for the assigning of moral rights to them, as well as to any sufficiently similar beings, is bound to be futile; for even the capacity of humans to experience pain and pleasure falls short of complete universality, as we have just seen. But then if we shift our attention instead to capacities that are nearly or virtually universal among humans, as we are forced to do, it will be seen that humans generally possess them and (probably) no animals do and, hence, that the concept of a moral right to equitable treatment makes no sense except as applied to humans.

Regan challenges the assertion that humans are different from animals in morally relevant ways by declaring that the opponents of his position bear the onus of providing adequate empirical evidence to support their claim and that such evidence does not at present exist. It seems to me, however, that (as I think most people would agree on the basis of experience) all animals—whatever their place on the evolutionary scale—are prima facie significantly different kinds of creatures from humans, in morally relevant as well as other ways, and that the onus of proof is therefore on those who would hold otherwise. Further, though experimental psychology, comparative anatomy and physiology, and the biological and ecological sciences are far from being able to yield all the evidence Regan demands, it is surely naive in the extreme to blithely brush aside as of no consequence (R, p. 191) all the data on the important differences between animals and humans which have been gathered to date. Let us assume, for the sake of argument, that it could be shown to everyone's satisfaction that animals experience pleasure and pain in the same way and to the same degree as humans and, further, that many also reason, have emotions, use some form of symbolic communication, and have a sense of self-identity. It still would not follow that these facts would qualify such animals to be recipients of moral rights. For, as H. J. McCloskey has recently pointed out,[7] to appreciate (1) that the existence of certain higher animals is intrinsically valuable because they possess some capacities (like sentience, intelligence, emotionality), the exercise of which enables them to enjoy a quality of life that humans can recognize as of value, (2) that they are capable of suffering psychologically as well as physically, and, (3) that as a consequence of 1 and 2, good reasons are required to be given for killing such beings is not tantamount to, and does not entail, assigning animals moral rights.

---

6 Singer actually appears to acknowledge 1 when he says, "The capacity for suffering and enjoyment is *a prerequisite for having interests at all* (p. 9; Singer's italics). But if so, then he owes us an account of the other prerequisites.

7 H. J. McCloskey, "The Right to Life," *Mind* 84 (July 1975): 410–13.

What other characteristics, then, that humans share in general should be cited in order to give an adequate account of the reasons why they have, and animals lack, moral rights? A complete list of these would have to include at least the following: the capacities to be critically self-aware, manipulate concepts, use a sophisticated language,[8] reflect, plan, deliberate, choose, and accept responsibility for acting. In a similar vein, McCloskey suggests that the crucial morally relevant characteristics of humans which we are seeking here are those which manifest the attributes of truly autonomous beings, where this entails being capable of acting freely, choosing and deciding rationally in the fullest sense, creating, and self-making (self-realizing).[9] I have drawn attention to certain cognitive capacities (critical self-awareness, concept manipulation, and the use of a sophisticated language) because these are the essential tools or vehicles by means of which an agent's autonomy is evolved, made known to himself reflexively, and manifested or expressed. The possession of these cognitive capacities, therefore, is a necessary pre-prequisite for autonomy, which is the capacity for self-conscious, voluntary, and deliberate action, in the fullest sense of these words. Autonomy, which thus entails certain cognitive capacities, is necessary (and, together with the capacity to enjoy and suffer, sufficient) for the possession of moral rights. It follows that all (and only) those beings which are members of a species of which it is true in general (i.e., typically the case at maturity, assuming normal development) that members of the species in question can be considered autonomous agents are beings endowed with moral rights.[10]

Now how can the above entailments be defended? I cannot give full treatment to this important topic here, but I should like to suggest that only autonomous beings, as just described, can and do belong to a moral community, which is the sort of social group within which (and only within which) such concepts as those of rights and duties have any meaning and application. For it is only in a community of interacting autonomous beings of this sort that there can be the kind of mutual recognition required for these concepts to evolve and be understood. Obligations and rights, as well as the moral discourse generated by these and ancillary notions, are functions of mutual recognition and accountability and are, consequently, inapplicable outside the context specified. It should be made clear that the foregoing is not an attempt merely to legislate concerning the kinds of beings which qualify as possessors of moral rights. Rather, my analysis is meant to suggest that, since the only species we know of that has developed the concepts of rights and obligations (and the institutions associated with them) is *Homo sapiens,* there must be something about this peculiar sort of social being that accounts for the phenomenon in question. And my argument is that the relevant features of humans (other than their capacity to suffer and enjoy) that explain why they have rights are their

---

8   Regan assumes that the use of language is an uncomplicated phenomenon and that granting animals the same language capacities as humans is unproblematic. This is certainly empirically false, but it is also philosophically naive. As McCloskey points out (ibid., p. 413), it is not just the capacity to use language that is involved when we refer to humans' linguistic endowment as a criterion for the assigning of rights; it is their capacity to use language "to express thoughts, decisions, wishes, choices."

9   Ibid., pp. 413–17.

10   To anticipate a possible objection, individual beings (say one or more extraterrestrials) may be granted moral rights on the same basis (i.e., if they show evidence of autonomy, etc.), without our knowing the general characteristics of their species.

possession of a certain kind of consciousness, particular cognitive and linguistic abilities, and the capacity to comprehend, undertake, and carry out obligations and to expect the same of like beings.

The considerations taken up briefly here should suffice to show that regarding the cognitive capacities of human beings as relevant to the question of possessing moral rights is not tantamount to invoking some simplistic notion of humans' rationality to settle a vastly more complex set of issues, as proponents of animal rights frequently suppose. Singer and Regan just conveniently leave the capacities I have mentioned out of the picture or else systematically misunderstand and underrate their significance.

I conclude, then, that it is difficult to see how an argument for ascribing specifically moral rights to animals can get started. And if it cannot get off the ground, then there also appears to be no case for saying either that animals ought not to be treated as means to human ends, provided that they are treated in as humane a manner as possible in the process, or that they have a right to life. But it seems to me that the overall obligation to prevent or minimize animal suffering should suffice as a moral basis for prohibiting the atrocious conditions of crowding and confinement that prevail on modern "factory farms," for drastically curtailing the use of animals in excruciating but pointless experiments in product testing, and for ending other inhumane practices (in slaughtering, trapping, the keeping of pets, hunting, racing, and so on). Undoubtedly animals should not be maltreated. They should not be made to suffer needlessly or excessively.[11] Singer and Regan are surely correct to single out animals' capacity to suffer as the reason why we should treat them humanely. But it is no more clear how this extends moral rights to them than how our dawning ecological sense that we ought not to waste natural resources and systematically ravage the environment would establish moral rights for trees, lakes, or mineral deposits. What should be said is that we have an obligation to avoid mistreating animals, but that this is an obligation without a corresponding right on the part of the beings affected by our behavior.[12]

The argument presented thus far undercuts Singer's surely exaggerated claim that philosophers have felt the need to posit "some basis for the moral gulf that is commonly thought to separate humans and animals, but can find no concrete difference that will do this without undermining the equality of humans ..." (S, pp. 266–67). It is difficult to see how Singer can maintain the position that there is no "moral gulf" separating humans from animals when he also makes the following (clearly speciesist)

---

11   Singer often talks as if we have an obligation to avoid ever deliberately causing an animal to suffer. Thus, for instance, we may not eat any organism, however rudimentary a form of life, if it shows any sign whatever that it has the capacity to suffer (S, pp. 185 ff.). But even our treatment of other human beings does not rest upon so unrealistic and stringent an attitude toward suffering. Punishment and the infliction of pain are often required in the pursuit of a greater long-range good for the individual concerned or sometimes for society as a whole.

12   I realize that denying the universal correlation of rights and obligations is controversial. It seems to me, however, that there is at least one clear case of an obligation which each of us has but for which it makes no sense to speak of anyone else possessing a corresponding right. The case I have in mind is the general duty of benevolence, where there is no individual or group that can justifiably claim a right to benevolent treatment from a given person. Another example would be duties toward oneself (supposing there to be such).

remark "It is not arbitrary to hold that the life of a self-aware being, capable of abstract thought, of planning for the future, of complex acts of communication, and so on, is more valuable than the life of a being without these capacities" (S, p. 23). For once it is admitted that certain forms of life are inherently more valuable than others (valuable to whom, incidentally, if not to humans?), then it has already been conceded that the allegedly "more valuable" beings have a greater claim to life, pleasure, and freedom from suffering than those lacking the capacities in question. And it becomes highly problematic how Singer can go on from there to defend such views as that animal pleasure and pain are both qualitatively and quantitatively the same as those of humans and that their capacity for enjoying life is the same.

There is another important weakness in Singer's central argument, arising from his own (otherwise carefully suppressed) speciesist commitments. At one point, he considers the objection that if it were shown that plants, too, are capable of suffering (though there seems to be no reason at all for thinking they are), then it would follow that humans would be morally obliged to starve themselves to death rather than cause suffering to sentient beings. Singer replies, "If we must inflict pain or starve, we would then have to choose the lesser evil. Presumably it would still be true that plants suffer less than animals, and therefore it would still be better to eat plants than to eat animals" (p. 263). But if human beings have this kind of (absolute?) right to live and are thereby licensed to "choose the lesser evil" in this way, then they are in a position of "moral superiority" after all vis-à-vis the rest of nature. The same point can be made in regard to Singer's claim (p. 260) that animal populations may legitimately be controlled if they threaten our food supply. How can this be so if their right to life is on a par with our own? No answer is given.

It would seem to follow that if "lesser evil" arguments are to be admitted into this discussion, then the use of animals in research may be justified by a similar (and, in fact, the usual) appeal: that it is a lesser evil to subject some animals to suffering and possible death than to allow many humans (including those yet unborn) to suffer and perhaps die for lack of the knowledge that could be attained by such research. Singer does document in vivid and sordid detail the extraordinary and often apparently pointless suffering to which many laboratory animals have been routinely forced to submit. One can agree that this situation is shameful and intolerable, if accurately reported. However, the reader is never provided with descriptions of experiments that have proved beneficial to mankind—or to animals, for that matter. Nor is he ever given a larger context into which to place the experiments depicted in order to be able to judge whether they are, indeed, pointless and whether the number of pointless experiments is within the margin of error that might be acceptable when so many experiments are being performed by so many different investigators. But without this larger context, and in light of the general failure of the case for animal rights, and for the consequent principle that animals may not justifiably be used for human ends where some degree of discomfort or suffering is caused, no grounds remain for Singer's assertion that "if the experimenter would not be prepared to use a human infant then his readiness to use nonhuman animals reveals an unjustifiable form of discrimination on the basis of species ..." (S, p. 79).

Singer's entire case against animal experiments is buttressed by carefully selected and one-sided accounts, partial information, and outright misinformation. Of course, there are some insensitive persons engaged in animal research, just as there are in research on humans. But why one should regard these as typical remains a mystery—unless one deliberately adopts an a priori assumption about the fiendish qualities of laboratory personnel. Singer conveniently neglects to acknowledge the degree to which researchers have come to realize that better and more consistent experimental results are obtained when their animals' total environments are controlled and made to simulate natural conditions as closely as possible. It has also been found that when this is done fewer animals are needed for a given experiment than would otherwise be used. This shows that even aside from humane considerations, intelligent researchers have a practical interest in treating their animals with the best of care. Though it is, of course, difficult to say how many have learned these lessons, there is reason to believe that there is a growing awareness of the need for better animal care in the laboratory.

Singer points out that there are alternatives to experiments on animals, such as the use of tissue cultures and computer simulations. No doubt further advances will be made in these areas. But he misleads the reader seriously when he suggests that virtually all animal experiments could be eliminated by such surrogates. For the biomedical researcher and the teacher there is no substitute for a complete and healthy cardiovascular or central nervous system.

It might be of interest to note here that in Canada (about which Singer says nothing), most animal experiments for research purposes are done under guidelines set down by the Canadian Council on Animal Care. Under its experiment assessment scheme, responsibility for appraising the amount of pain an animal will be likely to suffer, as well as its environment, housing, procurement and transportation, anesthesia and euthanasia, is assigned to local committees at each research facility. These guidelines, though voluntary rather than legislated, have proved highly effective in preventing the abuse of animals. In Ontario, these matters are the subject of broad-ranging legislation, covering everything from anticipated pain levels in experiments to all aspects of hygiene in the research facility; from the animal's total artificial environment to postoperative care. Ontario Regulation 139/71 frequently states that conditions must be "suitable for the health, comfort and welfare" of the animals concerned.[13] Maybe the lot of most research animals is not so fortunate, but at least we can see that the situation is not so hopeless as Singer would have us believe and is, in fact, improving.

Again, Singer paints a shocking and lamentable picture of the competitive and virtually unregulated large-scale animal-rearing methods utilized in the United States and Britain. Something clearly must be done to prevent and eventually ban the abuses he documents. But this issue has little to do with the "justification" for eating meat, if one is required. Singer gives a very distorted view of humans' position in nature. If humans are part of the larger ecological balance and are responsible for maintaining it, then why may they not be viewed as part of the carnivorous, as well as the herbivorous, food chain as well?

---

13 Ontario Regulation 139/71, "Research and Supply Facilities," *Regulations Made under the Animals for Research Act, 1968–69* (Toronto: William Kinmond, Queen's Printer and Publisher, 1971), passim.

How can these eating habits be regarded as antinature, so long as humans replenish (or allow to replenish) what they take away? And if intervening in the natural course of events to regulate the rampant population of certain species through fertility control (as we saw above Singer suggests) is not somehow immoral, then in what way is farming livestock or commercial fishing inherently wrong? These questions are never realistically or fully examined by Singer, Regan, or any other animal-rights spokesman, as far as I know. It is true that unlike other animals, humans have the capacity to weigh alternatives and make a conscious moral choice whether or not to kill animals for food, as Singer points out (S, p. 250). But what follows from this fact? Simply that meat-eating humans are morally obligated to address themselves to the problem of animal suffering caused by intensive farming methods and to demand that the rearing (and slaughtering) of animals be brought under strict regulation.

Singer admits that there is no logical inconsistency in thinking that animals should be guarded against cruel treatment and simultaneously including meat in one's diet. However, he tries to base part of his argument for becoming a vegetarian on the claim that

> ... practically and psychologically it is impossible to be consistent in one's concern for nonhuman animals while continuing to dine on them. If we are prepared to take the life of another being merely in order to satisfy our taste for a particular type of food, then that being is no more than a means to our end. In time we will come to regard pigs, cattle and chickens as things for us to use, no matter how strong our compassion may be; and when we find that to continue to obtain supplies of the bodies of these animals at a price we are able to pay it is necessary to change their living conditions a little, we will be unlikely to regard these changes too critically. The factory farm is nothing more than the application of technology to the idea that animals are means to our ends. [S, p. 172]

Here we have a classical "slippery slope" argument. Such arguments should always be considered suspect, since careful scrutiny usually shows them to be meretricious at best. In this case, it is not at all clear that people would fail, out of narrow self-interest, to challenge the abominable farming methods Singer describes, if they were confronted with the full facts. To declare otherwise is to assume an unwarrantably low estimate of human decency (a typical feature of slippery slope arguments, incidentally). To go beyond this and assert that "no one in the habit of eating an animal can be completely without bias in judging whether the conditions in which that animal is reared cause suffering" (S, p. 172) is plainly absurd (cf., "No radical can get a fair and impartial trial by jury"). Singer's own conversion from meat eater to vegetarian itself falsifies this extreme dictum. Finally, factory farms are only a technological triumph in the eyes of their greedy and unfeeling proprietors.

The strongest part of Singer's case against meat eating is his brief discussion of the world food crisis. It is a patent truth that by any conceivable health standards most North Americans are overfed.

More specifically, they eat far more meat than is necessary to maintain adequate nutrition. Surely some of the excess food they consume should be distributed, in some form, to the starving millions of the world. One can only agree. Modern livestock farming on a grand scale also wastes a colossal amount of feed grains on animals which, in times past, would simply have fed off the land Even if, contrary to fact, none of this feed grain could be used to nourish humans elsewhere in the world, at least the land which yields the grain could be sown with high-protein-yielding crops, such as soybeans, according to Singer. There is no doubt a good deal of truth in this last point as well, and we are here presented with a serious moral problem concerning the world food supply. But even this fails to establish a case for vegetarianism. All it establishes is that we should eat far less meat so that factory farms become obsolete and that, in conjunction with this, arable land should be turned over to the production of high-protein crops, where possible, so that world hunger can be alleviated somewhat.

We are given to believe that meat is merely a wasteful luxury and that vegetarians are probably healthier than meat eaters. But meat is not a wasteful luxury per se: ruminants can (whereas humans cannot) utilize cellulose to produce carbohydrates and, from these, synthesize certain essential amino acids, the constituents of protein. Not only this, but as Singer himself notes (S, p. 196), "animal foods ... have a very well-balanced amino acid composition" (which a diet that excludes all animal products can easily lack); they are also a natural source of vitamin B_{12}, which pure vegetarians (or "vegans") have to take as a dietary supplement for complete nutrition. Nor is it clear that being a vegetarian is inherently healthier, unless one is impressed by such statistics as that concerning "the 'mean transit time' of food through the digestive system" (76–83 hours for nonvegetarians, 42 hours for vegetarians), and the highly speculative inferences based on them (S, p. 193 n.).[14]

In closing his book, Singer emphasizes the rational approach he has taken toward the discussion of speciesism: "I have *argued* for it, appealing to reason rather than to emotion or sentiment" (p. 270; Singer's italics). In general this is true, and his arguments are often well constructed. But he likewise often falls considerably short of such objective detachment: "Flesh taints our meals. Disguise it as we may, the fact remains that the centerpiece of our dinner has come to us from the slaughterhouse, dripping blood. Untreated and unrefrigerated, it soon begins to putrefy and stink. When we eat it, it sits heavily in our stomachs, blocking our digestive processes until, days later, we struggle to excrete it" (p. 193). There are also repeated examples, both in Singer's book (pp. x, 81–82, 240–41) and in Regan's article (pp. 182, 213–14), of a disturbing penchant for equating experiments on animals with Nazi death-camp experiments performed on hapless, unanesthetized human beings. The overall impression one gains from such lurid passages, despite the legitimate points Singer and Regan may have to make regarding unjustified cruelty, is that in their zeal to help launch a new and popular

---

14   If a shorter "mean transit time" indicates a healthier diet, it follows that an alcoholic should be healthier than a vegetarian, since alcohol passes through the digestive system much faster than a vegetarian's diet. The reasons why a vegetarian diet is processed faster by the body than a nonvegetarian diet are: (*a*) roughage stimulates peristalsis and (*b*) the body can utilize less of the bulk of vegetable matter (cellulose) than that of meat and, hence, discards it more rapidly. This is an example of the tendency that many philosophers have of failing to get their facts straight when borrowing empirical data from other disciplines.

movement for animal rights they cast their usual caution to the breeze. Or are we, instead, merely being subjected to the self-righteousness of recent converts?

Is speciesism immoral, then? The only sensible verdict, I think, is "not proven." The effort to establish speciesism, on the one hand, and racism and sexism, on the other, as identical forms of unjust discrimination which flout basic moral rights cannot succeed because neither Singer nor Regan has shown any meaningful sense in which rights can and should be ascribed to animals to begin with.

It would seem, therefore, that while the issue of the infliction of unnecessary and excessive pain and suffering upon animals, which is not offset by a significant long-term gain in pleasure for humans or for animals, is a matter that ought to concern every thoughtful and caring person, the question of animals' rights in which it has unfortunately become embroiled—and hence, that of "animal liberation"—is a nonstarter. But Regan and Singer have an important moral to teach. As Regan rightly notes, "The onus of justification is always on anyone who supports a practice that is known to inflict nontrivial, undeserved pain on a sentient creature to show that, in doing so, he is not doing anything wrong" (R, p. 202). The point implicit here, it seems to me, is not that everyone who finds great animal suffering odious to contemplate should rush to dump the contents of his frozen meat locker and medicine cabinet or makeup kit in the garbage pail and don the nearest available (synthetic) hair shirt. Rather, it is that each concerned person should consider carefully the amount of meat a sensible diet, the world food crisis, and the cost of living really should allow him or her, and what sorts of drugs and cosmetics are really essential, and begin lobbying for the elimination of factory farms and for more stringent regulation of the use of animals in experiments and product testing.

Singer and Regan confine themselves to a consideration of the rights and wrongs of killing animals for purely human ends. If I may be permitted to append my own moral to this discussion, a somewhat wider perspective on the issues they have raised would suggest that political involvement aimed at effecting the redistribution of world food supplies and the control of proliferating consumer goods is also morally obligatory.

6A3. The Ethics of Respect for Nature

By Paul W. Taylor

Human-Centered and Life-Centered Systems of Environmental Ethics

In this paper I show how the taking of a certain ultimate moral attitude toward nature, which I call "respect for nature," has a central place in the foundations of a life-centered system of environmental ethics. I hold that a set of moral norms (both standards of character and rules of conduct) governing human treatment of the natural world is a rationally grounded set if and only if, first, commitment to those norms is a practical entailment of adopting the attitude of respect for nature as an ultimate moral attitude, and second, the adopting of that attitude on the part of all rational agents can itself be justified. When the basic characteristics of the attitude of respect for nature are made clear, it will be seen that a life-centered system of environmental ethics need not be holistic or organicist in its conception of the kinds of entities that are deemed the appropriate objects of moral concern and consideration. Nor does such a system require that the concepts of ecological homeostasis, equilibrium, and integrity provide us with normative principles from which could be derived (with the addition of factual knowledge) our obligations with regard to natural ecosystems. The "balance of nature" is not itself a moral norm, however important may be the role it plays in our general outlook on the natural world that underlies the attitude of respect for nature. I argue that finally it is the good (well-being, welfare) of individual organisms, considered as entities having inherent worth, that determines our moral relations with the Earth's wild communities of life.

In designating the theory to be set forth as life-centered, I intend to contrast it with all anthropocentric views. According to the latter, human actions affecting the natural environment and its nonhuman inhabitants are right (or wrong) by either of two criteria: they have consequences which are favorable (or unfavorable) to human well-being, or they are consistent (or inconsistent) with the system of norms that protect and implement human rights. From this human-centered standpoint it is to humans and only to humans that all duties are ultimately owed. We may have responsibilities *with regard to* the natural ecosystems and biotic communities of our planet, but these responsibilities are in every case based on the contingent fact that our treatment of those ecosystems and communities of life can further the realization of human values and/or human rights. We have no obligation to promote or protect the good of nonhuman living things, independently of this contingent fact.

A life-centered system of environmental ethics is opposed to human-centered ones precisely on this point. From the perspective of a life-centered theory, we have prima facie moral obligations that are owed to wild plants and animals themselves as members of the Earth's biotic community. We are morally bound (other things being equal) to protect or promote their good for *their* sake. Our duties to respect the integrity of natural ecosystems, to preserve endangered species, and to avoid environmental pollution stem from the fact that these are ways in which we can help make it possible for wild species populations to achieve and maintain a healthy existence in a natural state. Such obligations are due those living things out of recognition of their inherent worth. They are entirely additional to and independent of the obligations we owe to our fellow humans. Although many of the actions that fulfill one set of obligations will also fulfill the other, two different grounds of obligation are involved. Their well-being, as well as human well-being, is something to be realized *as an end in itself.*

If we were to accept a life-centered theory of environmental ethics, a profound reordering of our moral universe would take place. We would begin to look at the whole of the Earth's biosphere in a new light. Our duties with respect to the "world" of nature would be seen as making prima facie claims upon us to be balanced against our duties with respect to the "world" of human civilization. We could no longer simply take the human point of view and consider the effects of our actions exclusively from the perspective of our own good.

The Good of a Being and the Concept of Inherent Worth

What would justify acceptance of a life-centered system of ethical principles? In order to answer this it is first necessary to make clear the fundamental moral attitude that underlies and makes intelligible the commitment to live by such a system. It is then necessary to examine the considerations that would justify any rational agent's adopting that moral attitude.

Two concepts are essential to the taking of a moral attitude of the sort in question. A being which does not "have" these concepts, that is, which is unable to grasp their meaning and conditions of applicability, cannot be said to have the attitude as part of its moral outlook. These concepts are, first, that of the good (well-being, welfare) of a living thing, and second, the idea of an entity possessing inherent worth. I examine each concept in turn.

(1) Every organism, species population, and community of life has a good of its own which moral agents can intentionally further or damage by their actions. To say that an entity has a good of its own is simply to say that, without reference to any *other* entity, it can be benefited or harmed. One can act in its overall interest or contrary to its overall interest, and environmental conditions can be good for it (advantageous to it) or bad for it (disadvantageous to it). What is good for an entity is what "does it good" in the sense of enhancing or preserving its life and well-being. What is bad for an entity is something that is detrimental to its life and well-being.

We can think of the good of an individual nonhuman organism as consisting in the full development of its biological powers. Its good is realized to the extent that it is strong and healthy. It possesses whatever capacities it needs for successfully coping with its environment and so preserving its existence throughout the various stages of the normal life cycle of its species. The good of a population or community of such individuals consists in the population or community maintaining itself from generation to generation as a coherent system of genetically and ecologically related organisms whose average good is at an optimum level for the given environment. (Here *average good* means that the degree of realization of the good of *individual organisms* in the population or community is, on average, greater than it would be under any other ecologically functioning order of interrelations among those species populations in the given ecosystem.)

The idea of a being having a good of its own, as I understand it, does not entail that the being must have interests or take an interest in what affects its life for better or for worse. We can act in a being's interest or contrary to its interest without its being interested in what we are doing to it in the sense of wanting or not wanting us to do it. It may, indeed, be wholly unaware that favorable and unfavorable events are taking place in its life. I take it that trees, for example, have no knowledge or desires or feelings. Yet it is undoubtedly the case that trees can be harmed or benefited by our actions. We can crush their roots by running a bulldozer too close to them. We can see to it that they get adequate nourishment and moisture by fertilizing and watering the soil around them. Thus we can help or hinder them in the realization of their good. It is the good of trees themselves that is thereby affected. We can similarly act so as to further the good of an entire tree population of a certain species (say, all the redwood trees in a California valley) or the good of a whole community of plant life in a given wilderness area, just as we can do harm to such a population or community.

When construed in this way, the concept of a being's good is not coextensive with sentience or the capacity for feeling pain. William Frankena has argued for a general theory of environmental ethics in which the ground of a creature's being worthy of moral consideration is its sentience. I have offered some criticisms of this view elsewhere, but the full refutation of such a position, it seems to me, finally depends on the positive reasons for accepting a life-centered theory of the kind I am defending in this essay.[1]

It should be noted further that I am leaving open the question of whether machines—in particular, those which are not only goal directed, but also self-regulating—can properly be said to have a good of their own.[2] Since I am concerned only with human treatment of wild organisms, species populations, and communities of life as they occur in our planet's natural ecosystems, it is to those entities alone that the concept "having a good of its own" will here be applied. I am not denying that other living things, whose genetic origin and environmental conditions have been produced, controlled, and manipulated by humans for human ends, do have a good of their own in the same sense as do wild plants and animals. It is not my purpose in this essay, however, to set out or defend the principles that should guide our conduct with regard to their good. It is only insofar as their production and use by humans have good or ill effects upon natural ecosystems and their wild inhabitants that the ethics of respect for nature comes into play.

(2) The second concept essential to the moral attitude of respect for nature is the idea of inherent worth. We take that attitude toward wild living things (individuals, species populations, or whole biotic communities) when and only when we regard them as entities possessing inherent worth. Indeed, it is only because they are conceived in this way that moral agents can think of themselves as having validly binding duties, obligations, and responsibilities that are *owed* to them as their *due*. I am not at this juncture arguing why they *should* be so regarded; I consider it at length below. But so regarding them is a presupposition of our taking the attitude of respect toward them and accordingly understanding ourselves as bearing certain moral relations to them. This can be shown as follows:

What does it mean to regard an entity that has a good of its own as possessing inherent worth? Two general principles are involved: the principle of moral consideration and the principle of intrinsic value.

According to the principle of moral consideration, wild living things are deserving of the concern and consideration of all moral agents simply in virtue of their being members of the Earth's community of life. From the moral point of view their good must be taken into account whenever it is affected for better or worse by the conduct of rational agents. This holds no matter what species the creature belongs to. The good of each is to be accorded some value and so acknowledged as having some weight in the deliberations of all rational agents. Of course, it may be necessary for such agents to act in ways contrary to the good of this or that particular organism or group of organisms in order to further the good of others, including the good of humans. But the principle of moral consideration prescribes that, with respect to each being an entity having its own good, every individual is deserving of consideration.

The principle of intrinsic value states that, regardless of what kind of entity it is in other respects, if it is a member of the Earth's community of life, the realization of its good is something *intrinsically* valuable. This means that its good is prima facie worthy of being preserved or promoted as an end in itself and for the sake of the entity whose good it is. Insofar as we regard any organism, species population, or life community as an entity having inherent worth, we believe that it must never be treated as if it were a mere object or thing whose entire value lies in being instrumental to the good of some other entity. The well-being of each is judged to have value in and of itself.

Combining these two principles, we can now define what it means for a living thing or group of living things to possess inherent worth. To say that it possesses inherent worth is to say that its good is deserving of the concern and consideration of all moral agents, and that the realization of its good has instrinsic value, to be pursued as an end in itself and for the sake of the entity whose good it is.

The duties owed to wild organisms, species populations, and communities of life in the Earth's natural ecosystems are grounded on their inherent worth. When rational, autonomous agents regard such entities as possessing inherent worth, they place intrinsic value on the realization of their good and so hold themselves responsible for performing actions that will have this effect and for refraining from actions having the contrary effect.

...

The Justifiability of the Attitude of Respect for Nature

The attitude we take toward living things in the natural world depends on the way we look at them, on what kind of beings we conceive them to be, and on how we understand the relations we bear to them. Underlying and supporting our attitude is a certain belief system that constitutes a particular world view or outlook on nature and the place of human life in it. To give good reasons for adopting the attitude of respect for nature, then, we must first articulate the *belief system* which underlies and supports that attitude. If it appears that the belief system is internally coherent and well-ordered, and if, as far as we can now tell, it is consistent with all known scientific truths relevant to our knowledge of the object of the attitude (which in this case includes the whole set of the Earth's natural ecosystems and their communities of life), then there remains the task of indicating why scientifically informed and rational thinkers with a developed capacity of reality awareness can find it acceptable as a way of conceiving of the natural world and our place in it. To the extent we can do this we provide at least a reasonable argument for accepting the belief system and the ultimate moral attitude it supports.

I do not hold that such a belief system can be *proven* to be true, either inductively or deductively. As we shall see, not all of its components can be stated in the form of empirically verifiable propositions. Nor is its internal order governed by purely logical relationships. But the system as a whole, I contend, constitutes a coherent, unified, and rationally acceptable "picture" or "map" of a total world. By examining each of its main components and seeing how they fit together, we obtain a scientifically informed and well-ordered conception of nature and the place of humans in it.

This belief system underlying the attitude of respect for nature I call (for want of a better name) "the biocentric outlook on nature." Since it is not wholly analyzable into empirically confirmable assertions, it should not be thought of as simply a compendium of the biological sciences concerning our planet's ecosystems. It might best be described as a philosophical world view, to distinguish it from a scientific theory or explanatory system. However, one of its major tenets is the great lesson we have learned from the science of ecology: the interdependence of all living things in an organically unified order whose balance and stability are necessary conditions for the realization of the good of its constituent biotic communities.

...

The Biocentric Outlook on Nature

The biocentric outlook on nature has four main components. (1) Humans are thought of as members of the Earth's community of life, holding that membership on the same terms as apply to all the nonhuman members. (2) The Earth's natural ecosystems as a totality are seen as a complex web of interconnected elements, with the sound biological functioning of each being dependent on the sound biological functioning of the others. (This is the component referred to above as the great lesson that the science of ecology has taught us.) (3) Each individual organism is conceived of as a teleological center of life, pursuing its own good in its own way. (4) Whether we are concerned with standards of merit or with the concept of inherent worth, the claim that humans by their very nature are superior to other species is a groundless claim and, in the light of elements (1), (2), and (3) above, must be rejected as nothing more than an irrational bias in our own favor.

The conjunction of these four ideas constitutes the biocentric outlook on nature. In the remainder of this paper I give a brief account of the first three components, followed by a more detailed analysis of the fourth. I then conclude by indicating how this outlook provides a way of justifying the attitude of respect for nature.

Humans as Members of the Earth's Community of Life

We share with other species a common relationship to the Earth. In accepting the biocentric outlook we take the fact of our being an animal species to be a fundamental feature of our existence. We consider it an essential aspect of "the human condition." We do not deny the differences between ourselves and other species, but we keep in the forefront of our consciousness the fact that in relation to our planet's natural ecosystems we are but one species population among many. Thus, we acknowledge our origin in the very same evolutionary process that gave rise to all other species and we recognize ourselves to be confronted with similar environmental challenges to those that confront them. The laws of genetics, of natural selection, and of adaptation apply equally to all of us as biological creatures. In this light we consider ourselves as one with them, not set apart from them. We, as well as they, must face certain basic conditions of existence that impose requirements on us for our survival and well-being. Each animal and plant is like us in having a good of its own. Although our human good (what is of true value in human life, including the exercise of individual autonomy in choosing our own particular value systems) is not like the good of a nonhuman animal or plant, it can no more be realized than their good can without the biological necessities for survival and physical health.

When we look at ourselves from the evolutionary point of view we see that not only are we very recent arrivals on Earth, but that our emergence as a new species on the planet was originally an event of no particular importance to the entire scheme of things. The Earth was teeming with life long before we appeared. Putting the point metaphorically, we are relative newcomers, entering a home that has been the residence of others for hundreds of millions of years, a home that must now be shared by all of us together.

The comparative brevity of human life on Earth may be vividly depicted by imagining the geological time scale in spatial terms. Suppose we start with algae, which have been around for at least 600 million years. (The earliest protozoa actually predated this by several *billion* years.) If the time that algae have been here were represented by the length of a football field (300 feet), then the period during which sharks have been swimming in the world's oceans and spiders have been spinning their webs would occupy three quarters of the length of the field; reptiles would show up at about the center of the field; mammals would cover the last third of the field; hominids (mammals of the family *Hominidae*) the last two feet; and the species *Homo sapiens* the last six inches.

Whether this newcomer is able to survive as long as other species remains to be seen. But there is surely something presumptuous about the way humans look down on the "lower" animals, especially those that have become extinct. We consider the dinosaurs, for example, to be biological failures, though they existed on our planet for 65 million years. One writer has made the point with beautiful simplicity:

> We sometimes speak of the dinosaurs as failures; there will be time enough for
> that judgment when we have lasted even for one tenth as long. ...[3]

The possibility of the extinction of the human species, a possibility which starkly confronts us in the contemporary world, makes us aware of another respect in which we should not consider ourselves privileged beings in relation to other species. This is the fact that the well-being of humans is dependent upon the ecological soundness and health of many plant and animal communities, while their soundness and health does not in the least depend upon human well-being. Indeed, from their standpoint the very existence of humans is quite unnecessary. Every last man, woman, and child could disappear from the face of the Earth without any significant detrimental consequence for the good of wild animals and plants. On the contrary, many of them would be greatly benefited. The destruction of their habitats by human "developments" would cease. The poisoning and polluting of their environment would come to an end. The Earth's land, air, and water would no longer be subject to the degradation they are now undergoing as the result of large-scale technology and uncontrolled population growth. Life communities in natural ecosystems would gradually return to their former healthy state. Tropical forests for example, would again be able to make their full contribution to a life-sustaining atmosphere for the whole planet. The rivers, lakes, and oceans of the world would (perhaps) eventually become clean again. Spilled oil, plastic trash, and even radioactive waste might finally, after many centuries, cease doing their terrible work. Ecosystems would return to their proper balance, suffering only the disruptions of natural events such as volcanic eruptions and glaciation.

From these the community of life could recover, as it has so often done in the past. But the ecological disasters now perpetrated on it by humans—disasters from which it might never recover—these it would no longer have to endure.

If, then, the total, final, absolute extermination of our species (by our own hands?) should take place and if we should not carry all the others with us into oblivion, not only would the Earth's community of life continue to exist, but in all probability its well-being would be enhanced. Our presence, in short, is not needed. If we were to take the standpoint of the community and give voice to its true interest, the ending of our six-inch epoch would most likely be greeted with a hearty "Good riddance!"

The Natural World as an Organic System

To accept the biocentric outlook and regard ourselves and our place in the world from its perspective is to see the whole natural order of the Earth's biosphere as a complex but unified web of interconnected organisms, objects, and events. The ecological relationships between any community of living things and their environment form an organic whole of functionally interdependent parts. Each ecosystem is a small universe itself in which the interactions of its various species populations comprise an intricately woven network of cause–effect relations. Such dynamic but at the same time relatively stable structures as food chains, predator-prey relations, and plant succession in a forest are self-regulating, energy-recycling mechanisms that preserve the equilibrium of the whole.

As far as the well-being of wild animals and plants is concerned, this ecological equilibrium must not be destroyed. The same holds true of the well-being of humans. When one views the realm of nature from the perspective of the biocentric outlook, one never forgets that in the long run the integrity of the entire biosphere of our planet is essential to the realization of the good of its constituent communities of life, both human and nonhuman.

Although the importance of this idea cannot be overemphasized, it is by now so familiar and so widely acknowledged that I shall not further elaborate on it here. However, I do wish to point out that this "holistic" view of the Earth's ecological systems does not itself constitute a moral norm. It is a factual aspect of biological reality, to be understood as a set of causal connections in ordinary empirical terms. Its significance for humans is the same as its significance for nonhumans, namely, in setting basic conditions for the realization of the good of living things. Its ethical implications for our treatment of the natural environment lie entirely in the fact that our *knowledge* of these causal connections is an essential *means* to fulfilling the aims we set for ourselves in adopting the attitude of respect for nature. In addition, its theoretical implications for the ethics of respect for nature lie in the fact that it (along with the other elements of the biocentric outlook) makes the adopting of that attitude a rational and intelligible thing to do.

Individual Organisms as Teleological Centers of Life

As our knowledge of living things increases, as we come to a deeper understanding of their life cycles, their interactions with other organisms, and the manifold ways in which they adjust to the environment, we become more fully aware of how each of them is carrying out its biological functions according to the laws of its species-specific nature. But besides this, our increasing knowledge and understanding also develop in us a sharpened awareness of the uniqueness of each individual organism. Scientists who have made careful studies of particular plants and animals, whether in the field or in laboratories, have often acquired a knowledge of their subjects as identifiable individuals. Close observation over extended periods of time has led them to an appreciation of the unique "personalities" of their subjects. Sometimes a scientist may come to take a special interest in a particular animal or plant, all the while remaining strictly objective in the gathering and recording of data. Nonscientists may likewise experience this development of interest when, as amateur naturalists, they make accurate observations over sustained periods of close acquaintance with an individual organism. As one becomes more and more familiar with the organism and its behavior, one becomes fully sensitive to the particular way it is living out its life cycle. One may become fascinated by it and even experience some involvement with its good and bad fortunes (that is, with the occurrence of environmental conditions favorable or unfavorable to the realization of its good). The organism comes to mean something to one as a unique, irreplaceable individual. The final culmination of this process is the achievement of a genuine understanding of its point of view and, with that understanding, an ability to "take" that point of view. *Conceiving of it as a center of life, one is able to look at the world from its perspective.*

This development from objective knowledge to the recognition of individuality, and from the recognition of individuality to full awareness of an organism's standpoint, is a process of heightening our consciousness of what it means to be an individual living thing. We grasp the particularity of the organism as a teleological center of life, striving to preserve itself and to realize its own good in its own unique way.

It is to be noted that we need not be falsely anthropomorphizing when we conceive of individual plants and animals in this manner. Understanding them as teleological centers of life does not necessitate "reading into" them human characteristics. We need not, for example, consider them to have consciousness. Some of them may be aware of the world around them and others may not. Nor need we deny that different kinds and levels of awareness are exemplified when consciousness in some form is present. But conscious or not, all are equally teleological centers of life in the sense that each is a unified system of goal-oriented activities directed toward their preservation and well-being.

When considered from an ethical point of view, a teleological center of life is an entity whose "world" can be viewed from the perspective of *its* life. In looking at the world from that perspective we recognize objects and events occurring in its life as being beneficent, maleficent, or indifferent. The first are occurrences which increase its powers to preserve its existence and realize its good.

The second decrease or destroy those powers. The third have neither of these effects on the entity. With regard to our human role as moral agents, we can conceive of a teleological center of life as a being whose standpoint we can take in making judgments about what events in the world are good or evil, desirable or undesirable. In making those judgments it is what promotes or protects the being's own good, not what benefits moral agents themselves, that sets the standard of evaluation. Such judgments can be made about anything that happens to the entity which is favorable or unfavorable in relation to its good. As was pointed out earlier, the entity itself need not have any (conscious) *interest* in what is happening to it for such judgments to be meaningful and true.

It is precisely judgments of this sort that we are disposed to make when we take the attitude of respect for nature. In adopting that attitude those judgments are given weight as reasons for action in our practical deliberation. They become morally relevant facts in the guidance of our conduct.

The Denial of Human Superiority

This fourth component of the biocentric outlook on nature is the single most important idea in establishing the justifiability of the attitude of respect for nature. Its central role is due to the special relationship it bears to the first three components of the outlook. This relationship will be brought out after the concept of human superiority is examined and analyzed.[4]

In what sense are humans alleged to be superior to other animals? We are different from them in having certain capacities that they lack. But why should these capacities be a mark of superiority? From what point of view are they judged to be signs of superiority and what sense of superiority is meant? After all, various nonhuman species have capacities that humans lack. There is the speed of a cheetah, the vision of an eagle, the agility of a monkey. Why should not these be taken as signs of *their* superiority over humans?

One answer that comes immediately to mind is that these capacities are not as *valuable* as the human capacities that are claimed to make us superior. Such uniquely human characteristics as rational thought, aesthetic creativity, autonomy and self-determination, and moral freedom, it might be held, have a higher value than the capacities found in other species. Yet we must ask: valuable to whom, and on what grounds?

The human characteristics mentioned are all valuable to humans. They are essential to the preservation and enrichment of our civilization and culture. Clearly it is from the human standpoint that they are being judged to be desirable and good. It is not difficult here to recognize a begging of the question. Humans are claiming human superiority from a strictly human point of view, that is, from a point of view in which the good of humans is taken as the standard of judgment. All we need to do is to look at the capacities of nonhuman animals (or plants, for that matter) from the standpoint of *their* good to find a contrary judgment of superiority. The speed of the cheetah, for example, is a sign of its superiority to humans when considered from the standpoint of the good of its species.

If it were as slow a runner as a human, it would not be able to survive. And so for all the other abilities of nonhumans which further their good but which are lacking in humans. In each case the claim to human superiority would be rejected from a nonhuman standpoint

When superiority assertions are interpreted in this way, they are based on judgments of *merit*. To judge the merits of a person or an organism one must apply grading or ranking standards to it. (As I show below, this distinguishes judgments of merit from judgments of inherent worth.) Empirical investigation then determines whether it has the "good-making properties" (merits) in virtue of which it fulfills the standards being applied. In the case of humans, merits may be either moral or nonmoral. We can judge one person to be better than (superior to) another from the moral point of view by applying certain standards to their character and conduct. Similarly, we can appeal to nonmoral criteria in judging someone to be an excellent piano player, a fair cook, a poor tennis player, and so on. Different social purposes and roles are implicit in the making of such judgments, providing the frame of reference for the choice of standards by which the nonmoral merits of people are determined. Ultimately such purposes and roles stem from a society's way of life as a whole. Now a society's way of life may be thought of as the cultural form given to the realization of human values. Whether moral or nonmoral standards are being applied, then, all judgments of people's merits finally depend on human values. All are made from an exclusively human standpoint.

The question that naturally arises at this juncture is: why should standards that are based on human values be assumed to be the only valid criteria of merit and hence the only true signs of superiority? This question is especially pressing when humans are being judged superior in merit to nonhumans. It is true that a human being may be a better mathematician than a monkey, but the monkey may be a better tree climber than a human being. If we humans value mathematics more than tree climbing, that is because our conception of civilized life makes the development of mathematical ability more desirable than the ability to climb trees. But is it not unreasonable to judge nonhumans by the values of human civilization, rather than by values connected with what it is for a member of *that* species to live a good life? If all living things have a good of their own, it at least makes sense to judge the merits of nonhumans by standards derived from *their* good. To use only standards based on human values is already to commit oneself to holding that humans are superior to nonhumans, which is the point in question.

A further logical flaw arises in connection with the widely held conviction that humans are *morally* superior beings because they possess, while others lack, the capacities of a moral agent (free will, accountability, deliberation, judgment, practical reason). This view rests on a conceptual confusion. As far as moral standards are concerned, only beings that have the capacities of a moral agent can properly be judged to be *either* moral (morally good) *or* immoral (morally deficient). Moral standards are simply not applicable to beings that lack such capacities. Animals and plants cannot therefore be said to be morally inferior in merit to humans. Since the only beings that can have moral merits *or be deficient in such merits* are moral agents, it is conceptually incoherent to judge humans as superior to nonhumans on the ground that humans have moral capacities while nonhumans don't.

Up to this point I have been interpreting the claim that humans are superior to other living things as a grading or ranking judgment regarding their comparative merits. There is, however, another way of understanding the idea of human superiority. According to this interpretation, humans are superior to nonhumans not as regards their merits but as regards their inherent worth. Thus, the claim of human superiority is to be understood as asserting that all humans, simply in virtue of their humanity, have *a greater inherent worth* than other living things.

The inherent worth of an entity does not depend on its merits.[5] To consider something as possessing inherent worth, we have seen, is to place intrinsic value on the realization of its good. This is done regardless of whatever particular merits it might have or might lack, as judged by a set of grading or ranking standards. In human affairs, we are all familiar with the principle that one's worth as a person does not vary with one's merits or lack of merits. The same can hold true of animals and plants. To regard such entities as possessing inherent worth entails disregarding their merits and deficiencies, whether they are being judged from a human standpoint or from the standpoint of their own species.

The idea of one entity having more merit than another, and so being superior to it in merit, makes perfectly good sense. Merit is a grading or ranking concept, and judgments of comparative merit are based on the different degrees to which things satisfy a given standard. But what can it mean to talk about one thing being superior to another in inherent worth? In order to get at what is being asserted in such a claim it is helpful first to look at the social origin of the concept of degrees of inherent worth.

The idea that humans can possess different degrees of inherent worth originated in societies having rigid class structures. Before the rise of modern democracies with their egalitarian outlook, one's membership in a hereditary class determined one's social status. People in the upper classes were looked up to, while those in the lower classes were looked down upon. In such a society one's social superiors and social inferiors were clearly defined and easily recognized.

Two aspects of these class-structured societies are especially relevant to the idea of degrees of inherent worth. First, those born into the upper classes were deemed more worthy of respect than those born into the lower orders. Second, the superior worth of upper class people had nothing to do with their merits nor did the inferior worth of those in the lower classes rest on their lack of merits. One's superiority or inferiority entirely derived from a social position one was born into. The modern concept of a meritocracy simply did not apply. One could not advance into a higher class by any sort of moral or nonmoral achievement. Similarly, an aristocrat held his title and all the privileges that went with it just because he was the eldest son of a titled nobleman. Unlike the bestowing of knighthood in contemporary Great Britain, one did not earn membership in the nobility by meritorious conduct.

We who live in modern democracies no longer believe in such hereditary social distinctions. Indeed, we would wholeheartedly condemn them on moral grounds as being fundamentally unjust.

We have come to think of class systems as a paradigm of social injustice, it being a central principle of the democratic way of life that among humans there are no superiors and no inferiors. Thus we have rejected the whole conceptual framework in which people are judged to have different degrees of inherent worth. That idea is incompatible with our notion of human equality based on the doctrine that all humans, simply in virtue of their humanity, have the same inherent worth. (The belief in universal human rights is one form that this egalitarianism takes.)

The vast majority of people in modern democracies, however, do not maintain an egalitarian outlook when it comes to comparing human beings with other living things. Most people consider our own species to be superior to all other species and this superiority is understood to be a matter of inherent worth, not merit. There may exist thoroughly vicious and depraved humans who lack all merit. Yet because they are human they are thought to belong to a higher class of entities than any plant or animal. That one is born into the species *Homo sapiens* entitles one to have lordship over those who are one's inferiors, namely, those born into other species. The parallel with hereditary social classes is very close. Implicit in this view is a hierarchical conception of nature according to which an organism has a position of superiority or inferiority in the Earth's community of life simply on the basis of its genetic background. The "lower" orders of life are looked down upon and it is considered perfectly proper that they serve the interests of those belonging to the highest order, namely humans. The intrinsic value we place on the well-being of our fellow humans reflects our recognition of their rightful position as our equals. No such intrinsic value is to be placed on the good of other animals, unless we choose to do so out of fondness or affection for them. But their well-being imposes no moral requirement on us. In this respect there is an absolute difference in moral status between ourselves and them.

This is the structure of concepts and beliefs that people are committed to insofar as they regard humans to be superior in inherent worth to all other species. I now wish to argue that this structure of concepts and beliefs is completely groundless. If we accept the first three components of the biocentric outlook and from that perspective look at the major philosophical traditions which have supported that structure, we find it to be at bottom nothing more than the expression of an irrational bias in our own favor. The philosophical traditions themselves rest on very questionable assumptions or else simply beg the question. I briefly consider three of the main traditions to substantiate the point. These are classical Greek humanism, Cartesian dualism, and the Judeo-Christian concept of the Great Chain of Being.

The inherent superiority of humans over other species was implicit in the Greek definition of man as a rational animal. Our animal nature was identified with "brute" desires that need the order and restraint of reason to rule them (just as reason is the special virtue of those who rule in the ideal state). Rationality was then seen to be the key to our superiority over animals. It enables us to live on a higher plane and endows us with a nobility and worth that other creatures lack. This familiar way of comparing humans with other species is deeply ingrained in our Western philosophical outlook.

The point to consider here is that this view does not actually provide an argument *for* human superiority but rather makes explicit the framework of thought that is implicitly used by those who think of humans as inherently superior to nonhumans. The Greeks who held that humans, in virtue of their rational capacities, have a kind of worth greater than that of any nonrational being, never looked at rationality as but one capacity of living things among many others. But when we consider rationality from the standpoint of the first three elements of the ecological outlook, we see that its value lies in its importance for *human* life. Other creatures achieve their species-specific good without the need of rationality, although they often make use of capacities that human lack. So the humanistic outlook of classical Greek thought does not give us a neutral (nonquestion-begging) ground on which to construct a scale of degrees of inherent worth possessed by different species of living things.

The second tradition, centering on the Cartesian dualism of soul and body, also fails to justify the claim to human superiority. That superiority is supposed to derive from the fact that we have souls while animals do not. Animals are mere automata and lack the divine element that makes us spiritual beings. I won't go into the now familiar criticisms of this two-substance view. I only add the point that, even if humans are composed of an immaterial, unextended soul and a material, extended body, this in itself is not a reason to deem them of greater worth than entities that are only bodies. Why is a soul substance a thing that adds value to its possessor? Unless some theological reasoning is offered here (which many, including myself, would find unacceptable on epistemological grounds), no logical connection is evident. An immaterial something which thinks is better than a material something which does not think only if thinking itself has value, either intrinsically or instrumentally. Now it is intrinsically valuable to humans alone, who value it as an end in itself, and it is instrumentally valuable to those who benefit from it, namely humans.

For animals that neither enjoy thinking for its own sake nor need it for living the kind of life for which they are best adapted, it has no value. Even if "thinking" is broadened to include all forms of consciousness, there are still many living things that can do without it and yet live what is for their species a good life. The anthropocentricity underlying the claim to human superiority runs throughout Cartesian dualism.

A third major source of the idea of human superiority is the Judeo-Christian concept of the Great Chain of Being. Humans are superior to animals and plants because their Creator has given them a higher place on the chain. It begins with God at the top, and then moves to the angels, who are lower than God but higher than humans, then to humans, positioned between the angels and the beasts (partaking of the nature of both), and then on down to the lower levels occupied by nonhuman animals, plants, and finally inanimate objects. Humans, being "made in God's image," are inherently superior to animals and plants by virtue of their being closer (in their essential nature) to God.

The metaphysical and epistemological difficulties with this conception of a hierarchy of entities are, in my mind, insuperable. Without entering into this matter here, I only point out that if we are unwilling to accept the metaphysics of traditional Judaism and Christianity, we are again left without good reasons for holding to the claim of inherent human superiority.

The foregoing considerations (and others like them) leave us with but one ground for the assertion that a human being, regardless of merit, is a higher kind of entity than any other living thing. This is the mere fact of the genetic makeup of the species *Homo sapiens*. But this is surely irrational and arbitrary. Why should the arrangement of genes of a certain type be a mark of superior value, especially when this fact about an organism is, taken by itself, unrelated to any other aspect of its life? We might just as well refer to any other genetic makeup as a ground of superior value. Clearly we are confronted here with a wholly arbitrary claim that can only be explained as an irrational bias in our own favor.

That the claim is nothing more than a deep-seated prejudice is brought home to us when we look at our relation to other species in the light of the first three elements of the biocentric outlook. Those elements taken conjointly give us a certain overall view of the natural world and of the place of humans in it. When we take this view we come to understand other living things, their environmental conditions, and their ecological relationships in such a way as to awake in us a deep sense of our kinship with them as fellow members of the Earth's community of life. Humans and nonhumans alike are viewed together as integral parts of one unified whole in which all living things are functionally interrelated. Finally, when our awareness focuses on the individual lives of plants and animals, each is seen to share with us the characteristic of being a teleological center of life striving to realize its own good in its own unique way.

As this entire belief system becomes part of the conceptual framework through which we understand and perceive the world, we come to see ourselves as bearing a certain moral relation to nonhuman forms of life. Our ethical role in nature takes on a new significance. We begin to look at other species as we look at ourselves, seeing them as beings which have a good they are striving to realize just as we have a good we are striving to realize. We accordingly develop the disposition to view the world from the standpoint of their good as well as from the standpoint of our own good. Now if the groundlessness of the claim that humans are inherently superior to other species were brought clearly before our minds, we would not remain intellectually neutral toward that claim but would reject it as being fundamentally at variance with our total world outlook. In the absence of any good reasons for holding it, the assertion of human superiority would then appear simply as the expression of an irrational and self-serving prejudice that favors one particular species over several million others.

Rejecting the notion of human superiority entails its positive counterpart: the doctrine of species impartiality. One who accepts that doctrine regards all living things as possessing inherent worth—the *same* inherent worth, since no one species has been shown to be either "higher" or "lower" than any other. Now we saw earlier that, insofar as one thinks of a living thing as possessing inherent worth, one considers it to be the appropriate object of the attitude of respect and believes that attitude to be the only fitting or suitable one for all moral agents to take toward it.

Here, then, is the key to understanding how the attitude of respect is rooted in the biocentric outlook of nature. The basic connection is made through the denial of human superiority. Once we reject the claim that humans are superior either in merit or in worth to other living things, we are ready to adopt the attitude of respect. The denial of human superiority is itself the result of taking the perspective on nature built into the first three elements of the biocentric outlook.

Now the first three elements of the biocentric outlook, it seems clear, would be found acceptable to any rational and scientifically informed thinker who is fully "open" to the reality of the lives of nonhuman organisms. Without denying our distinctively human characteristics, such a thinker can acknowledge the fundamental respects in which we are members of the Earth's community of life and in which the biological conditions necessary for the realization of our human values are inextricably linked with the whole system of nature. In addition, the conception of individual living things as teleological centers of life simply articulates how a scientifically informed thinker comes to understand them as the result of increasingly careful and detailed observations. Thus, the biocentric outlook recommends itself as an acceptable system of concepts and beliefs to anyone who is clear-minded, unbiased, and factually enlightened, and who has a developed capacity of reality awareness with regard to the lives of individual organisms. This, I submit, is as good a reason for making the moral commitment involved in adopting the attitude of respect for nature as any theory of environmental ethics could possibly have.

Moral Rights and the Matter of Competing Claims

I have not asserted anywhere in the foregoing account that animals or plants have moral rights. This omission was deliberate. I do not think that the reference class of the concept, bearer of moral rights, should be extended to include nonhuman living things. My reasons for taking this position, however, go beyond the scope of this paper.[6] I believe I have been able to accomplish many of the same ends which those who ascribe rights to animals or plants wish to accomplish. There is no reason, moreover, why plants and animals, including whole species populations and life communities, cannot be accorded *legal* rights under my theory. To grant them legal protection could be interpreted as giving them legal entitlement to be protected, and this, in fact, would be a means by which a society that subscribed to the ethics of respect for nature could give public recognition to their inherent worth.

There remains the problem of competing claims, even when wild plants and animals are not thought of as bearers of moral rights. If we accept the biocentric outlook and accordingly adopt the attitude of respect for nature as our ultimate moral attitude, how do we resolve conflicts that arise from our respect for persons in the domain of human ethics and our respect for nature in the domain of environmental ethics? This is a question that cannot adequately be dealt with here. My main purpose in this paper has been to try to establish a base point from which we can start working toward a solution to the problem. I have shown why we cannot just begin with an initial presumption in favor of the interests of our own species. It is after all within our power as moral beings to place limits on human population and technology with the deliberate intention of sharing the Earth's bounty with other species. That such sharing is an ideal difficult to realize even in an approximate way does not take away its claim to our deepest moral commitment.

Notes

1. W.K. Frankena, "Ethics and the Environment," in *Ethics and Problems of the 21st Century*, ed. K.E. Goodpaster and K.M. Sayre, (South Bend: University of Notre Dame Press, 1979), pp. 3–20. I critically examine Frankena's views in "Frankena on Environmental Ethics," *Monist*, 64 (July 1981), no. 3: 313–324.

2. In the light of considerations set forth in Daniel Dennett's *Brainstorms: Philosophical Essays on Mind and Psychology* (Montgomery, Vermont: Bradford Books, 1978), it is advisable to leave this question unsettled at this time. When machines are developed that function in the way our brains do, we may well come to deem them proper subjects of moral consideration.

3. Stephen R. L. Clark, *The Moral Status of Animals* (Oxford: Clarendon Press, 1977), p. 112.

4. My criticisms of the dogma of human superiority gain independent support from a carefully reasoned essay by R. and V. Routley showing the many logical weaknesses in arguments for human-centered theories of environmental ethics. R. and V. Routley, "Against the Inevitability of Human Chauvinism," in *Ethics and Problems of the 21st Century*, ed. K. E. Goodpaster & K. M. Sayre, (South Bend: University of Notre Dame Press, 1979), pp. 36–59.

5. For this way of distinguishing between merit and inherent worth, I am indebted to Gregory Vlastos, "Justice and Equality," in *Social Justice*, ed. R. Brandt (Englewood Cliffs, N.J.: Prentice-Hall, 1962), pp. 31–72.

6. Editor's Note: For further discussion, see Paul Taylor, *Respect for Nature* (Princeton: Princeton University Press, 1986), pp. 245ff.

6B3. Against Biospherical Egalitarianism

By William C. French

Introduction

In an effort to overcome anthropocentric traditions of ethics, some in the various ecology movements have come to espouse a "biospherical egalitarian" position.[1] In its strict version, proponents of this view hold, first, that all life forms—trees, microorganisms, humans, wolves—have inherent value, and, second, that this inherent value is held equally, such that the members of one species cannot be considered superior (in terms of moral value) to any other. This biospherical egalitarian principle calls for a wide expansion of direct moral consideration, concern, and respect for the value of all life.

This expansion of what counts as the moral community far beyond the borders of the human community is, I believe, correct. What I find problematic, however, is the egalitarian view that not only do all living entities have inherent moral value, but that they all have *equal* inherent moral value. Biospherical egalitarian claims, as I show, tend to be developed inconsistently and often do not *in fact* govern the concrete moral reasoning of even the theorists who most strongly espouse such beliefs. Many biospherical egalitarians are not, on close examination, the radical egalitarians that they first appear to be. Rather they continue to allow certain species-ranking procedures to control their moral casuistry when they grapple with concrete cases of conflict between and among the interests of humans and other species.

In what follows, I first provide a close analysis of the claims about the moral equality of species made by Arne Naess and others of the deep ecology movement as well as those made by Paul Taylor in his book, *Respect for Nature.*[2] In the deep ecology literature, species equality is loudly stressed "in principle," while sotto voce it is acknowledged that vital human interests may legitimately override vital interests of nonhumans. Taylor develops a more consistent and indeed strident emphasis on species equality; yet, at the end of his book, when he addresses concrete cases of conflict between the interests of humans and nonhumans, he too argues that there are many occasions when it is morally proper for humans to kill or injure nonhuman life forms. While never backing off from his insistence on the equality of inherent moral value of all life forms, he too supports ranking procedures

---

1   This term and *ecological egalitarianism* are used interchangeably by Arne Naess in his now classic essay, "The Shallow and the Deep, Long-Range Ecology Movement: A Summary," *Inquiry* 16 (1973): 95–100. This position is also endorsed by some ecofeminists who are understandably suspicious of appeal to hierarchical models as a means of understanding either social or natural relationships.

2   Paul W. Taylor, *Respect for Nature: A Theory of Environmental Ethics* (Princeton.: Princeton University Press, 1986).

that in many cases permit human interests, even nonbasic ones, to override the basic interests of nonhumans.

Both deep ecologists and Taylor appear to toss species ranking out the front door of their arguments only to have it sneak around and into the house from the back. They attempt to preserve consistency by holding that our decisions to kill and injure plants and animals are performed under the aegis of necessity, not under the authority of some appeal to any superior inherent value of humans. Ranking procedures based on necessity and self-defense are permitted, but great efforts are taken to try to show that these in no way imply any rejection of species equality. This strategy, however, oddly suggests that ethical principles ought to be consigned solely to some ideal sphere of pure theory, while our concrete decisions about human action ought to be made outside the sphere of moral review and governed strictly by concerns of power and raw necessity. Biospherical egalitarian claims are secured, but at the cost of transforming them into utopian abstractions that exert no decisive normative weight in our moral decision and practice. By so separating moral principle from practice, this strategy prevents one from providing a clear account of why the necessity of human interests should be morally privileged over the necessity recognized to exist in the survival interests of nonhuman forms of life.

After exploring the claims of deep ecology and Taylor about species equality, in the next section I turn to an examination of a critical, species-ranking position developed in detail in Lawrence Johnson's recent book, *A Morally Deep World*.[3]

In the concluding section, I argue that the biospherical egalitarian ethic is utopian and, even in the hands of its proponents, fails to provide normative guidance in decision and action. If biospherical egalitarianism is promulgated as a moral principle, but is not actually employed as a controlling, normative principle, then ecologists would do well to drop claims of species equality. The growth of a broad-based, ecological movement is ill-served by "deeper than thou" postures and by conceptual and moral confusion.

Paul Taylor's Position

In his book *Respect for Nature*, Paul Taylor develops an endorsement of the radical equality of the inherent value of all life forms which is even more thoroughly sustained than that of the deep ecologists. Taylor holds that a "biocentric outlook on nature" entails a rejection of any hierarchical "idea of human superiority over other living things."[4] It requires that one commit oneself to "the principle of species-impartiality," according to which

---

3   Lawrence E. Johnson, *A Morally Deep World: An Essay on Moral Significance and Environmental Ethics* (Cambridge: Cambridge University Press, 1991).
4   Taylor, *Respect for Nature*, pp. 44–45.

... every species counts as having the same value in the sense that, regardless of what species a living thing belongs to, it is deemed to be prima facie deserving of equal concern and consideration on the part of moral agents. ... species-impartiality ... means regarding every entity that has a good of its own [humans, animals, and plants] as possessing inherent worth—the *same* inherent worth, since none is superior to another.[5]

While Naess regularly qualifies his commitment to a strict species-equality view, Taylor seems at first to allow no qualifications whatsoever. Taylor holds that animals and plants

... possess a degree or amount of inherent worth equal to that of humans. To say that they possess a worth equal to ours means that we owe duties to them that are prima facie as stringent as those we owe to our fellow humans.[6]

Yet Taylor, too, at the end of his book is forced to grapple with the inevitable conflict of interest cases that occur so often between humans and nonhumans. Those committed to both a respect for persons and a respect for nature must, according to Taylor, give equal consideration to moral claims that arise from both "systems of ethics."[7] The fact that conflict cannot be avoided leads him to elaborate and apply priority principles that provide a means for adjudicating these cases. Taylor articulates five such principles: self-defense, proportionality, minimum wrong, distributive justice, and restitutive justice. Methodologically, he is committed to developing and applying these principles so as to avoid any anthropocentric bias in order to respect species impartiality. While granting that humans "alone are full-fledged bearers of moral rights," Taylor insists that those who "adopt the attitude of respect for nature" will "consider morally irrelevant the fact that wild animals and plants, unlike human persons, are not bearers of moral rights."[8]

The principle of self-defense holds that "it is permissible for moral agents to protect themselves against dangerous or harmful organisms by destroying them." This measure may only be taken as a "last resort" after all other means to avoid the danger have been exhausted.[9] Taylor notes that, at first, this requirement seems biased in favor of humans, but he insists that "humans are not given an advantage simply on the basis of their humanity." His formulation of the principle, he insists, is "species-blind."

---

5   Ibid., p. 155.
6   Ibid., pp. 151–52.
7   Ibid., p. 259.
8   Ibid., pp. 261–62. For Taylor's argument that humans have "rights" and animals and plants do not, see pp. 150–52, 219–55, 262.
9   Ibid., pp. 264–65.

The fact that (most) humans are moral agents and (most) nonhumans are not is a contingent truth which the principle does not take to be morally relevant. Moral agents are permitted to defend themselves against harmful or dangerous organisms that are not moral agents. This is all the principle of self-defense allows.[10]

In elaborating his priority principles Taylor draws a distinction between basic and nonbasic interests. He also distinguishes between practices harmful to nonhuman nature that are intrinsically incompatible with the attitude of respect for nature and those practices that, while harmful to nonhuman nature, are not intrinsically incompatible with a stance of respect for nature. He restricts the scope of the principle of proportionality "to situations of conflict between the basic interests of wild animals and plants and those nonbasic human interests that are intrinsically incompatible with respect to nature."[11] Among the practices prohibited by this principle, Taylor lists: (a) the slaughtering of elephants for ivory to make tourist novelties, (b) "picking rare wildflowers" for private collections, (c) "capturing tropical birds" for sale as pets, (d) hunting "rare wild mammals" for the "luxury fur trade," and (e) "all sport hunting and recreational fishing."[12]

The principle of minimum wrong, likewise, is limited by Taylor to cases involving a clash between "basic interests of wild animals and plants" and nonbasic interests of humans. Additionally, this principle only covers cases in which the nonbasic human interests are "*not* intrinsically incompatible with respect for nature."[13] Interestingly Taylor holds that there is a class of human values and preferences which, though they themselves are not basic human interests, are still "so highly valued" that they often warrant the overriding of the basic interests of nonhumans. He cites among other practices the construction of museums, libraries, public parks, airports, harbors, highways, and hydroelectric dams, all of which disturb or destroy natural habitats. Such activities do not, Taylor believes, "express a purely exploitative attitude toward nature." This set of nonbasic, yet "highly valued," human interests, Taylor states, may properly "outweigh the undesirable consequences" of harming wild animals and plants. Such practices are only justified, of course, if all less ecologically damaging ways of reaching these human goals have been exhausted.[14]

Though nonbasic, this set of human interests are still, for Taylor, "so important that rational and factually informed people who have genuine respect for nature" would not be "willing to relinquish the pursuit of those interests even when they take into account the undesirable consequences for wildlife."[15] Such valued interests, Taylor believes, are "essential to a whole society's maintaining a high level of culture," "carry great weight" and, indeed, may legitimately override even the basic interests of

---

10 Ibid., pp. 266–67.
11 Ibid., pp. 277–78.
12 Ibid., p. 274.
13 Ibid., pp. 278, 280.
14 Ibid., pp. 276–77.
15 Ibid., pp. 280.

the "Earth's nonhuman inhabitants."[16] The principle of minimal wrong holds that when rational and informed persons "*who have adopted the attitude of respect for nature* are nevertheless unwilling to forgo" intrinsically valued social ends "shared by a whole society as the focus of its way of life," then it is "permissible for them to pursue those values" so long as they have opted for the policy that does the least harm to nonhuman living entities.[17]

The principle of distributive justice, for Taylor, covers cases in which the competing human and nonhuman interests are all basic ones and in which the nonhumans are not harmful to us. Given that all the interests are basic, they all must be accorded equal "moral weight." This principle requires that when "there exists a natural source of good that can be used for the benefit of any of the parties, each party must be allotted an equal share."[18] Yet, Taylor allows that if human survival requires the killing and eating of animals, fish, or plants, then it is morally permissible for humans to do so. Even here, however, he does not back off from his insistence that animals, plants, and humans have equal inherent worth. He sees no contradiction because he holds that humans have no obligation to sacrifice themselves "for the sake of animals" or plants. As he puts it: "Animals are not of *greater* worth, so there is no obligation to further their interests at the cost of the basic interests of humans." Similarly, for Taylor, plants are humans' "equals in inherent worth," but "we have no duty to sacrifice ourselves to them."[19]

Critique of Taylor's Account

If I understand Taylor's arguments correctly, then I find his system bizarre. Naess at least makes clear that his formulation of biospherical egalitarianism still accepts that human vital interests outweigh nonhuman interests. Taylor, while insisting throughout that all species have equal inherent value, sees no contradiction in allowing that even various nonbasic, human interests morally outweigh the basic interests of nonhumans. For Taylor, humans may kill animals and plants out of necessity. Humans may use animals and plants in many ways and may continue actively to develop the Earth to support our important cultural and societal values. How does this position square with his sustained, strict acceptance of species equality? If I follow his arguments correctly, only methodological contortion permits their reconciliation. In my critique, I focus on five points.

First, Taylor holds that the principle of proportionality requires that in conflict cases "greater weight is to be given to basic than to nonbasic interests, no matter what species, human or other, the competing claims arise from."[20] Yet, when he delineates the principle of minimum wrong, he holds the contradictory position, that in a wide range of cases it is proper for humans' "highly valued," but

---

16 Ibid., p. 281.
17 Ibid., pp. 282–83.
18 Ibid., p. 292.
19 Ibid., pp. 294–95.
20 Ibid., p. 278.

nonbasic interests to be given greater moral weight than the basic interests of animals and plants. In an ethical system that is supposed to provide substantive guidance for decision and action, should the normative bite of different moral principles clash so directly? Taylor seems to believe that there is no normative contradiction because each principle covers a different set of cases. I, however, do not believe that moral principles are best viewed as strictly separate from one another and only narrowly applicable to this, but not that, range of cases. There are significant continuities of value across the whole set of cases that Taylor's approach obscures.

Second, recall Taylor's attempt to defend the principle of self-defense as "species-blind." Although this principle privileges the interests of "moral agents" over beings who aren't agents, Taylor argues that it does not necessarily entail that only humans can possibly count as moral agents. Taylor dismisses as merely a "contingent truth" the fact that in the only world in which we live and act, almost all humans become moral agents and almost all nonhumans don't. He uses an analytical razor to cut remarkably formal distinctions. If ethics is primarily an exercise in practical reason, then the data of our common world should be treated not as a "contingent," but rather as a central truth of our moral experience. In the realm of decision and action, Taylor's formulation provides wide-ranging justification for acts by humans that harm animals, microorganisms, and plants. Analytical sleight of hand should not be allowed to hide this fact. Clarity would be promoted, I believe, by acknowledging directly that Taylor's normative privileging of moral agents over non-agents constitutes a general privileging (under normal conditions) of human over nonhuman life.

Third, Taylor's gravest contradiction seems to lie in his appeal to a shadowy set of human interests that while dubbed "nonbasic," are still of such "special importance" that they morally outweigh the basic interests of nonhumans. If nonbasic interests can outweigh basic interests, then the distinction between basic and nonbasic is rendered deeply problematic. If such human interests are so special, then why are they not classed as basic? More importantly, if such societal interests in maintaining a "high level of civilized life"[21] are normatively weighty, what is the moral basis of that weight? Even though high levels of human culture play a governing role in Taylor's ethical theory, his insistence upon strict species equality requires him simultaneously to refuse to grant any distinctive moral weight to the inherent value of human individuals—the beings who create and sustain that high culture. Taylor's strict commitment to species equality thus contorts his theory, pushing him to hold that human culture has especially weighty normative value, but human life does not.

Fourth, when Taylor analyzes the requirements of distributive justice, he first holds that all concerned parties must be accorded an equal share of some good—food, water, air, land. Yet, he concludes, it is permissible to kill animals and plants because they do not have greater value than humans, and because we have no obligation to sacrifice ourselves for them. But if a just distribution is an equal share, why not hold to that position in concrete decision and action? Why not prescribe a random method for deciding who or what should get the food or habitat space? Or perhaps the moral agent

---

21   Ibid., p. 281.

could work out a schedule whereby each privileging of the agent's own claims to the resources would next time be followed by an explicit privileging of the non-agent's claims. Taylor stresses normative equality; yet, he regularly formulates his principles so as to justify all sorts of cases in which humans may kill or injure animals and plants.

Fifth, these concerns taken together make it unclear just what scope Taylor wants the principle of species equality to play in his ethical system. He states that the adjudication between respect for nature and respect for human cultural and civilizational interests depends on "people's total systems of value."[22] However, by not delineating just how principles derived from our "respect for persons" are to be joined with principles derived from our "respect for nature" to form a coherent total system, Taylor leaves us unclear about the moral grounding of our final, concrete, normative weightings.

Especially vague is Taylor's use of the terms *equal concern* and *consideration*. Recall Taylor's view that species equality means that plants and animals "possess a worth equal to ours" and we thus "owe duties to them that are prima facie as stringent as those we owe to our fellow humans." Cases of conflict between the interests of humans and those of wild animals and plants are cases in which "validly binding prima facie duties of equal stringency … are in conflict."[23]

Nevertheless, almost immediately gaps appear in his argument. Taylor acknowledges that species equality does not rule out how the "duty not to destroy or harm animals and plants in natural ecosystems" may be legitimately overridden by "duties that moral agents owe to humans."[24] Far from cashing out his view at the normative level as a strict species-egalitarian position, Taylor holds, to the contrary, that various human practices harmful to nature may be justified on moral grounds when they are required for human survival. He backs this claim with an appeal to ethical principles rooted in "a system of human ethics" and "a priority principle that makes the duty to provide for human survival outweigh those duties of nonmaleficence, noninterference, and fidelity that are owed to nonhumans."[25]

Taylor can defend his position against the charge of contradiction in two ways. First, he seems to believe that there are two sharply distinct spheres of ethics—human ethics and environmental ethics. Perhaps he means that his claim of strict species equality only applies in the sphere of environmental ethics, and thus does not govern the "total system." This position would save his claim of species equality, but at the cost of radically qualifying its range of relevance and application. A concrete decision regarding what one's actual moral duty is in a given case would thus not be controlled by the principle of species equality, but by whether one's total ethical system allows human survival and cultural interests to override one's prima facie duties to animals and plants. If so, then, although Taylor may stress species equality, he still subscribes to an ethical view which, in fact, normatively gives a privileged position to the interests of moral agents—namely, most humans.

---

22   Ibid., p. 277.
23   Ibid., p. 152.
24   Ibid., p. 171.
25   Ibid., p. 183.

Second, Taylor may argue that his principle of species equality is only meant to hold for our prima facie duties but not for our judgment of our concrete duty at the point of decision and action, what W. D. Ross calls our "actual duty."[26] This position would allow Taylor to say that our prima facie duties to humans, animals, and plants are all equally stringent and yet hold that our actual duties—as he puts it, the "all-things-considered judgment that a certain action ought or ought not be done"[27]—at times rightly give priority to human survival and cultural interests. If so, then Taylor appears to want to have his cake and to eat it too. He loudly endorses what on first blush appears to be a radical species-equality position, but quietly constructs many methodological walls to hem in that position and to restrict sharply its authority at the point of a moral agent's final determination of his or her actual moral duty. If this reading of Taylor's position is correct, then he restricts his species-equality principle to a claim about prima facie duties, while allowing certain undeveloped species-ranking judgments and weightings to control the actual—the "all-things-considered"—normative judgment.

Lawrence Johnson's Species-Ranking Scheme

Biospherical egalitarianism, as I believe the preceding analyses of Naess' and Taylor's ethical theories shows, is unable to guide concrete normative judgments without reintroducing some normative ranking of species. If, finally, even the proponents of species equality must accept a normative privileging of human interests and worth, then, I believe, concerns for ethical consistency and clarity suggest that it is better to articulate our value hierarchy plainly, rather than having it remain cloaked and unarticulated. In what follows, I provide a brief sketch of such a critical, anti-anthropocentric, species-ranking position.

Lawrence Johnson in his recent book, *A Morally Deep World,* has given a sustained and well-nuanced account of a critical species-ranking ecological ethic. In opposition to anthropocentric traditions, which exclude all nonhumans from direct moral consideration, and hedonic utilitarian schemes, which exclude plants and microorganisms from such moral consideration, Johnson argues that *all* living beings and entities have morally significant interests in their own well-being that we humans must respect. Against Taylor and others who hold that only individual living beings have inherent moral worth, Johnson holds that both living individuals and living "holistic entities"—for example, species, discrete ecosystems, and the entire biosphere itself—have significant, inherent moral worth.

Johnson tries to chart a mid-course between atomism and ethical holism and between anthropocentrism and biospherical egalitarianism. For Johnson, although all the relevant interests of all living individuals and holistic entities potentially impacted by our decision must be considered, not

---

26 See W. D. Ross, *The Right and the Good* (1930; reprint ed., Oxford: Clarendon Press, 1973), pp. 19–20.
27 Ibid., p. 192.

all of these interests need be weighted equally in our normative consideration of our actual moral duty or duties. While stressing that "*all* genuine interests must be recognized as having some moral weight," Johnson holds that

> some interests have more weight than others. It is a matter of degrees. In arguing that the interests of a mouse are morally considerable, I am not claiming that setting a mousetrap is on a par with the premeditated murder of a human being. Normally, a human being has more interests than does a mouse.[28]

As he puts it later: "Although we ought to revere life ... some life is more valuable than other life. This is not because only some interests count while some do not—all interests count—but because not all interests are equivalent."[29] To illustrate his position concretely, he ranks a chimpanzee as having a morally more significant interest in life than an amoeba (under normal conditions). Likewise, he holds that the interests of individual plants are, under normal conditions, usually quite slight, certainly less than the interests of humans who eat them. However, the interests of a whole plant species threatened by extinction normally are morally privileged, thereby thwarting human interests in consuming the last few of that species in a salad for lunch.[30]

The key normative principle, for Johnson, is: "Give due respect to all the interests of all beings that have interests, in proportion to their interests."[31] He believes the "bad news" is that no moral theory can generate a complete set of principles to cover all possible ecological cases of conflict of interests.[32] Still, the "good news" is that we generally do well morally when we adopt a stance of genuine respect for the "well-being interests" of all. When doing so, we may well make mistakes, but at least we avoid utter callousness toward nature and thus avoid acting as sheer exploiters and vandals. If people ever came to view every animal, plant, species, and ecosystem as a valuable and morally significant "end in itself," they would have to develop terribly significant changes in moral perception, sensitivity, and habits of action, but still would not solve all dilemmas.[33]

Johnson sees inherent value running deeply throughout the full range of living beings and entities, and hence holds that the world is a "morally deep" one. Unlike the deep ecologists and Taylor, however, Johnson believes that we must adopt "a multilevel approach to multilevel problems in a multilevel world."[34]

---

28   Johnson, *Morally Deep World,* p. 7. For an important articulation of a position similar to Johnson's, see Louis G. Lombardi, "Inherent Worth, Respect, and Rights," *Environmental Ethics* 5 (1983): 257–70. See also Taylor's responses to Lombardi, "Are Humans Superior to Animals and Plants?" *Environmental Ethics* 6 (1984): 149–60 and *Respect for Nature*, pp. 147–52.

29   Ibid., pp. 135–36.

30   Ibid., pp. 136, 172.

31   Ibid., pp. 118, 185, 198.

32   Ibid., pp. 185, 189.

33   Ibid., pp. 189–200.

34   Ibid., p. 247.

Individuals of different species have different types of well-being interests, and, while all of these interests are morally significant, their significance is a "matter of degree."[35]

Johnson avoids Taylor's confusion over what it means to give different individuals of different species "equal moral consideration" by distinguishing clearly between giving something or someone moral consideration and holding that something or someone is morally significant. A being or entity either deserves or doesn't deserve moral consideration. *Moral consideration* tends not to be a scalar term mapping degrees or levels, but rather is used to register a claim about admission into, or denial from, the circle of beings or entities to which inherent value is ascribed. When a being or an entity is evaluated as being morally considerable, the level of its moral significance vis-à-vis other morally considerable beings and entities remains to be established. In Johnson's view, all interests are morally significant and thus should be taken into account in our moral decision making. However, some individuals, species, and ecosystems have greater moral significance than others.

What then for Johnson are the criteria of moral significance? He employs the notion of "interest packages" to chart how individuals of one species may share a particular well-being interest with individuals of another species and yet also have an additional, distinctive well-being interest that is not shared by the individuals of that other species.[36] As he puts it:

> Certainly rational beings have interests involving their rationality, interests that nonrational beings lack, and these interests are morally significant. ... Sentient beings have interests involving their sentience, interests that nonsentient beings lack, and these interests are morally significant. As these interests of different sorts are all morally significant, we must try to give them all their due weight—whatever that is.[37]

For Johnson, although humans, dogs, and trees all have "intrinsic moral importance," "they have very different interests" and thus "very different [moral] importance."[38]

Johnson holds that "any even moderately viable means of morally assessing a life or a life system would, at the very least, have to take into consideration the degree of complexity of the life system in question and its degree of coherent, integrated, functional organic unity." Thus, a human by virtue of his or her greater "complexity" over a dandelion has a "greater interest in life and a higher moral status."[39] Elsewhere, he argues that certain "well-being configurations are better than others, in terms of having greater complexity, diversity, balance, organic unity or integrity. ..."[40] He suggests that

---

35 Ibid., pp. 243, 278.
36 Ibid., p. 279.
37 Ibid., p. 198.
38 Ibid., p. 267.
39 Ibid., p. 188.
40 Ibid., p. 227.

"more highly developed individuals [of different species] will have greater self-identity" than less developed and less complex, so that amoebas have "much less moral importance" vis-à-vis their species than do individual humans vis-à-vis ours.[41]

Ranking as Response to Needs and Vulnerability

Both Taylor and the deep ecologists seem to believe that when we acknowledge any superiority of capacities of certain species, we immediately find ourselves on the slippery slope to flat-out anthropocentrism. Hence, they adopt the strategy of denying species ranking in principle, even if not in practice. Talk of certain species having inherent moral superiority over others seems to Taylor and the deep ecologists to violate the holistic ecological understanding of the interdependency of the community of life.

Johnson's approach is helpful because he suggests that the key issue in our ranking of species in conflict-of-interest cases is not some reward for merit based on some superiority of capacities, but rather is an appropriate response to protect, as best we can, individuals and species that have greater ranges of vulnerability than others. When Johnson claims that a human has a higher moral status than a dandelion, he is not granting some moral reward to the human for his or her superior capacities. Rather, Johnson's claim rightly flags the fact that the human not only has the well-being interests of a dandelion (for example, the need for air and water), but also has a whole range of additional well-being needs. The claim that certain individuals, species, and ecosystems have higher moral status than others is, I believe, at bottom, a comparative, normative claim that is supposed to draw attention to the fact that certain individuals, species, and ecosystems have greater development and complexity, and thus a greater range of vulnerability and need.

Species ranking is not some prize awarded to those having superior capacities. Rather, it is an appropriate attempt under the conditions of finitude to give special protection to *some* when we are not able to give equal protection to *all*. In a utopian world we would not need to make forced choices, and thus would not need to allow a harm to occur to one in order to protect another from harm. In our world, however, we often must make such choices.

Part of our problem arises from the use of the term *inherent value*. When using this term, we are usually trying to assert that some being or entity is a moral "end in itself"—that is, that it has its own worth independent of its instrumental worth for us. Unfortunately, some seem to hear in the term *inherent* some suggestion of a type of essentialist metaphysics according to which different levels of being have different levels of value wired into them. Species ranking from this point of view understandably appears methodologically crude and morally arrogant.

If ethics is understood, however, as a relational discipline centered on assessments of responsibility to diverse beings and entities in relation to each other and in relation to us, then species ranking is

---

41 Ibid., p. 243.

simply a necessary part of our moral practice of setting priorities. Rankings should not be thought of as static assessments of some mysterious and fixed levels of ontological value. Rather, rankings are relational assessments about where—in particular cases and under distinct conditions—our moral priority lies to defend those who have the greatest range of potential vulnerability. I think it best not to think of rankings as an assessment of some "inherent" superiority, but rather as a considered moral recognition of the fact that greater ranges of vulnerability are generated by broader ranges of complexity and capacities.[42] As Johnson suggests, species and ecosystem rankings are really based on a recognition that more developed, more complex individuals, species, and ecosystems are more vulnerable in the sense that they have more to lose. As Johnson puts it, both a dead mouse with bacterial growth and a mature rain forest constitute distinctive ecosystems. Yet, the growth in the "dead-mouse ecosystem" is in no way unique or complex and almost nothing "would be lost were that tiny ecosystem disrupted."[43] In contrast to Taylor, who fears ascribing greater inherent worth to species with wider ranges of capacities, Johnson rightly accepts normative priorities grounded in duties to protect vulnerability and to minimize loss. Species ranking is not, at bottom, based on human hubris, but rather on a commitment to responsible choice and action under the constraints imposed by conditions of finite resources, time, and energy.

Conclusion

Biospherical egalitarianism, even in the hands of its most consistent proponents, breaks down when dealing with the necessary choices that must be made under the conditions of life. In my analysis, I have tried to chart a pattern of argument, common to many egalitarians, in which they initially enunciate a broad principle of species equality, but later back away from it as they struggle to account for our moral responsibilities in conflict-of-interest cases. When those who most consistently reject notions of human superiority over nonhumans later reach for the functional equivalent of species-ranking procedures, one must conclude that no ecological ethic that attempts to be comprehensive can dispense with some sort of hierarchical ranking of moral priorities based, at least in part, on critical evaluations of the different capacities, needs, and vulnerabilities of different individuals, species, and ecosystems. An ecological ethical scheme that makes this point clear from the start avoids much methodological confusion.

Some, I suspect, are attracted to the species-egalitarian position because of the sheer force and sweep of its indictment of anthropocentric traditions of ethics. Its absolutism provides a strong

---

42 For an excellent account of how more advanced organisms pay for their increased capacities and vitalities by increased habitat and energy needs, see Hans Jonas, *The Phenomenon of Life: Toward a Philosophical Biology* (Chicago and London: University of Chicago Press, 1966, Phoenix edition, 1982), pp. 99–107, 183–87. Also see Robert E. Goodin, *Protecting the Vulnerable* (Chicago and London: University of Chicago Press, 1985) for an explicit attempt to analyze ethics as centered in our responsibilities for the vulnerable. See especially pp. 179–88, where he turns his attention to ecological issues.

43 Johnson, *Morally Deep World*, p. 278.

platform for radical prophetic indictment. Nevertheless, we must be mindful of the costs of this moral strategy. Those who wave the banner of biospherical egalitarianism may well score points with an already converted, radical few; yet, they may also be leading a broad segment of the general public to conclude that the radical wing of the ecology movement is, at best, unrealistic, or worse, anti-human.

Naess and other deep ecologists have made many important and timely points that deserve a broad hearing, particularly, their emphasis on the need for a radical identification with nature, their advocacy of appropriate technologies and sustainability, and their potent critiques of consumerism, high-growth economics, and population expansion. Taylor, too, makes important contributions with his analysis of what the attitude of "respect for nature" entails. However, the insistence of Taylor and the deep ecologists on biospherical egalitarianism, I fear, draws attention away from their other, more solid and serviceable contributions. Their insistence on a principle that does not finally seem intended to govern moral judgment about concrete duty and practice purchases little normative work at high cost in conceptual contortion.

If, as I have tried to show, both Naess and Taylor—two of the strongest advocates of biospherical egalitarianism—move away from that principle when adjudicating conflict-of-interest cases, then both the coherency and usefulness of that principle are called sharply into question. It would be a shame if the stress on biospherical egalitarianism led people to dismiss deep ecology as deeply confused, for many of deep ecology's other affirmations are significant and deserve a broad hearing. Until more consistent and stronger defenses of biospherical egalitarianism can be marshalled, I believe, deep ecologists and other ecological theorists would do well to drop this principle from their portfolio of affirmations.

CHAPTER 7

Feminist Environmental Ethics: Is It Sound? Culturally Limited?

7A. The Power and Promise of Ecological Feminism

By Karen J. Warren

E cological feminism is the position that there are important connections—historical, symbolic, theoretical between the domination of women and the domination of nonhuman nature. I argue that because the conceptual connections between the dual dominations of women and nature are located in an oppressive patriarchal conceptual framework characterized by a logic of domination, (1) the logic of traditional feminism requires the expansion of feminism to include ecological feminism, and (2) ecological feminism provides a framework for developing a distinct feminist environmental ethic. I conclude that any feminist theory and any environmental ethic which fails to take seriously the interconnected domination of women and nature is simply inadequate.

Introduction

Ecological feminism (ecofeminism) has begun to receive a fair amount of attention lately as an alternative feminism and environmental ethic. Since Francoise d'Eaubonne introduced the term *ecofeminisme* in 1974 to bring attention to women's potential for bringing about an ecological revolution,[1] the term has been used in a variety of ways. As I use the term in this paper, ecological feminism is the position that there are important connections—historical, experiential, symbolic, theoretical—between the domination of women and the domination of nature, an understanding of which is crucial to both feminism and environmental ethics. I argue that the promise and power of ecological feminism is that *it provides a distinctive framework both for reconceiving feminism and for developing an environmental ethic which takes seriously connections between the domination of women and the domination of nature.* I do so by discussing the nature of a feminist ethic and the ways in which ecofeminism provides a feminist and environmental ethic. I conclude that any feminist theory *and* any environmental ethic which fails to take seriously the twin and interconnected dominations of women and nature is at best incomplete and at worst simply inadequate.

Feminism, Ecological Feminism, and Conceptual Frameworks

Whatever else it is, feminism is at least the movement to end sexist oppression. It involves the elimination of any and all factors that contribute to the continued and systematic domination or subordination of women. While feminists disagree about the nature of and solutions to the subordination of women, all feminists agree that sexist oppression exists, is wrong, and must be abolished.

Karen J. Warren, "The Power and Promise of Ecological Feminism," *Environmental Ethics*, vol. 12, pp. 125-146.

A "feminist issue" is any issue that contributes in some way to understanding the oppression of women. Equal rights, comparable pay for comparable work, and food production are feminist issues wherever and whenever an understanding of them contributes to an understanding of the continued exploitation or subjugation of women. Carrying water and searching for firewood are feminist issues wherever and whenever women's primary responsibility for these tasks contributes to their lack of full participation in decision making, income producing, or high status positions engaged in by men. What counts as a feminist issue, then, depends largely on context, particularly the historical and material conditions of women's lives.

Environmental degradation and exploitation are feminist issues because an understanding of them contributes to an understanding of the oppression of women. In India, for example, both deforestation and reforestation through the introduction of a monoculture species tree (e.g., eucalyptus) intended for commercial production are feminist issues because the loss of indigenous forests and multiple species of trees has drastically affected rural Indian women's ability to maintain a subsistence household. Indigenous forests provide a variety of trees for food, fuel, fodder, household utensils, dyes, medicines, and income-generating uses, while monoculture-species forests do not.[2] Although I do not argue for this claim here, a look at the global impact of environmental degradation on women's lives suggests important respects in which environmental degradation is a feminist issue.

Feminist philosophers claim that some of the most important feminist issues are *conceptual* ones: these issues concern how one conceptualizes such mainstay philosophical notions as reason and rationality, ethics, and what it is to be human. Ecofeminists extend this feminist philosophical concern to nature. They argue that, ultimately, some of the most important connections between the domination of women and the domination of nature are conceptual. To see this, consider the nature of conceptual frameworks.

A *conceptual framework* is a set of *basic* beliefs, values, attitudes, and assumptions which shape and reflect how one views oneself and one's world. It is a socially constructed lens through which we perceive ourselves and others. It is affected by such factors as gender, race, class, age, affectional orientation, nationality, and religious background.

Some conceptual frameworks are oppressive. An *oppressive conceptual framework* is one that explains, justifies, and maintains relationships of domination and subordination. When an oppressive conceptual framework is *patriarchal*, it explains, justifies, and maintains the subordination of women by men.

I have argued elsewhere that there are three significant features of oppressive conceptual frameworks: (1) value-hierarchical thinking, i.e., "up-down" thinking which places higher value, status, or prestige on what is "up" rather than on what is "down"; (2) value dualisms, i.e., disjunctive pairs in which the disjuncts are seen as oppositional (rather than as complementary) and exclusive (rather than as inclusive), and which place higher value (status, prestige) on one disjunct rather than the other (e.g., dualisms which give higher value or status to that which has historically been identified as "mind," "reason," and "male" than to that which has historically been identified as "body," "emotion," and "female"); and (3) logic of domination, i.e., a structure of argumentation which leads to a justification of subordination.

The third feature of oppressive conceptual frameworks is the most significant. A logic of domination is not just a logical structure. It also involves a substantive value system, since an ethical premise is needed to permit or sanction the "just" subordination of that which is subordinate. This justification typically is given on grounds of some alleged characteristic (e.g., rationality) which the dominant (e.g., men) have and the subordinate (e.g., women) lack.

Contrary to what many feminists and ecofeminists have said or suggested, there maybe nothing inherently problematic about "hierarchical thinking" or even "value-hierarchical thinking" in contexts other than contexts of oppression. Hierarchical thinking is important in daily living for classifying data, comparing information, and organizing material. Taxonomies (e.g., plant taxonomies) and biological nomenclature seem to require some form of "hierarchical thinking." Even "value-hierarchical thinking" may be quite acceptable in certain contexts. (The same may be said of "value dualisms" in non-oppressive contexts). For example, suppose it is true that what is unique about humans is our conscious capacity to radically reshape our social environments (or "societies"), as Murray Bookchin suggests.[3] Then one could truthfully say that humans are better equipped to radically reshape their environments than are rocks or plants—a "value-hierarchical" way of speaking.

The problem is not simply that value-hierarchical thinking and value dualisms are used, but the way in which each has been used in oppressive conceptual frameworks to establish inferiority and to justify subordination.[4] It is the logic of domination, coupled with value-hierarchical thinking and value dualisms, which "justifies" subordination. What is explanatorily basic, then, about the nature of oppressive conceptual frameworks is the logic of domination.

For ecofeminism, that a logic of domination is explanatorily basic is important for at least three reasons. First, without a logic of domination, a description of similarities and differences would be just that—a description of similarities and differences. Consider the claim, "Humans are different from plants and rocks in that humans can (and plants and rocks cannot) consciously and radically reshape the communities in which they live; humans are similar to plants and rocks in that they are both members of an ecological community." Even if humans are "better" than plants and rocks with respect to the conscious ability of humans to radically transform communities, one does not thereby get any morally relevant distinction between humans and nonhumans, or an argument for the domination of plants and rocks by humans. To get those conclusions one needs to add at least two powerful assumptions, viz., (A2) and (A4) in argument A below:

(A1) Humans do, and plants and rocks do not, have the capacity to consciously and radically change the community in which they live.

(A2) Whatever has the capacity to consciously and radically change the community in which it lives is morally superior to whatever lacks this capacity.

(A3) Thus, humans are morally superior to plants and rocks.

(A4) For any X and Y, if X is morally superior to Y, then X is morally justified in subordinating Y.

(A5) Thus, humans are morally justified in subordinating plants and rocks.

Without the two assumptions that humans are morally superior to (at least some) nonhumans, (A2), and that superiority justifies subordination, (A4), all one has is some difference between humans and some nonhumans. This is true even if that difference is given in terms of superiority. Thus, it is the logic of domination, (A4), which is the bottom line in ecofeminist discussions of oppression.

Second, ecofeminists argue that, at least in Western societies, the oppressive conceptual framework which sanctions the twin dominations of women and nature is a patriarchal one characterized by all three features of an oppressive conceptual framework. Many ecofeminists claim that, historically, within at least the dominant Western culture, a patriarchal conceptual framework has sanctioned the following argument B:

(B1) Women are identified with nature and the realm of the physical; men are identified with the "human" and the realm of the mental.

(B2) Whatever is identified with nature and the realm of the physical is inferior to ("below") whatever is identified with the "human" and the realm of the mental; or, conversely, the latter is superior to ("above") the former.

(B3) Thus, women are inferior to ("below") men; or, conversely, men are superior to ("above") women.

(B4) For any X and Y, if X is superior to Y, then X is justified in subordinating Y.

(B5) Thus, men are justified in subordinating women.

If sound, argument B establishes patriarchy, i.e., the conclusion given at (B5) that the systematic domination of women by men is justified. But according to ecofeminists, (B5) is justified by just those three features of an oppressive conceptual framework identified earlier: value-hierarchical thinking, the assumption at (B2); value dualisms, the assumed dualism of the mental and the physical at (B1) and the assumed inferiority of the physical vis-à-vis the mental at (B2); and a logic of domination, the assumption at (B4), the same as the previous premise (A4). Hence, according to ecofeminists, insofar as an oppressive patriarchal conceptual framework has functioned historically (within at least dominant Western culture) to sanction the twin dominations of women and nature (argument B), both argument B and the patriarchal conceptual framework, from whence it comes, ought to be rejected.

Of course, the preceding does not identify which premises of B are false. What is the status of premises (B1) and (B2)? Most, if not all, feminists claim that (B1), and many ecofeminists claim that (B2), have been assumed or asserted within the dominant Western philosophical and intellectual tradition.

As such, these feminists assert, as a matter of historical fact, that the dominant Western philosophical tradition has assumed the truth of (B1) and (B2). Ecofeminists, however, either deny (B2) or do not affirm (B2). Furthermore, because some ecofeminists are anxious to deny any ahistorical identification of women with nature, some ecofeminists deny (B1) when (B1) is used to support anything other than a strictly historical claim about what has been asserted or assumed to be true within patriarchal culture—e.g., when (B1) is used to assert that women properly are identified with the realm of nature and the physical. Thus, from an ecofeminist perspective, (B1) and (B2) are properly viewed as problematic though historically sanctioned claims: they are problematic precisely because of the way they have functioned historically in a patriarchal conceptual framework and culture to sanction the dominations of women and nature.

What all ecofeminists agree about, then, is the way in which the logic of domination has functioned historically within patriarchy to sustain and justify the twin dominations of women and nature.[5] Since all feminists (and not just ecofeminists) oppose patriarchy, the conclusion given at (B5), all feminists (including ecofeminists) must oppose at least the logic of domination, premise (B4), on which argument B rests—whatever the truth-value status of (B1) and (B2) outside of a patriarchal context.

That *all* feminists must oppose the logic of domination shows the breadth and depth of the ecofeminist critique of B: it is a critique not only of the three assumptions on which this argument for the domination of women and nature rests, viz., the assumptions at (B1), (B2), and (B4); it is also a critique of patriarchal conceptual frameworks generally, i.e., of those oppressive conceptual frameworks which put men "up" and women "down," allege some way in which women are morally inferior to men, and use that alleged difference to justify the subordination of women by men. Therefore, ecofeminism is necessary to any feminist critique of patriarchy, and, hence, necessary to feminism (a point I discuss again later).

Third, ecofeminism clarifies why the logic of domination, and any conceptual framework which gives rise to it, must be abolished in order both to make possible a meaningful notion of difference which does not breed domination and to prevent feminism from becoming a "support" movement based primarily on shared experiences. In contemporary society, there is no one "woman's voice," no woman (or human) *simpliciter*: every woman (or human) is a woman (or human) of some race, class, age, affectional orientation, marital status, regional or national background, and so forth. Because there are no "monolithic experiences" that all women share, feminism must be a "solidarity movement" based on shared beliefs and interests rather than a "unity in sameness" movement based on shared experiences and shared victimization.[6] In the words of Maria Lugones, "Unity—not to be confused with solidarity—is understood as conceptually tied to domination."[7]

Ecofeminists insist that the sort of logic of domination used to justify the domination of humans by gender, racial or ethnic, or class status is also used to justify the domination of nature. Because eliminating a logic of domination is part of a feminist critique—whether a critique of patriarchy, white supremacist culture, or imperialism—ecofeminists insist that *naturism* is properly viewed as an integral part of any feminist solidarity movement to end sexist oppression and the logic of domination which conceptually grounds it.

Ecofeminism Reconceives Feminism

The discussion so far has focused on some of the oppressive conceptual features of patriarchy. As I use the phrase, the "logic of traditional feminism" refers to the location of the conceptual roots of sexist oppression, at least in Western societies, in an oppressive patriarchal conceptual framework characterized by a logic of domination. Insofar as other systems of oppression (e.g., racism, classism, ageism, heterosexism) are also conceptually maintained by a logic of domination, appeal to the logic of traditional feminism ultimately locates the basic conceptual interconnections among all systems of oppression in the logic of domination. It thereby explains at a conceptual level why the eradication of sexist oppression requires the eradication of the other forms of oppression. It is by clarifying this conceptual connection between systems of oppression that a movement to end sexist oppression—traditionally the special turf of feminist theory and practice—leads to a reconceiving of feminism as a movement to end all forms of oppression.

Suppose one agrees that the logic of traditional feminism requires the expansion of feminism to include other social systems of domination (e.g., racism and classism). What warrants the inclusion of nature in these "social systems of domination"? Why must the logic of traditional feminism include the abolition of "naturism" (i.e., the domination or oppression of nonhuman nature) among the "isms" feminism must confront? The conceptual justification for expanding feminism to include ecofeminism is twofold. One basis has already been suggested: by showing that the conceptual connections between the dual dominations of women and nature are located in an oppressive and, at least in Western societies, patriarchal conceptual framework characterized by a logic of domination, ecofeminism explains how and why feminism, conceived as a movement to end sexist oppression, must be expanded and reconceived as also a movement to end naturism. This is made explicit by the following argument C:

(C1) Feminism is a movement to end sexism.
(C2) But Sexism is conceptually linked with naturism (through an oppressive conceptual framework characterized by a logic of domination).
(C3) Thus, Feminism is (also) a movement to end naturism.

Because, ultimately, these connections between sexism and naturism are conceptual—embedded in an oppressive conceptual framework—the logic of traditional feminism leads to the embracement of ecological feminism.

The other justification for reconceiving feminism to include ecofeminism has to do with the concepts of gender and nature. Just as conceptions of gender are socially constructed, so are conceptions of nature. Of course, the claim that women and nature are social constructions does not require anyone to deny that there are actual humans and actual trees, rivers, and plants. It simply implies that how women and nature are conceived is a matter of historical and social reality. These conceptions vary cross-culturally and by historical time period. As a result, any discussion of the "oppression or domination of nature" involves reference to historically specific forms of social domination of nonhuman nature by humans, just as discussion of the "domination of women" refers to historically specific forms of social domination of women by men. Although I do not argue for it here, an ecofeminist defense of the historical connections between the dominations of women and of nature, claims (B1) and (B2) in argument B, involves showing that within patriarchy the feminization of nature and the naturalization of women have been crucial to the historically successful subordinations of both.[8]

If ecofeminism promises to reconceive traditional feminism in ways which include naturism as a legitimate feminist issue, does ecofeminism also promise to reconceive environmental ethics in ways which are feminist? I think so. This is the subject of the remainder of the paper.

Climbing from Ecofeminism to Environmental Ethics

Many feminists and some environmental ethicists have begun to explore the use of first-person narrative as a way of raising philosophically germane issues in ethics often lost or underplayed in mainstream philosophical ethics. Why is this so? What is it about narrative which makes it a significant resource for theory and practice in feminism and environmental ethics? Even if appeal to first-person narrative is a helpful literary device for describing ineffable experience or a legitimate social science methodology for documenting personal and social history, how is first-person narrative a valuable vehicle of argumentation for ethical decision making and theory building? One fruitful way to begin answering these questions is to ask them of a particular first-person narrative.

Consider the following first-person narrative about rock climbing:

> For my very first rock climbing experience, I chose a somewhat private spot, away from other climbers and on-lookers. After studying "the chimney," I focused all my energy on making it to the top. I climbed with intense determination, using whatever strength and skills I had to accomplish this challenging feat. By midway I was exhausted and anxious. I couldn't see what to do next—where to put my hands or feet. Growing increasingly more weary as I clung somewhat desperately to the rock, I made a move. It didn't work. I fell. There I was, dangling midair above the rocky ground below, frightened but terribly relieved that the belay rope had held me. I knew I was safe. I took a look up at the climb that remained. I was determined to make it to the top. With renewed confidence and concentration, I finished the climb to the top.

On my second day of climbing, I rappelled down about 200 feet from the top of the Palisades at Lake Superior to just a few feet above the water level. I could see no one—not my belayer, not the other climbers, no one. I unhooked slowly from the rappel rope and took a deep cleansing breath. I looked all around me—really looked—and listened. I heard a cacophony of voices—birds, trickles of water on the rock before me, waves lapping against the rocks below. I closed my eyes and began to feel the rock with my hands—the cracks and crannies, the raised lichen and mosses, the almost imperceptible nubs that might provide a resting place for my fingers and toes when I began to climb. At that moment I was bathed in serenity. I began to talk to the rock in an almost inaudible, child-like way, as if the rock were my friend. I felt an overwhelming sense of gratitude for what it offered me—a chance to know myself and the rock differently, to appreciate unforeseen miracles like the tiny flowers growing in the even tinier cracks in the rock's surface, and to come to know a sense of being in relationship with the natural environment. It felt as if the rock and I were silent conversational partners in a longstanding friendship. I realized then that I had come to care about this cliff which was so different from me, so unmovable and invincible, independent and seemingly indifferent to my presence. I wanted to be with the rock as I climbed. Gone was the determination to conquer the rock, to forcefully impose my will on it; I wanted simply to work respectfully with the rock as I climbed. And as I climbed, that is what I felt. I felt myself *caring* for this rock and feeling thankful that climbing provided the opportunity for me to know it and myself in this new way.

There are at least four reasons why use of such a first-person narrative is important to feminism and environmental ethics. First, such a narrative gives voice to a felt sensitivity often lacking in traditional analytical ethical discourse, viz., a sensitivity to conceiving of oneself as fundamentally "in relationship with" others, including the nonhuman environment. It is a modality which takes relationships themselves seriously. It thereby stands in contrast to a strictly reductionist modality that takes relationships seriously only or primarily because of the nature of the relators or parties to those relationships (e.g., relators conceived as moral agents, right holders, interest carriers, or sentient beings). In the rock-climbing narrative above, it is the climber's relationship with the rock she climbs which takes on special significance—which is itself a locus of value—in addition to whatever moral status or moral considerability she or the rock or any other parties to the relationship may also have.

Second, such a first-person narrative gives expression to a variety of ethical attitudes and behaviors often overlooked or underplayed in mainstream Western ethics, e.g., the difference in attitudes and behaviors toward a rock when one is "making it to the top" and when one thinks of oneself as "friends with" or "caring about" the rock one climbs.[9] These different attitudes and behaviors suggest an ethically germane contrast between two different types of relationship humans or climbers may have toward a rock: an imposed conqueror-type relationship, and an emergent caring-type relationship. This contrast grows out of, and is faithful to, felt, lived experience.

The difference between conquering and caring attitudes and behaviors in relation to the natural environment provides a third reason why the use of first-person narrative is important to feminism and environmental ethics: it provides a way of conceiving of ethics and ethical meaning as emerging out of particular situations moral agents find themselves in, rather than as being imposed on those situations (e.g., as a derivation or instantiation of some predetermined abstract principle or rule). This emergent feature of narrative centralizes the importance of *voice*. When a multiplicity of cross-cultural voices are centralized, narrative is able to give expression to a range of attitudes, values, beliefs, and behaviors which may be overlooked or silenced by imposed ethical meaning and theory. As a reflection of and on felt, lived experiences, the use of narrative in ethics provides a stance from which ethical discourse can be held accountable to the historical, material, and social realities in which moral subjects find themselves.

Lastly, and for our purposes perhaps most importantly, the use of narrative has argumentative significance. Jim Cheney calls attention to this feature of narrative when he claims, "To contextualize ethical deliberation is, in some sense, to provide a narrative or story, from which the solution to the ethical dilemma emerges as the fitting conclusion."[10] Narrative has argumentative force by suggesting what counts as an appropriate conclusion to an ethical situation. One ethical conclusion suggested by the climbing narrative is that what counts as a proper ethical attitude toward mountains and rocks is an attitude of respect and care (whatever that turns out to be or involve), not one of domination and conquest.

In an essay entitled "In and Out of Harm's Way: Arrogance and Love," feminist philosopher Marilyn Frye distinguishes between "arrogant" and "loving" perception as one way of getting at this difference in the ethical attitudes of care and conquest.[11] Frye writes:

> The loving eye is a contrary of the arrogant eye.
>
> The loving eye knows the independence of the other. It is the eye of a seer who knows that nature is indifferent. It is the eye of one who knows that to know the seen, one must consult something other than one's own will and interests and fears and imagination. One must look at the thing. One must look and listen and check and question.
>
> The loving eye is one that pays a certain sort of attention. This attention can require a discipline but *not* a self-denial. The discipline is one of self-knowledge, knowledge of the scope and boundary of the self. ... In particular, it is a matter of being able to tell one's own interests from those of others and of knowing where one self leaves off and another begins. ...
>
> The loving eye does not make the object of perception into something edible, does not try to assimilate it, does not reduce it to the size of the seer's desire, fear and imagination,

and hence does not have to simplify. It knows the complexity of the other as something which will forever present new things to be known. The science of the loving eye would favor The Complexity Theory of Truth [in contrast to The Simplicity Theory of Truth] and presuppose The Endless Interestingness of the Universe.[12]

According to Frye, the loving eye is not an invasive, coercive eye which annexes others to itself, but one which "knows the complexity of the other as something which will forever present new things to be known."

When one climbs a rock as a conqueror, one climbs with an arrogant eye. When one climbs with a loving eye, one constantly "must look and listen and check and question." One recognizes the rock as something very different, something perhaps totally indifferent to one's own presence, and finds in that difference joyous occasion for celebration. One knows "the boundary of the self," where the self—the "I," the climber—leaves off and the rock begins. There is no fusion of two into one, but a complement of two entities acknowledged as separate, different, independent, yet in relationship; they are in relationship if only because the loving eye is perceiving it, responding to it, noticing it, attending to it.

An ecofeminist perspective about both women and nature involves this shift in attitude from "arrogant perception" to "loving perception" of the nonhuman world. Arrogant perception of nonhumans by humans presupposes and maintains sameness in such a way that it expands the moral community to those beings who are thought to resemble (be like, similar to, or the same as) humans in some morally significant way. Any environmental movement or ethic based on arrogant perception builds a moral hierarchy of beings and assumes some common denominator of moral considerability in virtue of which like beings deserve similar treatment or moral consideration and unlike beings do not. Such environmental ethics are or generate a "unity in sameness." In contrast, "loving perception" presupposes and maintains difference—a distinction between the self and other, between human and at least some nonhumans—in such a way that perception of the other as other is an expression of love for one who/which is recognized at the outset as independent, dissimilar, different. As Maria Lugones says, in loving perception, "Love is seen not as fusion and erasure of difference but as incompatible with them."[13] "Unity in sameness" alone is an erasure of difference.

"Loving perception" of the nonhuman natural world is an attempt to understand what it means for humans to care about the nonhuman world, a world acknowledged as being independent, different, perhaps even indifferent to humans. Humans are different from rocks in important ways, even if they are also both members of some ecological community. A moral community based on loving perception of oneself in relationship with a rock, or with the natural environment as a whole, is one which acknowledges and respects difference, whatever "sameness" also exists.[14] The limits of loving perception are determined only by the limits of one's (e.g., a person's, a community's) ability to respond lovingly (or with appropriate care, trust, or friendship)—whether it is to other humans or to the nonhuman world and elements of it.[15]

If what I have said so far is correct, then there are very different ways to climb a mountain and how one climbs it and how one narrates the experience of climbing it matter ethically. If one climbs with "arrogant perception," with an attitude of "conquer and control," one keeps intact the very sorts of thinking that characterize a logic of domination and an oppressive conceptual framework. Since the oppressive conceptual framework which sanctions the domination of nature is a patriarchal one, one also thereby keeps intact, even if unwittingly, a patriarchal conceptual framework. Because the dismantling of patriarchal conceptual frameworks is a feminist issue, how one climbs a mountain and how one narrates—or tells the story—about the experience of climbing also are feminist issues. In this way, ecofeminism makes visible why, at a conceptual level, environmental ethics is a feminist issue. I turn now to a consideration of ecofeminism as a distinctively feminist and environmental ethic.

Ecofeminism as a Feminist and Environmental Ethic

A feminist ethic involves a twofold commitment to critique male bias in ethics wherever it occurs, and to develop ethics which are not male-biased. Sometimes this involves articulation of values (e g., values of care, appropriate trust, kinship, friendship) often lost or underplayed in mainstream ethics.[16] Sometimes it involves engaging in theory building by pioneering in new directions or by revamping old theories in gender sensitive ways. What makes the critiques of old theories or conceptualizations of new ones "feminist" is that they emerge out of sex–gender analyses and reflect whatever those analyses reveal about gendered experience and gendered social reality.

As I conceive feminist ethics in the pre-feminist present, it rejects attempts to conceive of ethical theory in terms of necessary and sufficient conditions, because it assumes that there is no essence (in the sense of some transhistorical, universal, absolute abstraction) of feminist ethics. While attempts to formulate joint necessary and sufficient conditions of a feminist ethic are unfruitful, nonetheless, there are some necessary conditions, what I prefer to call "boundary conditions," of a feminist ethic. These boundary conditions clarify some of the minimal conditions of a feminist ethic without suggesting that feminist ethics has some ahistorical essence. They are like the boundaries of a quilt or collage. They delimit the territory of the piece without dictating what the interior, the design, the actual pattern of the piece looks like. Because the actual design of the quilt emerges from the multiplicity of voices of women in a cross-cultural context, the design will change over time. It is not something static.

What are some of the boundary conditions of a feminist ethic? First, nothing can become part of a feminist ethic—can be part of the quilt—that promotes sexism, racism, classism, or any other "isms" of social domination. Of course, people may disagree about what counts as a sexist act, racist attitude, classist behavior. What counts as sexism, racism, or classism may vary cross-culturally.

Still, because a feminist ethic aims at eliminating sexism and sexist bias, and (as I have already shown) sexism is intimately connected in conceptualization and in practice to racism, classism, and naturism, a feminist ethic must be anti-sexist, anti-racist, anti-classist, anti-naturist and opposed to any "ism" which presupposes or advances a logic of domination.

Second, a feminist ethic is a *contextualist* ethic. A contextualist ethic is one which sees ethical discourse and practice as emerging from the voices of people located in different historical circumstances. A contextualist ethic is properly viewed as a collage or mosaic, a tapestry of voices that emerges out of felt experiences. Like any collage or mosaic, the point is not to have one picture based on a unity of voices, but a pattern which emerges out of the very different voices of people located in different circumstances. When a contextualist ethic is feminist, it gives central place to the voices of women.

Third, since a feminist ethic gives central significance to the diversity of women's voices, a feminist ethic must be structurally pluralistic rather than unitary or reductionistic. It rejects the assumption that there is "one voice" in terms of which ethical values, beliefs, attitudes, and conduct can be assessed.

Fourth, a feminist ethic reconceives ethical theory as theory in process which will change over time. Like all theory, a feminist ethic is based on some generalizations.[17] Nevertheless, the generalizations associated with it are themselves a pattern of voices within which the different voices emerging out of concrete and alternative descriptions of ethical situations have meaning. The coherence of a feminist theory so conceived is given within a historical and conceptual context, i.e., within a set of historical, socioeconomic circumstances (including circumstances of race, class, age, and affectional orientation) and within a set of basic beliefs, values, attitudes, and assumptions about the world.

Fifth, because a feminist ethic is contextualist, structurally pluralistic, and "in-process," one way to evaluate the claims of a feminist ethic is in terms of their inclusiveness: those claims (voices, patterns of voices) are morally and epistemologically favored (preferred, better, less partial, less biased) which are more inclusive of the felt experiences and perspectives of oppressed persons. The condition of inclusiveness requires and ensures that the diverse voices of women (as oppressed persons) will be given legitimacy in ethical theory building. It thereby helps to minimize empirical bias, e.g., bias rising from faulty or false generalizations based on stereotyping, too small a sample size, or a skewed sample. It does so by ensuring that any generalizations which are made about ethics and ethical decision making include—indeed cohere with—the patterned voices of women.[18]

Sixth, a feminist ethic makes no attempt to provide an "objective" point of view, since it assumes that in contemporary culture there really is no such point of view. As such, it does not claim to be "unbiased" in the sense of "value-neutral" or "objective." However, it does assume that whatever bias it has as an ethic centralizing the voices of oppressed persons is a better bias—"better" because it is more inclusive and therefore less partial—than those which exclude those voices.[19]

Seventh, a feminist ethic provides a central place for values typically unnoticed, underplayed, or misrepresented in traditional ethics, e.g., values of care, love, friendship, and appropriate trust.[20] Again, it need not do this at the exclusion of considerations of rights, rules, or utility. There may be many contexts in which talk of rights or of utility is useful or appropriate. For instance, in contracts or property relationships, talk of rights may be useful and appropriate. In deciding what is cost effective or advantageous to the most people, talk of utility may be useful and appropriate. In a feminist *qua* contextualist ethic, whether or not such talk is useful or appropriate depends on the context; other values (e.g., values of care, trust, friendship) are not viewed as reducible to or captured solely in terms of such talk.

Eighth, a feminist ethic also involves a reconception of what it is to be human and what it is for humans to engage in ethical decision making, since it rejects as either meaningless or currently untenable any gender-free or gender-neutral description of humans, ethics, and ethical decision making. It thereby rejects what Alison Jaggar calls "abstract individualism," i.e., the position that it is possible to identify a human essence or human nature that exists independently of any particular historical context.[21] Humans and human moral conduct are properly understood essentially (and not merely accidentally) in terms of networks or webs of historical and concrete relationships.

All the props are now in place for seeing how ecofeminism provides the framework for a distinctively feminist and environmental ethic. It is a feminism that critiques male bias wherever it occurs in ethics (including environmental ethics) and aims at providing an ethic (including an environmental ethic) which is not male biased—and it does so in a way that satisfies the preliminary boundary conditions of a feminist ethic.

First, ecofeminism is quintessentially anti-naturist. Its anti-naturism consists in the rejection of any way of thinking about or acting toward nonhuman nature that reflects a logic, values, or attitude of domination. Its anti-naturist, anti-sexist, anti-racist, anti-classist (and so forth, for all other "isms" of social domination) stance forms the outer boundary of the quilt: nothing gets on the quilt which is naturist, sexist, racist, classist, and so forth.

Second, ecofeminism is a contextualist ethic. It involves a shift *from* a conception of ethics as primarily a matter of rights, rules, or principles predetermined and applied in specific cases to entities viewed as competitors in the contest of moral standing, *to* a conception of ethics as growing out of what Jim Cheney calls "defining relationships," i.e., relationships conceived in some sense as defining who one is. As a contextualist ethic, it is not that rights, or rules, or principles are not relevant or important. Clearly they are in certain contexts and for certain purposes. It is just that what makes them relevant or important is that those to whom they apply are entities in relationship with others.

Ecofeminism also involves an ethical shift from granting moral consideration to nonhumans exclusively on the grounds of some similarity they share with humans (e.g., rationality, interests, moral agency, sentiency, rightholder status) to "a highly contextual account to see clearly what a human being is and what the nonhuman world might be, morally speaking, for human beings."[22] For an ecofeminist, how a moral agent is in relationship to another becomes of central significance, not simply that a moral agent is a moral agent or is bound by rights, duties, virtue, or utility to act in a certain way.

Third, ecofeminism is structurally pluralistic in that it presupposes and maintains difference—difference among humans as well as between humans and at least some elements of nonhuman nature. Thus, while ecofeminism denies the "nature/culture" split, it affirms that humans are both members of an ecological community (in some respects) and different from it (in other respects). Ecofeminism's attention to relationships and community is not, therefore, an erasure of difference but a respectful acknowledgment of it.

Fourth, ecofeminism reconceives theory as theory in process. It focuses on patterns of meaning which emerge, for instance, from the storytelling and first-person narratives of women (and others) who deplore the twin dominations of women and nature. The use of narrative is one way to ensure that the content of the ethic—the pattern of the quilt—may/will change over time, as the historical and material realities of women's lives change and as more is learned about women-nature connections and the destruction of the nonhuman world.

Fifth, ecofeminism is inclusivist. It emerges from the voices of women who experience the harmful domination of nature and the way that domination is tied to their domination as women. It emerges from listening to the voices of indigenous peoples such as Native Americans who have been dislocated from their land and have witnessed the attendant undermining of such values as appropriate reciprocity, sharing, and kinship that characterize traditional Indian culture. It emerges from listening to voices of those who, like Nathan Hare, critique traditional approaches to environmental ethics as white and bourgeois, and as failing to address issues of "black ecology" and the "ecology" of the inner city and urban spaces.[23] It also emerges out of the voices of Chipko women who see the destruction of "earth, soil, and water" as intimately connected with their own inability to survive economically.[24] With its emphasis on inclusivity and difference, ecofeminism provides a framework for recognizing that what counts as ecology and what counts as appropriate conduct toward both human and nonhuman environments is largely a matter of context.

Sixth, as a feminism, ecofeminism makes no attempt to provide an "objective" point of view. It is a social ecology. It recognizes the twin dominations of women and nature as social problems rooted both in very concrete, historical, socioeconomic circumstances and in oppressive patriarchal conceptual frameworks which maintain and sanction these circumstances.

Seventh, ecofeminism makes a central place for values of care, love, friendship, trust, and appropriate reciprocity—values that presuppose that our relationships to others are central to our understanding of who we are.[25] It thereby gives voice to the sensitivity that in climbing a mountain, one is doing something in relationship with an "other," an "other" whom one can come to care about and treat respectfully.

Lastly, an ecofeminist ethic involves a reconception of what it means to be human, and in what human ethical behavior consists. Ecofeminism denies abstract individualism. Humans are who we are in large part by virtue of the historical and social contexts and the relationships we are in, including our relationships with nonhuman nature. Relationships are not something extrinsic to who we are, not an "add on" feature of human nature; they play an essential role in shaping what it is to be human. Relationships of humans to the nonhuman environment are, in part, constitutive of what it is to be a human.

By making visible the interconnections among the dominations of women and nature, ecofeminism shows that both are feminist issues and that explicit acknowledgment of both is vital to any responsible environmental ethic. Feminism must embrace ecological feminism if it is to end the domination of women because the domination of women is tied conceptually and historically to the domination of nature.

A responsible environmental ethic also must embrace feminism. Otherwise, even the seemingly most revolutionary, liberational, and holistic ecological ethic will fail to take seriously the interconnected dominations of nature and women that are so much a part of the historical legacy and conceptual framework that sanctions the exploitation of nonhuman nature. Failure to make visible these interconnected, twin dominations results in an inaccurate account of how it is that nature has been and continues to be dominated and exploited and produces an environmental ethic that lacks the depth necessary to be truly inclusive of the realities of persons who at least in dominant Western culture have been intimately tied with that exploitation, viz., women. Whatever else can be said in favor of such holistic ethics, a failure to make visible ecofeminist insights into the common denominators of the twin oppressions of women and nature is to perpetuate, rather than overcome, the source of that oppression.

This last point deserves further attention. It may be objected that as long as the end result is "the same"—the development of an environmental ethic which does not emerge out of or reinforce an oppressive conceptual framework—it does not matter whether that ethic (or the ethic endorsed in getting there) is feminist or not. Hence, it simply is not the case that any adequate environmental ethic must be feminist. My argument, in contrast, has been that it does matter, and for three important reasons. First, there is the scholarly issue of accurately representing historical reality, and that, ecofeminists claim, requires acknowledging the historical feminization of nature and naturalization of women as part of the exploitation of nature. Second, I have shown that the conceptual connections between the domination of women and the domination of nature are located in an oppressive and, at least in Western societies, patriarchal conceptual framework characterized by a logic of domination. Thus, I have shown that failure to notice the nature of this connection leaves at best an incomplete, inaccurate, and partial account of what is required of a conceptually adequate environmental ethic. An ethic which does not acknowledge this is simply not the same as one that does, whatever else the similarities between them. Third, the claim that, in contemporary culture, one can have an adequate environmental ethic which is not feminist assumes that, in contemporary culture, the label feminist does not add anything crucial to the nature or description of environmental ethics. I have shown that at least in contemporary culture this is false, for the word feminist currently helps to clarify just how the domination of nature is conceptually linked to patriarchy and, hence, how the liberation of nature, is conceptually linked to the termination of patriarchy. Thus, because it has critical bite in contemporary culture, it serves as an important reminder that in contemporary sex-gendered, raced, classed, and naturist culture, an unlabeled position functions as a privileged and "unmarked" position.

That is, without the addition of the word *feminist*, one presents environmental ethics as if it has no bias, including male-gender bias, which is just what ecofeminists deny: failure to notice the connections between the twin oppressions of women and nature is male-gender bias.

One of the goals of feminism is the eradication of all oppressive sex–gender (and related race, class, age, affectional preference) categories and the creation of a world in which *difference does not breed domination*—say, the world of 4001. If in 4001 an "adequate environmental ethic" is a "feminist environmental ethic," the word *feminist* may then be redundant and unnecessary. However, this is not 4001, and in terms of the current historical and conceptual reality the dominations of nature and of women are intimately connected. Failure to notice or make visible that connection in 1990 perpetuates the mistaken (and privileged) view that "environmental ethics" is not a feminist issue, and that *feminist* adds nothing to environmental ethics.

Conclusion

I have argued in this paper that ecofeminism provides a framework for a distinctively feminist and environmental ethic. Ecofeminism grows out of the felt and theorized about connections between the domination of women and the domination of nature. As a contextualist ethic, ecofeminism refocuses environmental ethics on what nature might mean, morally speaking, for humans, and on how the relational attitudes of humans to others—humans as well as nonhumans—sculpt both what it is to be human and the nature and ground of human responsibilities to the nonhuman environment. Part of what this refocusing does is to take seriously the voices of women and other oppressed persons in the construction of that ethic.

A Sioux elder once told me a story about his son. He sent his seven-year-old son to live with the child's grandparents on a Sioux reservation so that he could "learn the Indian ways." Part of what the grandparents taught the son was how to hunt and kill the four leggeds of the forest. As I heard the story, the boy was taught, "to shoot your four-legged brother in his hind area, slowing it down but not killing it. Then, take the four legged's head in your hands, and look into his eyes. The eyes are where all the suffering is. Look into your brother's eyes and feel his pain. Then, take your knife and cut the four-legged under his chin, here, on his neck, so that he dies quickly. And as you do, ask your brother, the four-legged, for forgiveness for what you do. Offer also a prayer of thanks to your four-legged kin for offering his body to you just now, when you need food to eat and clothing to wear. And promise the four-legged that you will put yourself back into the earth when you die, to become nourishment for the earth, and for the sister flowers, and for the brother deer. It is appropriate that you should offer this blessing for the four-legged and, in due time, reciprocate in turn with your body in this way, as the four-legged gives life to you for your survival." As I reflect upon that story, I am struck by the power of the environmental ethic that grows out of and takes seriously narrative, context, and such values and relational attitudes as care, loving perception, and appropriate reciprocity, and doing what is appropriate in a given situation—however that notion of appropriateness eventually gets filled out. I am also struck by what one is able to see, once one begins to explore some of the historical and conceptual connections between the dominations of women and of nature. A re-conceiving and re-visioning of both feminism and environmental ethics, is, I think, the power and promise of ecofeminism.

Notes

1. Francoise d'Eaubonne, *Le Feminisme ou la Mort* (Paris: Pierre Horay, 1974).

2. I discuss this in my paper, "Toward an Ecofeminist Ethic."

3. Murray Bookchin, "Social Ecology versus 'Deep Ecology'", in *Green Perspectives: Newsletter of the Green Program Project*, no. 4–5 (Summer 1987): 9.

4. It may be that in contemporary Western society, which is so thoroughly structured by categories of gender, race, class, age, and affectional orientation, that there simply is no meaningful notion of "value-hierarchical thinking" which does not function in an oppressive context. For purposes of this paper, I leave that question open.

5. I make no attempt here to defend the historically sanctioned truth of these premises.

6. See, e.g., Bell Hooks, *Feminist Theory: From Margin to Center* (Boston: South End Press, 1984), pp. 51–52.

7. Maria Lugones, "Playfulness, 'World-Travelling,' and Loving Perception," *Hypatia* 2 (Summer 1987): 3.

8. See, e.g., Gray, *Green Paradise Lost*: Griffin, *Women and Nature*; Merchant, *The Death of Nature*; and Ruether, *New Woman/New Earth*.

9. It is interesting to note that the image of being friends with the Earth is one which cytogeneticist Barbara McClintock uses when she describes the importance of having "a feeling for the organism," "listening to the material [in this case the corn plant]," in one's work as a scientist. See Evelyn Fox Keller, "Women, Science, and Popular Mythology," in *Machina Ex Dea: Feminist Perspectives on Technology*, ed. Joan Rothschild (New York: Pergamon Press, 1983), and Evelyn Fox Keller, *A Feeling For the Organism: The Life and Work of Barbara McClintock* (San Francisco: W. H. Freeman, 1983).

10. Cheney, "Eco-Feminism and Deep Ecology," 144.

11. Marilyn Frye, "In and Out of Harm's Way: Arrogance and Love," *The Politics of Reality* (Trumansburg, New York: The Crossing Press, 1983), pp. 66–72.

12. Ibid., pp. 75–76.

13. Maria Lugones, "Playfulness," p. 3.

14. Cheney makes a similar point in "Eco-Feminism and Deep Ecology," p. 140.

15. Ibid., p. 138.

16. This account of a feminist ethic draws on my "Toward an Ecofeminist Ethic."

17. Marilyn Frye makes this point in her illuminating paper, "The Possibility of Feminist Theory," read at the American Philosophical Association Central Division in Chicago, 1986. My discussion of feminist theory is inspired largely by that paper and by Kathryn Addelson's paper "Moral Revolution," in *Women and Values: Reading in Recent Feminist Philosophy*, ed. Marilyn Pearsall (Belmont: Wadsworth, 1986) pp. 291–309.

18. Notice that the standard of inclusiveness does not exclude the voices of men. It is just that those voices must cohere with the voices of women.

19. For a more in-depth discussion of the notions of impartiality and bias, see my paper, "Critical Thinking and Feminism," *Informal Logic* 10, no. l (Winter 1988): 31–44.

20. The burgeoning literature on these values is noteworthy. See, e.g., Carol Gilligan, *In a Different Voice: Psychological Theories and Women's Development* (Cambridge: Harvard University Press, 1982); *Mapping the Moral Domain: A Contribution of Women's Thinking to Psychological Theory and Education*, ed. Carol Gilligan, Janie Victoria Ward, and Jill McLean Taylor, with Betty Bardige (Cambridge: Harvard University Press, 1988); Nel Noddings, *Caring: A Feminine Approach to Ethics and Moral Education* (Berkeley: University of California Press, 1984); Maria Lugones and Elizabeth V. Spelman, "Have We Got a Theory for You! Feminist Theory, Cultural Imperialism, and the Women's Voice," *Women's Studies International Forum 6* (1983): 573–81; Maria Lugones, "Playfulness"; Annette C. Baier, "What Do Women Want in a Moral Theory?" *Nous* 19 (1985): 53–63.

21. Alison Jaggar, *Feminist Politics and Human Nature* (Totowa: Rowman and Allanheld, 1980): pp. 42–44.

22. Cheney, "Eco-Feminism and Deep Ecology," p. 144.

23. Nathan Hare, "Black Ecology," in *Environmental Ethics*, ed. K. S. Shrader-Frechette (Pacific Grove, Calif.: Boxwood Press, 1981), pp. 229–36.

24. For an ecofeminist discussion of the Chipko movement, see my "Toward an Ecofeminist Ethic," and Shiva's *Staying Alive*.

25. See Cheney, "Eco-Feminism and Deep Ecology," p. 122.

7B1. Some Problems With Ecofeminism

By Susan Feldman

K aren Warren claims that there is an interconnection between the domination of nature by humans and the domination of women by men. She uses the following argument schemas to set out the 'logic of domination'.

A1. Humans do, and plants and rocks do not, have the capacity to consciously and radically change the community in which they live.

A2. Whatever has the capacity to consciously and radically change the community in which it lives is morally superior to whatever lacks this capacity.

A3. Thus, humans are morally superior to plants and rocks.

A4. For any X and Y, if X is morally superior to Y, then X is morally justified in subordinating Y.

A5. Thus, humans are morally justified in subordinating plants and rocks. (1)

She points out that the assumptions A2 and A4 are critical, since without them, all that can be shown is that people are different from plants and rocks. A4 in particular expresses the logic of domination. (269) This key assumption recurs in the reasoning justifying male domination of females:

B1. Women are identified with nature and the realm of the physical; men are identified with the "human" and the realm of the mental.

B2. Whatever is identified with nature and realm of the physical is inferior to ("below") whatever is identified with the "human" and the realm of the mental; or conversely, the latter is superior to ("above") the former.

B3. Thus, women are inferior to ("below") men; or conversely, men are superior to ("above") women.

B4. For any X and Y, if X is superior to Y, then X is justified in subordinating Y.

B5. Thus, men are justified in subordinating women.

Claims of superiority, moral or otherwise, justify the subordination of the alleged inferior by the alleged superior, via the justifiable domination assumption 4. Feminism involves the principled opposition to domination, hence it opposes B4. But since B4 is virtually the same as A4, and since women are culturally identified with nature, feminism should also involve an opposition to A4, and its use in the A argument justifying the subordination of nature by people. "That *all* feminists must oppose the logic of domination shows the breadth and depth of the ecofeminist critique of B; it is a critique not only of the three assumptions on which this argument for the domination of women and nature rests, viz. the assumption at B1, B2 and B4; it is also a critique of patriarchal conceptual frameworks generally, i.e. of those oppressive conceptual frameworks which put men "up" and women "down". ... Therefore, ecofeminism is necessary to any feminist critique of patriarchy, and hence necessary to feminism ..." (270) That is, feminism involves a rejection of the logic of domination, value dualisms, and value hierarchical thinking, which treats differences as grounds for moral rankings of superiority and inferiority, and which justifies domination, as reflected in B4. But that same logic of domination operates to justify the human domination of nature, so feminists must be as opposed to the latter as to men's domination of women.

(In what follows I will use the term domination of X by Y to express the relation of subordination of X by Y, since Warren objects primarily to the 'logic of domination' although she couches her arguments in terms of subordination.)

I have no doubt that a feminist's principled objection to the logic of domination *could* lead her to reject that logic when applied to natural objects such as plants or rocks. However, it does not follow from this possibility, or from Warren's parallel reasoning that this objection *must* lead to her to reject 'naturism' (Warren's term for the unjust domination of nature by people, in parallel to 'sexism'). There are undoubtedly multiple theories of domination and its wrongness, but in at least the enlightenment tradition, which played a major role in the development of contemporary feminism, the conditions for there being grounds to object to domination do apply to the domination of women by men, but do not apply to the domination of nature by people.

Modern western feminism is very much the product of enlightenment political thought. This is not to say all enlightenment thinkers were in fact feminists—far from it. Kant and Rousseau, for example, were thoroughly anti-feminist and indeed misogynist. However, certain key notions for feminism and feminist objections to unjust domination arise from the enlightenment framework, exemplified by Kant's moral theory: moral autonomy, involving the moral agency and rights of rational beings, and moral equality of persons, independent of factual equality. The domination of women by men, women's lack of political and legal standing, their social inferiority inside and outside of the home, offends the enlightenment sensibility (and should have offended Kant) because it violates the autonomy and equality requirements: that all persons, by virtue of their rationality, (whatever the particulars of their actual abilities) are entitled to self rule, in the moral and social sphere. Subordination of other persons, whether in the form of human slavery, denial of political rights, or conventional treatment of women as not full political, and social actors is morally offensive. It treats rational agents as non-rational patients, "thingifying" them. Even under the guise of being for their own good, the control of women's choices and activities by men ignores the fact of women's moral agency and concomitant responsibility. Treating women as moral inferiors whose choices must be more carefully controlled and constrained than those of most men, on this enlightenment view is a paradigm of disrespectful, immoral treatment.

This enlightenment view objects to the domination of women by men not because it is domination but because it is *unjust* domination. B4 becomes moot because factual equality for persons is delinked from moral equality. (2) Just being the same *kind* : human, and putatively rational, is sufficient proof of moral equality. Either B1 reports a false belief (one that identifies women with nature) or B2 is a false premise: if women are culturally identified with nature, it is illegitimate to leap to claims of inferiority. Thus, the conclusions B3 and B5 do not stem from a sound argument.

So far, I have been outlining the broad enlightenment picture in which the moral equality of women with men has been advanced. On this picture, that the domination of women by men is unjust provides no grounds to object to domination of other beings. It is unjust domination, not domination itself, which is the target of moral objection. And much of contemporary feminism emerges from this enlightenment tradition. Hence, a contemporary feminist may easily separate objection to sexism from objection to 'naturism'.

But more, and worse for ecofeminism, follows from the reflection on the enlightenment rejection of the unjust domination of women by men. The rationale for finding domination unjust involves moral objection to "thingifying" an agent: bending or ignoring the will of the one being dominated for the satisfaction of the dominator. This requires, at the very least, that the one being dominated has a will, and raises the question of the intelligibility of applying the characterizations of justice/injustice to the domination of non-conscious, non-volitional objects for the reason of that domination. (3) Consider the options:

a. If domination of X by Y can be taken to be unjust and morally objectionable for the reason of that domination, then X must have some kind of will.
b. If X has no will, then domination of X by Y is not unjust because of that domination. (It might be unjust for other reasons, but not from the simple fact of the domination relationship; additionally, it might be taken to be connected to a vice, in the same way that gluttony is taken to be a vice, but such vices are defects in character and are not unjust conduct).

Re:a. As the line of reasoning concerning the enlightenment view of the domination of women suggests, the reason that it is wrong to dominate women lies in the control of the rational or moral will by another. Ignoring someone's choices, overriding them, or forbidding the conditions for the consciousness and articulation of those choices are paradigmatically immoral acts. The value and dignity of each rational individual lies in her rational will:the source of the moral law. Subordinating her capacity of choice to that of another, controlling, overriding or ignoring the choices stemming from this will treats the person disrespectfully, as a thing, ignoring in that individual the source of her unique and priceless worth:the capacity to be a moral agent. Thus, a necessary condition for the domination of X by Y to be morally objectionable is that X is conscious and volitional.

Re b: A species can be said to dominate an ecosystem or an eagle can be said to dominate a mountaintop. However, in these cases, it would be unintelligible to characterize this domination as unjust or morally objectionable, without further explanation. A fact about the proliferation of one species, and its dominant role in an ecosystem, by itself implies nothing about its value. There may be reasons to deplore the domination in particular cases: e.g. the proliferation of a given species might disrupt the balance of an ecosystem, and this could be judged wrong, say, by a land ethicist. This judgement, however, although negative, is not one of injustice, and is based on valuing balance and integrity of ecosystems, so it is in content and grounds different than the judgment of wrongness of the domination of women by men. In different cases, there is no reason for a moral judgement about the fact of domination: that an eagle dominates the mountaintop, or that dogs are subordinate to the dominant member in a dog pack, invites no moral concern. In the case of humans and nature, e.g. logging an old growth forest, it is not domination as such which raises concerns for environmental ethics, but rather that the logging destroys an increasingly rare functioning ecosystem. Ethical concerns about the treatment of natural objects can, and for a true environmental ethic, *should* stem from commitments to the value of these natural objects, and their functioning and biological integrity, and not from concerns about justice.

We can now return to A4. If Y has no will, then either moral justification of this relationship is irrelevant, or if this is an issue of moral concern, it is because of other features of the treatment of Y by X, and the context in which it occurs.

The ecofeminist claim that the plundering of nature and the oppression of women represent the same logic of domination and are both wrong for the same reason is thus problematic. On the historically influential enlightenment view of unjust domination, the claim is unintelligible. Yet the enlightenment framework provided a decent explanation of the wrongness of domination of women.

Of course an ecofeminist such as Warren will object to the importation of enlightenment views to analyse domination:after all, the enlightenment celebrated human control over nature, and most of its adherents fudged the case for the moral equality of women. However, to link every feminist position with the rejection of naturism, Warren has to debunk, and not simply ignore, enlightenment feminism. She must argue either that the enlightenment tradition is incompatible with feminism, which is historically false, or that enlightenment feminism is conceptually unstable, so that while such feminists try to separate the domination of nature from the domination of women, the grounds for doing so are incoherent. However, that case has yet to be made.

It is at this point that we can see the artificiality of Warren's B argument: while her reconstruction of patriarchal reasoning in B is supposed to reveal the deep motivations underlying the acceptance of the sexist premise B3, as a point of fact B3 has been supported in multiple fashions throughout intellectual history. For example, the inferiority of women to men is fashioned, by Aristoteleans, in terms of the weakness of women's faculty of reason and inability to control appetites and passion by reason. This might tend to support Warren's view, if we assume the passions are identified with nature, and not just, say, with animal life. Yet, in contrast, the enlightenment misogynist Rousseau justifies training women for inferiority and submission to men for the purpose of upholding family order. The point is that the reasons for misogyny are various and premise B1 and B2 are entirely replaceable in the argument for patriarchal control of women. B, in short, is not a sketch of the only argument supporting the domination of women, or even an influential one; rather B represents ecofeminist conjectures about the deep cultural/cognitive reasons for belief in B3. These conjectures then reconstruct intellectual history to cast patriarchy and the domination of nature as evil twins when in fact, in other genealogies, they might not even be in the same family.

The upshot is that the 'logic of domination' is not a single logic after all, at least in the tradition which gave clear articulation to the moral objection to unjust domination.

Notes

1. Karen Warren, "The Power and Promise of Ecological Feminism". Reprinted in Donald Van DeVeer and Christine Pierce. *The Environmental Ethics and Policy Book* (Belmont, CA.: Wadsworth Publishing Co., 1994.) pp. 267–281).Originally in *Environmental Ethics*, Vol 12, No.2 (Summer 1990) 125–146.

2. The enlightenment feminism view a): that women as well as men hold rights naturally, and b): that women are men's moral equals runs through writers such as Mary Wollenstonecraft and later John Stuart Mill. In both writers, however, there is a question mark concerning women's factual equality with men. Are women as capable as men in certain activities? Mill raises his famous objections to claims about factual equality in this connection: we cannot at present tell what women are naturally like because no one has ever seen them absent their domination by men. John Stuart Mill. *The Subjection of Women*. (Cambridge, MA: MIT Press. 1970). p. 22.

3. Non-human animals pose a complication, to both the enlightenment view and to Warren's A2, since many have wills, and are conscious, yet are not considered to be agents, capable of making choices. In what follows, I will bracket the issue of whether human domination of non-human animals is unjust (although I will assume that animal domination of other animals (as in the dominance hierarchy of a wolf pack) is not subject to moral characterization.

7B2. Can Africana Women Truly Embrace Ecological Feminism?

By Fainos Mangena

Introduction

There are different forms of ecological feminism with all of them agreeing that there are important connections between the oppression of women and the ill-treatment of non-human animals by humans. My task in this essay is to reflect on Warren's defense of ecological feminism as contained in her classic essay entitled: "The Power and Promise of Ecological Feminism" with a view to establishing whether this theory is transferrable to sub-Saharan Africa. In this essay, Warren begins by making the observation that there are important connections between the domination of women and the domination of nature. Warren links this connection with what she calls the *Oppressive Patriarchal Conceptual Framework* which, according to her, looks down upon women the same way it looks down upon non-human creatures. Using the Africana Womanist theory conceptualized by Clenora Hudson-Weems and the method of deduction in philosophy, I argue that while the discourse on feminism has received worldwide acclaim and while feminists have raised genuine concerns about how they are oppressed by their male counterparts, I find it difficult to apply or transpose the idea of feminism, let alone ecological feminism to Africa since the history of feminism, and by extension ecological feminism precludes the values and experiences of women of African descent. As a result of this charge and given the spiritual character of African environments, I argue that there is no correlation between the oppression of women and the ill-treatment of nature in Africa. In the final analysis, this reasoning automatically allows me to draw the conclusion that: "No Black African women are ecological feminists." Below, I outline and explain the deductive method in philosophy which I use partly to dismiss both African feminism and the idea of African ecological feminism.

The Deductive Method in Philosophy

The deductive method in Philosophy stipulates that the conclusion of an argument must necessarily follow from its premises (COPI 1994, 54). Thus, when the reasoning in a deductive argument is correct, that argument becomes *valid*; when the reasoning in a deductive argument is incorrect, that argument becomes *invalid* (1994, 56). In every deductive argument, either the premises succeed in providing conclusive grounds for the truth of the conclusion, or they do not succeed. If they do, the

Fainos Mangena, "Can Africana Women Truly Embrace Ecological Feminism?" *Filosofia Theoretica: Journal of African Philosophy, Culture and Religions*, vol. 3, no. 2, pp. 124-139. Copyright © 2014 by The Calabar School of Philosophy (CSP). Reprinted with permission.

argument becomes valid and sound. If they don't, the argument may remain valid but unsound. So, *validity* has to do with the formal or syntactic relational aspect of the premises and conclusion in an argument, while *soundness* has to do with the semantic aspect of the premises and conclusion in an argument. But in all cases, validity is a pre-condition for soundness, that is to say, an argument cannot be sound without being valid.

The three examples below show how valid and sound arguments are structured, with argument **A** representing a valid argument and argument **B** and **C** representing sound arguments:

A

1. All Black African feminists are unmarried Women

2. All unmarried women are Ecological feminists

   Therefore, all Ecological feminists are Black African feminists

B

1. All Feminists are White supremacists

2. No White supremacists are Black African women

   Therefore, No Black African women are feminists

Note that if we take the conclusion of argument **B** above to be the premise of argument **C**, below, we can draw the conclusion: "No Black African women are Ecological feminists" as illustrated by argument **C** below:

C

1. No Black African women are feminists

   Therefore, No Black African women are Ecological feminists

Notice that the conclusion of argument **A**, "All ecological feminists are Black African women," follows from premises 1 and 2. This makes the argument valid. But in deductive inferences, validity does not always translate to soundness or truthfulness. Thus, while argument **A** is valid, it is not sound because it is not true that "All Black African feminists are unmarried women," or that "All unmarried women are ecological feminists." The conclusion drawn from these two premises is also not true, that is, "All ecological feminists are Black African women." Having said this, it is important to note that argument B is valid and sound in the following ways: In my view and judging from the nature and character of feminism which I shall outline later in this essay, it is true that "All feminists are White supremacists." It is also true that "No Black African women are White supremacists." The conclusion—"No Black African women are feminists"—which is drawn from two premises above is also true in my view.

I also take argument **C**, which is a development of argument **B** to be an example of a valid and sound argument. In my view, if the premise "No Black African women are feminists" is based on a truism, then the conclusion "No Black African women are ecological feminists" should immediately follow. Note that arguments **A** and **B** are mediate inferences as the conclusion is drawn from two premises but argument **C** is an immediate inference as the conclusion is drawn from one premise. In the rest of the essay, I outline and explain the premises that lead to the conclusion that "No Black African women are feminists" and "No Black African women are ecological feminists" as represented by arguments **B** and **C**. To kick start this important debate, I now present Warren's ecological feminism.

Warren's Presentation of Ecological Feminism

According to Warren, *ecological feminism* is the position that there are important connections—historical, symbolic and theoretical—between the domination of women and the domination of nature (WARREN 1990, 342). Warren argues that because the conceptual connections between the dual dominations of women and nature are located in an *Oppressive Patriarchal Conceptual Framework* characterized by the logic of domination, (1) traditional feminism must expand feminism to include ecological feminism (2) ecological feminism must provide a framework for developing a distinctively feminist environmental ethic (1990, 342).

But how are these *Oppressive Patriarchal Conceptual Frameworks* to be explained by ecological feminists? Warren begins by defining and explaining Conceptual frameworks in general before defining and explaining *Oppressive Patriarchal Conceptual Frameworks*. For Warren, a *Conceptual Framework* is a set of basic beliefs, values, attitudes and assumptions which shape and reflect how one views oneself and one's own world (1990, 342). It is a socially constructed lens through which we perceive ourselves and others. It is affected by such factors as gender, race, class, age, nationality and religious background (1990, 342). Lynn White observes that:

> What people do about their ecology depends on what they think about themselves in relation to things around them. Human ecology is deeply conditioned by beliefs about our nature and destiny—that is, by religion. (WHITE 1967, Web. N. P.)

The above position by White, sets us right into the philosophical discourse of *Oppressive Conceptual Frameworks* which Warren defines as frameworks that explain, justify and maintain relationships of domination and subordination (WARREN 1990, 342). When an *Oppressive Conceptual Framework* is patriarchal, it explains, justifies and maintains the subordination of women by men (1990, 342).

For Warren, there are three significant features of *Oppressive Patriarchal Conceptual Frameworks*, namely: 1. Value-hierarchical thinking, which is a kind of thinking that places higher value, status or prestige on what is "up" rather than on what is "down." 2. Value dualisms, that is, disjunctive pairs in which the disjuncts are seen as oppositional (rather than as complementary) and exclusive (rather than as inclusive) and which place higher value or status to that which has historically been identified as "mind," "reason" and "male" than to that which has historically been identified as "body," "emotion" and "female." 3. The logic of domination, that is, a structure of argumentation which leads to a justification of subordination (1990, 342).

For Warren, this third feature of *Oppressive Patriarchal Conceptual Frameworks* is the most significant. The logic of domination is not just a logical structure. It also involves a substantive value system, since an ethical premise is needed to permit or sanction the "just" subordination of that which is subordinate (1990, 342). This justification typically is given on grounds of some alleged characteristic (for example, rationality) which the dominant (for example, men) have and the subordinate (for example, women) lack (1990, 342). Warren argues that contrary to what many feminists and eco-feminists have said or suggested, there may be nothing inherently problematic about "hierarchal thinking" or even "value-hierarchical thinking" in contexts other than contexts of oppression (1990, 342).

Warren argues that hierarchal thinking is important in daily living for classifying data, comparing information and organizing material (1990, 342). Even "value-hierarchical thinking" can be quite acceptable in certain contexts. For Warren, the problem is not simply that value-hierarchal thinking and value dualisms are used, but the way in which each has been used in *Oppressive Conceptual Frameworks* to establish inferiority and justify subordination (1990, 342). It is the logic of domination coupled with value hierarchal thinking and value dualisms, which justify subordination (1990, 342).

For Warren, what is explanatorily basic, then, about the nature of *Oppressive Conceptual Frameworks* is the logic of domination and that the logic of domination is explanatorily basic is important for at least three reasons: First, without the logic of domination, a description of similarities and differences would be just that—a description of similarities and differences (1990, 342). Consider the claim, "Humans are different from rocks in that humans can radically and consciously re-shape the communities in which they live; humans are similar to plants and rocks in that they are both members of the ecological community" (1990, 342).

Even if humans are better than plants and rocks with respect to the conscious ability of humans to radically transform communities, one does not thereby get any morally relevant distinction between humans and non-humans, or an argument for the dominance of plants and rocks by humans (1990, 342). To get these conclusions, one need to add at least two powerful assumptions; namely, (A2) and (A4) in argument A below:

> (A1) Humans do, and plants and rocks do not, have the capacity to consciously and radically change the community in which they live.
>
> (A2) Whatever has the capacity to consciously and radically change the community in which it lives is morally superior to whatever lacks this capacity.
>
> (A3) Thus, humans are morally superior to plants and rocks
>
> (A4) For any X and Y, if X is morally superior to Y, then X is morally justified in subordinating Y.
>
> (A5) Thus, humans are morally justified in subordinating plants and rocks (1990, 342).

Without the two assumptions that humans are morally superior to (at least some) non-humans, (A2), and that superiority justifies subordination, (A4), all one has is some difference between humans and some non-humans (1990, 342). This is true even if that difference is given in terms of superiority. Thus, it is the logic of domination, (A4), which is the bottom line in ecological feminist discussions of oppression (1990, 342).

Second, ecological feminists argue that, at least in Western societies, the *Oppressive Conceptual Framework* which sanctions the twin dominations of women and nature is patriarchal, one characterized by all three features of an *Oppressive Conceptual Framework* (1990, 342). Many ecological feminists claim that, historically, within at least the dominant Western culture, a patriarchal framework has sanctioned the following argument:

(B1) Women are identified with nature and the realm of the physical; men are identified with the "human" and the realm of the mental.

(B2) Whatever is identified with nature and the realm of the physical is inferior to (below) whatever is identified with the human and the realm of the mental; or, conversely, the latter is superior (above) to the former.

(B3) Thus, women are inferior to (below) men; or, conversely, men are superior to (above) women.

(B4) For any X and Y, if X is superior to Y, then X is justified in subordinating Y.

(B5) Thus, men are justified in subordinating women (1990, 342).

Having outlined and explained Warren's ecological feminism, I now try to establish and explain the premises that will lead to the conclusions that "No Black African women are feminists" and "No Black African Women are Ecological feminists." I do this in two ways: First, I trace the history of feminism with a view to establish whether or not Africana women are part of the project of feminism, and second, I then try to find out if the idea of ecological feminism is all-encompassing, that is, is it cross-cultural to the effect that it can also address the concerns of Africana women?

A Brief History of Feminism

The true history of feminism, its origin and participants reveal its blatant racist background, thereby establishing its incompatibility with Africana women (that is, continental African women and those in the Diaspora) (WEEMS 1993, 18). Feminism, earlier called the Woman's Suffrage Movement (WSM), started when a group of liberal white women, whose concerns then were for the abolition of slavery and equal rights for all people regardless of race, class and sex, dominated the scene on the national level during the early to middle century (1993, 18). At the time of the civil war in America, such leaders as Susan B. Anthony and Elizabeth Cady Stanton held the universalist philosophy on the natural rights of women (both white and black) to full citizenship, which included the right to vote.

However, in 1870, the fifteenth Amendment to the constitution of the United States of America ratified the voting rights of African men leaving women, White women, in particular and their desire for the same rights unaddressed (1993, 342). Middle class White women were naturally disappointed, for they had assumed that their efforts toward securing full citizenship for Africana people would ultimately benefit them, too, in their desire for full citizenship, as voting citizens (1993, 18). The result was a racist reaction to the amendment and to Africans in particular (1993, 18). In 1890, the National American Woman Suffrage Association (NAWSA) was founded by northern White women … epitomizing the growing race chauvinism of the late nineteenth century (1993, 18).

The organization, which brought together the National Woman Suffrage Association (NWSA) and the American Woman Suffrage Association (AWSA) departed from Susan B Anthony's original women suffrage posture (1993, 18). They asserted that the vote for women should be utilized chiefly by middle class White women, who could aid their husbands in preserving the virtues of the Republic from the threat of unqualified and biological inferiors (Africana men) who with the power of the vote, could gain a political foothold in the American system (1993, 18). This is how feminism was born.

Note of course, that Africana women were not even part of the equation and never became part of the equation in the minds of these White women. This raises a lot of eye brows for those Africana women who, today, claim to be feminists. They face hard questions such as: On what basis do they justify feminism? How can they claim to own an idea that is foreign to them? Aren't they championing the White women's interests? These hard questions and many others only help to complicate the puzzle for Africana women who claim to be feminists when in actual fact feminism excluded them right from the onset.

Critical Remarks

Having looked at this brief history of feminism, it is important to answer two critical questions: What is feminism? Who is a feminist? To begin with, *feminism*, a term conceptualized and adopted by White women involves an agenda that was designed to meet the needs and demands of that particular group (1993, 19). For this reason, it is quite plausible for white women to identify with feminism and the feminist movement (1993, 18). Although this definition of feminism automatically excludes Black African women or Africana women, later on feminism expanded to include White men who were also interested in seeing women being treated equally.

In fact, elsewhere I argue that the emphasis on feminists as male or female is important because it is wrong to assume that only white women can be feminists since being a feminist or a non-feminist is not a biological construct but a way in which one look at life (MANGENA 2011, 118). The emergency of homosexual practices in the West also meant that those men who assumed the role of "wives" also had to identify with feminism and to fight for the liberation of women from the yoke of patriarchy. So, in proper terminology, a *feminist* is someone [male or female] who believes that men and women are inherently equal in all respects relevant to how they should be treated (BARCALOW 1994, 95).

Judging from the way the history of feminism is presented above, it is probably clear that in her definition of feminism, Barcalow fell short of saying that a feminist was someone [white male or female] who believes that White men and women were inherently equal in all respects relevant to how they should be treated. If feminism is a Western concept as demonstrated above, then why are there designations such as *Black feminism* or *African feminism*? Don't they point or attest to the fact that feminism can be cross-cultural?

In my response to the questions above, I argue that those women who have adopted feminism and named it either *Black feminism* or *African feminism* either do not know the history of feminism or ignore this history to deliberately mislead other Africana women for selfish reasons. This is so because the objectives of, for instance, Black Feminism are not any different from those of traditional feminism. In fact, Black feminism is simply an imitation of traditional feminism. Weems (1993, 35) captures this point succinctly when she says:

> Black feminism is some Africana women's futile attempt to fit into the constructs of an established White female paradigm. At best, Black feminism may relate to sexual discrimination outside of the Africana community, but cannot claim to resolve the critical problems within it which are influenced by racism and classism.

Despite variations in the source of their daily struggles (That is, Black/African or White Women), they both blame patriarchy for their inferior positions in society. For instance, while feminists in the West have focused on issues of reproduction and sexuality; the so-called African feminists have attached importance to heterosexuality, issues of motherhood as well as bread and butter issues, culture and power (1993, 38). However, both feminists in the West and the so-called African feminists blame patriarchy for marginalizing them. But what is more worrying is that African feminists do not have a thorough-bred African theory to justify their claims. Instead, they use Western feminism as their template as well and they justify this use by arguing that feminism can be re-defined to suit the needs of Africana women.

My challenge with this thinking is that, it gives the impression that Africana people cannot invent and defend anything of their own but they can only discover and modify other people's ideas or theories. This is fortunately not true as Africana people are capable of inventing and defending their own ideas or theories. For instance, Africanas have successfully invented and defended the theory of *hunhu, ubuntu* or *botho* (as is the case with Southern Africa), *omundu* (as is the case with some countries in East Africa), *Umunna* and *Okra* (as is the case with some countries in West Africa, for instance, Nigeria and Ghana respectively) and *Ma'at* (as is the case with some countries in North Africa, for example, Egypt). These are theories that define Africa's ethical, metaphysical and epistemological thought. The theories attach importance to the value of group belonging and collective responsibility subsumed under communalism. The theory proceeds by noting that the importance or value of any person can only be expressed through that person's contribution to the betterment of the group. A *hunhu* or *ubuntu* theory says, *munhu munhu muvanhu* or *umuntu ngumuntu ngabantu* (a person is a person through other persons). A *hunhu* or *ubuntu* theory does not create gender binaries as is the case with feminism which divides people based on biology and sexuality. It prefers to focus on roles and responsibilities of men and women which roles point to the fact that men and women work together for the betterment of their communities. Thus, *hunhu* or *ubuntu* is a world view ... and a way of life for the African (MANGENA 2012, 11).

It is from such African moral theories as *hunhu* or *ubuntu* that Africana women like Weems have successfully invented and defended *Africana womanism* in the face of stiff resistance from the so-called Black feminists or African feminists whose main agenda is Western. By definition, *Africana womanism* is an ideology created and designed for all women of Africana descent and it is grounded in African culture, and therefore, it necessarily focuses on the unique experiences, struggles, needs and desires of African women (WEEMS 1993, 22). As Weems maintains, Africana womanism sits well with the cultures of sub-Saharan Africa because of its emphasis on the centrality of self-definition, self-naming and the place of the family or community (1993: 22). Weems remarks, thus:

> Africana womanism emerged from the acknowledgement of a long standing authentic agenda for that group of women of African descent who needed only to be properly named and officially defined according to their own unique historical and cultural matrix, one that would reflect the co-existence of a man and a woman in a concerted struggle for the survival of their entire family/community. (WEEMS 2007, 289)

The above paragraph shows that Africana womanism puts the interests of men and women, their families or communities ahead of the interests of individual men and individual women as is the case with feminism, including ecological feminism. Thus, any Africana woman who embraces feminism is most likely to be isolated by her peers at one end and vilified by those people whose ideas or theories she wants to embrace at the other end.

So, the problem with discovering and modifying theories and concepts like feminism to suit particular cultures like those of Africa are that an African (man or woman) cannot wholly own such theories and concepts making it difficult for him or her to fully identify with the theory. In most cases, the one who discovers the theory or idea cannot claim to belong to the inner circle of those who invented it—he or she remains cast as *the other*. It is like somebody who gatecrashes a wedding party and suddenly wants to control the wedding proceedings or wants to sit at the high table with the newly-weds.

The point I am putting across is that as a result of colonialism, some Africana women adopted the feminist discourse by white colonialists while others did not. Those who adopted feminism are the ones who today call themselves Black or African feminists and those who declined to associate themselves with feminism are today called Africana womanists. The latter decided to define their experiences and challenges in the context of their experiences, traditions and cultures. In other words, they did not look elsewhere for answers to their challenges. To this end, Weems (1993, 34) notes, thus:

> Too many Blacks have taken the theoretical framework of "feminism" and have tried to make it fit their particular circumstances. Rather than create their own paradigm and name and define themselves, some Africana women, scholars in particular, have been persuaded by white feminists to adopt or adapt to the White concept and terminology of feminism. The real benefit of the amalgamation of Black feminism and White feminism goes to White feminists who can increase their power base by expanding their scope with the convenient consensus that sexism is their commonality and primary concern.

Patricia Hill Collins (1996, 11) highlights what she considers to be drawbacks to buying into a feminist ideology that is outside of one's culture (1996, 11). First, she points out that gender works with racism to maintain oppression (1996, 11). Second, she argues that an acceptance of feminism by Africana women translates into the rejection of Africana men, given the theoretical underpinnings of the movement (1996, 12). Remember at its formative stages, feminism was meant to challenge the American constitution which had given Africana men voting rights ahead of White women.

Any attempt by women of Africana descent to accept feminism leaving men alone to fight against racism and classicism will leave men vulnerable. Third, feminism is based on individualism rather than communalism and yet Africans are communal by orientation. Besides, communalism is a life style and value more akin to African Americans and continental Africans and their ancestry than individualism (1996, 12). As I mentioned earlier, this lifestyle and value is subsumed under *hunhu* or *ubuntu or botho* (in Southern Africa), *omundu* (in some parts of East Africa), *ma'at* (in Egypt) and *Okra* (in Ghana) among others.

Those Africana women who have embraced feminism have done so for two reasons, (1) feminism's theoretical and methodological legitimacy in the academy and their desire to remain a legitimate part of the academic community, and (2) the absence of a suitable framework for their individual needs as Africana women (WEEMS 1993, 16). Collins (1996, 16) thinks that feminism cannot be a viable methodology for Black women. In particular, she challenges the acceptance of the concept of feminism *ipso facto* by Black women arguing that some of the characteristics of feminism are in conflict with the moral ethos of an oppressed people whose past is marred by the collective actions of the oppressor group (COLLINS 1996, 16).

In her full scale attack on feminism and by extension, African feminism; Filomina Chioma Steady argues that the designation *African feminism* is problematic as it naturally suggests an alignment with feminism, a concept that has been alien to the plight of Africana women from its inception (STEADY cited in WEEMS 1993, 17). This is particularly the case in reference to racism and classism which are prevailing obstacles in the lives of Africana people. Steady puts it thus:

> Regardless of one's position, the implications of the feminist movement for the black woman are complex ... Several factors set the black woman apart as having a different order of priorities. She is oppressed not simply because of her sex but ostensibly because of her race, and for the majority, essentially because of their class. Women belong to different socio-economic groups and do not represent a universal category. Because the majority of black women are poor, there is likely to be some alienation from the middle class aspect of the women's movement which perceives feminism as an attack on men rather than on a system which thrives on inequality. (1993, 17)

What I can discern from the above paragraph by Steady is that by virtue of having a different order of priorities compared to those of White women, black women cannot be feminists. For instance, Black women are still fighting poverty, race and class and this is different from White women who overcame these evils a long time ago. Hence, feminism and more specifically, Black feminism or African feminism is extremely problematic as labels for the true Africana woman (WEEMS 1993, 16).

Is Ecological Feminism Applicable in Africa, and Among Africana Women in the Diaspora?

To begin with, the history of feminism as presented above seems to show no connections between the oppression of women of Africana descent and the ill-treatment of nature. This is so because this history does not recognize the existence and contribution of Africana women in the feminist discourse in the first place. As noted above, feminism as a political movement that was meant to address the concerns of White women whose rights to vote were not respected. Later on, it spread to other spheres of life but its main thrust was to advance the interests of the White women. Thus, it was and still remains a project by and for White women even today. If this history is anything to go by, then it follows that ecological feminism is also a White women's project, for the simple reason that it is a type of feminism that seeks to link the oppression of women with the ill-treatment of nature.

While many academics uncritically adopt feminism, most Africana women, in general do not identify with the concept in its entirety and thus cannot see themselves as feminists (1993, 15). This also means that the conceptual connections between the dual dominations of women and nature as put by Warren are only cultural and not cross-cultural. That is, they only apply to Warren's context and not the context of Africa. For instance, traditional feminism cannot expand to include ecological feminism in sub-Saharan Africa since feminism by its nature is only a White women's project restricted to Western cultures. On the basis of this critique, a conclusion can be drawn from this premise that –*No Black African women are Ecological feminists.*

It is also not possible for ecological feminism to develop a distinctively feminist environmental ethic that can be applied across cultures given that most Africans do not identify with the concept of feminism because of its history and scope. In fact, most Africana women identify with Womanism and not Feminism. By extension, this also means that Africana women cannot identify with ecological feminism. It was easier for White women like Warren to coin the phrase *Ecological feminism* but this cannot be applied to sub-Saharan Africa in the sense that the genesis of the word "womanism" shows that there is no correlation between women's oppression at the hands of men and the ill-treatment of nature. In her definition of womanism, Weems (1993, 21) observes that:

> The term "woman," and by extension "womanism," is far more appropriate than female ("feminism") because of one major distinction—only a female of the human race can be a woman. "Female," on the other hand, can refer to a member of the animal or plant kingdom as well as to a member of the human race.

As the above paragraph shows, it is easier for feminists to talk of ecological feminism, than it is for Africana womanists to talk about the same without distorting African social and environmental realities and experiences given—as shown above—that the word "feminist" comes from the word "female" which applies to both human beings and animals or plants and yet as Weems put it above, womanism refers only to a female of the human race. Thinkers like White also believe that although the idea of conceptual frameworks cannot be ruled out in Western Europe, the only link or connection that exists is that between men and nature.

For White, this relationship is brought to bear by the advent of Science and Technology. Science and Technology—hitherto quite separate activities, joined to give mankind powers which, to judge by many of the ecologic effects, are out of control (WHITE 1967, Web. N. P.). This led men to conclude that they were superior to nature, contemptuous of it, willing to use it to their slightest whim (WHITE 1967, Web. N. P.). No attempt is made to look at the connection between men and women. This also means that Warren's idea of *Oppressive Conceptual Frameworks* when pitched against this position is found wanting. Warren's *Oppressive Conceptual Frameworks* are also found wanting in that they are out of sync with African social and environmental realities.

In sub-Saharan Africa, the environment is owned by the ancestral spirits. In Shona culture, in particular, these ancestral spirits are referred to as *varidzi ve masango* (custodians of the environment and its content). This means that human beings (men and women) have no control over the behavior of the environment to warrant a comparison between the oppression of women and the ill-treatment of the environment. It is also critical to note that in sub-Saharan Africa, men and women are victims of racism and classism which means that there is no such thing as value-hierarchical thinking as men do not look at themselves as being of higher status or prestige than women. They consider women to be their equal partners in their fight against racism and classims. Against this background, Joyce Ladner (cited in WEEMS 1993, 21) notes that "Black women do not perceive their enemy to be black men, but rather the enemy is considered to be oppressive forces in the larger society which subjugate black men, women and children".

The above arguments do not only eliminate value hierarchal thinking but the other two features of *Oppressive Conceptual Frameworks* as well, that is, value dualisms and the logic of domination which divides people based on both socially constructed characteristics and biological characteristics such as "reason and emotion" as well as "male and female" respectively. I argue that in sub-Saharan Africa such binaries do not exist as the emphasis is not on whether men are more rational than women or women are more emotional than men as is the case with Warren's value dualisms and the logic of domination.

The emphasis is on how intellectual assets like "reason" and "emotion" can be used for the betterment of the community. These assets appeal at the community level than at individual level. Hence, we talk of communal/group rationality rather than individual rationality (MANGENA 2012, 10). In this kind of set up no one [male or female] can dominate the other. In fact, a man (the male category) can play the role of a mother to his sister's children in the event that the biological mother is dead or absent and all mothers are women (the female category).

Conversely, a woman (the female category) can play the role of a father to her brother's children in the event that the biological father has passed on and fathers are men (the male category) (MANGENA and MUHWATI 2013) What does this mean logically speaking? It probably means that if the argument I am presenting is pointing to the fact that feminism is out of sync with African realities/experiences, it follows necessarily that ecological feminism which is best explained by the three features of *Oppressive Conceptual Frameworks* discussed above is also out of sync with African realities/experiences. Thus, the conclusion—*No Black African women are ecological feminists*—would follow with necessity.

Conclusion

This essay was an attempt to establish whether or not a conclusion can be drawn to the effect that there is something called African ecological feminism. The essay progressed through the use of Africana womanism as a theory and the deductive method in philosophy to draw its warranted conclusions. The argument was put thus, if it can be ascertained that there is something called Black or African feminism, then that there is African ecological feminism should be a matter of deduction. The essay began by presenting Warren's ecological feminism before looking at the history of feminism and showing that this history precludes the values, experiences and aspirations of Africana women. By deduction, this automatically meant that the designations Black or African feminism were not conceivable as the suffix 'feminism' was and still is a foreign concept. On the basis of this understanding, it was, therefore, easier to draw the conclusion: "No Black African women are ecological feminists."

Relevant Literature

1. BARCALOW, E. [Moral Philosophy; Theory and Issues], 1994. Wardsworth Publishing Company: Belmont. Paperback.

2. COLLINS, P. H. "What is in a Name? Womanism, Black Feminism and Beyond," [The Black Scholar], pp 9–17, Winter/Spring 1996. Vol 1. No 26. Paperback.

3. COPI, I.M. [Introduction to Logic], 1994. Prentice Hall: Eaglewood Cliffs, New Jersey. Paperback.

4. LADNER, J. 'Tomorrow's tomorrow: The Black Woman." [Africana Womanism: Reclaiming Ourselves, C.H Weems, Ed.], 1993. Bedford Publishers: Michigan. Paperback.

5. MANGENA, F. and MUHWATI, I. "Kelland on Rape and Objectification: An Africana Feminist Response," 2013. Unpublished article.

6. _____. "Towards a *Hunhu/Ubuntu* Dialogical Moral Theory," [Journal of the South African Society for Greek Philosophy and the Humanities], pp 1–17, December 2012. Vol 13. No 2. Paperback.

7. _____. "Teaching African Feminist Ethics in the Era of HIV and AIDS: A University of Zimbabwe Study," [BOLESWA: Journal of Theology, Religion and Philosophy], pp 117–133, December 2011. Vol 3. No 3. Paperback.

8. MAPPES, T.A and ZEMBATY, J. S. [Social Ethics: Morality and Social Policy], 1997. McGraw-Hill: New York. Paperback.

9. STEADY, F.C. "The Black Woman Cross-Culturally," [Africana Womanism: Reclaiming Ourselves, C.H Weems, Ed.], 1993. Bedford Publishers: Michigan. Paperback.

10. WARREN, K. "The Power and Promise of Ecological Feminism," [Ethics: Theory and Contemporary Issues, B Mackinnon, Ed.], 1998. Wadsworth Publishing Company: Belmont. Paperback.

11. WEEMS, C.H. "Nomo/Self-Naming, Self-Definition and the History of Africana Womanism," [Contemporary Africana: Theory, Thought and Action, C.H Weems, Ed.], 2007. Africa World Press: Trenton. Paperback.

12. _____. [Africana Womanism: Reclaiming Ourselves], 1993. Bedford Publishers: Michigan. Paperback.

13. WHITE, L. "The Historical Roots of our Ecological Crisis," N.P., March 1967. Retrieved 10 July 2013. Web.

CHAPTER 8

Consumption and Environmental Ethics: Is Consumption a Way to Discover Ourselves or a Vice?

8A. I Shop Therefore I Know That I Am

The Metaphysical Basis of Modern Consumerism

By Colin Campbell

Introduction

I would hazard a guess and suggest that metaphysics is not a term that most people would normally associate with the activity of consumption. Indeed it seems more likely that these two would be regarded as polar opposites; the one concerned—as the dictionary puts it—with 'first principles, especially in relation to being and knowing', the other with the routine, the practical and the mundane. How then is it that I am suggesting that there might be a connection between the two? Well I arrived at the intimation of a link largely as a consequence of my attempts to seek an answer to the question of why consuming has come to occupy such a central place in our lives. Why, in other words, are the activities generally associated with the term 'consumption', such as the searching out, purchasing and using goods and services that meet our needs or satisfy our wants, regarded as so extraordinarily important? Because it seems self-evident to me that, in general and with some significant exceptions, that is precisely how they are regarded by the majority of people in contemporary society, as especially important if not actually central to their lives. It also seems largely self-evident that this has not been the case in previous eras.

Now this is not the same question as 'why do we consume?' For there are several widely accepted answers to that question, ranging from the satisfaction of needs, the emulation of others, the pursuit of pleasure, the defence or assertion of status, etc. However, in seeking to understand why consumption has such importance in people's lives one is implying that it might be fulfilling a function above and beyond that of satisfying the specific motives or intentions that prompt its individual component acts. In other words, it might possess a dimension that relates it to the most profound and ultimate questions that human beings can pose, questions concerning the nature of reality and the very purpose of existence—with issues of 'being and knowing' in fact. That, at least, will be the thesis upon which—in true metaphysical fashion—I wish to speculate in this [reading].

The Nature of Modern Consumerism

In order for my argument to make sense it is important that I make it quite clear, at the very beginning, just what I consider to be the two crucial defining features of modern consumerism, that is those that distinguish it most clearly from earlier, more traditional forms. The one is the central place occupied by emotion and desire, in conjunction to some degree with imagination. This is an argument that I have developed elsewhere and hence shall not repeat at length here (see Campbell 1987).

So let me just emphasize my belief that it is the processes of wanting and desiring that lie at the very heart of the phenomenon of modern consumerism. This is not to say that issues of need are absent, or indeed that other features, such as distinctive institutional and organizational structures, are not important. It is simply to assert that the central dynamo that drives such a society is that of consumer demand, and that this is in turn dependent upon the ability of consumers to experience continually the desire for goods and services. In this respect it is our affectual states, most especially our ability 'to want', 'to desire' and 'to long for', and especially our ability to experience such emotions repeatedly, that actually underpins the economies of modern developed societies.[1]

The second, and closely associated, critical defining characteristic of modern consumerism I take to be its unrestrained or unrestricted individualism. Obviously not all consumption is individualistic in nature; for there continues to be a significant element of collective consumption even in the most modern and capitalist of societies, that is goods and services which are consumed by the community (such as defence or law and order) or owned by the community and then allocated to individuals rather than purchased on the open market (local government housing, for example). Yet it is quite clear that a distinctive hallmark of modern consumption is the extent to which goods and services are purchased by individuals for their own use. Again this is in marked contrast to the earlier pattern, in which these were either purchased by, or on behalf of, social groups, most especially the extended kin or household, or the village or local community, or alternatively allocated to individuals by governing bodies. Even more characteristic of modern consumerism is the associated ideology of individualism. That is the extraordinary value attached to this mode of consumption in conjunction with the emphasis placed on the right of individuals to decide for themselves which goods and services they consume.[2]

Now these two features strongly support each other, combining to define the nature of modern consumerism. And the crucial link between the two is the simple fact that modern consumerism is by its very nature predominately concerned with the gratification of wants rather than the meeting of needs. The significance of this development being that, while needs can be, and indeed generally are, objectively established, wants can only be identified subjectively. That is to say, others can always tell you what it is that you need. Indeed you may not be qualified to assess those needs for yourself and hence have to seek the assistance of experts in order to identify them, as in the case of one's medical 'needs'. But no one but you is in a position to decide what it is that you want. When it comes to wanting only the 'wanter' can claim to be an 'expert' (Campbell 1998). Naturally therefore it follows that such a mode of consumption is inherently individualistic, with the authority for decision-making located firmly within the self.[3] To summarize modern consumerism is more to do with feeling and emotion (in the form of desire) than it is with reason and calculation, while it is fiercely individualistic, rather than communal, in nature. And these two features provide the most obvious connection with the larger culture as well as providing the basis for the claim that modern consumerism rests on metaphysical assumptions.

Ontology and the Search for Meaning: Identity as Defined by Desire

In my initial remarks I observed that there seemed little obvious connection between the subject of consumption and metaphysical matters. There is however one topic where it is relatively easy to see a connection between the two, and that concerns the issue of identity. This is an issue central to many discussions of modern consumerism, where an emphasis is frequently placed on the significance of consuming in relation to the affirmation, confirmation or even the creation of identity. At the same time it is fairly obvious that the question 'who am I?' is one of the most fundamental and basic that human beings can pose.

It is at this point that I become acutely conscious of the fact that the spectre of postmodern thought is hovering at my shoulder, and much as I would like to ignore its presence this is hardly possible. So I shall briefly acknowledge it and hope that by doing so it will be persuaded to fade into the shadows. For my position on the 'postmodern phenomenon' or the 'postmodern movement' is that this should be the object of sociological investigation. I regard it as a mistake to view this body of philosophical speculation as an intellectual or academic 'resource', useful as an aid to an understanding of the social and cultural world. To adopt this attitude is to my mind equivalent to assuming that astrology can serve as a useful guide to an understanding of the universe. What we need, as Mike Featherstone has said, is a sociology of postmodernism, not a postmodern sociology (1991: x). Unfortunately few social scientists seem to have followed this eminently sensible suggestion, with the result that many postmodern speculations concerning the contemporary world are frequently repeated as if they were indeed established truths. And one of the more widely reported of these concerns personal identity and the activity of consumption. Here the widespread presumption is that the contemporary or 'postmodern' self is exceptionally open and flexible. That is to say, it is assumed that individuals—by making use of the wide-ranging and ever-changing products on offer in a modern consumer society—are regularly engaged in the process of recreating themselves: first adopting and then casting off identities and lifestyles in just as easy and casual a manner as they do their clothes. This is made possible because, as Ewen and Ewen have put it, 'Today there are no … rules, only choices.' And hence 'Everyone can be anyone.' (Ewan & Ewan 1982: 249–51). At the same time it is commonly suggested that individuals have little choice but to behave in this manner since what Lyotard has called 'grand narratives' are no longer credible, with the direct consequence that there is no longer any firm cultural anchorage for the individual's sense of identity. Thus one commonly encounters the view that the activities of consumers should be understood as both a response to a postulated 'crisis of identity' and an activity that in effect only serves to intensify that very crisis.[4]

I fully accept that it is probably true to say that an individual's sense of identity is no longer clearly determined, as once it was, by their membership of specific class or status groupings (Bocock & Thompson 1992: 149). I also accept that consumption is central to the process through which individuals confirm, if not create, their identities. But what I would dispute is the suggestion that individuals in contemporary society have no unitary or fixed concept of the self (Hollinger 1994: 113–14). While I would wish to maintain that consumption, far from exacerbating the 'crisis of identity' is indeed the very activity through which individuals commonly resolve just this issue.

The 'personal ads' sections of newspapers and magazines make fascinating reading and it could be that you, like me, are drawn to them because of what they reveal about our fellow human beings. This section of a newspaper or magazine is the place where individuals advertise for 'partners' either with just short-term friendship and fun in mind, or alternatively with a view to establishing a long-term, if not necessarily permanent, relationship. And, in order to attract the right kind of person, individuals set out to describe themselves (as well very often as the person they are looking for) in the advertisement. Now they usually only have a few lines in which to do this, so obviously they need to think carefully about what to say. What most people want to do is to give as clear and accurate impression of the sort of person they consider themselves to be—even if in the process there is a tendency to convey something of an over-flattering image. So what, typically, do people say when given only a restricted space in which to describe themselves? Well they say things like this: 'Bohemian cat-lover, 46 going on 27, totally broke and always working, likes red wine, working out, Pratchet, Tolkein & Red Dwarf.' Or 'Outdoor Girl, 50s, loves long country walks, jive dancing & Tate Modern. Seeks partner to share interests and maybe more.' One final example, 'Slim, professional, lively, reflective 40 year-old, enjoys Moby, Mozart, the Arts, and watching sports, seeks compatible male.'

Now what I find especially interesting about these ads is that the individuals concerned appear to be defining themselves—that is specifying what they see as their essential identity—almost exclusively in terms of their *tastes*. That is to say in terms of their distinctive profile of wants and desires. For, if we set aside the inclusion of what we might call the 'fixed basic facts' about a person, that is their gender and age together with some indication of appearance, occupation or class, then what is provided in these ads relates almost entirely to an individual's tastes. The things most commonly specified being, as my examples suggest, their tastes in music, literature, the arts, food and drink, together with leisure-time pursuits. Now why should that be? Why should people concentrate upon defining themselves in terms of their tastes? Well I would suggest that it is because these are what we feel define us more clearly than anything else, and that when it comes to the crucial issue of our 'real' identity then we effectively consider ourselves to be defined by our desires, or profiled by our preferences.

Let me be quite clear that I am not suggesting that it is our 'interests' or 'hobbies' that define us. Those people who define themselves in these ads in terms of their liking for red wine or country walks are unlikely to be looking for a partner to join them in organized wine-tastings, or in meetings of The Ramblers Association. After all, if these are indeed your hobbies then you can meet people with similar interests simply by joining the relevant societies concerned. No, what these people are identifying are less their serious interests or hobbies, than their 'tastes' (similar in effect to their sexual 'tastes', details of which do indeed appear in the more specialized and salacious variety of personal ad.). Nor am I suggesting that what we might call 'tribal identity' has ceased to be significant. Clearly these identities still matter, especially after what Americans call 9/11. In that sense the answer to the question 'Who Am I?' will still include such basic definers as gender, race, nationality, ethnicity and religion. But what I would like to suggest is that these identifiers do no more than 'frame' the parameters of who we consider ourselves to be. They do not specify the fine lines of our identity—merely its general outline. While the person we really consider ourselves to be, the 'real me' if you like, is to be found in our special mix or combination of tastes. This is where we are most likely to feel that our uniqueness as individuals—our individuality—actually resides.

Now of course if this argument is valid it means that the proliferation of choice characteristic of a modern consumer society is essential if we are ever to discover 'who we are'. For a wide range of variation in products is crucial for us to 'test ourselves', as we continually seek to answer the question, do I like this or that? Do I like this fabric, or this colour? Does this music, or those images, turn me on? Do I enjoy this experience, or does it turn me off? Viewed in this way the activity of consuming can be considered as the vital and necessary path to self-discovery, while the marketplace itself becomes indispensable to the process of discovering who we really are.

It should be clear that I am not suggesting that identity derives from the product or service consumed, or that, as the saying goes, 'people are what they purchase' (Ritzer, Goodman & Wiedenscroft 2002: 413). Of course, what we buy says something about who we are. It could not be otherwise. But what I am suggesting is that the real location of our identity is to be found in our reaction to products, and not in the products themselves. Hence I am not arguing that as consumers we 'buy' identity through our consumption of particular goods and services. Rather I am suggesting that we 'discover' it by exposing ourselves to a wide variety of products and services, and hence it is by monitoring our reaction to them, noting what it is that we like and dislike, that we come to 'discover' who we 'really are'.

It is important to realize that this manner of conceiving of self-identity is very new. Indeed considered against the backdrop of historical time it has only just happened. It is very unlikely that our grandparents, if not our parents, would ever have conceived of themselves in this way. For them, identity was far more likely to be primarily a matter of their status and position in various institutions and associations, with family, occupation, religious adherence, race, ethnicity and nationality all counting for more than something as insignificant as taste. Consequently their self-definitions would have tended to emphasize such statuses as farmer, fisherman, father, Presbyterian, Catholic, Englishman or Swede, etc., and not their taste in wine, literature, music or leisure-time activities.

If the suggestion that identity is discovered rather than purchased sounds a little too abstract or far-fetched let me quote April Benson on the subject of shopping. She writes,

> Shopping … is a way we search for ourselves and our place in the world. Though conducted in the most public of spaces, shopping is essentially an intimate and personal experience. To shop is to taste, touch, sift, consider, and talk our way through myriad possibilities as we try to determine what it is we need or desire.

To shop consciously is to search not only externally, as in a store, but internally, through memory and desire. Shopping is an interactive process through which we dialogue not only with people, places, and things, but also with parts of ourselves. This dynamic yet reflective process reveals and gives form to pieces of self that might otherwise remain dormant ... the act of shopping is one of self-expression, one that allows us to discover who we are ... (2000: 505)

'I Shop Therefore I Am'

These quotes come from a book entitled *I Shop Therefore I Am*, which might seem an apt slogan in the context of the argument I have just advanced. However, strictly speaking, 'I shop in order that I might discover who I am' would be a more accurate summary of the claim I have just made. By contrast, 'I shop, therefore I am', modelled as it obviously is on Descartes's famous 'I think, therefore I am', implies something a little different. It suggests not so much that the activity of shopping is a means through which people discover who they are than that it provides them with the basic certainty of their existence. Now April Benson's book is about compulsive shopping so it is possible that the title is meant to indicate—if humorously—a situation in which this activity has come to totally dominate the lives of those subject to this addiction. Viewed in this light it simply refers to people for whom there is no other activity of any significance in life except that of shopping. I do believe however that this slogan is applicable to all consumers in modern society, whether compulsive shoppers or not, and in relation to exactly the same ontological issue that was of concern to Descartes. However before developing this argument I need to say something about the nature of the epistemology that underlies modern consumerism.

A Consumerist Epistemology

There are two popular sayings that are important pointers to the nature of the epistemology that is implicit in the metaphysical assumptions that I am suggesting underlie modern consumerism. The one is *'de gustibus non est disputandum',* or in English, 'there is no disputing about tastes'. This saying originally referred to the fact that it was simply a waste of time trying to convince someone, by means of rational argument, to like or dislike certain foods or drink. However, it also resonates very clearly with the point I have just made about the self-defining significance of personal taste. That is to say, our tastes are unquestionably 'ours' in the sense that they cannot be legitimately challenged by others. The second well-known, if not well-worn, saying, is that 'the customer is always right'. This originally gained currency because it was the motto that store managers or proprietors were wont to instil in their staff in order that their particular retail outlet or chain might acquire, or keep, a reputation for good service. It was, of course, never intended to be taken literally, that is in the sense of being a statement of epistemological principle. However, I would suggest that this is indeed precisely what it has become; that is, in the form 'the consumer is always right.' Indeed I would suggest that the assumptions embodied in these two sayings—that there is no disputing tastes, and that the customer is always right—have become the basis for a widespread and largely taken-for-granted individualist epistemology, one in which the 'self' is the only authority in matters of truth.

We can see ample evidence to support this claim in the growing tendency to reject both the authority of tradition and that of experts in favour of the authority individuals claim for their own wants, desires and preferences. This is apparent in an area like health, for example, where there has been a rapid growth of complementary and alternative medicine at the expense of more conventional medical practice (see Fuller 1989). For it is clear that this development is a direct consequence of the assumption that the consumer is better placed than any so-called 'experts' to judge what treatment is in his or her best interests. Another area where exactly the same change is apparent is religion. Here too the authority of the churches, in the form of the clergy, is rejected in favour of the individual's claim to select his or her own version of 'eternal truth'; a process that has led to the development of what is often referred to as the 'spiritual supermarket'.[6]

In effect what has happened is that the authority of the old-style 'expert', that is someone who told you what you 'needed' and who gained their authority primarily from their institutional role, has been rejected, while their place has been taken by 'gurus' or 'enlightened ones', that is people whose role is to help you discover what it is that you really 'want', or 'desire'. Of course this is precisely what we would expect to happen in a society in which the gratification of wants has come to displace the satisfaction of needs. For as noted, when it comes to the identification of wants, 'the customer or consumer is of course necessarily always right'; always right, that is, in their judgment of what is ultimately true. In precisely the same way that it is generally assumed that no one else is in a position to tell you what you want so too is it assumed that no one else is in a position to tell you what is true. Hence we arrive at the popular notion of 'your truth, my truth' and the rampant relativizing of all claims to veracity that accompanies such a slogan. At the same time the process through which individuals discover what is true for them is always and everywhere the same, and it is modelled on the manner in which they 'know' what they want. For a consumerist epistemology now prevails in which 'truth' is established in the same manner as the existence of wants; that is, through a scrutiny of one's internal emotional states.

The Search for Ontological Security

I would now like to return to the issue of ontology and the Descartes-style quote mentioned earlier, the famous 'I shop therefore I am'. So far I have suggested that modern consumerism embodies, or is predicated upon, a specific theory of personal identity together with a distinctive individualistic epistemology. But it is clear that it also contains a distinct ontology, or theory of reality, one that follows logically from the distinctive features of modern consumerism noted earlier. In fact, in the contemporary world epistemology is little more than an adjunct of ontology anyway, as I shall imply.

That is to say, the former is commonly treated as simply an indicator of the latter; there being a greater desire to experience the real than to know the true.

I suggested earlier that consumption, and more especially perhaps shopping, could be seen as a process through which individuals resolve the 'problem' of personal identity. That is they 'discover who they are' by monitoring their responses to various products and services and therefore establish their distinctive tastes or desires. But, as the postmodernists are fond of emphasizing, individuals in contemporary society may change their tastes and preferences as, either following fashion or seeking higher status, they undergo the process of 'recreating' themselves. Now this may seem to argue against the suggestion that consumption enables people to discover who they really are, since if they had indeed found the answer to this question why would they subsequently abandon that particular identity in favour of another? Indeed, why would they continue to engage as enthusiastically as before in the search for new products and services if they have already resolved the issue of personal identity? I believe that the answers to these questions can be found in an understanding of the ontological function that modern consumerism currently fulfils.

The first critical point to appreciate is that if individuals do indeed change their pattern of tastes or preferences this does not represent any change in the *manner* in which identity is recognized or conceived, for this is still primarily a matter of the self being defined by desire, of having our profile traced through preference. In this respect, the much-emphasized variability and changeability in the perceived content of identity is not as significant as the continuity manifest in the processes involved in its 'discovery'. In fact the changes in content become quite understandable once one shifts the focus from the nature and content of individual identity to the deeper underlying human need for reassurance concerning the reality of the self. For consumption, which in the sense I have emphasized here can be viewed as an activity that involves the exploration of the self, can also be seen as constituting a response to ontological insecurity or existential angst. That is to say, it can comfort us by providing us with the certain knowledge that we are real authentic beings—that we do indeed exist. In this respect, the slogan 'I shop therefore I am' should indeed be understood in a truly literal sense.

Obviously in order to accept the truth of this assertion it is necessary to appreciate the extent to which we live in a culture that embraces an 'emotional ontology' and consequently accords consumption a remarkable significance. By emotional ontology I mean that the true judge of whether something is real or not is taken to be its power to arouse an emotional response in us. The more powerful the response experienced, the more 'real' the object or event that produced it is judged to be. At the same time, the more intense our response, the more 'real'—or the more truly ourselves—we feel ourselves to be at that moment. Very simply put, we live in a culture in which reality is equated with intensity of experience, and is hence accorded both to the source of intense stimuli and to that aspect of our being that responds to them. If then we apply this doctrine to the question of identity and the 'self' we can conclude that it is through the intensity of feeling that individuals gain the reassurance they need to overcome their existential angst and hence gain the reassuring conviction that they are indeed 'alive'. Thus although exposure to a wide range of goods and services helps to tell us who we are (by enabling us to formulate our tastes), this self-same exposure fulfils the even more vital function of enabling us to be reassured that our self is indeed 'authentic' or 'real'. Hence while what I desire (and also dislike) helps to tell me who I am, the fact that I do desire intensely helps to reassure me that I do indeed exist. To quote again from April Benson, 'I believe that reframing shopping as a process of search, a vital activity that reaches far beyond traditional associations with buying or having, can aid in [the] quest for identity and meaning.' (2002: 498). She continues, 'Conscious shopping, shopping as a process of search, is not about buying, it's about *being*' (2002: 502 emphasis added)

Of course one does not have to go shopping, or indeed engage in any other consumption activity, to undertake the quest for identity and meaning; let alone in order to gain reassurance concerning the reality of one's own existence. Any experience that provides an opportunity for a strong emotional response can serve this purpose; a fact that perhaps helps to explain the popularity of extreme sports and adventure holidays in our culture as well as the continuing popularity of horror and science fantasy films, as well too of course as romantic love, with its promise of passion, intimacy and desire. Yet it is worth observing that shopping is an ideal context in which to pursue this quest for meaning. Ideal because there is a purity of self-expression attached to the activity that is not commonly experienced in these other activities (as long as one is not thinking of routine provisioning or gift purchasing but activity directed to meeting the wants of the self). This purity derives from the absence of any need to consider either the feelings or demands of others on the one hand, and the sheer volume and variety of stimuli on offer on the other.

However, to return to the issue of changes in taste and preference and hence in identity, the key point here is that gaining reassurance concerning the 'reality' or if you like the 'authenticity' of one's existence through exposure to experiences that produce an emotional response in oneself is not a one-off requirement. Rather it is a psychological need that requires repeated satisfaction. However, it is impossible for the same stimuli—that is to say, the same products and services—to produce the same intensity of response in us when we are exposed to them a second or third time as they did on the first occasion. On the contrary it is more than probable that we will become bored as habituation sets in. Consequently, we need regular exposure to fresh stimuli if boredom is to be avoided and the continuing need for ontological reassurance satisfied. In this respect, boredom is seen as threatening because it undermines our sense of identity—we risk losing our sense of who we are once boredom sets in—hence our grip on reality falters. As a result there is a continuing need for fresh stimuli, ones that will produce a strong reaction in us. Hence the importance of fashion—as a mechanism for the regular and controlled introduction of 'new' products—as well as the fact that consumers may indeed be tempted to make significant changes to their 'identity' on a regular basis.

These changes should not be seen, however, as indicating that earlier attempts to establish the 'real' or 'true' nature of the self had failed. On the contrary, since the desires and preferences that defined that identity were experienced intensely at the time this 'proves' that it was 'real', just as the intensity attached to the new desires similarly demonstrates the authenticity of the novel 'replacement' self. The fact that such different selves can both be viewed as equally 'real' is reconciled—if indeed any reconciliation is seen to be necessary—by perceiving the true identity of the individual as being 'developmental' in nature. That is to say, as individuals we are conceived of as beings who are in an endless process of 'becoming', such that each new 'identity' emerges butterfly-like—from a deeper and hence more authentic level of the self—out of the discarded chrysalis of its predecessor.

A Consumerist Ontology

It should be clear by now that what I am claiming is that an emanationist or idealist ontology, or theory of reality, provides the foundation for modern consumerism. Of course an emanationist assumption has always underpinned the traditional economic paradigm for the analysis of consumption, being embodied in the central concept of the 'latent want'. That is to say, this paradigm necessarily presupposes that real consumer activity in the world, the selecting, purchasing and using of products, is to be understood as a process that results from the manifesting or 'making real' of something that previously was merely latent. Now I have criticized this concept in the past, pointing out not merely that the only evidence for the existence of latent wants is the actual behaviour they are supposed to explain, but also that wants should be considered as emergent constructs, the products of psychological 'work' on the part of consumers (Campbell 1987: 43–4). I still believe that these criticisms are valid. However this is not to deny that modern consumption rests on fundamentally emanationist assumptions. For, as I have already emphasized, its dynamic is built upon the ability of individuals to perform a particular psychological 'trick', that of producing desire where none previously existed. For consumers to accomplish this however—that is to perform the 'trick' of wanting what they had never wanted before—they have to engage in a highly creative process. In effect they have to 'conjure up' a specific positive feeling for an object or experience out of thin air. It is then the ensuing 'want', which has been conjured in this way, that becomes the cause (assuming they possess the necessary resources) of the subsequent and very real gratifying experience. It is thus not entirely fanciful to suggest that consumers do indeed create their own reality. That is to say they are themselves responsible for creating the necessary conditions for their consumption experiences. I believe that it is this fundamentally idealist and emanationist ontology that has in effect become the underlying paradigm for the modern consumerist view of the world; one in which all of reality, and not just the items we consume, is regarded as capable of being 'conjured up' in a similar fashion.

This claim might seem unduly fanciful, but I think it appears less so if we stop and consider just how the many objects that surround us in our own homes have actually come to be there. For most, if not all, of the products that we have purchased, and which now fill our homes—such as the furniture, the books, the CDs, the pictures and works of art, etc.—are only really there because at some stage we 'wanted' them. In that particular sense their presence in our world is the direct outcome or result of our emotional state, specifically of our desire. If we had not felt desire for them they would not be part of our everyday reality. Of course one could argue that these goods would still exist, even if we had not desired them, since they would probably have remained on the shelf in the shop where we first saw them. However it can also be argued that it is still primarily desire, one which in this case is shared with very many other people, that has brought these goods into existence in the first place, manufactured, as the producers might say, simply in order to 'meet demand'. Hence one could argue that it is not simply our purely personal world of possessions that should be regarded as 'conjured up' through a process of wanting but that the whole modern consumer economy is built upon a similar 'magical' process.

It was while I was speculating along these lines—that is on the possible pervasive nature of such an idealist and emotionalist ontology in our society—that I was prompted to think of the modern phenomenon of the 'wannabe'. Usually a young person, a 'wannabe' is an individual who is characterized by an intense desire (or 'want') to be famous and successful, most commonly as a pop star. What I find so interesting is the extent to which these young people appear to believe that their wanting—if intense enough—will be sufficient to secure the outcome they desire. Typically this belief is fiercely adhered to despite both the astronomical odds against their being successful and the fact—obvious to others if not to most wannabes themselves—that they lack the requisite talent. In this respect they are the supreme example of the now widespread belief that anyone can have, or do, anything, if only they *want* it enough. Now I used to imagine that when people uttered this sentiment they were endorsing the belief that success would come to those whose desire was such that they were prepared to put in the long, hard hours of work or practice required to achieve success. But now—and in line with the argument that I have just outlined—I am increasingly inclined to believe that contemporary wannabes actually interpret this phrase in a far more literal sense. That is to say, they actually believe that the wanting itself will bring them success, provided of course that it is intense enough. In other words, these young people exemplify just that idealist and emotionalist ontology that I have claimed underlies consumption, the idea that feeling—if intensely experienced—can directly change the external world.

Now of course the belief that you can change the world through mental or emotional effort alone conventionally goes by the name of 'magic'; something that most of us might associate either with the world of music-hall entertainment and children's parties, or a much earlier, more primitive and superstitious stage in human evolution. However, to think in this way would be to reveal just how out of touch one is with the contemporary world. It is not just in the world of children's books and the cinema that magic currently features so prominently, dominated as these are by the persona of Harry Potter and fantasy epics such as *The Lord of The Rings*. Magic also features prominently in both the New Age and neo-pagan movements that are currently enjoying such success in modern Western societies.[7] And how is magic defined by the spokespersons for these movements? Well it is defined as the ability to alter oneself and one's environment through attitudes, thoughts and emotions alone.[8] While if we take the trouble to examine the precise nature of that New Age philosophy which has found so many adherents in recent years we find that it contains an idealist ontology. In other words,

New Agers believe that reality is really ideational and spiritual in form, not material. So here we find exactly that ontology which I have speculated might underlie modern consumerism, and in a very explicit form. In fact we can discern in the New Age world-view all those elements of a consumerist metaphysic that I have indicated above.

The New Age World-view and a Consumerist Metaphysic

This, of course, raises a very interesting question concerning cultural change and the nature of contemporary society. Could it be that the very extent and pervasiveness of the activity of consuming has helped to change our view of reality? That the marked degree to which the world that we experience is one that has increasingly been molded by us to meet our desires means that we now accept—if only implicitly—a theory which regards reality as the product of our wishes? With the result that the New Age world-view can be regarded as coming into existence as a consequence of a process of extrapolation from the assumptions that underlie modern consumerism? Or could it be that, on the other hand, we should understand modern consumerism as gaining its explicit cultural legitimation from a cultural development—the New Age movement—that had its origins elsewhere (see Heelas 1993). These are fascinating questions concerning the dynamics of cultural change. However this is not the place to explore the precise nature of the relationship between a New Age-style world-view and modern consumerism. Hence I shall restrict myself to noting the close parallels between the two.

Before doing so however it might be wise of me briefly to anticipate the objection that the New Age movement is so insignificant—and indeed in the twenty-first century so passé, so 70s and 80s,—that it cannot really be credited with a significant role in contemporary society. Now it is quite clear that nothing is further from the truth. For in fact New Age beliefs and attitudes are now so widespread and pervasive in our society and its culture as to effectively dominate all areas of life (just look carefully at the shelves in your local bookshop next time you are there if you don't believe me) (York 1995; Heelas 1996).

There are three principal parallels that we can discern between the metaphysic underlying modern consumption and a New Age world-view. The first—and most obvious—is what Roy Wallis has called epistemological individualism (1984: 100). This is the assumption that authority lies with the self, and that there is no true authority outside the self. As the New Age spokesman Sir George Trevelyan expresses it, 'Only accept what rings true to your own inner self (quoted by Heelas 1996: 21).' This, as we have seen, is also the central tenet of the modern consumer ideology, the assumption that personal experience and personal experience alone—largely in the form of wants and desires—constitutes the highest authority. Second, as we have also seen there is a shared ontological idealism or emanationism. This is the belief that reality consists of mind and spirit rather than matter. While the third, as suggested, is the fact that they share a basically 'magical' philosophy in which the 'external' or 'material world' is generally considered to be directly subject to the power of human thoughts and desires.

The second of these similarities, the shared belief in an idealistic metaphysic, provides me with an opportunity to cite the last of those well-known and popular phrases that have commonly been applied to consumption. In this case the term I have in mind is 'retail therapy'; a phrase that, in my experience, is almost always employed in a humorous context, or at least spoken of in a light-hearted or flippant manner. However, once again I would like to suggest that we should treat it with all seriousness, regarding it not as a metaphor or as a joke but as an accurate and meaningful descriptor. For when the belief in an idealistic ontology is applied to individuals it leads to the idea that the 'authentic self' is located deep within the human psyche and can only be discovered through what are essentially processes that 'express' or 'release' this underlying reality. Naturally this belief casts all restraint or constraint of any kind, whether imposed on the individual from without, or more significantly by individuals themselves through excessive self-control or inhibition, as the cause of all that is false, inauthentic or harmful. Now the term 'retail therapy' is commonly used to mean little more than that the activity of shopping, understood as a form of self-indulgence, may have the effect of making us feel better. However I would like to suggest that the term, if taken seriously, actually means that we should regard this activity as directly comparable with something like participation in an encounter group; that is, as an important means of overcoming inhibitions or 'psychic blocks' and directly expressing powerful feelings. Obviously I don't mean by this that people regularly hit out at irritating shop assistants, or for that matter routinely hug the kind and helpful ones. What I mean is that in selecting and purchasing products that we want (not ones we 'need') we are directly acting out our feelings—and hence throwing off unhelpful restraints—in just the same basic fashion as in the self-consciously constructed therapeutic contexts. Certainly shopping does indeed commonly (although obviously not always) resemble therapy as New Agers understand that term (see Button & Bloom 1992: 131–46; Heelas 1996, ch. 3). That is to say it is essentially a process in which healing and 'self-transformation' is achieved by encouraging direct emotional expression, and hence can indeed be seen as one means of 'liberating' the 'real self'. Indeed at least one New Age author explicitly identifies shopping as a means to this end (Ray 1990: 135–7).

Conclusion

The aim of this [reading] was to explore some of the fundamental assumptions that could be considered to lie behind the phenomenon of modern consumption; to seek out those ideas concerning the nature of knowing and being that are implied in the beliefs and attitudes typically associated with such apparently mundane consumption practices as shopping. The conclusion I have reached is that there are indeed significant metaphysical assumptions underpinning modern consumerism, assumptions that, intriguingly, do not appear to be limited to the sphere of consumption itself but are also present in many other areas of contemporary life. What this could be seen to indicate is that the activity of consuming—with its implied emanationism and faith in the power of 'magic'—has become a kind of template or model for the way in which citizens of contemporary Western societies have come to view all their activities. Since, as we have seen, more and more areas of contemporary society have become assimilated to a 'consumer model' it is perhaps hardly surprising that the underlying metaphysic of consumerism has in the process become a kind of default philosophy for all of modern life. Viewed in this light the fact that consuming has acquired a central significance in our lives could indicate something very different from the common suggestion that we are all victims of a selfish materialism and acquisitiveness. Quite the contrary in fact, it could be seen as implying an acceptance of a fundamentally idealistic metaphysic. If so, then this would mean that consuming should no longer be viewed as a desperate and necessarily futile response to the experience of meaninglessness, but rather as the very solution to that experience. The suggestion being that consumption itself can provide the meaning and identity that modern humans crave, and that it is largely through this activity that individuals discover who they are, as well as succeed in combating their sense of ontological insecurity. Hence it is exactly in this aspect of their lives that most people find the firm foundations upon which their grasp of the real and the true are based, while also providing them with their life's goal. Consequently it is on the basis of this diagnosis that I would suggest that it is justifiable to claim not simply that we live in a consumer society, or are socialized into a consumer culture, but that ours is in a very fundamental sense, a consumer civilization.

Notes

1. In relation to this point I do find it interesting that economists increasingly appear to recognize that our economy is ultimately dependent on the psychological capacities and mental states of individuals. That is to say they generally recognize the important role played by what they call 'consumer confidence'. Yet this simple concept does not really encompass the full extent to which our economy is dependent on the psychic skills and mental dispositions of individuals. For it is our ability continually to manufacture wants that really provides its underpinning.

2. See, for one example among many, Kumar's observation that one of the key features of modernity is individualization, by which he means that 'the structures of modern society take as their unit the individual rather than, as with agrarian or peasant society, the group or community' Kumar (1988: 10).

3. These two characteristics can also be seen to largely account for most of the other characteristic features of modern consumerism, such as the importance of fashion for example, and the extensive proliferation of choice of products offered for sale.

4. See for example Don Slater's observation that 'Consumerism simultaneously exploits mass identity crisis … and in the process intensifies it' (1997: 85).

5. These ads have been taken from 'Soulmates' *The Observer Review,* 9 June 2002, p.19.

6. 'The Spiritual Supermarket: Religious Pluralism in the 21st Century' was the title of a conference organised by INFORM and CESNUR held in London in April 2001.

7. For accounts of the rise of the New Age and neo-pagan movements see Michael York, *The Emerging Network: A Sociology of the New Age and Neo-Pagan Movements,* New York: Rowman & Littlefield, 1995; and Paul Heelas, *The New Age Movement: The Celebration of the Self and the Sacralization of Modernity,* London: Blackwell, 1996.

8. See William Bloom's discussion in Button and Bloom 1992: 89.

References

Bocock, R. & Thompson, K. A. (1992) *Social and cultural forms of modernity,* Cambridge: Polity.

Button, J. & Bloom, W, (1992), (eds.) *The Seeker's Handbook: A New Age Resource Book,* London: Aquarian/Thorsons

Campbell, C. (1987) *The Romantic Ethic and the Spirit of Modern Consumerism,* Oxford: Blackwell.

———— (1998) 'Consumption and the Rhetorics of Need and Want' *Journal of Design History* 11(3): 235–46.

Featherstone, M. (1991), *Consumer Culture and Postmodernism,* London: Sage.

Fuller, R. C. (1989), *Alternative Medicine and American Religious Life,* New York: Oxford University Press.

Heelas, P. (1993) 'The New Age in Cultural Context: the Premodern, the Modern and the Postmodern', *Religion* 23 (2): 103–16.

Heelas, P. (1996). *The New Age Movement: The Celebration of the Self and the Sacralization of Modernity,* London: Blackwell

Hollinger, R. (1994), *Postmodernism and the Social Sciences,* Thousand Oaks, CA: Sage.

Kumar, K. (1988), *The Rise of the Modern West: aspects of the social and political development of the West,* Oxford: Blackwell.

Lane Benson, A. (ed.) (2000), *I Shop Therefore I Am: Compulsive Buying and the Search for Self,* Northvale, New Jersey: Jason Aronson Inc.

Ray, S. (1990), *How to be Chic, Fabulous and Live Forever,* Berkeley, CA: Celestial Arts.

Ritzer, G. Goodman D. & Wiedenscroft, W. (2002) 'Theories of Consumption', in Ritzer, G. & Smart, B. (eds), *The Handbook of Social Theory,* London: Sage.

Slater, D. (1997) *Consumer Culture and Modernity,* Cambridge: Polity. 'Soulmates', *The Observer Review,* 9 June 2000.

Wallis, R. (1984), *The Elementary Forms of the New Religious Life,* London: Routledge.

York, M. (1995), *The Emerging Network: A Sociology of the New Age and Neo-Pagan Movements,* New York: Rowman & Littlefield.

8B. Gluttony, Arrogance, Greed, and Apathy

An Explication of Environmental Vice

By Philip Cafaro

Search on *vice* in the *Philosopher's Index* and not much comes up. Along with a lot of articles with "vice versa" in their abstracts there is one book, which is not about vice but about just political arrangements, and half a dozen articles, none well known, actually dealing with vice or particular vices.[1] Yet there are good reasons to explore vice. Dramatically speaking, vice is more interesting than virtue: think *Inferno* versus *Paradiso*; think Lucifer versus any other character, including God, in *Paradise Lost*. More important, the exploration of moral character has been one of the great steps forward in the "virtue ethics" revival of the past two decades, and considering vice in addition to virtue leads to a more complete treatment of moral character. How human beings fail can tell us much about ourselves. Perhaps nowhere are our failures more apparent than in our treatment of nature.

Public opinion polls repeatedly have shown that most Americans self-identify as "environmentalists" and support strong policies to protect the environment.[2] Yet these same people routinely behave in environmentally irresponsible ways. They plant thirsty bluegrass lawns and pour poisons on them to keep them free of dandelions. They buy gas-guzzling SUVs and drive them four blocks for a loaf of bread. We need to ask why, when it comes to the environment, our actions are so out of sync with our professed values, and we need to ask why in a way that leaves room for both political and personal answers.

To some degree our political, economic, and technological systems present us with environmentally unsustainable choices or strongly incline us in those directions. Our politicians fund highways, not bike paths or mass transit; corporate advertising stimulates environmentally costly desires, rather than encouraging contentment with what we have. Still, as consumers and citizens we usually have real choices, and we often choose the environmentally worse ones. No one forces us to buy big SUVs, build three-car garages, or let our bicycles rust. This [reading] argues that we do these things because we are not the people we should be. Our poor environmental behavior stems, in part, from particular character defects or vices. Among the most important of these are gluttony, arrogance, greed, and apathy.[3]

To anticipate one criticism, exploring environmental vice at the individual level does not mean ignoring the larger, systemic causes of environmental degradation. Creating sustainable societies will demand fundamental political change. Citizens across the globe should work for the passage and enforcement of strong antipollution laws, more national parks and wilderness areas, funding for mass transit and taxes on personal cars, and measures to limit human population growth. Above all, we should work to end the power of large corporations to set environmental policy, directly or through their political tools. At the same time, those of us who care about nature have a responsibility to choose wisely in our everyday environmental decisions. The failures of our neighbors, or our leaders, do not absolve us from our personal environmental responsibilities. The world is an unjust place, but we should live justly within it.

Vice Defined

In common usage, a "vice" is a personal habit, a social practice, or an aspect of human character of which we disapprove.[4] We may speak of a person's habitual lying and nose picking as vices, of more or less widely practiced activities such as smoking and gambling as vices, and of character traits such as greed and gluttony as vices. From here on in, when I speak of a vice, I mean it in the sense of a character trait.

In many cases, when people call a character trait a vice, there is nothing more in their minds than a picture of certain behaviors and a swirl of negative emotions. Thinking human beings aspire to something more than this. We believe that our vice judgments can be right or wrong—or at least more or less plausible. We try to correct or improve them. How?

Traditionally, Western philosophers have invoked the concept of *harm* in order to clarify and justify their judgments about vice.[5] A vice harms the vicious person, those around him, or both. So, for example, gluttony may undermine the health of the glutton or predispose him to pay insufficient attention to what is really important in life. Avarice may tempt us to cheat our business partners or neglect the claims of justice and charity. Sloth undermines our ability to pursue valuable projects that give our lives meaning and which benefit society.

Judgments about the vices are thus derivative: they rest on particular conceptions of the "goods" that make up a good human life and on the general presupposition that the flourishing of the individual and society are important.[6] Lists of key vices and specific conceptions of particular vices have changed, as notions of flourishing have changed. Aristotle imagined human flourishing to consist largely in fulfilling the roles of friend, householder, and citizen in a fourth-century Greek polis. His "vices of character" hinder our performance of these roles and cut us off from the benefits they provide.[7] For Thomas Aquinas, human happiness finds completion in knowledge of and right relationship to God, in this world and the next. Hence, he defined the vices partly in terms of them separating human beings from God. Hence "worldliness" became a vice in the medieval tradition in a way that would not have made sense to the Greeks. For Montaigne and increasingly in the modern world, a sense of the preciousness and fragility of the individual self comes to the fore. Thus, cruelty emerges as a major vice (and diversity becomes a societal virtue).[8] Once again as in Greek times, a vice's evil is described not in terms of disobedience to God but in terms of how it undermines the happiness of individuals or their unlucky neighbors.

Throughout the evolution of the Western tradition and despite much variety, four commonalities tend to hold. First, selfishness and self-centeredness are condemned, whereas legitimate self-concern and self-development are praised. For Aristotle, "every virtue causes its possessors to be in a good state and to perform their functions well"; the vices undermine proper human functioning and well-being.[9] For Aquinas, too, the notion of virtue "implies the perfection of a power," whereas vice leads to weakness, failure, and, in extreme cases, a sort of disintegration of the self.[10] Even Kant, despite his caution that love of "the dear self" lies at the root of immorality, also argues that we have a duty to develop our talents and capabilities.[11] Vices hinder this legitimate self-development.

Second, and as a consequence, the tradition insists that vice is both bad for individuals and harmful to their communities. Indeed, individual writers have sometimes gone to extreme lengths here, arguing, for example, that we never benefit ourselves when we wrong others.[12] More sensibly, the tradition has argued that moral shortcuts to happiness in fact *tend* to place us on winding roads toward unhappiness. Sharp dealing in business leads people to distrust us, and hence we do not prosper; avarice helps us amass great wealth at the expense of our fellow citizens, who then hate us or plot our demise. In this way, the tradition often appealed to a broadened self-interest in order to convince people to act morally: our happiness is bound up with the happiness of others. This approach has largely been abandoned by modern moral philosophy, which has focused on direct appeals to altruism.

Third, the tradition sees vice as contradicting and eventually undermining reason, hence destroying our ability to understand our proper place in the world and act morally. Aristotle expresses this in his distinction between incontinence (the tendency to pursue pleasure even when we know it is wrong to do so) and the full-blown vice of intemperance (where the continued pursuit of illicit pleasure has so clouded our judgment that we no longer recognize right from wrong).[13] The vices are habits of thought and action. Left unchecked, they tend to cloud reason, the voice of both conscience and prudence.

Fourth, and partly as a consequence of this diminished rationality, the tradition sees vice as cutting us off from reality or at least from what is most important in life. This is most obvious in the late ancient and medieval periods; for Augustine and Aquinas, sin and vice cut us off from God, the highest reality.[14] But we also see this notion at work in Aristotle, where intemperance leads people to pursue gross physical pleasures at the expense of activities such as science and contemplation that connect us to higher things.[15] We see it in early modern times in Montaigne, where the vice of certainty blocks sustained inquiry into existence, and intolerance blinds us to our common humanity and a true understanding of the human condition.[16]

What holds these four aspects of vice together is that they all involve harm: to ourselves, to those around us, or to both. What constitutes harm, particularly beyond a core of obviousness, has varied widely in the tradition, along with the particular conceptions of human nature and the ultimate commitments held by philosophers. And until recently, philosophers have paid scant attention to human harms to the environment—or to the potential for those harms to rebound and harm us in turn.

Vice and Environmental Harm

Take a look at the arguments for environmental protection in op-ed pieces in the newspapers, in articles in *Sierra* or *Audubon* magazines, or in the classic works of Aldo Leopold or Rachel Carson.[17] Sometimes environmentalists appeal to human altruism. Air pollution from Midwestern power plants is killing trees and acidifying lakes in the Appalachian Mountains; a proposed dam out West will drown a river and perhaps extinguish a rare fish species. This harm to nature is, or would be, wrong, based on nature's intrinsic worth—a worth that may be expressed more in aesthetic or spiritual terms than directly in what philosophers recognize as ethical terms. As we are powerful, these arguments assert, so we should be just and merciful.

At least as often, environmentalists' arguments appeal to human self-interest. We should rein in water and air pollution because they harm human health. We should preserve an undeveloped tract of prairie, an unroaded forest, a wild and undammed river, because opportunities to know and appreciate nature will disappear if we do not do so. Scientists and artists will lose chances to study and appreciate wild nature; hunters, fishermen, and backpackers will lose recreational opportunities. We might be able to live without these activities, but at least some of us would not be able to live well or live the way we want to live.[18]

Both sorts of arguments are ubiquitous in the environmental literature. Both can be effective. One need not preclude the other. The first sort of argument finds direct (or intrinsic) value in nature's flourishing; the second sees human flourishing as dependent on nature's flourishing, which thus has derivative (or instrumental) value. In either case, harms to nature are ethically important. During the past thirty years, most environmental philosophers have focused on making the case for altruism, refining and developing the first sort of argument. Recently some philosophers have focused on refining and justifying the second sort of approach, arguing that we will be better and happier people if we appreciate and protect nature.[19]

The key idea behind such an *environmental virtue ethics* is that we cannot harm nature without harming ourselves. A basic human flourishing depends on a healthy environment (lead exposure can damage children's brains, leading to lower intelligence, mental retardation, and death, at progressively higher levels of exposure). Full human flourishing depends on a varied and stimulating environment, including accessible wild areas that preserve the native flora and fauna (children who grow up without chances to experience wild nature miss opportunities to appreciate beauty, understand human history and prehistory, and reflect on their place in the world). The complementary insight is that human flourishing does *not* depend on high levels of material consumption. In fact, when the acquisition of material possessions leads us to ignore higher pursuits, or when society's overconsumption undermines nature's health and integrity, our own lives suffer.

In her book *Dirty Virtues,* Louke van Wensveen shows that environmentalists often assert that certain vices are at the base of environmentally harmful behavior.[20] A *greedy* factory owner dumps untreated pollutants into a stream, even though she knows that it may harm fish in the stream or people who eat the fish. *Gluttonous* Americans consume too much food, energy, or raw materials; thus, we take more than we need from the Earth. To justify such vice judgments, environmental philosophers must provide convincing accounts of the motivations behind antienvironmental behavior. And they must show harm.

Consider how Aristotle discusses vice. In the *Ethics*, certain persistent and cohesive aspects of human personality are defined as character traits, and certain character traits are judged vices because they harm vicious individuals and those around them. Because for Aristotle a human being can only flourish in a polis and because one's happiness cannot be completely divorced from that of one's family, friends, and descendants, even the vices that seem primarily to harm others have a potentially self-destructive aspect. There are a number of well-worn paths by which other-directed harms may harm a selfish person, including poisoning his relationships with others and undermining the social cohesion on which a functioning polis depends. Ultimately, self-harms and other-directed harms cannot be completely separated.

The way to justify environmentalists' vice talk is similar. We need to show how environmental vices—which may be largely the same as the traditional vices or may include many new ones—harm the vicious person directly. We need to show how they harm those around him and future generations, people about whom he should care (for one thing, the selfish person's happiness is not so easily separated from theirs as he thinks). We must also show that there is another legitimate circle of moral concern, not recognized by Aristotle or the philosophical tradition, pleaded for in Leopold's *Sand County Almanac* and by legions of environmentalists since then: the wider circle of nonhuman nature. Harm within this circle is bad in itself, for it is real harm to entities that can flourish and are wonderful when they do flourish. And such harm rebounds, harming human communities and (sometimes) the individuals inflicting the environmental harms. Aristotle places us in a social environment and defines human flourishing accordingly. The fact that we also live in physical environments shows the need for this more encompassing view of human flourishing and moral concern.[21]

To anticipate another criticism, some philosophers will say that only when we show how vices harm vicious persons themselves have we given the strongest possible argument for their viciousness. Although I do think that showing the connection between vice and self-harm is one benefit of a virtue ethics approach, I see no reason to limit our conception of harm to self-harm. Self-concern and concern for others are both legitimate and necessary within ethics. There is something wrong with a person who brings all of her actions to the test of her own happiness, even when they obviously affect others. Similarly, there is something wrong with ethical philosophies that do so. An environmental virtue ethics may give us good self-interested reasons to rein in our environmental vices; it does not seek to reduce all vice to self-interest.

On the other hand, I see nothing wrong with curbing our vices because we believe that it is in our self-interest to do so. My colleague Holmes Rolston is worried that you will treat nature right for the wrong reasons.[22] I am more worried that you will not treat nature right at all, and I believe that any reason that convinces you to treat nature more gently is a good reason. Furthermore, a better understanding of our self-interest should lead to less materialistic lifestyles and more time exploring nature. Rolston's arguments for nature's intrinsic value deserve to prevail; they are more likely to prevail among people who have had experiences that help them understand and appreciate them.

In the end, as in interpersonal ethics, a complete environmental ethics will have to make a place for both altruism and enlightened self-interest. In truth we are all self-interested, although not exclusively so. In truth, our flourishing and nature's flourishing are intertwined. In what follows, I discuss four key environmental vices: gluttony, arrogance, greed, and apathy.[23] If I can show how these vices lead to harm, that will be all the justification you should need that they are worth reforming (certainly it is all the justification you will ever be able to get). The greater the harm—to oneself, to others, to nature, or to all three—the greater the incentive to reform.

Gluttony

"Gluttony: excess in eating and drinking" says my *American Heritage Dictionary;* the *Oxford English Dictionary* adds that the word may also refer to an excessive *desire* for food and drink and by a natural extension to many kinds of overindulgence (I may be a glutton for punishment, learning, or cheap romance novels). Despite the word's pejorative connotations, we tend to take a relatively benign view of this vice today. Few moralists treat overeating as a serious personal failing, on a par with such qualities as selfishness or cruelty. Earlier thinkers took gluttony more seriously. Aristotle devoted extensive attention to intemperance, defined as the vice regarding the pleasures of touch: primarily food, drink, and sex. Saint Paul inveighed against those "whose God is their belly." Not only was *gula* considered one of the seven deadly sins, but early church thinkers often put it at the head of the list.[24]

Perhaps the classic picture of the glutton is a man at table, stuffing in food with both hands, sauces dribbling down his chins, belly pushing back the table as he occasionally lurches into it. Unconcerned with quality, he is going for quantity. He does not talk to his dinner companions, even to comment on the food. He is all desire; there is something brutal and inhuman about him. Another picture of gluttony involves two women sitting in a fancy restaurant, simpering over the tomato bisque. One compares it with the soup she had at another restaurant three weeks ago; the other describes a version she made from a recipe taken from *Gourmet* magazine. We might call these women epicures rather than gluttons, and many would see nothing wrong with their behavior. Gregory the Great, who helped define the seven deadly sins for the medieval tradition, took a sterner and more encompassing view: "In another manner are distinguished the kinds of gluttony, according to Saint Gregory. The first is, eating before it is time to eat. The second is when a man gets himself too delicate food or drink. The third is when men eat too much, and beyond measure. The fourth is fastidiousness, with great attention paid to the preparation and dressing of food. The fifth is to eat too greedily. These are the five fingers of the Devil's hand wherewith he draws folk into sin."[25] Monkish quibbling? Or a recognition that beyond the health harms of gross gluttony, gourmandizing wastes our time and causes us to pay less attention to what is truly important? It depends on your view of human flourishing and the purpose of life.

Neither of these pictures is particularly appealing, yet our disapproval could be merely aesthetic. To show why gluttony is *morally* wrong, we must discuss the harms it generates. In the case of gluttonous eating, the most obvious harms fall on the glutton himself. Excessive eating leads to obesity, and the health dangers of obesity are well documented in the scientific literature. Of the ten leading causes of death in America, four show positive correlation to being overweight or the diet and activity patterns that lead to being overweight.[26] These include the three leading proximate causes of death—heart disease, cancer, and cerebrovascular disease (stroke)—as well as diabetes mellitus, the seventh leading cause. In addition to direct harms to health, obesity decreases happiness and well-being in less obvious ways that are harder to measure.[27] Overweight people tend to feel more lethargic. Obese individuals participate less often in many enjoyable physical activities, from sports to sex (this is a positive feedback problem: less physical activity leads to less energy, leading to less physical activity, etc.). The surgeon general has concluded that obesity is a major health problem in the United States.[28]

With fine gluttony, the argument that it harms the glutton is less clear. Gourmands may find a lot of pleasure savoring the sauces and comparing the wines. Gregory did not have to worry about whether his monks were enjoying themselves, but for most of us today pleasure is at least part of what we want out of life. Even from a hedonistic perspective, however, we may wonder whether developing a taste for finer things will lead to happiness in the long run. If we are no longer able to enjoy simple meals, or forget Seneca's words that "hunger is the best spice," or pay more attention to how our cooking turned out than to the friends around our table, or eat such rich foods that we get gout, the gourmet life may lead away from happiness. Too, our time is limited. Attention to trivia can lead us to neglect more important things.

So gluttony takes a direct toll on gluttons, but it also has environmental costs. In America, 1,265 species are listed as threatened or endangered under the Endangered Species Act: 519 animals and 746 plants.[29] The causes of extinction are complex, but scientists generally agree that habitat loss is primary. A comprehensive study has found habitat degradation/loss implicated as a cause for 85 percent of threatened and endangered species in the United States.[30] Crucially, in analyzing the causes of habitat loss, the study identifies agriculture (principally row cropping) as the leader, affecting fully 38 percent of all endangered species. Livestock grazing is also important, affecting 22 percent. In addition, agriculture is an important contributor to several other major causes of endangerment, including water developments such as reservoirs and dams (affecting 30 percent of species) and pollutants (20 percent).[31]

Now just as food consumption drives agricultural production, so food *over*consumption fuels a more environmentally harmful and intensive agriculture. A recent, comprehensive study by the U.S. Department of Agriculture's Economic Research Unit estimated that in 2000, Americans consumed an average of 2,800 calories per day, 25 percent more than the 2,200 calories needed to supply their nutritional and energy needs.[32] This translates directly into increased agricultural demand. All else being equal, Americans' habit of consuming approximately 25 percent more calories than necessary increases the amount of land needed to grow crops and graze animals by 25 percent. It increases the amount of pollutants dumped onto agricultural lands and running off into rivers and streams by 25 percent.[33] Excess food consumption harms Americans' health; if we take *ecosystem* health to include clean rivers and streams and robust populations of our native flora and fauna, we must conclude that excess food consumption also harms environmental health.

Because ecosystem health and human health are connected, a complete account of the harms of gluttony must extend further. Unhealthy ecosystems lead to direct human harms, for example, when people sicken from the air or water pollution generated by huge livestock confinement facilities. Ecosystem sickness also leads to intellectual and spiritual losses, as a dull and lifeless agricultural landscape becomes a bore to live and work in. Even if this landscape remains productive of agricultural products, it may no longer be productive of happy and healthy human beings.[34] In Illinois only one-ten thousandth of the original 37 million acres of tall-grass prairie remains: 3,500 acres occurring in small, isolated conservation areas.[35] Living in a monotonous sea of corn and soybeans has probably taken a toll on the minds of Illinois farmers.

Gluttony reminds us that the vices, although often selfish, harm both ourselves and others. Food overconsumption harms our health and lowers life expectancy, but it also harms nature. These harms to nature rebound, in turn, and cause new kinds of harm to human and nonhuman beings. So that in the end, it becomes difficult to separate harms to self and harms to others, harms to people and harms to nature. Our flourishing is tied up with the flourishing of others.

On the other hand, the example of gluttony reminds us that the calculus of harms does not always come out as neatly as moralists want it to. For the past thirty years, books like Frances Moore Lappé's *Diet for a Small Planet* have argued that overeating in the wealthy nations leads to Third World hunger.[36] The argument has developed momentum by virtue of endless repetition, but empirical studies show that the connection does not hold. Work by Amartya Sen and others suggests instead that political and economic factors within Third World countries are most important in causing famines and malnutrition: particularly civil war, indifferent governments, and terrible poverty.[37] This does not mean that rich, fat Americans should not do more to help the world's poor; it means that eating less food is unlikely to help feed them. However, eating less *will* lessen our agricultural footprint, helping all those other species that compete with us for habitat and resources. Gluttony's other-directed harms fall primarily on nonhuman others.

Again, the moralist may want to say that gluttony, like all vices, inevitably harms the glutton herself. But gluttony shows us that we may refine our vices, so as to direct more of their harm—perhaps *all* of their harm—toward others. I may dine out three times a week in spectacular restaurants, eating and drinking my way through my children's inheritance—without neglecting to hit the gym the next day, thus staying quite healthy. I may cook spectacular meals for myself and my friends, thoroughly enjoy both, and maximize my own pleasure—while greatly increasing my environmental harms. On average, it takes one cup of oil to grow, harvest, store, ship, and sell each cup of food (dry weight) consumed by Americans. Fine gluttony greatly increases this aspect of our agricultural footprint, as "the market" flies fish from New Zealand to Denver or strawberries from Chile to New York in January. This causes *us* no harm; furthermore, we may still get out and enjoy nature, perhaps even flying to New Zealand or Chile to hike and ski. Still, a more comprehensive and accurate account of harm will teach us that we should limit our agricultural footprint and accommodate ourselves more to locally available foods. All important, unnecessary harm is wrong. Although it is possible to live a life in which we largely externalize the costs of our gluttony, we should not do so.

Virtue ethicists emphasize the childishness of gluttony. Aristotle believed that there is something crude and undeveloped in a person who seeks all happiness in the simplest ways.[38] "The gross feeder is a man in the larva state," wrote Henry Thoreau, "and there are whole nations in that condition, nations without fancy or imagination, whose vast abdomens betray them."[39] Similarly, virtue ethicists assert that self-development and lasting satisfaction come not through gluttony but through pursuing more adult pleasures and activities. "When someone lacks understanding," wrote Aristotle, "his desire for the pleasant is insatiable and seeks indiscriminate satisfaction."[40] In contrast, the pleasures of love and friendship, aesthetic appreciation and the pursuit of knowledge, will not pale or lead us to behave unjustly.

Traditionally, the virtue opposed to gluttony was *temperance* or moderate use. We may also speak of *gratitude* as a complementary virtue. Consider an American Thanksgiving. Originally it was a day set aside to thank the Lord for physical and spiritual sustenance, with roots in Indian green corn ceremonies with similar motivations. Now Thanksgiving is often just another excuse for Americans to pig out. The next day, we go shopping. I do not think that the answer to this is to fast on Thanksgiving but, rather, to give thanks, thoughtfully and sincerely. With gratitude will come understanding and acceptance of our environmental responsibilities.

Arrogance

With no other virtue/vice complex have Western attitudes varied so much as with pride, humility, and arrogance. The Sermon on the Mount exhorts us to live lives of meekness and humility. For Christians pride is a vice, because human beings are infinitely inferior to God and essentially equal to one another. We often go wrong in our social dealings precisely through a desire to assert our superiority over others. Contrarily, the ancient pagans tended to view pride as a necessary part of a good life. Because self-knowledge and striving to live well helped define the good life, if one lived well, one knew it and commended oneself for it. Humility was at best a just judgment of one's own mediocrity and at worst a failure to understand true human excellence and whether one had achieved it.[41]

We are heirs to this complex heritage. On the one hand, we condemn those who lord it over others. We dislike braggarts and prefer heroes who credit others for their successes or who downplay them.

On the other hand, we scoff at obsequious people. We encourage our children to take pride in their schoolwork and other efforts and are proud of their achievements.

If we look to the harm criterion, I believe we will make a place for a proper pride as a virtue, with obsequiousness as one vice and arrogance as another. As Kant, our greatest exponent of egalitarian morality, puts it, we have no right to disrespect humanity in our own person; nor should we encourage others to do so through excessive meekness. Furthermore, part of our legitimate motivation for treating others morally is a sense that we exalt our own humanity in the process.[42] Still, arrogance—an overvaluation of ourselves and an undervaluation of others—remains a vice. The human harms that arrogance leads to are obvious, as we selfishly place our own interests far ahead of other people's.

Environmentalists and environmental philosophers see a similar arrogance in much of our treatment of nature. "Christian as well as non-Christian ecowriters warn against the prideful attitude that makes us humans think we are number one in the universe," Louke van Wensveen writes, "that we are ... 'central and in control'." She notes that "the Latin term for pride, *superbia,* translates the Greek *huperbios,* which means 'above life'," and "the Latin term *humilitas* literally suggests closeness to 'humus', i.e., 'soil' or 'ground'."[43] An early attempt to articulate a better environmental ethics was titled "the arrogance of humanism."[44] Today philosophers speak of the arrogance of "anthropocentrism," the vain and selfish view that human beings alone are worthy of respect, whereas everything else in the world, including several million other species of life, only has value if it is useful to humans.

Arrogant indifference to nature and arrogant indifference to people often go together. For four decades, Chevron and Shell have been drilling for oil in the Niger Delta, making billions of dollars for their companies, their shareholders, and Nigeria's successive military and civilian dictators. Little of this wealth has made its way into the hands of the delta's inhabitants, who have had to bear the brunt of the environmental harms of oil drilling. These have included poisoned water and diminished fisheries, leading to sickness and hunger for many inhabitants. Efforts to protect the environment and other local interests have been brutally suppressed. Ken Saro-Wiwa and eight other leaders of the Ogoni people were executed following a show trial in 1995. Since then other activists have been jailed and tortured, as documented in a 200-page report from Human Rights Watch.[45]

In May 1998, more than 100 activists from the Ilaje people occupied a Chevron drilling platform and service barge in an effort to force the company's management to negotiate with them. Activists' demands included clean drinking water, electricity, environmental reparations for nearby villages, and rebuilding of eroding riverbanks. With work on the barge stopped, Chevron was losing money. After four days and while the activists believed they were still in negotiations, Chevron flew in members of the Nigerian military, who opened fire on the unarmed occupiers, shooting two of them dead. The rest were taken off to prison and tortured.[46]

The Nigerian armed forces were brought in on Chevron contractors' helicopters and given bonus pay by the contractor; the decision to bring them in was made by Chevron management. Nigeria's armed forces and police are notorious for human rights abuses. By bringing in the military and sending the activists off to jail, oil company managers knew what they were buying.

Bola Oyinbo, one of eleven protesters arrested, reported being handcuffed and hung from a ceiling hook for five hours, in an effort to extract a confession of piracy and destruction of property. The radio program *Democracy Now* asked Bill Spencer, a Chevron contractor in charge of servicing the barge, what he thought of the torture endured by Oyinbo and others:

> *Spencer:* I don't think anybody here was under the impression that when you go to jail in Nigeria, it's pleasant.
>
> *Q:* Was there concern about the young people who were held in detention. Was there any follow up?
>
> *A:* By me? Not at all. No.
>
> *Q:* Were you concerned about them in detention?
>
> *A:* I was more concerned about 200 people who work for me. I could care less about the people from the village, quite frankly.
>
> *Q:* Once your people were safe …
>
> *A:* Did I personally have any concern for them, not one little bit. No.

The arrogance here is blatant. With this view of the Niger Delta's inhabitants, it is hard to imagine Spencer or the other oil men working there having much concern for the delta's fisheries or wildlife. Indeed, coming to Nigeria seems to provide them with a well-paid moral holiday. As Spencer puts it: "I'm not leading a moral campaign. We're just here to work. Strictly commercial venture. Not a political one."

But Chevron's and Shell's activities have enormous political consequences. Oil provides the government with 80 percent of its revenues. That money helped prop up military dictatorships for more than thirty years. The oil companies got what they wanted: zero accountability for the environmental and human harms caused by their activities, hence maximum profits. Only the Nigerian people suffered. Here is Bill Spencer again, on that subject:

> *Democracy Now:* Do you have any reservation about working with those forces [Nigerian armed forces and police] knowing or acknowledging they can in fact be ruthless?
>
> *Spencer:* No, I don't know. Life is tough here. And people, you often hear it said, that life is cheap here. I guess it is. It's looked at a little differently. I think that

that's something that doesn't happen in our society. Life is a little more maybe precious or something. I think here or any of these developing countries it tends to be a little cheaper.

It is fascinating to see how arrogance can dim a man's sense of moral responsibility. This is how it *is* here, Spencer says, as if he and the oil companies are not helping to create the conditions in Nigeria from which they profit. But read the words of the activists describing what they hope to achieve: clean water, secure food, education for their children, and some say in how they are governed and how their environment is managed. *They* seem to think that their lives and the lives of their children are precious. Now we can begin to understand why Chevron managers prefer to send in the armed forces to kill these people and crush their spirit, rather than meet with them. If they heard them speak and looked them in the eyes, they would be forced to see them as human beings. That might get in the way of maximizing profits.

Examples of corporate arrogance are legion; arrogant environmental destruction by individuals is just as common. A good example in the United States is off-road vehicle (ORV) use. Over the past three decades, ORVs have created major, well-documented harms to our public lands.[47] Four-wheelers have carved tens of thousands of miles of illegal roads onto our national forests, degrading wildlife habitat and causing erosion. Snowmobiles in Yellowstone National Park stampede wildlife and cause such serious air pollution that entrance guards have been forced to wear respirators. Jet skis dump up to one-quarter of their oil and gas directly into lakes and rivers, polluting them. While they trash nature, ORV users ruin the experience of other recreationists—who happen to be the vast majority of visitors to national parks and national forests.

The arrogance of many ORV users is palpable. Magazines such as *Petersen's 4-Wheel & Off-Road* or *4-Wheel Drive and Sport Utility Magazine* are filled with macho posturing. "Bud Vandermel chose to display some attitude coupled with Chevy prowess when building his '78 Scottsdale off-roader," begins a typical article: "Wanting to run with the big trucks, or wanting them to follow, Bud's off-road machine needed to be tall, and it needed to display dominance. To get the altitude, Bud installed 8-inch Skyjacker Softride leaf springs."[48] When Bud revs up his truck and heads into the backcountry, crashing through small trees and leaving tire tracks in the streams are part of the experience. At a minimum, ORVers do not care about their effects on the places they are tearing up. For some of them, harming nature is part of the fun.

These arrogant practices showcase important aspects of the vices. First, they tend to make us *selfish*. The ORV magazines rarely mention the obvious environmental harms ORVs cause or how annoying they are to other public lands users. In an extensive review, the few mentions I found of environmental harms all focused on the "environmental extremists" or "eco-wackos" complaining about them. Second, as Aristotle emphasizes, the vices *corrupt our reasoning abilities*.[49] In eight years teaching environmental ethics, I have read term papers on most major environmental issues, and some of the most illogical, rhetorically overblown, and willfully confused ones have been discussions of the ethics of ORV use by ORV enthusiasts. Third, vices come from and lead to *crude views of the good life* and make it hard to appreciate better ones. In discussing the experience of off-roading the emphasis is on fun, excitement, "the adrenaline rush." That is what people want—and it has nothing to do with understanding or appreciating nature. Indeed, it makes it harder for ORVers or anyone else to do so.

Vice cuts us off from reality, according to Thomas Aquinas. The arrogance of anthropocentrism cuts people off from the reality of nature. ORV users arrogantly destroy the wild nature that others want to appreciate and whiz through it so fast that they learn nothing about it themselves. In the Niger Delta, Chevron and Shell are arrogantly displacing traditional ways of life based on small-scale agriculture and sustainable fishing. Anthropocentrism as an intellectual outlook also cuts us off from reality, as we ignore nature's stories and tell truncated and false stories about ourselves.[50]

In the pursuit of virtue, *practices and laws* are crucial. ORV use is a good example of a practice that encourages anthropocentrism. If we want to live environmentally responsible lives, we will have to cultivate practices that lock in habits and ways of looking at the world that are nonanthropocentric. As Aristotle says, we learn to act morally by instilling proper habits, not by arguments. Activities such as bird-watching, trout fishing, wildlife photography, and backcountry camping instruct us in nature's diversity and beauty each time we engage in them. They teach us nature's stories, sharpening our senses and quieting our minds enough to appreciate them.[51] We should encourage our children in these practices—and we should keep them from engaging in what might seem like harmless fun on ORVs.[52]

For the irredeemably arrogant, of course, we need laws. Current efforts in the United States to replace strong environmental laws with voluntary environmental protection must be exposed and defeated. And as Peter Singer has recently argued, we must create an international legal order in which Chevron, Shell, and other corporations are held accountable for encouraging human rights abuses and propping up tyrannical regimes that abuse their own people.[53] Similarly, we must develop strong, binding international agreements to halt global warming, preserve endangered species and ecosystems, and reverse human population growth. Nothing less than this will succeed in preserving the flourishing natural world that an environmental virtue ethics insists is the prerequisite for human flourishing.

We cannot be good people without appreciating and developing those aspects of our humanity that distinguish us from the rest of nature: our abstract reason, our complex culture. Yet exalting our humanity does not mean focusing exclusively on these differences or setting ourselves up as tyrants over the rest of creation. Rather, the more we preserve and appreciate nature's beauty, the more we will flourish ourselves. The greater our moral restraint, the more a proper human pride will be justified.[54]

Greed

Greed is "an excessive desire to acquire or possess more than what one needs or deserves, especially with respect to material wealth."[55] It is natural to enjoy material possessions; it is necessary, in modern society, to deal with money. But the desire for wealth may prove excessive for several reasons. It may leave us perpetually unsatisfied; as one philosopher puts it, greed is "an insatiable longing" that actual possession cannot slake.[56] The greedy person is often portrayed as rich. He has more than most people, more, perhaps, than he knows what to do with. Still, it is not enough. Greed may also lead us to neglect other, more important aspects of life. Another picture of greed is the miser counting gold pieces, alone in a windowless room, without friends, without interest in the world outside. The clink, clink, clink of each coin as it hits the pile echoes hollowly down the empty halls.

These are just images, of course, proving nothing. To show greed's viciousness, we must explore how too great an emphasis on money or possessions leads to harm. We must show, too, that there are limits to what we need, deserve, or really can use here.

Greed is perhaps the most selfish-making vice; in its grip we become incapable of generosity and immune to the demands of justice. When Andrew Carnegie and Henry Clay Frick broke the Homestead steelworkers strike in 1892, they were among the wealthiest men in America, but they had no intention of sharing any more of that wealth with their workers than they could possibly avoid. No claims of justice, no consideration of the good uses their workers could put that money to or the sheer pointlessness of *them* amassing any more wealth, made any impression.

Cases such as Homestead or the oil companies' injustices in Nigeria show how greed can lead to great injustice. But even everyday, small-scale greed can lead to important harms, accentuating differences in wealth, fueling envy in the poor and vanity in the rich, and undermining the social bonds necessary for a happy society. Christians have criticized avarice above all for these social harms. "Now shall you understand that the relief for avarice is mercy and pity in large doses," Chaucer's Parson says: "Certainly, the avaricious man shows no pity nor any mercy to the needy man; for he delights in keeping his treasure and not in the rescuing or relieving of his fellow Christian."[57] Aquinas condemned the hoarding of unnecessary possessions in clear terms, stating that "whatever a man has in superabundance is owed, of natural right, to the poor for their sustenance."[58] To grasp possessions beyond this limit is unjust and idolatrous: the worship of Mammon.

To the traditionally recognized social harms of greed, environmentalists add harms to nature. Greed leads to environmental harms in three ways. First, when profit is placed over all other goals, greed leads businesspeople to break environmental laws or do the minimum necessary to comply with them. For example, a factory hog farm might be highly profitable; still, its owner wants more money. He doubles his hog sheds, increasing the stink breathed by the neighbors and his poorly paid workers. The resultant increase in manure overstresses his waste lagoons, causing overflows into a nearby river. This kills fish and other wildlife, drives anglers and canoers from the river, and decreases property values for dozens of his neighbors. Unfortunately, it is easy to find real examples where businesspeople break or bend environmental laws in pursuit of profit.[59]

Second, greed undermines the democratic political process. In his final year as CEO of Halliburton, an oilfield services and construction firm, Dick Cheney earned $26.4 million in compensation.[60] Upon taking office as U.S. vice president a year later, Cheney's main job was to chair a task force charged with setting U.S. energy policy. Its recommendations, developed in meetings closed to the public but open to friends and colleagues from the energy industries, read like a wish list from those same industries, including rollbacks of environmental regulations and tens of billions of dollars in unnecessary subsidies for new energy development. In the Bush administration, in one governmental department after another, industry lobbyists and managers are "regulating" their own industries, lining their friends' pockets just as their own pockets will be lined when they return to private life. In Cheney's case he does not even have to wait, for he continues to receive compensation from Halliburton while serving as vice president.[61] These are clear cases of greed trumping the public interest.

Third, greed leads to environmental harms by helping drive overconsumption among the general populace. Americans use vastly more oil, coal, water, metals, and other resources than our grandparents did, largely because we purchase lots of unnecessary things. Four and five year olds badger their parents for the latest plastic action figures and video games, which soon enough are dispatched to overflowing landfills. Middle-aged men with flagging libidos acquire mysterious desires for large, powerful cars—no matter that they already own cars or that the new Porsche or Hummer gets one-third the gas mileage and generates three times the CO_2 of the family's Taurus. All this overconsumption makes a pitiful enough spectacle, but the more important point is that it leads to great harms to nature. Human beings compete with millions of other species for the habitat and resources needed to survive. Like Carnegie and Frick 100 years ago we are willing to destroy other lives or monopolize the resources needed to preserve them for the most trivial reasons. At a minimum, justice would seem to demand that we avoid consumption that does *nothing* to further our happiness. But greed leads us on to ever more consumption.

In these ways, greed harms nature. But it also harms greedy people themselves. In the first place, there is no strong connection between increased wealth and happiness. Sages and philosophers have taught that "money can't buy happiness" for millennia—now science is starting to confirm it. Numerous studies in America have shown that beyond the poorest 10 to 15 percent of the population, there is no statistically significant correlation between wealth and subjective or objective measures of happiness.[62] You are no more likely to be happy earning $4,000,000 per year than $40,000. The factors that correlate most strongly with happiness are *security* of income—having some assurance that you and your family will have enough—and getting along well with your fellow workers and your spouse. But having some assurance that one has enough depends on being able to *recognize* that one has enough. Greedy people find this hard to do. Furthermore, studies have shown that people with more materialistic outlooks on life tend to have poor interpersonal relationships.[63] So the most proven, effective means to happiness tend to be beyond the reach of greedy people—no matter how wealthy they are.

Beyond the fact that material possessions are largely irrelevant to happiness, psychological studies show that a materialistic *outlook* on life tends to undermine happiness. One group of psychologists report:

A growing body of research demonstrates that people who strongly orient toward values such as money, possessions, image, and status report lower subjective well-being. For example, [several studies] have shown that when people rate the relative importance of extrinsic, materialistic values as high in comparison to other pursuits (e.g., self-acceptance, affiliation, community feeling), lower quality of life is also reported. Late adolescents with a strong materialistic value orientation report lower self-actualization and vitality, as well as more depression and anxiety.[64]

Other studies have replicated these findings with college students and older adults.

Why are materialists less satisfied with life? One review article has considered various hypotheses and concluded that there is good evidence for three of them. First, materialists have poorer social lives, thus undermining their subjective well-being (but whether materialism is cause or effect remains unclear; unhappy people may grasp at materialistic values like straws). Second, it appears that "working toward material goals is less rewarding in the moment than working toward other goals." Anyone who has worked jobs that were enjoyable and challenging and jobs that were not knows this already. Third, the evidence suggests that the gap between what people have and what they want is more pronounced in the material realm than in other areas of life; hence focusing on material goals fosters dissatisfaction. It leads to a race to get and spend that leaves many people feeling hurried and harassed.[65]

Philosophers, following Thomas Aquinas, will add that materialism pales because it involves turning away from real goods to apparent goods.[66] When we are greedy, we neglect the real goods of activities for mere passive possession (the bird-watcher with top-of-the-line Zeiss binoculars who rarely gets up to hear the dawn chorus, the spoiled teenager with a fifteen-piece drum kit sitting unused in the basement). We reject the real goods of relationships for the apparent goods of triumphing over others (the CEO who cheats his employees out of their expected pension benefits and trades in his wife for a younger model). We neglect fulfilling, socially useful work for the trappings of status or success (the millionaire plastic surgeon specializing in boob jobs versus the humble pediatrician who volunteers at a free clinic twice a month).

In an excellent study of the seven deadly sins, Henry Fairlie notes that different societies predispose their members to different vices.[67] In America, we are raised to be greedy. Never before has a nation been so relentlessly bombarded by advertising; the average American child sees hundreds of thousands of television commercials by the time he or she reaches adulthood. Advertising emphasizes consumption as the primary means to happiness and works by increasing our dissatisfaction with life. As one marketer puts it: "Advertising at its best is making people feel that without their product, you're a loser. Kids are very sensitive to that. … You open up emotional vulnerabilities, and it's very easy to do with kids because they're the most emotionally vulnerable."[68]

This education in greed does not stop with childhood. Our colleges and universities teach applied avarice in their economics classes and business schools. At election time, candidates work to convince us that they can increase economic growth, without asking whether that growth will make us happier or better people. Institutions that once spoke out against materialism, above all the churches, have largely fallen silent about its dangers.[69]

We cannot eradicate the vices from human beings. However, there are practical steps we can take to limit greed and promote its contrasting virtues: thrift, modesty, generosity, and contentment. Individuals can focus on engaging in activities, rather than purchasing things. We can *share* things: buying a new lawnmower with several neighbors, for example, rather than buying one alone. We can stop watching television, eliminating much of the commercial incitement to greed from our lives. We can find alternatives to "recreational shopping" and other activities that cause wasteful consumption and leave us feeling unsatisfied.

At the political level, communities should ban billboards and commercial advertising in public schools. They should *require* recycling: current voluntary systems ensure that those who most need to learn restraint do not do so. More ambitiously, communities could pass sumptuary laws: limiting the size of houses, for example, to decrease human impacts on the landscape and standing incitements to envy. Beyond their direct environmental benefits, such measures would send a powerful, socially sanctioned message that greed is bad. Taking these personal and political steps would be good for us and good for nature.

Apathy

"Apathy" comes from the Greek *apatheia,* "without feeling"; one synonym in old English was *unlust*.[70] It is perhaps best understood as a lack: "lack of interest or concern, especially regarding matters of general importance or appeal ... lack of emotion or feeling; impassiveness."[71] There is a close connection between apathy and laziness. Over the course of the Middle Ages, the two vices of *tristitia* (pessimism, despair) and *accidia* (apathy, "dryness of spirit") merged and morphed into the cardinal sin of sloth.[72] Calling apathy and sloth vices, or sins, emphasizes the active nature of a good human life.

Apathy is a key environmental vice, for several reasons. Our default procedures typically harm the environment, whereas doing better takes work, especially initially: bicycling to work rather than driving a car, setting up recycling bins rather than just tossing our garbage. One pop philosopher connects *all* our moral failures to laziness, and if this perhaps goes too far, it is true that doing right requires effort.[73] Often, we need to *think* our way toward better environmental solutions, and apathy shows itself in lazy thinking as well as in halfhearted action or inaction. Sluggish thinking tends to be selfish, short-term, and unimaginative. It reinforces passivity, as when my students' inability to imagine any way forward beyond American car culture, combined with their understanding of its environmental harms, leaves them feeling defeated and hopeless.

Thankfully, some of my students are not apathetic but, rather, are filled with passion and energy: to save Yellowstone's buffalo or Colorado's prairie dogs, to convince the university to purchase more recycled paper and wind power. Here, though, another problem can crop up, for too often their passions burn bright and flare out after a semester or two of activity, leaving them apathetic and disengaged. This is not just an issue for students learning about environmental issues for the first time; "burnout" among activists is a major problem for environmental groups, which depend on grassroots strength to combat the overwhelming monetary advantages of their opponents. When activists burn out, particular environmental efforts lose continuity and focus.[74]

The harms to nature from apathy are obvious: the old growth is cut, the refuge is drilled, the endangered species disappears. Polls might say that the great majority of the population supports preserving old growth, wilderness areas, or endangered species, but it is no matter if an active, eloquent few do not speak up on their behalf. "The broadest and most prevalent error requires the most disinterested virtue to sustain it," wrote Henry Thoreau, discussing his own society's apathetic acceptance of slavery.[75]

Apathy's harms to people are just as clear. Most simply, *apatheia* feels bad. A passive life is dull and boring. It lacks the engagement and interest in the world that are keys to happiness. It makes life seem meaningless, and meaning is as important as bread for living a fully human life.[76] Environmental apathy is especially pernicious for environmentalists; arguably, a person who has a strong sense of nature's beauty and worth, yet who cannot summon the energy to try to protect it, fails to live up to his or her full humanity.[77] Nothing makes us more fully human than the ability to articulate and live up to our ethical values. Environmentalists who do not act on their beliefs forfeit moral integrity.

With its focus on human flourishing, the virtue ethics tradition has generally praised the active life.[78] According to Aristotle, "Virtue is an ability [or power; *dynamis*] that is productive and preservative of goods, and an ability for doing good in many and great ways, actually in all ways in all things."[79] "By *virtue* and *power* I mean the same thing," wrote Spinoza: a power that allows us to become more fully ourselves.[80] Giving in to apathy means acquiescing in powerlessness. It means allowing others to circumscribe your life and your children's lives. Fighting for a special place or a beloved species, although it opens us up to disappointment, engages a basic human capability for political action. One of my students astutely suggests *vulnerability* and *ambition* as two virtues opposed to apathy.

A fear of vulnerability was partly behind the Stoic cultivation of *apatheia* as a virtue. Indifference toward "externals" beyond one's control allowed a person to take charge of his life and achieve happiness, the Stoics believed, while an unemotional rationality helped further just and successful action out in the world. The Stoic approach holds some appeal. It can further focus, hence effectiveness. Environmentalists do need to avoid fretting about events beyond our control, in a world with immense environmental problems and too much information about them. Nevertheless, cultivating environmental apathy seems misguided, for our happiness and flourishing depend, to an important degree, on flourishing natural and human communities. These must be defended. Environmentalists also *want* to explore and connect with these communities, which necessarily involves caring for them. There are many benefits to caring—but they cannot be divorced from the pain we feel when that which we care for is harmed.

Still, a person sometimes might be happier not caring about the environment and just living in it. From an individual point of view, being a free rider might make sense. In my home state of Colorado, many people take the attitude: "I'll float the rivers and ski the mountains, build my second home in prime elk habitat, enjoy it while I can, and not worry about tomorrow." These people may be happier than the people sitting through four-hour-long city council meetings, waiting nervously for a chance to speak for two minutes in favor of a new zoning ordinance. After all, you cannot sit in a meeting room and ski fresh powder at the same time. But with too many free riders, too much selfishness, the environment will be degraded, and soon enough the people living within it will suffer. I believe that those of us who enjoy nature's benefits have a duty to try to preserve it: for our communities and for future generations, for nature's sake and for our own.

In a recent article, Louke van Wensveen argues that genuine virtues must help ensure ecosystem sustainability.[81] As the virtues are virtues because they contribute to human flourishing and as flourishing is an ongoing project, the virtues must help secure the conditions necessary for their own cultivation. Traditionally, philosophers have emphasized the need to sustain the *social* conditions necessary for flourishing; today the evidence is clear that sustaining necessary *environmental* conditions is just as important. Wensveen's position seems unassailable.[82] It sets minimum standards for environmental concern that any plausible virtue ethics needs to uphold. Generalizing the point and shifting the focus from virtue to vice, I contend that any character trait, habit, institution, or way of life that cannot be sustained indefinitely is vicious. Furthermore, any character trait, habit, institution, or way of life whose current pursuit jeopardizes the well-being of others, now or in the future, is unjust. Apathy and indifference are socially and environmentally unsustainable. They cause, or allow, great harm. By these criteria, they are vices.

To fight apathy, we must find sustainable ways to engage in politics. Ideally, we will find political roles that we enjoy. Failing that, we will have to come up with tasks that we can tolerate for restricted amounts of time. Here we see particularly well the limits of general rules and prescriptions in ethics. People are different and suited to different social roles. The idea that you *should* engage in particular political activities will almost certainly fail to motivate sustained action. Instead, find out what you are good at and what you find enjoyable. Perhaps you like the excitement and combat of political campaigns; or the fleeting, minor celebrity of writing newspaper editorials; or the quiet, anonymous analysis of complex government policy proposals. Perhaps you would prefer teaching children the names of the flowers and birds in the local woods. All these activities are necessary in the ongoing struggle for nature.

To fight apathy and despair, we also need to find ways to *escape* from politics.[83] Aldo Leopold wrote that the price of an ecological education is to walk through a world of wounds. Leopold spent a good part of his life speaking out for wildlife and wilderness preservation, working politically to heal the wounds. But he also spent many hours planting trees and filling gullies on his sand county farm and many more hours hunting, fishing, bird-watching, snowshoeing, canoeing, and horse packing. No matter how dismal the environmental policies of the Soil Conservation Service or the State of Wisconsin were, Leopold could see the slow healing of land on his farm. No matter how often the Forest Service or Park Service punched roads into wilderness or exterminated predators, he found opportunities to explore and connect with wild nature. Leopold crafted a life that he found enjoyable and meaningful, that sustained him and made possible his lasting contributions to conservation. Our challenge is to do likewise. In the end, action is the only answer to apathy.[84]

Conclusion

Why do we harm nature? Because we are ignorant. Because we are selfish. Because we are gluttonous, arrogant, greedy, and apathetic. Because we do not understand our obligations to others or our own self-interest. We falsely assume that we can keep separate harms to nature and harms to humanity, harms to others and harms to ourselves. We do not see that environmental vices do not just harm nature; they harm us and the people around us. As I have shown in this essay, many of these harms are scientifically verifiable; the rest can be understood by anyone with open eyes and an open heart. The environmental vices are bad for us and bad for the Earth. For better and for worse, we really are all in this together.

Notes

1. Why is vice so little discussed in contemporary philosophy? Perhaps the failure comes from a discomfort with appearing too judgmental. When we assert that a particular action is wrong, we typically assume that people are free to act otherwise. Vice terms imply a deeper evil in people, harder to reform, certainly not to be shaken off by an argument or two. Similarly, when we assert that particular social arrangements are unfair or unjust, we locate the primary evil in "the system." Vice terms, in contrast, locate evil squarely within people. It is fine to criticize particular acts or social arrangements; criticize people generally and you trespass on the sacred, humanity having replaced God as the divine object in modern secular philosophy. Locate a *persistent* evil in individuals, and you verge on a pessimism at odds with the Enlightenment optimism still at the heart of most moral philosophy.

2. See recent Gallup Earth Day polls, available at www.gallup.com (accessed 18 February 2004).

3. My sense is that these are our four most important, or cardinal, environmental vices because they are fundamental and lead to the greatest environmental harms. Justification of this claim lies beyond the scope of this essay, depending as it would on a fully developed moral psychology and a comprehensive account of environmental degradation.

4. See the *American Heritage Dictionary of the English Language* and the *Oxford English Dictionary* (3d ed.).

5. Louke van Wensveen, *Dirty Virtues: The Emergence of Ecological Virtue Ethics* (Amherst, NY: Humanity Books, 2000), 103–6.

6. In this way vice judgments are similar to virtue judgments. See Martha Nussbaum, "Non-relative Virtues: An Aristotelian Approach," in *The Quality of Life,* ed. Martha Nussbaum and Amartya Sen (Oxford: Oxford University Press, 1993), 242–69.

7. Aristotle also described human flourishing in terms of higher activities such as philosophical study and contemplation, leading to a different set of virtues and vices. These two different conceptions of happiness and virtue are incompletely integrated in his ethical philosophy.

8. See the essays "Of Cruelty" and "Cowardice, Mother of Cruelty" in Michel de Montaigne, *Essays.*

9. Aristotle, *Nicomachean Ethics* (Indianapolis: Hackett, 1999), 23 (bk. 2, chap. 6).

10. Thomas Aquinas, *Treatise on the Virtues* (Englewood Cliffs, NJ: Prentice-Hall, 1966), 57 (*Summa,* pt. 2, question 56).

11. Immanuel Kant, *Groundwork of the Metaphysic of Morals,* AK 397; Immanuel Kant, *The Doctrine of Virtue: Part II of The Metaphysic of Morals,* AK 384–91, 443–45.

12. If we take moral character to be the sole determinant of personal well-being, or infinitely more important than other aspects of personal well-being, then it becomes true that we cannot improve our own well-being by wronging others. However, these Socratic and Stoic views give morality more importance than it deserves. Morality is important, but it is not all-important. We can preserve the nobility behind the view that we can never benefit ourselves by harming others by saying instead that we never *should* benefit ourselves by harming others.

13. Aristotle, *Nicomachean Ethics,* 110–11 (bk. 7, chap. 8).

14. See, for example, Augustine's account of his theft of the pears in the *Confessions,* bk. 2.

15. Aristotle, *Nicomachean Ethics,* 48–49 (bk. 3, chap. 12), 160-61 (bk. 10, chap. 5).

16. Both these themes are treated in Montaigne's final essay, "Of Experience." On tolerance, see also "Of Cannibals."

17. See Bill Shaw, "A Virtue Ethics Approach to Aldo Leopold's Land Ethic," in this volume; and Philip Cafaro, "Rachel Carson's Environmental Ethics," *Worldviews: Environment, Culture, Religion* 6 (2002): 58–80.

18. This last point is important. We need not show that some aspect of environmental protection is a *necessary* condition for the happiness of *all* members of society; to show that it is an *important* condition for the happiness of *some* members of society may be all the justification we need for environmental protection. As Aldo Leopold wrote: "Mechanized recreation already has seized nine-tenths of the woods

and mountains; a decent respect for minorities should dedicate the other tenth to wilderness" (*A Sand County Almanac with Essays on Conservation from Round River* [New York: Ballantine, 1970], 272).

19. The most comprehensive study so far, setting the agenda for future scholarship in this area, is Wensveen, *Dirty Virtues.*

20. Wensveen, *Dirty Virtues,* 97–103.

21. To be fair to Aristotle, he already had some sense of the importance of environmental protection to human flourishing. See Aristotle, *Politics,* bk. 7, chaps. 4–6, 11–12.

22. See Holmes Rolston III, "Environmental Virtue Ethics: Half the Truth but Dangerous as a Whole," in this volume.

23. Once again, though I believe that these are our cardinal environmental vices, sustaining that claim would require further elaboration and defense. Selfishness, injustice, and ignorance are also plausible candidates for cardinal environmental vices.

24. Morton Bloomfield, *The Seven Deadly Sins: An Introduction to the History of a Religious Concept, with Special Reference to Medieval English Literature* (East Lansing: Michigan State University Press, 1967), 59, 69. Bloomfield (*The Seven Deadly Sins,* 74–75) documents how, early in the medieval period, gluttony lost its place at the head of the list to pride; he speculates that as the list began to be used to guide moral life outside monasteries, sins of the flesh such as gluttony and lust came to seem less important than more socially damaging sins such as pride and avarice.

25. Geoffrey Chaucer, *Canterbury Tales* (New York: Covici and Friede, 1934), 603.

26. J. M. McGinnis and W. H. Foege, "Actual Causes of Death in the United States," *Journal of the American Medical Association* 270, no. 18 (1993): 2207–12.

27. One study notes that "aside from mortality rate ... obesity substantially increases morbidity and impairs quality of life" (D. B. Allison, K. R. Fontaine, J. E. Manson, J. Steens, and T. B. Van Itallie, "Annual Deaths Attributable to Obesity in the United States," *Journal of the American Medical Association* 282, no. 16 [1999]: 1530).

28. U.S. Department of Health and Human Services, *The Surgeon General's Call to Action to Prevent and Decrease Overweight and Obesity* (Rockville, MD: Public Health Service, Office of the Surgeon General, 2001).

29. U.S. Fish and Wildlife Service, "Summary of Listed Species," available at http://ecos.fws.gov/tess_public/ TESSBoxscore?format=display&type=archive&sysdate=5/01/2004 (accessed 14 May 2004).

30. D. S. Wilcove, D. Rothstein, J. Dubow, A. Phillips, and E. Losos, "Quantifying Threats to Imperiled Species in the United States: Assessing the Relative Importance of Habitat Destruction, Alien Species, Pollution, Overexploitation, and Disease," *BioScience* 48, no. 8 (1998): 607–15.

31. Wilcove et al., "Quantifying Threats to Imperiled Species in the United States." A more recent study has confirmed agriculture's leading role in species endangerment; see B. Czech, R. Krausman, and P. K. Devers, "Economic Associations among Causes of Species Endangerment in the United States," *BioScience* 50, no. 7 (2000): 593–601.

32. J. Putnam, J. Allshouse, and L. S. Kantor, "U.S. Per Capita Food Supply Trends: More Calorics, Refined Carbohydrates, and Fats," *FoodReview* 25, no. 3 (2002): 2–15.

33. Of course, all else is not equal. For one thing, approximately 20 percent of the food produced in the United States is exported (see M. Reed, *International Trade in Agricultural Products* [Upper Saddle River, NJ: Prentice-Hall, 2001]). But this point cuts both ways: much of the food consumed today in America is imported, and its growing, harvesting, and shipping have environmental costs.

34. Robert Pyle, *The Thunder Tree: Lessons from an Urban Wildland* (New York: Lyons Press, 1993); Kent Meyers, *The Witness of Combines* (Minneapolis: University of Minnesota Press, 1998).

35. D. H. Chadwick, "American Prairie: Roots of the Sky," *National Geographic* 184 (October 1993): 116.

36. Frances Moore Lappé, *Diet for a Small Planet* (New York: Ballantine, 1991).

37. Amartya Sen, *Poverty and Famines: An Essay on Entitlement and Deprivation* (Oxford: Oxford University Press, 1981).

38. Aristotle, *Nicomachean Ethics,* 46, 48–49 (bk. 3, chaps. 10, 12), 157 (bk. 10, chap. 3).

39. Henry Thoreau, *Walden* (Princeton: Princeton University Press, 1971), 215.

40. Aristotle, *Nicomachean Ethics,* 49 (bk. 3, chap. 12).

41. Readers interested in the ancient pagan view should review Aristotle's discussion of magnanimity or "great-souledness" (*Nicomachean Ethics,* bk. 4, chap. 3). Aristotle there defines magnanimity (Greek *megalnpsuchid*) as a virtue specifying the proper attitude toward honor, stating that the magnanimous man "thinks himself worthy of great honors, and is worthy of them." The associated vices are overvaluation of oneself, on the one hand, and pusillanimity, thinking oneself worthy of little, on the other. Interestingly, Aristotle thinks that the latter vice is more usual than the former.

42. For a good discussion of Kantian self-respect, see Thomas Hill Jr., "Servility and Self-Respect," *Monist* 57 (1973): 87–104.

43. Wensveen, *Dirty Virtues,* 98.

44. David Ehrenfeld, *The Arrogance of Humanism* (New York: Oxford University Press, 1978).

45. Bronwen Manby, *The Price of Oil: Corporate Responsibility and Human Rights Violations in Nigeria's Oil Producing Communities* (Washington, DC: Human Rights Watch, 1999).

46. This account of events in the Niger Delta, and the quotes from Chevron contractor Bill Spencer that follow, come from the *Democracy Now* radio program "Drilling and Killing: Chevron and Nigeria's Oil Dictatorship," produced by Amy Goodman and Jeremy Scahill, 30 September 1998, available at www. pacifica.org/programs/nigeria (accessed 13 February 2004).

47. For a comprehensive discussion and bibliography, see American Land Alliance, *Off-Road Vehicles: A Growing Threat to Public Lands and Waters,* available at www.americanlands.org/forestweb/offroad.htm.

48. Kevin McNulty, "Off-Road Attitude," available at www.off-roadweb.com/features/0202or_covertruck/index.html (accessed 12 February 2004).

49. Aristotle, *Nicomachean Ethics,* bk. 7, chaps. 7–8.

50. The arrogance of someone who holds to belief in a literal biblical creation, its combination of stubbornness and laziness, has a lot in common with the justifications for corporate crime and personal irresponsibility above. Anthropocentrism is not just a faulty value system but also a faulty way of understanding the world. In Aristotle's terms, it is an intellectual vice as well as a character vice.

51. It is no accident that most of our environmental heroes have been naturalists. See Philip Cafaro, "The Naturalist's Virtues," *Philosophy in the Contemporary World* 8, no. 2 (2001): 85–99.

52. For similar reasons, federal and state land management agencies should ban ORVs from our public lands. By allowing and often encouraging such use, they are creating a whole constituency of people who do not respect nature. They are training people *on* public lands to *trash* public lands.

53. Peter Singer, *One World: The Ethics of Globalization* (New Haven: Yale University Press, 2002), 104–5.

54. Ron Sandler makes the good point that arrogance is as much about what we think we can do as what we think we are worth. It is the former that is most in play in genetic engineering, damming and straightening rivers, industrial agriculture, and so on.

55. See the *American Heritage Dictionary.* Greed can also refer to an extreme desire for anything; as Chaucer says, "Avarice ne stont not oonly in lond ne in catel, but som tyme in science and in glorie" (quoted in the *Oxford English Dictionary* definition for *avarice).*

56. Wensveen, *Dirty Virtues,* 233.

57. Chaucer, *Canterbury Tales,* 601.

58. Thomas Aquinas quoted in Singer, *One World,* 185.

59. For examples of businessmen and businesswomen who are building profitable businesses that *enhance* environmental protection, see Steven Lerner, *Eco-pioneers: Practical Visionaries Solving Todays Environmental Problems* (Cambridge: MIT Press, 1998).

60. Gary Strauss, "Cheney as VP Faces a Serious Cut in Pay," *USA Today,* 26 June 2000. Available at www.usatoday.com/news/opinion/e2415.htm (accessed 15 June 2004).

61. John King, "Cheney Aide Rejects Halliburton Questions," *CNN.com/Inside Politics,* 16 September 2003. Available at www.cnn.com/2003/ALLPOLITICS/09/16/cheney.halliburton/index.html (accessed 15 June 2004).

62. These studies are summarized in Robert Lane, *The Market Experience* (Cambridge: Cambridge University Press, 1991), 524–47.

63. Tim Kasser, Richard Ryan, Charles Couchman, and Kennon Sheldon, "Materialistic Values: Their Causes and Consequences," in *Psychology and Consumer Culture: The Struggle for a Good Life in a Materialistic World,* ed. Tim Kasser and Allen Kanner (Washington, DC: American Psychological Association, 2004), 19.

64. Kasser et al., "Materialistic Values," 29 (in-text citations silently removed).

65. Emily Solberg, Edward Diener, and Michael Robinson, "Why Are Materialists Less Satisfied?" in *Psychology and Consumer Culture: The Struggle for a Good Life in a Materialistic World,* ed. Tim Kasser and Allen Kanner (Washington, DC: American Psychological Association, 2004), 45.

66. Bloomfield, *The Seven Deadly Sins,* 88.

67. Henry Fairlie, *The Seven Deadly Sins Today* (Washington, DC: New Republic Books, 1978), 25. Fairlie argues that American society instills avarice, gluttony, and lust in its members.

68. Nancy Shalek, quoted in Tim Kasser, *The High Price of Materialism* (Cambridge: MIT Press, 2002), 91.

69. Of course, one can take the view that our contemporary acceptance of greed is all to the good. Almost 300 years ago, Bernard Mandeville, in his *Fable of the Bees: Or, Private Vices, Public Virtues,* argued that the vices are in fact necessary to a happy and flourishing nation.

70. Bloomfield, *The Seven Deadly Sins,* 251.

71. See the *American Heritage Dictionary.*

72. Wensveen, *Dirty Virtues,* 100; Bloomfield, *The Seven Deadly Sins,* 96.

73. M. Scott Peck, *People of the Lie: The Hope for Healing Human Evil* (New York: Simon and Schuster, 1983).

74. Randy Larsen, "Tenacity as a Virtue," unpublished MS, 8. For a good discussion of issues surrounding apathy and activism, see Randy Larsen, "Environmental Virtue Ethics: Nature as Polis" (M.A. thesis, Colorado State University, Fort Collins, 1996), chap. 3.

75. Henry Thoreau, *Reform Papers* (Princeton: Princeton University Press, 1973), 72.

76. See Matthew 4:4.

77. David Schmidtz, "Are All Species Equal?" in *Environmental Ethics: What Really Matters, What Really Works,* ed. David Schmidtz and Elizabeth Willot (New York: Oxford University Press, 2002), 100.

78. Still, passivity remains a live option within virtue ethics, embraced in ancient times by Eastern Taoists and Western Cynics. Given how much environmental harm is caused by the human need to act, regardless of whether action is justified, an environmental focus may challenge the traditional preference for activity within virtue ethics. Perhaps the most radical aspect of the U.S. National Environmental Protection Act is its requirement that federal managers consider a "no action" option before proceeding with projects.

79. Aristotle, *On Rhetoric* (New York: Oxford University Press, 1991), 79 (bk. 1, chap. 9).

80. Baruch Spinoza, *The Ethics and Selected Letters* (Indianapolis: Hackett, 1982), 156 (pt. 4, definitions). We see this equation of virtue, power, and activity in various archaic uses of the word *virtue,* when botanists or physicians write of the virtues of medicinal plants, for instance. Contrarily, many contemporary philosophers could agree with Ambrose Bierce's definition of virtue in his *Devil's Dictionary,* "virtues: certain abstentions."

81. Louke van Wensveen, "Ecosystem Sustainability as a Criterion for Genuine Virtue," *Environmental Ethics* 23 (2001): 232–34.

82. Wensveen's approach is challenged in Ronald Sandler, "The External Goods Approach to Environmental Virtue Ethics," *Environmental Ethics* 25 (2003): 279–93.

83. For a discussion of hope, despair, and political activism in environmental virtue ethics, sec Philip Cafaro, *Thoreau's Living Ethics:* Walden *and the Pursuit of Virtue* (Athens: University of Georgia Press, 2004), 174–204.

84. Ed Abbey echoes Leopold and well sums up the claims of an environmental virtue ethics when he writes: "Do not burn yourselves out. Be as I am—a reluctant enthusiast … a part-time crusader, a half-hearted fanatic. Save the other half of yourselves and your lives for pleasure and adventure. It is not enough to fight for the land; it is even more important to enjoy it. … Enjoy yourselves, keep your brain in your head and your head firmly attached to the body, the body active and alive, and I promise you this much: I promise you this one sweet victory over our enemies, over those desk-bound people with their hearts in a safe deposit box and their eyes hypnotized by desk calculators. I promise you this: you will outlive the bastards" (quoted in Steve Van Matre and Bill Weiler, eds., *The Earth Speaks* [Greenville, WV: Institute for Earth Education, 1983], 57). Randy Larsen points out the appropriateness of this quote in his "Environmental Virtue Ethics."

The Proposed Concept of the "Anthropocene": Should We Accept It as Science, Reject It as Ideology, or Both?

9A. The "Anthropocene"

By P. J. Crutzen and E. F. Stoermer

The name Holocene ("Recent Whole") for the post-glacial geological epoch of the past ten to twelve thousand years seems to have been proposed for the first time by Sir Charles Lyell in 1833, and adopted by the International Geological Congress in Bologna in 1885 (1). During the Holocene mankind's activities gradually grew into a significant geological, morphological force, as recognised early on by a number of scientists. Thus, G.P. Marsh already in 1864 published a book with the title "Man and Nature", more recently reprinted as "The Earth as Modified by Human Action" (2). Stoppani in 1873 rated mankind's activities as a "new telluric force which in power and universality may be compared to the greater forces of earth" [quoted from Clark (3)]. Stoppani already spoke of the anthropozoic era. Mankind has now inhabited or visited almost all places on Earth; he has even set foot on the moon.

The great Russian geologist V.I. Vernadsky (4) in 1926 recognized the increasing power of mankind as part of the biosphere with the following excerpt "... the direction in which the processes of evolution must proceed, namely towards increasing consciousness and thought, and forms having greater and greater influence on their surroundings". He, the French Jesuit P. Teilhard de Chardin and E. Le Roy in 1924 coined the term "noosphere", the world of thought, to mark the growing role played by mankind's brainpower and technological talents in shaping its own future and environment.

The expansion of mankind, both in numbers and per capita exploitation of Earth's resources has been astounding (5). To give a few examples: During the past 3 centuries human population increased tenfold to 6000 million, accompanied e.g. by a growth in cattle population to 1400 million (6) (about one cow per average size family). Urbanisation has even increased tenfold in the past century. In a few generations mankind is exhausting the fossil fuels that were generated over several hundred million years. The release of SO_2, globally about 160 Tg/year to the atmosphere by coal and oil burning, is at least two times larger than the sum of all natural emissions, occurring mainly as marine dimethyl-sulfide from the oceans (7); from Vitousek et al. (8) we learn that 30–50% of the land surface has been transformed by human action; more nitrogen is now fixed synthetically and applied as fertilizers in agriculture than fixed naturally in all terrestrial ecosystems; the escape into the atmosphere of NO from fossil fuel and biomass combustion likewise is larger than the natural inputs, giving rise to photochemical ozone ("smog") formation in extensive regions of the world; more than half of all accessible fresh water is used by mankind; human activity has increased the species extinction rate by thousand to ten thousand fold in the tropical rain forests (9) and several climatically important "greenhouse" gases have substantially increased in the atmosphere: CO_2 by more than 30% and CH_4 by even more than 100%. Furthermore, mankind releases many toxic substances in the environment and even some, the chlorofluorocarbon gases, which are not toxic at all, but which nevertheless have led to the Antarctic "ozone hole" and which would have destroyed much of the ozone layer if no international regulatory measures to end their production had been taken. Coastal wetlands are also affected by humans, having resulted in the loss of 50% of the world's mangroves. Finally, mechanized human predation ("fisheries") removes more than 25% of the primary production of the oceans in the upwelling regions and 35% in the temperate continental shelf regions (10). Anthropogenic effects are also well illustrated by the history of biotic communities that leave remains in lake sediments. The effects documented include modification of the geochemical cycle in large freshwater systems and occur in systems remote from primary sources (11–13).

Considering these and many other major and still growing impacts of human activities on earth and atmosphere, and at all, including global, scales, it seems to us more than appropriate to emphasize the central role of mankind in geology and ecology by proposing to use the term "anthropocene" for the current geological epoch. The impacts of current human activities will continue over long periods. According to a study by Berger and Loutre (14), because of the anthropogenic emissions of CO_2, climate may depart significantly from natural behaviour over the next 50,000 years.

To assign a more specific date to the onset of the "anthropocene" seems somewhat arbitrary, but we propose the latter part of the 18th century, although we are aware that alternative proposals can be made (some may even want to include the entire holocene). However, we choose this date because, during the past two centuries, the global effects of human activities have become clearly noticeable. This is the period when data retrieved from glacial ice cores show the beginning of a growth in the atmospheric concentrations of several "greenhouse gases", in particular CO_2 and CH_4 (7). Such a starting date also coincides with James Watt's invention of the steam engine in 1784. About at that time, biotic assemblages in most lakes began to show large changes (11–13).

Without major catastrophes like an enormous volcanic eruption, an unexpected epidemic, a large-scale nuclear war, an asteroid impact, a new ice age, or continued plundering of Earth's resources by partially still primitive technology (the last four dangers can, however, be prevented in a real functioning noösphere) mankind will remain a major geological force for many millennia, maybe millions of years, to come. To develop a world-wide accepted strategy leading to sustainability of ecosystems against human induced stresses will be one of the great future tasks of mankind, requiring intensive research efforts and wise application of the knowledge thus acquired in the noösphere, better known as knowledge or information society. An exciting, but also difficult and daunting task lies ahead of the global research and engineering community to guide mankind towards global, sustainable, environmental management (15).

We thank the many colleagues, especially the members of the IGBP Scientific Committee, for encouraging correspondence and advice.

References

1. Encyclopaedia Britannica, Micropaedia, IX, (1976).

2. G.P. Marsh, The Earth as Modified by Human Action, Belknap Press, Harvard University Press, 1965.

3. W. C. Clark, in *Sustainable Development of the Biosphere,* W. C. Clark and R. E. Munn, Eds., (Cambridge University Press, Cambridge, 1986), chapt. 1.

4. V. I. Vernadski, *The Biosphere, translated and annotated version from the original of 1926,* (Copernicus, Springer, New York, 1998).

5. B.L. Turner II et al., The Earth as Transformed by Human Action, Cambridge University Press, 1990.

6. P J. Crutzen and T E. Graedel, in *Sustainable Development of the Biosphere,* W. C. Clark and R. E. Munn, Eds., (Cambridge University Press, Cambridge, 1986). chapt. 9.

7. R. T. Watson, et al, in *Climate Change. The IPCC Scientific Assessment* J. T. Houghton, G. J. Jenkins and J. J. Ephraums, Eds., (Cambridge University Press, 1990), chapt. 1.

8. P. M. Vitousek et al., Science, **277**, 494, (1997).

9. E.O. Wilson, The Diversity of Life, Penguin Books, 1992.

10. D. Pauly and V. Christensen, Nature, **374**, 255–257, 1995.

11. E. F. Stoermer and J. P. Smol Eds. The Diatoms: Applications for the Environmental and Earth Sciences (Cambridge University Press, Cambridge, 1999).

12. C. L. Schelske and E. F. Stoermer, *Science,* 173, (1971); D. Verschuren et al. *J. Great Lakes Res.,* **24**, (1998).

13. M. S. V. Douglas, J. P Smol and W. Blake Jr., *Science* **266** (1994).

14. A. Berger and M.-F. Loutre, C. R. Acad. Sci. Paris, **323**, II A, 1–16, 1996.

15. H.J. Schellnhuber, Nature, **402**, C19–C23, 1999.

9B. Against the Idea of an Anthropocene Epoch

Ethical, Political, and Scientific Concerns

By Christine J. Cuomo

Introduction

Talk of an "anthropocene" era has become a popular way to describe the fact that human beings (anthropos) are now influencing Earth's systems and other species like never before, producing unpredictable and long-lasting changes, and threatening ecological stability and health nearly everywhere. Climate change due to greenhouse gas pollution is perhaps the most obvious evidence that Earth itself is in a state unprecedentedly driven by decisions and actions of people, or at least certain people, rather than by "natural" forces alone. But atmosphere and climate are not the only systems where recent anthropogenic interventions are creating intense quantitative and qualitative changes in Earth's physical and living systems. Along with global warming and skyrocketing rates of species endangerment, the gross impacts of mining, deforestation and chemical agriculture are emblematic of the so-called "anthropocene" age. In the anthropocene, capital- and technology-intensive practices, such as the widespread use of synthetic fertilizers (which has altered Earth's nitrogen cycle), leave undeniable detrimental traces, at monumental scales.

The informal idea of an anthropocene cultural age is similar to concepts like "modernity," "post-modernity," or "the age of television," but with a dismal environmental twist. However, the informal concept of the anthropocene is inspired by a more formal scientific concept, which is the focus of my comments here. The formal idea of an "Anthropocene" age is linked to an effort in the geosciences to officially declare the beginning of a new geological epoch, marked by the scientifically traceable impacts of invasive anthropogenic practices in Earth's strata, systems and biosphere. By definition, declaring the beginning of a new "Anthropocene" geological epoch amounts to the formal end of the current Holocene epoch, for geological epochs follow in succession just as years do.

Method: Alleging the Anthropocene

The idea that a new Anthropocene epoch is supplanting the Holocene was first put forth in a 2000 essay proposing a new geological age, marked by the central role of "mankind" in shaping Earth's atmosphere, ecology and geology (Crutzen and Stoermer, 2000). A scientific movement developed, aiming to formally designate the beginning of a new Anthropocene age "at the same hierarchical

Christine J. Cuomo, "Against the Idea of an Anthropocene Epoch: Ethical, Political, and Scientific Concerns," *Biogeosystem Technique*, vol. 4, no. 1, pp. 4-8. Copyright © 2017 by Christine J. Cuomo. Reprinted with permission.

level as the Pleistocene and the Holocene epochs" (Zalasiewicz et al., 2015). As journalist Elizabeth Kolbert has pointed out, if the movement to formalize the Anthropocene is successful, every geology textbook in the planet will immediately become obsolete (Kolbert, 2014).

The proposal for an Anthropocene epoch has been endorsed by a working group of the International Union of Geological Sciences, a professional organization whose members determine the scientifically accurate portrayal of Earth's geological history. The website of the Working Group on the Anthropocene (WGA) describes the presumed new epoch as an age uniquely marked by "many geologically significant conditions and processes profoundly altered by human activities. These include changes in: erosion and sediment transport associated with a variety of anthropogenic processes, including colonisation, agriculture, urbanisation and global warming, the chemical composition of the atmosphere, oceans and soils, with significant anthropogenic perturbations of the cycles of elements" (Working Group on the Anthropocene, 2017).

Beyond advocating for a new geological epoch, the WGA also identifies the beginning of the Anthropocene (and by implication the end of the Holocene) as "the time of the world's first nuclear bomb explosion, on July 16, 1945 at Alamogordo, New Mexico," which produced a clear and indelible mark on Earth in the form of a "worldwide fallout easily identifiable in the chemostratigraphic record" (Zalasiewicz et al., 2015).

Although the drive to formally declare a new Anthropocene epoch has gained traction in a number of circles, there are serious questions that need to be raised about the wisdom and accuracy of formalizing the "signals of the anthropocene" as the definitive signs of a new geological epoch. There are important differences between noticing and publicizing a geological signal, and interpreting or defining that signal as the sign of an inevitable 'new normal'. Rather than interpreting troubling signals such as nuclear fallout, changes in the nitrogen cycle and mining tailings as marking the death of the Holocene, I argue that we should understand them as dire warning signs, demonstrating beyond a doubt the perilous legacies of highly invasive industries, and signaling the unprecedentedly urgent need to terminate and transform harmful practices, and to move our cultures and economies in Earth-friendly directions.

Results and Discussion

Protecting the Holocene

It is difficult to imagine a reason to rush to define away the Holocene epoch, or to regard its threatened demise as anything other than an absolute tragedy calling for unprecedented ethical responses. Yet scientists have been surprisingly sanguine about the proposed end of the Holocene epoch, as though they are considering the end of a cultural era, rather than the existential demise of our uniquely life-friendly planetary home. The WGA of the IUGS would like us to conclude that because there are clear stratigraphical marks of human interventions in Earth's ecology and geology, "the Holocene has terminated" (Working Group on the Anthropocene, 2017). But there are scientific and philosophical questions to be raised about the ontological status of the Holocene. And, as I discuss in more detail below, there are very troubling ethical implications in declaring that the decidedly human-friendly planetary and ecological realities dominant over the last twelve thousand years are officially "over." In fact, there is no underestimating the potential moral costs of killing off the Holocene epoch.

Although no epoch can last forever, given the unique and uniquely mammal-friendly character of Earth's Holocene, its preservation is of utmost importance for human communities. The Holocene, which began after Earth's Pleistocene period and the last major ice age, established itself around 10,000 BCE, and was designated by scientists in 1895. While "Holocene" is just a name, it designates particular ecosystemic realities for Earth, and a plethora of specific ideals, norms, and benchmarks embedded in those realities. Earth's diverse and dynamic ecologies in its Holocene forms are the fecund states that have been humanity's contexts, worlds, food, fuel and constitutive relationships since long before known human history began. Holocene ecosystems and species are central to all indigenous and subsistence cultures worldwide, and the material foundation for all human conceptions of ecological sustainability, coexistence and health. Ideals and norms provided by Holocene-identified states are what allow us to evaluate and measure environmental harm and endangerment, and to identify specific requirements for restoration. For example, it was various measurements and comparisons against Holocene-identified (i.e. early twentieth century) states of ecological and human health that enabled biologists Rachel Carson and Barry Commoner to show that willful and careless pollution was creating moral atrocities, inspiring the development of environmental law and policy (Carson, 1962; Commoner, 1971). Environmental values and movements the world over, especially those focused on the preservation or restoration of wilderness, sacred lands, animal well-being, traditional subsistence ecosystems, natural monuments, or healthy waterways are still based in material realities of the Holocene epoch.

Without Holocene realities, what can ground the sound ecological policies, laws, ideals and ethics needed in an age such as ours? Anthropocene values cannot be ecologically sound or protective, for the ideology that fuels the practices identified with the proposed human-driven epoch *require* the philosophical and economic reduction of the natural world into exploitable resources. The phenomena referred to in discourses of the anthropocene are catastrophic harms that should be ameliorated in the present and avoided in the future, rather than institutionalized into a new epoch.

Novel anthropogenic signals caused by war and other catastrophes should be regarded as crucial lessons and urgent warning signs, rather than as conclusive evidence that Holocene Earth—arguably the most precious physical location in the universe—has expired. Perilous environmental changes and compromised systems at planetary scales are trends we should work at all costs to terminate, rather than normalize for the future. Instead of dismal science declaring "game over" for the Holocene, realistic science can interpret the lasting environmental traces of war, pollution and disruption as crucial warnings *within* the current epoch, encouraging ethical and empowering responses rather than fatalism and denial.

The Anthropocene as Moral Atrocity

A New York Times headline recently asked, "Is the 'Anthropocene' epoch a condemnation of human interference, or a call for more?" (Yang, 2017). The geological signals scientists propose as the marks of a new epoch represent colonial and 'neocolonial' interventions and changes that have been catastrophically harmful, and that currently threaten to produce even more extensive harm (Whyte, 2017). If what is distinct about the proposed new geological phase is that it leaves physical signals like mining tailings, nuclear fallout, ocean acidification and anthropogenic species extinction, then the Anthropocene represents an atrocity rather than a promising new trend.

The philosopher Claudia Card developed a secular conception of moral atrocities that emphasizes the obligations of perpetrators and the importance of remediation, without relying on controversial metaphysics or the notion that atrocities necessarily follow from evil intentions. According to Card, a moral atrocity is an intense, extensive harm that "1) is reasonably foreseeable ... 2) is culpably inflicted (or tolerated, aggravated, or maintained), and 3) deprives, or seriously risks depriving, others of the basics that are necessary to make a life possible and tolerable or decent" (Card, 2002, 8). The actions of wealthy industries, governments and individuals who knowingly pollute and harm others seemingly fit the paradigm. Not surprisingly, Card argued that ecocide, "the threat to life on our planet posed by environmental poisoning, global warming, and the destruction of rain forests and other natural habitats," was among the paradigmatic moral evils of the twentieth century (Card, 2002, 8).

In asserting that a new epoch has already permanently replaced the Holocene epoch, the working group advocates for a position that deprives humanity of the opportunity to protect and restore the Holocene. They also present a pessimistic and insufficiently founded prediction of the future of human societies and Earth's ecologies. Whether any discipline can predict how human communities will ultimately respond as we come to better understand our environmental impacts and vulnerabilities, it is fatalistic and disempowering to assume that effective collective responses to global threats are categorically impossible. The last decade has seen a massive shift toward global recognition of climate change and the importance of climate justice, and a huge and broadly cross-cultural sector of humanity now expresses serious concern about the issues. Both social and ecological systems can turn out to be quite resilient, when provided with the right forms of support.

Instead of normalizing moral atrocities by proclaiming the birth of a new epoch, ethical interventions are required to address the serious and systematic harms of the last century, and restore ecological health. In addition to assessing culpability, positive ethical interventions include taking responsibility, healing, caring, restoring, acting justly, divesting, protecting, enabling autonomy, respecting rights, and showing respect. Rather than settling for the idea that the practices that currently threaten life on Earth are destined to grow into more of the same, scientists and others noticing the so-called "signals of the anthropocene" might expand and multiply efforts to protect and restore ecological health.

What's in a Name?

Finally, like other commentators who have suggested alternatives such as "capitalist-scene", I think it is important to consider the accuracy and implications of the name "anthropocene" (Hailwood, 2016; Haraway, 2016; Cuomo, 2014; Cuomo, 2017). The term supposedly identifies the agents behind the extensive and lasting impacts of technological interventions on Earth's vital systems. But is humanity, *anthropos*, or *Homo Sapiens* really the responsible party behind mass species endangerment, ocean acidification, fossil fuel pollution, deforestation, and nuclear fallout? Clearly it is some humans, and not others, who have devised, propagated and profited from the characteristic industries (and moral atrocities) of the so-called anthropocene. Phenomena identified with the anthropocene are quite recent, and though they have near-global reach, their origins are specific and often traceable. Describing the harms of the anthropocene as acts of 'humanity' represents the actions of few as universally chosen and preferred. It denies humanity's phenomenal historical and philosophical diversity, and feeds into a dismal and misanthropic conception of human nature as ultimately anti-nature, violent, and destructive. Furthermore, attributing the catastrophic changes Earth is experiencing to an abstract, diffuse non-actor like "humanity" hides the influence of specific ideologies, industries, and cultures, and allows everyone to avoid taking responsibility.

There is a unique hubris in characterizing your own culture's destructive patterns, which have been used against other cultures, as definitively human, and then defining those destructive patterns as the harbinger of an already-established new age destined to define the future. Instead of rendering them invisible, now is the time to highlight and learn from living and remembered human cultures who have realized more harmonious, mutually beneficial relationships within nature. Of fundamental importance will be the ability to sense, allow and support nature's autonomy, grounded in ethics of recognition and respect.

Conclusion

It is not the actions or inclinations of *anthropos* that produced the fallout resulting from the United States Army's detonation of nuclear weapons in 1945, or our current frightening eco-crises. But if not humanity as a species, who deserves the credit or blame for the troubling "man-made" global changes we are witnessing, working against, and working with? Many have emphasized the roles of "mankind" and "Western values" in endangering the health of the Holocene (White, 1967). In fact it is the economically powerful classes of recent colonial and capitalist regimes-mostly but certainly not only men—who masterminded, enacted and have directly benefited from the disruptions to Earth's "geologically significant conditions and processes" in question. We with massive greenhouse gas footprints can help write the next chapters of the Holocene by prioritizing practices to effectively support a thriving biosphere healthy and fertile enough to supplant current anti-Earth trends.

Acknowledgments

Thank you to Amy Ross, Clement Loo (on the matter of prediction), Amber Katherine, Jim Stockton, Kyle Powys Whyte, the University of Georgia Willson Center for the Humanities and Office of the Vice President for Research, Mark A. Farmer and Valery P. Kalinitchenko.

References

Card, 2002—*Card, C.* (2002). The Atrocity Paradigm: A Theory of Evil, London: Oxford University Press

Carson, 1962—*Carson, R.* (1962). Silent Spring, Boston: Houghton Mifflin.

Commoner, 1971—*Commoner, B.* (1971). The Closing Circle: Man, Nature and Technology. New York: Knopf.

Crutzen and Stoermer, 2000—*Crutzen, P, and E. Stoermer* (2000). "The Anthropocene." *Global Change Newsletter* 41: 17–18.

Cuomo, 2014—*Cuomo, C.* (2014). "Who is the 'Anthro' in the Anthropocene?" Anthropocene Lecture Series, University of Georgia, November 20.

Cuomo, 2017—*Cuomo, C.* (2017). 'Anthropocene': An Ethical Crisis, Not a Geological Epoch, *Geophysical Research Abstracts* Vol. 19, EGU2017-17142.

Hailwood, 2016—*Hailwood, S.* (2016). "Anthropocene: Delusion, celebration and concern." In P. Pattberg, & F. Zelli (Eds.), *Environmental Politics and Governance in the Anthropocene*, Abingdon: Routledge.

Haraway, 2016—*Haraway, D.* (2016). Staying with the Trouble: Making Kin in the Chthulucene, Durham: Duke University Press.

Kolbert, 2014—*Kolbert, E.* (2014). The Sixth Extinction: An Unnatural History, New York: Henry Holt and Company.

Working Group on the Anthropocene, 2017—Working Group on the Anthropocene, Subcommission on Quarternary Stratigraphy, (2014) "What is the Anthropocene?" URL: http://quarternary.stratigraphy.org/workinggroups/anthropocene retrieved June 28, 2017.

Yang, 2017—Yang, Wesley (2017). "Is the 'Anthropocene' Epoch a Condemnation of Human Interference—or a Call for More?" *The New York Times Magazine*, February 14.

White, 1967—White, L. (1967). The historical roots of our ecologic crisis, *Science*, Vol. 155, No. 3767:1203–1207.

Whyte, 2017—*Whyte, K.* (2017). "Indigenous climate change studies: Indigenizing futures, decolonizing the Anthropocene, *English Language Notes* 55 (1–2): 153–162.

Zalasiewicz et al., 2015—*Zalasiewicz, J., et al.* (2015). "When did the Anthropocene begin? A mid-twentieth century boundary is stratigraphically optimal", *Quarternary International*, 383, 196–203.

Index

tribal identity, 276

twin dominations of women and nature, 236, 237, 246

U

"unity in sameness" perception as an erasure of difference, 237, 242

universal correlation of rights and obligations, 193

universality, 116, 191, 317

universal perspective of ethics, 26

unjust domination, 252, 253, 254, 255

unrestricted, 274

"up-down" thinking, 234

utilitarianism, 24

V

validity, 258

value dualism, 234, 235, 236

value hierarchical thinking, 252

value objectivism, value realism, 122

values, 136, 148, 151

value skepticism, value relativism, value subjectivism, 122

Vaughn, Lewis, 21

vice, 178, 253, 271

virtue ethics, 289, 292, 301, 306

volition, 253

vulnerability of different species, 227

W

Walking by Henry David Thoreau, 12

"wannabes" in consumer society, 283

Warren, Karen J., 233

water pollution, 296

Western Civilization, 123

White, Lynn, Jr., 45, 85, 95

wildness and life, 79

will, 35, 37, 45

womanism, 264, 267, 268

womb of nature, 60, 67

worldview, 116, 117, 120, 124

Z

Zoocentrism, or nonhuman animals' moral equality with humans, 9